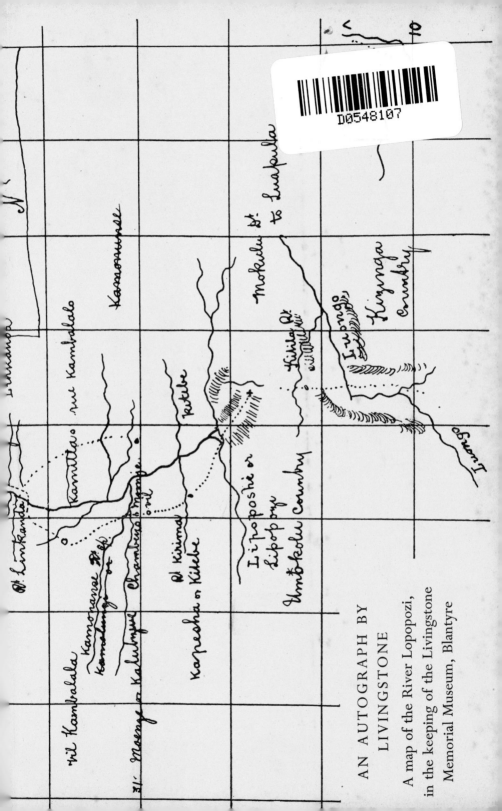

AN AUTOGRAPH BY
LIVINGSTONE

A map of the River Lopopozi,
in the keeping of the Livingstone
Memorial Museum, Blantyre

LIVINGSTONE'S TRAVELS

DAVID LIVINGSTONE AGED ABOUT 50

From the plaque by C. d'O. Pilkington Jackson at the
Livingstone Memorial, Blantyre, Scotland

LIVINGSTONE'S
TRAVELS

edited by

Dr James I. Macnair

Chairman of the Scottish National Memorial to
David Livingstone, Blantyre, Scotland.
Author of 'Livingstone the Liberator'

with geographical sections by

DR RONALD MILLER

Professor of Geography in the
University of Glasgow

Illustrated with
16 pages of photographs,
and maps

LONDON
J. M. DENT & SONS LTD

An act of piety to the memory
of David Livingstone

Contents

CONTENTS

BOOK FOUR: THE CENTRAL AFRICAN RIVERS

Illustrations

PHOTOGRAPHS

MAPS

ix

Preface

THE purpose of this book is to give, in one volume of moderate size, and in Dr Livingstone's words, an account of the travels that made him famous.

It is curious that, in spite of his worldwide reputation as an explorer, this has never been done before. The main facts of his romantic story are well known. Biographies in great numbers have been written, but in these the interest has been centred, in the main, upon his character and on his philanthropic and missionary achievements. They contain only meagre accounts of his epoch-making discoveries and but brief quotations from his voluminous diaries.

The published records of Livingstone's explorations are found in three very large books all printed by John Murray, London. The first, *Missionary Travels and Researches in South Africa*, issued in 1857, achieved a very wide popularity. Over seventy thousand copies were sold.

The second, *The Zambezi and its Tributaries*, published in 1865, though it did not have the same phenomenal success, attained a large circulation, as did also the third book (in two volumes), *Livingstone's Last Journals*. This was produced posthumously in 1874 and was edited by his intimate friend, the Rev. Horace Waller.

The last two of these books have been long out of print and the modern reader has no access to them except in some public libraries. Yet the journals are stocked with great stuff, and Livingstone knew how to tell his story.

The width of his interest was amazing. He had an eye that missed nothing and a curiosity that to the very end remained unquenched.[1] He was indefatigable in recording all that he saw

---

[1] As an illustration of Livingstone's 'insatiable curiosity,' take this extract from a letter to his brother-in-law, J. S. Moffat, who was starting on a journey to Matabeleland.

'As you wend your way north you will be inclined to note any point that comes before you. The size of the Cape elephants. See if you meet any man who has measured them. Are ostriches monogamists or polygamists? You will see them. Try and count their paces with your watch, when in full speed, and measure the length of his stride. Any information as to the

or learned of native customs; of birds and beasts and their habits; of trees and flowers in immense variety. His keen sensitiveness to the beauties of nature enlivened his painstaking geographical records, the accuracy of which has compelled the admiration of all travellers who have followed him.

Indeed it is the very opulence of the material that makes the books, in their original form, heavy going for the modern reader. In parts they resemble one of those jungle-streams in flat country, that the Explorer often describes, where the progress of the canoe is hindered by the density of the vegetation. Livingstone's interests were so varied, and his energy so continuous, that he tended to cumber his story with an overweight of detail. When it is stated that the three books together contain over three-quarters of a million words, it will be realized that the editor's first duty is that of judicious omission.

The story is given here, as far as is possible, in the Traveller's own words, but because severe condensation has been necessary, much dovetailing has been called for, and not infrequently some liberty has been taken with the text. Prominence has been given to the travel-tale, but an attempt has also been made to give a balanced account of the immense range of the geographical, geological, zoological, anthropological, and other researches that the journals contain. Livingstone had no scientific training in any of these subjects, his access to books was very limited, and yet such was the force of his genius that he became, and remained throughout his life, the highly valued correspondent of several of the first scientists of his time.

HOW LIVINGSTONE BECAME AN EXPLORER

Though, from youth up, Livingstone had read with avidity all the books of travel he could reach, he went out to Africa, for the first time, from the missionary motive alone and was, as far as can

cause of the migration of springboks, wildebeests, and the times and numbers. Try to discover the root and plant by which the Hottentots make their mead to ferment. Is there anything really irreligious in the boguera ceremonies? Is there anything besides wool-gathering that would be a profitable investment for the Bechuana? Take note of the diseases of the country, and observe the absence of pulmonary diseases.'

(From *The Matabele Mission of John and Emily Moffat*, page 10. Chatto and Windus),

be judged, quite unconscious of the passion for exploration that was so deeply embedded in him. For the first eleven years in Africa he lived on mission stations and performed, with characteristic enterprise and efficiency, the ordinary duties of a missionary. But these did not exhaust his tireless energy. Ever and anon he undertook tours, long or short, into country to the north, till then untrodden by white people. He disliked, however, to have these excursions described as 'explorations' as, no doubt, his somewhat critical colleagues were apt to call them, for each had for him a missionary purpose.

In his earlier short journeys the Doctor's main object was to discover localities where healthy mission stations might be established. Malaria was in those days the dreaded scourge of most parts of Africa, and the toll of European lives was terribly heavy. This quest continued to be a dominating purpose till the end of the Zambezi expedition.

But a different and even more urgent problem became distressingly plain as time passed. At this period the Boer farmers from the Cape were moving steadily northward and, by relentless pressure, depriving the Bechuana tribes, among whom he was then working, of their lands and water springs, and pushing them into a cul-de-sac against the dreaded Kalahari Desert. It was principally to find a relief for these unfortunate peoples, and a wider sphere for his own missionary efforts, that Livingstone undertook the exhausting marches of which the journals tell in their earlier chapters. To him every need was a call, and one thing leading to another, his tireless energy fitting itself to ever-wider tasks, he gradually ceased to be a missionary in the ordinary sense and became more and more the explorer. But he remained missionary-philanthropist to the end of his days, and nothing vexed him more keenly than to have his sacred vocation called in question.

ON THE WRITING OF THE JOURNALS

It may be safely claimed that no traveller ever kept a more copious or more meticulously careful day-by-day record than did Livingstone. No matter how difficult his situation nor how complete his exhaustion, it was rare for him to fail to make some entry, long or short, for each day.

A brief account of his method may be interesting. It was

his custom to carry in his jacket pocket a stiff-covered little book
in which he made notes, sketches, and rough maps.   Later, as
opportunity offered, these jottings were elaborated and entered,
carefully written, in large, strongly bound, locked volumes of the
size of a family Bible.   The penmanship of the rough notes is of
a very rapid writer, but is generally easy to read.

It was, further, his custom during longer periods of rest or
delay, as at Linyanti in 1855 and Tabora in 1872, to gather
together and arrange systematically the masses of other material
that he had so sedulously gathered.

It was from these records that, when on furlough during 1856
and 1864, his journals were written.   Happily the Explorer was
able to continue this method during the first part of the 'Last
Journals,' but after parting with Stanley, probably because he had
no longer a large tome in which to write, he ceased to 'post up'
his entries, so that his observations recorded in the last four little
pocket-books are quoted by the Rev. Horace Waller, the editor,
almost verbatim.[1]   When writing material gave out entirely he
wrote his memoranda on odd slips of paper and, later, even on
bits of newsprint, using for ink the juice of a plant.   It was only
his invariable habit of putting the date on every record that
prevented hopeless confusion.   But thanks to the care of the
African 'boys,' and to the ingenuity and pertinacity of the editor,
these scraps have been made to fit, and the record is complete.

For the sake of consistency the current usage for the spelling of
place-names has been in general adopted.

[1] The set of these little pocket-books—almost complete—is on exhibition
at the Livingstone Memorial, Blantyre.

Note

Grateful thanks are made to The Scottish National Memorial to David Livingstone and to The Carnegie Trust for the Universities of Scotland for assistance in making possible the publication of this work.

Acknowledgments

THANKS are accorded to the Rev. J. H. L. Burns, M.A., formerly of the London Missionary Society, Bechuanaland Protectorate, for his assistance in proof-correcting and for the help that his local knowledge has been to the editor. Also to J. R. Peddie, Esq., C.B.E., D.Lit., of the Carnegie Trust, for his encouragement at a critical point; to Dr Robert Common and Mr Ronald Paul for help in the preparation of maps, and to my wife.

Gratitude is due for use of illustrative material to Mr C. D'O. Pilkington Jackson, the Rev. Alexander Sandilands, M.B.E., the Rev. Edwin W. Smith, D.D., The London Missionary Society, Lieut.-Col. J. W. C. Kirk, and Miss M. L. Maitland Moir.

The complete title of the volume from which the first two
books of this narrative are compiled is:

MISSIONARY TRAVELS

and

RESEARCHES IN SOUTH AFRICA

including a sketch of

SIXTEEN YEARS' RESIDENCE IN THE
INTERIOR OF AFRICA

and a journey from the Cape of Good Hope to Loanda
on the West Coast; thence across the Continent, down
the River Zambezi, to the Eastern Ocean.

By DAVID LIVINGSTONE, LL.D., D.C.L.

Fellow of the Faculty of Physicians and Surgeons,
Glasgow, Corresponding Member of the Geographical
and Statistical Society of New York, and Gold Medallist
and Corresponding Member of the Royal Geographical
Societies of London and Paris.   F.S.A. etc. etc.

London
John Murray   Albemarle Street
1857

BOOK ONE

The Early Journeys, 1841–1845

I
Livingstone's Autobiography

My own inclination would be to say as little as possible about myself; but several of my friends have suggested that as the reader likes to know something about the author, a short account of my origin and early life would lend additional interest to this book. Such is my excuse for what follows.

My great-grandfather fell in the Battle of Culloden fighting for the old line of kings; and my grandfather was a small farmer in Ulva, where my father was born. It is one of that cluster of the Hebrides thus alluded to by Walter Scott:

> And Ulva dark and Colonsay
> And all the group of islets gay
> That guard famed Staffa round.

My grandfather was intimately acquainted with all the legends which that great writer has since made use of in *Tales of a Grandfather* and other works. As a boy I remember listening to him with delight. Many of his never-ending stock of stories were wonderfully like those I have since heard while sitting by African evening fires. My grandfather could give particulars of his ancestors for six generations before him; and the only point in the tradition of which I feel proud is this. One of these poor hardy islanders was renowned in the district for great wisdom. When he was on his deathbed he called his children around him and said: 'I have searched carefully through all the traditions of our family, and I never could discover that there was one dishonest man among our forefathers. If, therefore, any of you should take to dishonest ways, it will not be because it runs in our blood. I leave this precept with you: "Be honest."' Should I, in the following pages, perchance fall into error, I hope it will be regarded as unintentional, and not as indicating that I have forgotten his injunction

3

Finding his farm in Ulva insufficient to support a numerous family, my grandfather removed to Blantyre Works, a large cotton factory on the beautiful Clyde above Glasgow, and his sons, who had received the best education the Hebrides afforded, were gladly taken as clerks by the proprietors, Montieth & Co. He himself was highly esteemed for his unflinching honesty, and was employed for the conveyance of large sums of money from Glasgow to the works, and in his old age, according to the custom of the company, he was pensioned off, so as to spend his declining years in ease and comfort.

My uncles all entered His Majesty's Service during the last French war, either as soldiers or sailors; but my father remained at home. Too conscientious to grow rich as a small tea dealer, by his winning ways he made the hearts of his children twine round him as firmly as if he had bestowed upon them every worldly advantage.

He reared us in the Kirk of Scotland, a religious establishment that has been of incalculable blessing to that country; but he afterwards left it and for the last twenty years of his life was a deacon of an independent church in Hamilton. He is deserving of our lasting gratitude for presenting us from infancy with that consistent example of piety so beautifully portrayed by Burns in *The Cottar's Saturday Night*.

Early Education

The earliest recollection of my mother recalls a picture often seen among the Scottish poor—that of the anxious housewife striving to make both ends meet.

At the age of ten I went to the factory as a 'piecer.' With part of my first week's wages I purchased *Rudiments of Latin* and studied the language for many years with unabated ardour at an evening school, which met between the hours of eight and ten. I continued my labours when I got home till midnight or even later, if my mother did not interfere by snatching the books out of my hands. I had to be back in the factory by six in the morning, and my work lasted, with intervals for breakfast and dinner, till eight o'clock at night. I read in this way many of the classical authors, and knew Virgil and Horace better at sixteen than I do now.

I read everything I could lay my hands on, except novels. Scientific works and books of travel were my special delight, though my father, believing, as did many who ought to have known better, that the former were inimical to religion, would have preferred to see me poring over *The Cloud of Witnesses*[1] or Boston's *Fourfold State*.[2] Our differences of opinion reached the point of open rebellion on my part, and his last application of the rod was on my refusal to peruse Wilberforce's *Practical Christianity*.[3] This dislike of religious reading continued for years, but having lighted on those admirable works by Dr Thomas Dick,[4] *The Philosophy of Religion* and *The Philosophy of a Future State*, it was gratifying to find that he enforced my own conviction that religion and science were friendly to each other.

In the glow of love that Christianity inspires I soon resolved to devote my life to the alleviation of human misery. I felt that to be a pioneer of Christianity in China might lead to the material benefit of some small portion of that immense empire, and therefore set myself to obtain a medical education in order to qualify for that enterprise.

In identifying the herbs mentioned in my first medical treatise, that extraordinary old work on astrological medicine, Culpeper's *Herbal*,[5] I had the guidance of a book on the plants of Lanarkshire by Patrick. Limited as my time was, I managed to scour the whole countryside 'collecting simples.' Deep and anxious were my studies on the still deeper and more perplexing profundities of astrology, and I believe I got as far into the abyss of fantasies as my author said he dared to lead me. It seemed perilous ground to tread on farther, for the dark hint appeared to my youthful mind to

[1] Stories of the Scottish Covenanters (1714).
[2] An Exposition of Calvinistic Theology, by Thomas Boston of Ettrick (1720).
[3] *Practical View of Christianity* (1797), by William Wilberforce.
[4] A writer on Christian Apologetics (1775–1857).
[5] By Nicholas Culpeper, astrologer and physician (1616–54).

loom towards 'selling soul and body to the devil.' These
excursions gratified my intense love of nature.

On one of those exploring tours—long before geology was
the popular science it is now—we entered a limestone
quarry. It is impossible to describe the wonder with which
I began to collect the shells of the carboniferous limestone
which crops up in High Blantyre and Cambuslang. A
quarryman looked at me with that pitying eye which the
benevolent assume in viewing the insane. I asked him:
'How ever did these shells come into these rocks?' 'When
God made the rocks He made the shells in them,' was the
damping reply.

My reading in the factory was carried on by placing the
book on a portion of the spinning-jenny, so that I could catch
sentence after sentence as I passed at my work. I thus kept
up a pretty constant study undisturbed by the roar of the
machinery. To this part of my education I owe my present
power of completely abstracting my mind from surrounding
noises, so as to read and write in perfect comfort amidst the
play of children, and near the dancing and songs of savages.
The labour of the cotton factory, to which I was promoted in
my nineteenth year, was excessively severe for a slim loose-
jointed lad; but it was well paid, and it enabled me to
support myself while attending medical and Greek classes
in Glasgow in winter, and also the divinity lectures of Dr
Wardlaw, by working with my hands in summer.

Looking back now on that life of toil, I cannot but feel
thankful that it formed such a material part of my education;
and were it possible I should like to begin life again in the
same lowly style, and pass through the same hardy training.

I never received a farthing from anyone, and should have
accomplished my project of going to China as a medical
missionary had not some of my friends advised me to join the
London Missionary Society on account of its unsectarian
character. It 'sends neither episcopacy nor presbyterianism
or independency, but the Gospel of Christ, to the heathen.'
This exactly agreed with my idea of what a Missionary Society

ought to do; but it was not without a pang that I offered myself, for it was not agreeable to one accustomed to work his own way to become, in a measure, dependent on others.

Appointed to Africa

Having finished my medical curriculum and presented a thesis on a subject which required the use of the stethoscope for its diagnosis, I unwittingly procured for myself an examination rather more severe than usual, in consequence of a difference of opinion between me and the examiners on the use of the stethoscope. However, I was admitted a licentiate of the Faculty of Physicians and Surgeons (Glasgow), and it was with unfeigned delight that I became a member of the medical profession.

But now, though qualified for my original plan, the opium war was raging, and it was deemed inexpedient for me to proceed to China. I had fondly hoped to gain access to that, then, closed empire by means of the healing art, but as there was no prospect of early peace I was induced to turn my thoughts to Africa.

I embarked in 1840, and after a voyage of three months reached Cape Town.

(The Journal is resumed at the foot of page 19.)

Geographical Note

THE AFRICAN BACKGROUND

WE all, rightly, marvel at the extent of Livingstone's journeys: we ought equally to marvel that so much of the earth's surface remained unknown to us till he drew aside the veil less than a century ago. It will help us to understand the setting of his travels if we can understand something of the reasons why this continent of Africa, on whose northern flank, in Egypt, one of the earliest civilizations had developed, remained until quite recently the Dark Continent. It was circumnavigated by the Phoenicians at an early date and outlined again by navigators from the fifteenth century onwards, but in spite of fairly accurate fixing of the latitude and longitude of most parts of its coasts, details of the interior were drawn from hearsay and imagination rather than fact.

> Geographers in Afric maps
> With savage pictures fill their gaps.

A variety of reasons accounts for the long isolation of Africa. The coast is singularly devoid of natural harbours and even where landings are possible, avenues of penetration are usually lacking. The great rivers of Africa are without exception failures as routes to the interior. The Congo flood, that might have been one of the greatest transport arteries of the world, had it resembled in its make-up the humblest of our European navigable rivers, is barred by great cataracts at its mouth; and, by perverse contrast, up-stream from this its gradient is so slight, that it spreads out to such enormous widths that its depth rarely exceeds three feet. Beyond this, falls and cataracts again break the continuity. The next large river, the Niger, has so braided a delta that in none of the mouths is the flow sufficient to maintain a deep-water channel. The Zambezi, so impressive at Victoria Falls, has a shallow sandy mouth that denies access to all but small ships, while on the west side of the continent the Orange River, though comparable with the Danube in length, almost withers up in desert before reaching the sea. Even behind their uninviting mouths, these rivers do not lend themselves to navigation, for the seasonal

8

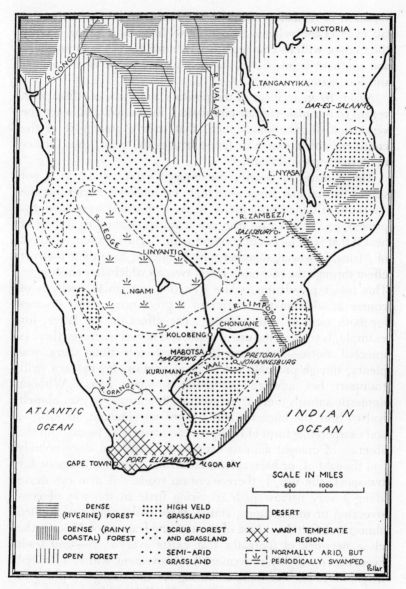

L.VICTORIA

R. CONGO

R. LUALABA

L. TANGANYIKA

DAR-ES-SALAAM

L. NYASA

R. ZAMBEZI

SALISBURY o

R. TEOGE

LINYANTIO

L. NGAMI

R. LIMPOPO

CHONUANE

KOLOBENG

MABOTSA

MAFEKING

PRETORIA

JOHANNESBURG

KURUMAN

R. VAAL

R. ORANGE

ATLANTIC
OCEAN

INDIAN
OCEAN

CAPE TOWN

PORT ELIZABETH

ALGOA BAY

SCALE IN MILES
500   1000

DENSE (RIVERINE) FOREST	HIGH VELD GRASSLAND	DESERT
DENSE (RAINY COASTAL) FOREST	SCRUB FOREST AND GRASSLAND	WARM TEMPERATE REGION
OPEN FOREST	SEMI-ARID GRASSLAND	NORMALLY ARID, BUT PERIODICALLY SWAMPED

Pollar

Livingstone's Africa: The Natural Setting

variation in rainfall is normally so great as to lead to a rise and fall in level and velocity that seriously impedes shipping. Only the Congo, with its compensatory tributaries from both northern and southern hemispheres, has a moderate range between high and low water.

Again, by an accident of the position and shape of Africa with regard to our planetary air circulation, the rainfall and hence the vegetation distribution is such, that over a great part of the continent either desert or forest fringes the coast, thus further rendering ingress difficult.

The climate, of course, discouraged exploration. It is not simply that temperatures were high, for medieval stories that the sea south of Cape Verde boiled in the tropic heat were soon disproved, and in any case man can stand an astonishing degree of heat if that is all he has to contend with.   The high temperatures of Africa, however, together with humidity, have their indirect effect through the enormous insect swarms which they encourage. This insect population, while irritating enough in itself, is of course in addition the carrier of a great many lethal diseases for both man and his animals. The effect on the latter, for example, is to deny the use of cattle and horses wherever there is infected tsetse—and even in Livingstone's time there was plenty, though probably not so many as now, for modern swift transport has infected previously immune areas. Without domestic animals there were no draught animals, so man himself had to bear the burdens, and a more uneconomic, unreliable, and exasperating form of transport can scarcely be found.   In the absence of draught animals over large areas, and since nobody had thought of, or been able to construct, that vital necessity for transport, the wheel, there were no roads.   A man can move along a very narrow path requiring little in the way of construction or maintenance, and so these paths can be multiplied almost indefinitely.   One of the amazing features of Africa is the close network of footpaths that exists everywhere—and leads everywhere—highly convenient for movement within a limited neighbourhood, but most confusing for the stranger wishing to make a long cross-country traverse; and placing him at the mercy of guides who may mislead him, deliberately or accidentally, or draw him into an ambush, or simply immobilize him by withdrawing their services.   Thus we find Livingstone, like many other African travellers, subjected to expensive and infuriating delays by the refusal of chiefs to supply guides. He navigated and fixed the framework of his maps by means of sextant observations, of course, but these could not tell him which fork of the path led merely to an outfield, and which to the next village on his route; which to a swamp and which to the ford on the river.

But insects, and the parasites they carry, affect man as gravely as his animals. Africa has all our diseases, coughs and colds, pneumonia and smallpox, and in addition a multitude of its own, of which perhaps malaria and intestinal parasites are in the long run the most serious. In Livingstone's time drugs were not available to treat all these afflictions, much less prevent infection. As a result, like the natives, he suffered from chronic malaria, but unlike them had no inbred resistance, though his magnificent physique bore the strain better than most—we have only to refer to the casualties among his compatriots on the second expedition to realize that. References to dysentery show that he—as was inevitable—succumbed like every other creature in Africa, man and beast, to parasites. Water everywhere is infected; game animals and cattle transmit the pests which they have swallowed with their food or water. Some parasites do not even require to be swallowed—they can penetrate the skin or are injected by insects. Some authorities believe that parasites account, more than all the other factors, for the crushing burden of ill health that has kept Africa down. Livingstone certainly carried his share of this burden. The fact that he surmounted not only the physical drag but the, in many ways, more serious psychological strain—for both malaria and dysentery cause periods of the most demoralizing depression and despair—can only make us marvel the more at the spirit that was within him.

The heavy incidence of disease in Africa was of course well known from the time of the early Portuguese discoverers onwards, and until recently 'The White Man's Grave' was a familiar expression. Brave men who were prepared to venture tempest and flood, heat and cold, in explorations elsewhere, could not be blamed if they did not seek death in the many painful and disgusting ways which Africa had to offer: death which was the more demoralizing in that its cause was unseen, and so could neither be avoided nor combated.

But in addition to these and other difficulties, another factor operated to delay the exploration of Africa—indifference. It is only recently, as history goes, that the scientific motive for exploration began to operate. Previously the main attraction was gain, either by plunder or trade, with sometimes a missionary effort as a secondary consideration. In respect of gain, however, Africa had few attractions to offer other than small quantities of gold, and these only on the west coast, its most unhealthy part. America had its Eldorados, real and imaginary, the Orient its spices and silks and superb craftsmanship in metal, wood, and stone. Africa, by contrast, was a land of miserable poverty; indeed it was indebted to Europeans for some of its staple food crops—maize, ground-nuts, cassava, and some others. But if Africa had no other natural resources to attract the exploring trader or adventurer, it had the ultimate human asset, the body. Traffic in human beings has been a feature of Africa's contact with the outside world for millennia. Even the Pharaohs had their black slaves, but the traffic that touches us most closely is that from the two main centres south of the Sahara. One was on the west coast, whence Europeans, including ourselves, transported slaves to the Americas. On the east coast, where a regularly reversing monsoon wind has, since earliest times, helped the mariner to cross and recross the Indian Ocean, Arab slavers not only provided the ocean transport but in Livingstone's time were penetrating inland and regularly participated in slave-hunts themselves.

While this traffic in human bodies was an index of poverty, it also, of course, greatly intensified the destitution of the people. Africa was never an easy land to live in, but when to natural poverty was added the disorganization, waste, and pain caused by the slave-trade, the areas of Africa so cursed probably offered less in human comfort and happiness than any other part of the globe. It was into such areas that Livingstone frequently penetrated, where his heart, like that of many other Europeans, was profoundly moved by the utter misery in which so many Africans were condemned to live. The Africans, on their part, could hardly fail to associate him, by virtue of his colour, with their oppressors, and he had to face a barrier of suspicion and distrust, if not of active hostility.

Apart from such considerations, Livingstone was fortunate compared with other travellers in that most of the areas he

African travel about 1850

Mirage: the salt-pans of Nchokotsa (Chukutsa)

explored lay at considerable altitudes—higher than the summits of the Scottish hills, for example—where the heat was less oppressive than in, say, West Africa. Much of the area opened up by Livingstone has proved less unsuitable for white occupation than most of tropical Africa, so that the present population of European origin is denser there than in the more lowlying parts.

In order to appreciate Livingstone's journals it is necessary to know something of the build and plan of these highlands, over which he travelled so extensively. Here again we find that Africa differs from the rest of the world. The normal story of the building of a country is one involving the repetition, over many millions of years, of the cycle that is usually the basis of the geological pattern. Earth movements heave up some parts of the earth's crust, usually folding and even over-folding them in the process. Frequently great shearing movements take place, by which rocks of one character are slid into juxtaposition with those of another. Wind and rain and sun and frost set to work weathering away the highlands so formed and the debris is carried in the rivers or by wind to be deposited, some in hollows on the land, some in the oceans; there eventually to form new rocks which some day are in their turn heaved up to form the highlands of yet another cycle in the earth's history. This kind of story, slowly repeated over aeons of time, naturally results in great complexity in most instances. Here in our small British Isles we are accustomed to the great variety of land forms which such a geological history produces. We have hills and dales, plains and plateaus, limestones and sandstones, granites and clays, coal and iron ore, salt, and even oil. Above all, our land is broken into regions each with its own characteristics; the whole is thus compartmented into units whose people feel themselves an entity, with a regional patriotism often quite intense, but never destroying its sense of kinship with neighbouring regions nor obscuring the fact of the greater unity which constitutes our nation.

Africa is quite different. This ancient block of the earth's crust has stubbornly resisted the earth movements to which most other continents yielded. The forces which folded rocks elsewhere induced in tropical Africa only gentle warpings; and while great stretches of the other continents were alternately above and below the sea, Africa has moved but little, and particularly in its southern half has experienced marine invasion only in a relatively narrow coastal zone.   In recent times, geologically speaking, the great earth movements that account for most of the present major mountain ranges of the world did succeed in making an impression on Africa, not by folding but by faulting.   Great cracks fissured East Africa along roughly parallel lines and the portions of crust between them moved in an uneven way to form alternately high and low ground.   So profound were these faults that in many cases they offered vents by which molten material from the interior reached the surface and piled up to form the great volcanoes of East Africa.

This special build, then, has as might be expected its special land forms.   If we confine ourselves to Africa south of the Sudan and east of Lake Chad—the area Livingstone was particularly concerned with—we see that over great areas the original crustal complex is at the surface or buried in its own ruins.   The processes of erosion have been at work for so long that the whole is reduced to gently rolling plains of a size and monotony rarely found elsewhere.   The only relief is an occasional relict hill representing either the residue of a primeval hill mass, or simply a plug of rock, often granite, in the original complex, whose greater resistance has left it upstanding as its surroundings weathered away.   Drainage is often quite indeterminate on such surfaces, and the rivers may make great purposeless detours or even lose themselves in swamps, particularly where some down-warping has occurred.

One must hasten to add, however, that the plains of Africa are not continuous.   Uplifts of the land in the geological past, by accelerating the lower courses of the rivers, transformed them there from sluggish old age to vigorous youth, in which the seaward edges of the plains were deeply dissected by the network of watercourses and, in conjunction with the usual weathering, a great layer of country was removed.   As their force became spent by the cutting away of the very slopes that gave them vigour, the rivers cut laterally again rather than vertically and smoothed off the surface at the new, lower level.   Such a relevelling must have spread inwards to attack the older, upper smooth surfaces, but in most cases a fresh rejuvenation of the rivers supervened before the process was complete.   The same kind of thing has happened elsewhere in the world, but nowhere was such a great compact land mass involved and in practically no case has the process been extended, as it has in Africa, over such an enormous stretch of geological time without any wiping of the slate clean by a general submergence beneath the sea.

As a result, the extensive smooth surfaces so typical of Africa are characteristically tiered one above the other in great terraces, with normally quite sharp breaks of slope between. Over these edges the rivers tumble either in sheer falls like those Livingstone called 'Victoria,' or in cataracts none the less prohibitive to transport. We thus have the paradox that Africa, of all continents the least mountainous and least distinguished by rushing streams, has the greatest potential hydro - electric power of all.

This terraced effect is also produced by some of the rocks formed from very ancient deposits in hollows of the land. These, usually sandstones, are being attacked by erosion round the edges, so that again a sharp break of slope occurs between the surrounding plains and the flat upper surface of the sandstones.

In East Africa, the great series of faults is often represented at the surface by massive scarps, so that while the upper surfaces of the blocks of crust here are smooth, the fractured edges are often virtually cliffs. In this area, of course, occur the only real mountains of Africa, the volcanoes, for while Africa as a whole is higher than other continents—its plateaus pile up to above 6,000 feet—it has only a relatively minute area above 10,000 feet.

This, then, was the setting in which Livingstone worked. Only in the extreme south, in Cape Province, was there anything resembling the rich diversity of Europe. Elsewhere great monotonous plains piled one above the other, separated always by something of a step and occasionally by a major feature like the Drakensberg scarp. Monotony and repetition are the keynotes, and their influence on the native peoples is profound. Nowhere had nature set limits to a people's wanderings, limits that might have caused them to live together long enough to learn to know each other, and wish to live together better: that might have given rise to the political organization that makes a state and demands the behaviour, which we call civilization, that is

B

necessary if large bodies of people are to live together in harmony. Instead, lacking cohesion, groups wandered off and budded in their turn, to scatter a sparse population of small units broadcast over the land. Except where a great leader arose for some special purpose, like a Zulu war-chief, there was no cohesion and thus no strength, no progress; and nothing like our nation-states of Western Europe ever developed. Even allowing for the initial advantage of fire-arms it is astonishing how small parties of Boer pioneers, as few as a family unit, were able to penetrate inland and maintain themselves amidst vastly superior numbers of natives. On the other hand, a solitary traveller like Livingstone had constantly to win the confidence of yet another petty chief in order to make progress, whereas had there been large political organizations, far fewer warrants to travel would have served.

Such, then, were the people amongst whom Livingstone moved. Politically and economically they were little removed from a patriarchal (sometimes matriarchal) communal life.

Their basis of life in the moister areas was agriculture; in the drier, stock-rearing, with sometimes a combination of both and usually some hunting. Over most of the area the rainfall tends to be rather scanty, and except in the Congo basin is restricted to the summer half-year, while in the south-west, the Kalahari, the season is so short as practically to amount to desert conditions. Temperatures are such that in combination with the summer rains the staple food is grain, either maize in the moister parts or millets in the drier. Now a fact that we bread-eaters often overlook is that wheat, with its peculiarly high gluten content, is the only grain save rye that forms a flour which can be made to 'rise' on cooking, i.e. to form a light, palatable food-stuff. Like oatmeal, neither maize nor millet will rise, and thus has to be eaten as porridge. Africans of Livingstone's time, as now, had an extremely dull diet in that the greater proportion of it was porridge: not porridge as we know it, oatmeal porridge, taken with milk or cream, and perhaps sugar, but porridge whose natural insipidity is relieved only by condiments. Little wonder then that salt has in Africa a very high value, and that fiery peppers and tasty seasonings like smoked fish and even putrid meat are popular. Even so, a porridge diet is not only dull, but has the drawback that so much bulk has to be taken to achieve adequate nutrition that some lassitude, if not discomfort, is common after meals.

It is tempting to point to the special success of the Scotsmen—Bruce, Park, Clapperton, and Livingstone—in living off the land in Africa, and ascribe their gifts of endurance under difficulties of diet to a background of porridge-eating at home, as contrasted with the traditionally more carnivorous Englishman, who must have sadly missed his beef in a continent where the slaughtering of cattle for food was a rare luxury.

While differing widely in background and personal character, the explorers just mentioned have, it must be noted, something in common beyond country of birth. Like some other explorers of their time they were seeking the truth: they represent the flowering in Europe of the spirit of scientific inquiry into our physical world. But Livingstone was more: there burned in him a flame of the spirit, a determination to overthrow the slave-trade. The others had noted and regretted its presence but it was not their concern: Livingstone on the other hand *made* it his concern to bring the weight of public opinion in Britain against it, and so enlist the material power of the state in the campaign. He was successful, and the great power of Britain began to operate against slavery and ended in a way that was not foreseen. By the turn of this century we had acquired an empire in Africa, and the whole continent had been partitioned among the European powers. From being lonely travellers obliged to seek the favour of the chiefs in whose territories they travelled, from having to use the indigenous languages and respect, if not adopt, local customs and manners, Europeans passed to a state of generic superiority and a mode of life which is often African only in climate. There can be little doubt that as far as understanding and mutual esteem is concerned the change has not been for the better. Little is left of the fellow feeling that could tend the utterly destitute Mungo Park and sing of him:

> Let us pity the white man,
> No mother has he,

and it is very doubtful if we can in these days match the deep devotion that bore the mortal remains of Livingstone from Ilala to the sea.

II

The Kalahari Desert

LIVINGSTONE spent a month in Cape Town with Dr John Philip, secretary in South Africa of the London Missionary Society and prominent as champion of the Hottentots, and then made his way by ship to Algoa Bay. From there he trekked by ox-wagon to Kuruman [1] (or Lattako), at that time the most northerly station of the society. His instructions were to await the arrival from Scotland of Dr Robert Moffat.

The Moffats' coming was, however, delayed, and Livingstone's overflowing energy found congenial outlet in various short expeditions towards the north, in company with a senior colleague called Edwards. [2]

The purpose of these 'prentice' trips was to discover a healthy and otherwise suitable site for the new station he hoped to build and occupy, in hitherto unexplored country. During these short excursions, and especially during a solitary stay in the village of Lepelole, the young missionary laid the foundation of that intimate and sympathetic understanding [3] of Bantu ideas and customs, and especially of language, that was to prove of supreme value in later life.

At the end of 1843 the Moffat family arrived, and about a year later, in Kuruman on 2nd January 1845, Livingstone married the eldest daughter, Mary. It proved an ideal marriage. [4] They built and lived in, successively, three stations: Mabotsa (near

---

[1] 125 miles north-west of Kimberley.   [2] See Notes on Persons, page 404.

[3] *Livingstone's Peculiar Gift.* 'Of seeing what lay at the back of the native mind. Irrational suspicions, mysterious motives, ridiculous arguments—he could understand and deal with them all. If they obstructed his progress, he never roughly overrode them. He argued, and if argument was useless he waited, waited sometimes for weeks before he gained his point. But he never gave up. He never turned back. Of all the qualities which enabled him to succeed, nothing was more vital than this tenacity.' (Note the whole of this fine passage, *Kirk on the Zambezi*, by Sir Reginald Coupland, page 40.)

[4] 'Mary speaks the language like a native without knowing as much as I do. I have a foreign accent—a heelandman! The native children are fond of her and maybe, so am I.'—From a letter to his brother Charles. See *Some Letters from David Livingstone*, by David Chamberlin, page 132.

Zeerust), Chonuane, forty miles farther north, and Kolobeng. They remained in the last place for several years, and four children were born during this period.

The Missionary, however, became increasingly uncomfortable under the restrictions of his situation, and pined for the wider and, as he pictured them, more fruitful fields lying on the farther side of the Kalahari Desert.

At this date Lake Ngami had become, in a measure out of all proportion to its importance, the lodestar of African explorers. Soon after his arrival in the country Livingstone writes of his ambition to be its discoverer. Indeed in one of his jaunts in his first year he had come within eight days' travel of the lake. But the expense of these long excursions was prohibitive. His salary as missionary was only £100 a year. On this sum it was possible, at that date, to support a family with difficulty, but to finance, in addition, long expeditions was more than even Mrs Livingstone's gifts of economy could compass.

A timely circumstance, however, presented itself. At this date South Africa was the favourite haunt of big-game hunters, and several of these, men of position and culture, became Livingstone's intimate friends and admirers. Indeed some of them became almost yearly visitors. And so it happened that in their company, and to a considerable extent with their financial assistance, from 1849 onwards he was able to undertake the journeys towards Lake Ngami that it had so long been his ambition to attempt.

Mary and the family remained behind at Kolobeng.

The Journal resumed

The true position of Lake Ngami had, for half a century at least, been correctly located by the natives who visited it when the rains were more copious in the desert than in recent times.[1] Many attempts had been made to reach it, but this was found impossible even by Griquas,[2] who may be supposed to be more capable of enduring thirst than Europeans. It

[1] *Missionary Travels*, page 46.
[2] A tribe of half-caste Dutch and Hottentots who spoke Dutch, cast off by whites and disowned by their mothers' people. They formed their own tribe, and being better armed than the Bantu had considerable power.

was clear that our only chance of success was by going round the desert rather than through it.

I communicated my intention to an African traveller, Colonel Steele.[1] He made it known to another gentleman, Mr Oswell,[2] who undertook to bear the entire expense of the guides and fully executed his generous intention. When he joined me he brought Mr Murray with him.

Before beginning my narrative I will give some account of the great Kalahari Desert. The space from the Orange River in the south to Lake Ngami in the north, and from about 24° east long. to near the west coast, has been called a desert because, though intersected by beds of ancient rivers, it contains no running water and very little in wells. Far from being destitute of vegetation, it is covered with grass and creeping plants, and there are large patches of bushes and even trees. It is remarkably flat, and prodigious herds of antelopes roam over the plains. The Bushmen [3] and Bakalahari [4] prey on the game, and on the countless *rodentia* and small species of the feline race.

In general the soil is light-coloured soft sand, nearly pure silica. The quantity of grass is remarkable. It usually rises in tufts with bare spaces between, or the intervals are occupied by creeping plants which, having their roots buried beneath the soil, feel little effect from the scorching sun. The number of those which have tuberous roots is very great, a structure which is intended to supply moisture during the long droughts. A plant named leroshúa is a blessing to the inhabitants of the desert. It is a small plant with linear leaves and a stalk not thicker than a crow quill, but on digging down a foot beneath the soil we come to a tuber often as large as the head of a young child. When the rind is removed we

---

[1] See Notes on Persons, page 407.   [2] See Notes on Persons, page 406.
[3] Now usually called Masarwa. Nomads living on antelopes and the roots and sparse fruits of the Kalahari. Chief Khama induced many of them to adopt a settled agricultural life.
[4] Though not now called a tribe, they were, Livingstone thought, the oldest of all the Bechuana tribes. They live in small groups on the fringes of the Kalahari.

find a mass of cellular tissue filled with a fluid much like that of a young turnip, which, owing to the depth it grows beneath the surface, is generally deliciously cool.

But the most surprising plant of the desert is the water-melon (*Kengwe* or *Keme*: *Cucumis caffer*). In years when more than a usual quantity of rain falls, vast tracts of the country are literally covered with these melons. This commonly happens every ten or eleven years. Then the animals of every sort and name, including man, rejoice in a rich supply. The elephant, true lord of the forest, revels in this fruit, and so do different species of rhinoceros, although naturally so diverse in their choice of pasture. The various kinds of antelope feed on it with avidity, and lions, hyenas, jackals, and mice all seem to appreciate the common blessing.

The inhabitants of this tract of country consist of Bushmen and Bakalahari. The former are probably the aborigines of the southern part of the continent; the latter the remnants of the first emigration of Bechuana. The Bushmen live in the desert from choice, the Bakalahari from compulsion, and both possess an intense love of liberty. The Bushmen are distinct in race and habits, language and appearance, and are the only real nomads in the country. They never cultivate the soil nor rear any animals save wretched dogs. They are intimately acquainted with the habits of game, and chiefly subsist on their flesh, eked out with roots and beans and fruits of the desert. Those who inhabit the hot sandy plains generally possess thin wiry forms capable of great exertion and of severe privations. Many are of low stature, though not dwarfish.

The Bakalahari are supposed to be the oldest of the Bechuana tribes, and are said to have possessed enormous herds of the large-horned cattle mentioned by Bruce, until they were driven into the desert by fresh migrations of their own nation. Living for centuries on the same plains with the Bushmen, subject to the same influences of climate, enduring the same thirst, and subsisting on similar food, they seem to supply a proof that locality is not always sufficient to account for differences in races.   The Bakalahari retain in undying vigour the Bechuana love of agriculture and domestic animals.

The dread of visits from Bechuanas of strange tribes causes the Bakalahari to reside far from water, and they not infrequently hide their supplies by filling the pits with sand and making a fire over the spot.   When they wish to draw water the women come with a bag or net on their backs, in which there are twenty or thirty ostrich egg-shells, with a hole in the end of each, such as would admit one's finger. Tying a bunch of grass to one end of a reed about two feet long, they insert it in a hole dug as deep as the arm will reach, and ram the wet sand firmly round it.   The grass absorbs the water, which is then sucked up by the woman through the reed.   A straw goes from her mouth to one of the egg-shells on the ground, and as she draws mouthful after mouthful from below, she makes the water trickle along the *outside* of the straw into the shell.   The whole stock is thus passed through the woman's mouth, taken home, and carefully buried.   I have visited villages where, had we acted the domineering part and rummaged every hut, we should have found nothing; but by waiting with patience the people were led to form a favourable opinion of us, and bring us a shellful of the precious fluid.

Crossing the Desert

Such was the desert which we were now preparing to cross [1] —a region formerly terrible to the Bechuanas from the number of serpents which infested it, and from the extreme thirst which these people often endured when their water vessels were insufficient to hold the requisite supply till the next well could be reached.

Just before the arrival of my companions a party of the people of the lake came to ask me to visit their country. They brought flaming accounts of the amount of ivory to be found there, and talked of the cattle-pens made of elephants' tusks.

[1] *Missionary Travels*, page 53.

We started for the unknown region on 1st June 1849. Proceeding northwards and passing through a range of tree-covered hills to Shokuane, formerly the residence of the Bakwains [1] we soon after entered the high road to the Bamangwato,[2] which lies mainly in the bed of an ancient river or wadi which must formerly have flowed north to south. There are indications here and there that at places which are now waterless then were formerly wells and cattle stations. The adjacent country is perfectly flat, but covered with forest, bush, and abundance of grass. The trees are mostly of a kind of acacia called Monáto that is common as far as Angola.

At Mashüe we came upon a never-failing supply of pure water in a sandstone rocky hollow. Here we left the road to the Bamangwato hills and struck away to the north into the desert. We next proceeded to Serotli, a real Kalahari fountain. The country around was covered with bushes and trees of a kind of *leguminosae*, with lilac flowers. At Serotli we found only a few hollows, like those made by buffalo and rhinoceros when they roll in the mud. In a corner of one of these there appeared water, which would have been quickly lapped up by our dogs, if we had not driven them away. This was all the apparent supply for some eighty oxen, twenty horses, and about a score of men, and it was to serve for the next seventy miles, a journey of three days with wagons.

Our guide, Ramotobi, who had spent all his youth in the desert, declared that there was plenty of water at hand. By the aid of spades and fingers, two of the holes were cleared out so as to form pits six feet deep and about as many broad. Our guides were earnest in their injunctions not to break through the hard crust of sand at the bottom, in which case 'the water would go away.' The value of this advice was

[1] *Bakwains* or *Bakwena*. The Bantu tribe with which Livingstone had closest connection, at Shokuane, at Lepelole, and later at Kolobeng. Their present headquarters are at Molepolole, Bechuanaland Protectorate.

[2] The tribe of Sekomi (Sekgoma), father of Chief Khama. Present chief town Serowe, Bechuana Protectorate.

* B

proved in the case of an Englishman who dug through the sandy stratum in the wells at Mohotluáni, when the water immediately disappeared downwards. Enough water accumulated for the horses that evening, but as there was not sufficient for the oxen we sent them back to Lobotani, where they got a good supply after thirsting for four full days. Next morning we found the water had flowed in faster than at first, which invariably happens in these reservoirs, owing to the passages widening by the flow. The supply, which at the beginning was only enough for a few men, becomes in a few days sufficient for the oxen as well. These sucking places are generally in the hollows of ancient river-beds.

In the evening of the second day at Serotli a hyena appeared in the grass and raised a panic among the cattle. This false mode of attack is the plan which this cowardly animal always adopts. His courage closely resembles that of a turkey-cock: he will bite only if an animal is running away. Seventeen of our draught oxen fled into the hands of Sekomi,[1] who was unfriendly to our expedition. He sent them back with a message strongly dissuading us from attempting to cross the desert: 'Where are you going? You will be killed by sun and thirst, and then all the white men will blame me for not saving you.'

We replied by assuring the messengers that the white men would attribute our deaths to our own stupidity, as we did not intend to allow our guides to return till they had put us into our graves. We sent a handsome present to Sekomi, with the promise that if he allowed the Bakalahari to keep the wells open for us, we would repeat the gift on our return.

All around Serotli the country is perfectly flat and composed of soft white sand. There is a peculiar glare of bright sunlight from a cloudless sky over the whole scene. One clump of trees looks so exactly like another, that if you leave the wells and walk a quarter of a mile in any direction, it is difficult to return. On one occasion Oswell and Murray,

---

[1] Chief of the Bamangwato. Father of the well-known Christian chief, Khama.

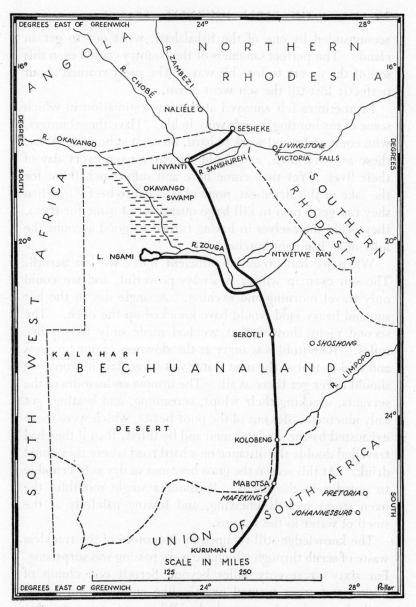

The Early Journeys

accompanied by one of the Bakalahari, went out to get an eland. The perfect sameness of the country caused even this son of the desert to lose his way. The party roamed about perfectly lost till the sun went down.

I sometimes felt annoyed at the low estimation in which some of my hunting friends were held. 'Have these hunters, who come so far and work so hard, no meat at home? Why, these are rich men, and could slaughter oxen every day of their lives. Yet they come here and suffer such thirst for the sake of this dry meat, none of it equal to beef!' When they can get a man to kill large quantities of game for them, they pride themselves in having turned to good account the folly of an itinerant butcher!

When we had procured sufficient water we left Serotli. The sun even in winter is always powerful, and we could only travel morning and evening. A single day in the hot sun and heavy sand would have knocked up the oxen. The second night showed that we had made only twenty-five miles. Ramotobi was angry at the slowness of our progress and told us that as the next water was three days in front, we should never get there at all. The utmost endeavours of the servants, cracking their whips, screaming, and beating, got only nineteen miles out of the poor beasts, which were more exhausted by the sandy ground and by thirst, than if they had travelled double the distance on a hard road where they could drink. At this season the grass becomes so dry as to crumble to powder in the hands. Without a single mouthful the oxen stood wearily chewing, and lowing painfully at the smell of water in the wagons.

The knowledge still retained by Ramotobi of the trackless waste of scrub through which we were passing was surprising. For sixty or seventy miles beyond Serotli one clump of bushes and trees seemed exactly like another; but as we walked together he remarked: 'When we come to that hollow we shall light on the highway to Sekomi, and beyond that lies the River Mokóko.' After breakfast some of the men who had gone forward along a little path which showed

The Zouga or Botletle River

the footprints of water-loving animals, returned with the joyful tidings of *metse* (water), and showed the mud on their knees as evidence. The pool of rain-water was called Mathuluáni. The thirsty oxen rushed in until the water was nearly level with their throats, and then they slowly drew long refreshing mouthfuls until their collapsed sides distended as if they would burst.

When we left the Mokóko, Mr Oswell saw a Bushwoman running away in a bent position to escape observation. He took her for a lion and galloped after her. She thought herself captured, and offered to deliver up her property, a few traps made of cord. When I explained that we only wanted water and would pay her if she led us to it, she walked briskly before our horses for eight miles and brought us to Nchokotsa.[1] We rewarded her with a piece of meat and a good large bunch of beads. At the sight of the latter she burst into a merry laugh.

At Chukutsa we came upon the first of a great number of salt-pans, covered with an efflorescence of lime, probably the nitrate. When this pan, which is twenty miles in circumference, burst upon our view, the setting sun was casting a beautiful blue haze over the white incrustations, making the whole expanse look exactly like a lake. Oswell threw his hat into the air and shouted out a huzzah which made the poor Bushwoman and the Bakwains think him mad. I was as completely deceived as he. We had no idea that the long-looked-for lake was still more than three hundred miles distant. The mirage on these salinas was marvellous. The waves danced, and the shadows of the trees were reflected in such a perfect manner, that the loose cattle, horses, dogs, and even Hottentots hastened towards the deceitful pools. A herd of zebras looked in the mirage exactly like elephants, and Oswell began to saddle a horse in order to hunt them. A sort of break in the haze dispelled the illusion.

---

[1] Modern name Chukutsa.

III

The Discovery of Lake Ngami

On 4th July we went forward on horseback, and again and again did we seem to see the lake. At last we came to the Zouga,[1] and found it to be a river running to the north-east. A village of Bakurutse lay on the opposite bank, and the people informed me that this water came out of Ngami. The news gladdened our hearts. We had the River Zouga (Botletle) at our feet and by following it we should at last reach the broad water.

When we had gone up the bank of this beautiful river about ninety-six miles from the point where we first struck it, the Bechuana chief of the district ordered his people to assist us. We were received by the Bakóba, whose language clearly shows that they bear affinity to the tribes of the north. They call themselves Bayeíye, i.e. men, but the Bechuanas call them Bakóba, a term that carries the idea of slaves. They have a tradition that their forefathers, in their first essays at war, made their bows from Palma Christi, and when these broke they gave up fighting altogether. They have never been known to use arms, and have invariably submitted to the rule of every horde which has overrun the countries adjacent to the rivers on which they specially love to dwell. They are thus the Quakers of the body politic in Africa.

The canoes of these inland sailors are primitive craft, hollowed with iron adzes out of single trees. If the tree has a bend so has the canoe. I found they regarded their rude vessels as an Arab does his camel. They have always fires in them, and prefer sleeping in them while on a journey to spending the night on shore. 'On the land,' they say, 'you have lions, serpents, hyenas, and your enemies, but in a canoe behind a bank of reeds nothing can harm you.'

While ascending the beautifully wooded river we came to a large stream flowing into it. This was the Tamunak'le.

[1] *Missionary Travels*, page 63.

28

I inquired whence it came. 'Oh, from a country full of rivers. So many that no one can tell their number, and full of large trees.' This was a confirmation of what I had heard from the Bakwains, that the country beyond was not the 'large sandy plateau' of the philosophers. The prospect of a highway capable of being traversed by boats to an un-explored and populous region, grew from that time stronger and stronger in my mind, and when we actually came to the lake this idea was so dominant that the actual discovery seemed of little importance.

It was on 1st August 1849 that we reached the north-east end of Lake Ngami,[1] and for the first time this fine-looking sheet of water was beheld by Europeans.[2] The direction of the lake to be north-north-east and south-south-west by compass. We could detect no horizon from where we stood, nor could we form any idea of the extent of the lake, except from the reports of local people: they pro-fessed to go round it in three days, which would make it about seventy miles in circumference.

It is shallow and can never be of much value as a com-mercial highway. In the months preceding the annual supply of water from the north it is with difficulty that cattle can approach to drink through the boggy, reedy banks. We were informed by the Bayeíye that during the annual inundation, not only trees of great size but antelopes, are swept down its rushing waters.

[1] Ngami is no longer a lake, but a wide stretch of flat land, marshy in parts. This is an extreme case of the problem of which Livingstone had so much experience in his early days, the growing desiccation of large parts of the south.

[2] *The discovery of Lake Ngami*. The charge has been made by not a few that Livingstone accepted the credit for this great discovery, while it should have gone by rights to Oswell, who financed the expedition. This seems unfair. It was natural that, as the news reached home first through him, he should have been the most closely connected in the public mind with the success. But he made no special claims. That Oswell seems to have kept in the back-ground may well have been due to his characteristic generosity. He knew that the kudos meant much more to his friend than to him. It should not be forgotten, moreover, that it was Livingstone who initiated the expedition. (See *The Personal Life of David Livingstone*, by Blaikie, page 102; *Livingstone the Liberator*, by James I. Macnair, page 117, also *Missionary Travels*, page 46.)

My chief object in coming to the lake was to visit Sebituane, the great chief of the Makololo, who was reported to live some two hundred miles beyond. We had come to a half-tribe of the Bamangwato, called the Batauána. Their chief was a young man called Lechulatébe. He had just come into power and was ambitious. I applied to him for guides to Sebituane's country but he objected, fearing lest other white men should go there also and give Sebituane guns, whereas he hoped to get a monopoly of fire-arms and thus obtain ascendancy.

He at last unwillingly provided us with guides, then again declined, and sent his men with orders to the Bayeíye to refuse us a passage across the river. I tried hard to form a raft but the dry wood was so worm-eaten that it would not bear the weight of a single person. I worked many hours in the water, for I was not aware of the number of alligators in the Zouga, and never think of my labour without feeling thankful that I escaped their jaws.

The season was now far advanced, and as Mr Oswell volunteered to go to the Cape to bring a boat, we resolved to make our way south.

The discovery of Lake Ngami was the starting point of Livingstone's public career. He lost no time in communicating the great news to the London Missionary Society and through Captain Steele to the Royal Geographical Society. The event caused a small sensation and brought the Missionary for the first time to public notice. The Kalahari Desert had previously foiled several well-equipped expeditions and there was no question that it was, in the main, to Livingstone's knowledge of African ways and his influence over the natives that the success of this one was due. To his keen gratification he received from Queen Victoria, through the Royal Geographical Society, the gift of twenty-five guineas.[1]

[1] *Queen Victoria's Gift.* In spite of the narrow position financially in which the Livingstone family had to live, it is characteristic that the Explorer spent this money in buying a watch for the observing of the occultation of the stars by the moon, for finding latitudes. Nor is it less remarkable that Mrs Livingstone agreed!

In one important respect, however, the effort had failed. He had not been able to make contact with the Paramount Chief Sebituane of the Makololo tribe, who was known to be most anxious to meet him. It was in this man's territory that the Doctor was hoping to found the new station that had become so important an element in his future plans.

So we find him in April 1850, once more on the track and moving northwards, and this time the family went with him. For some unexplained reason he did not wait for Oswell, though that had been apparently the arrangement.

This second attempt to reach Makololo territory was a complete failure. The tsetse-fly, met with in an unexpected quarter, led to a change of route, and an epidemic of fever, which affected two of the children and some of the servants, compelled a return to Kolobeng.

But a year later, in April 1851, a caravan, which included the family and was strengthened by the presence of Cotton Oswell, once more started on the arduous quest. Thanks to the latter's generous help, this expedition was fully equipped and the wells in the desert route had been deepened by men sent in advance.

This adventure, though it included one grim and very perilous episode, was completely successful.

Almost a Tragedy

When in April 1851 we set out on our journey, Sekomi, chief of the Bamangwato, was more than usually gracious and even furnished us with a guide. No one, however, knew the path beyond Chukutsa. When we reached that point we found that the mainspring of the gun of a man who was well acquainted with the Bushmen, through whose country we should pass, had opportunely broken. I never undertook to mend a gun with greater zest. Under the promise of the guidance of its owner we went north instead of westward.

One of the Bushmen, named Shobo, consented to be our guide over the waste between the springs and the country of Sebituane. Shobo gave us no hope of water in less than a month. Providentially, however, we came sooner than we had expected to rain-water in a chain of pools.

It is impossible to convey an idea of the dreary scene on which we entered after leaving this spot; the only vegetation was low scrub in deep sand. Not a bird or insect enlivened the landscape. To make matters worse our guide wandered to all points of the compass on the trail of elephants that had been here in the rainy season and then would sit down in the path and in his broken Sichuána say: 'No water, all country only'; and then coolly curl himself up and go to sleep. The oxen were terribly fatigued and thirsty, and on the morning of the fourth day Shobo, after professing ignorance of everything, vanished altogether. We went on in the direction in which we last saw him and at about eleven o'clock began to see birds and the trail of a rhinoceros. At this we unyoked the oxen, and they, apparently knowing the sign, rushed along towards the River Mabábe, which comes from the Tamunak'le and lay to the west of us. The supply of water in the wagons had been wasted by one of the servants, and only a small portion remained for the children. This was a bitterly anxious night, and in the morning the less there was of water the more thirsty the little rogues became. The idea of their perishing before our eyes was terrible. It would almost have been a relief to me to have been reproached with having been the entire cause of the catastrophe; but not one syllable of upbraiding was uttered by their mother, though the tearful eye told of the agony within. In the afternoon of the fifth day, to our inexpressible relief, some of the men returned with a supply of that fluid of which we never before had felt the true value.[1]

[1] Livingstone has frequently been censured for lack of consideration for his wife and children; for leaving them for months and unprotected among barbarous tribes, and with taking them with him through terrible country. This is undiscerning criticism. He could not have done the magnificent work he did without a formidable share of the burdens falling on his family. Mary Livingstone, on her part, accepted her fate proudly.

Further, fearsome adventures like that described above were very far from

The cattle, in rushing along the Mabábe, probably crossed a small patch of trees containing tsetse, an insect that was shortly to become a perfect plague to us.

Shobo had found his way to the Bayeíye and appeared when we came up the river, at the head of a party. As he wished to show his importance before his friends he walked up boldly and commanded our whole cavalcade to stop and bring forth tobacco and fire while he coolly sat down and smoked his pipe. We stopped to admire the acting, and though he had left us in the lurch we all liked this wonderful specimen of that wonderful people, the Bushmen.

A few remarks on the tsetse or *Glossina morsitans* may be here appropriate.[1] It is not much larger than a common house-fly, and is nearly the same brown colour as the common honey-bee. The after-part of the body has three or four yellow bars across it. It is remarkably alert, evading most dexterously all attempts to capture it with the hand in common temperatures. In the cool of the morning and evening it is less agile. Its peculiar buzz once heard can never be forgotten, for it is well known that the bite of this poisonous insect is certain death to the ox, horse, and dog. Though in this journey we were not aware of any great number having at any time alighted on our cattle we lost forty-three fine oxen by its bite. We watched the animals carefully and believe that not a score of flies were ever upon them. In the ox, a few days after the bite, the eyes and nose begin to run, the coat stares, and a swelling appears under the jaw and sometimes at the navel. Emaciation commences, accompanied by a curious flaccidity of the muscles. This proceeds unchecked until, perhaps some months afterwards, purging comes and the victim perishes in a state of extreme exhaustion.

---

being typical of the life on trek. Ordinarily it was for the children a joyous time. They went only where the great Cape-wagon could go—a house on wheels. Of such travel Livingstone writes: 'It is a prolonged system of picnicking, excellent for health and agreeable to those who are not over-fastidious about trifles and who delight in fresh air.'

[1] *Missionary Travels*, page 80.

IV

The Chief of the Makololo

THE Makololo, whom we met on the Chobe, were delighted to see us. As their chief Sebituane [1] was about twenty miles down the river, Mr Oswell and I proceeded in canoes to his temporary residence. [2] He had come from the Barótse town of Naliéle down to Seshéke as soon as he heard that white men were in search of him, and now came one hundred miles more, to welcome us to his country. He was upon an island with all his principal men around him, engaged in singing. It was more like church music than the sing-song ē ē ē, ae ae ae of the Bechuanas in the south. They continued their singing for some seconds after our approach. He signified his joy and added: 'Your cattle are all bitten by the tsetse and will certainly die; but never mind, I have oxen and will give you as many as you need.' He presented us with an ox and a jar of honey, and handed us over to the care of Mahále. Prepared skins as soft as cloth were given as a covering for the night, and since nothing could be returned to the chief, Mahále became the owner of them.

Long before it was day Sebituane came and sat down by the fire that was lighted for our benefit behind the hedge where we lay. As his career has been most remarkable and he was unquestionably the greatest man in all that country, I will give a short account of his life.

He was about forty-five years of age, of tall wiry form, of olive or coffee-and-milk colour, and slightly bald. He was cool and collected, and more frank in his answers than any other chief I ever met. He was the greatest warrior ever heard of beyond the colony, and always led his men

[1] See Notes on Persons, page 406.
[2] *Missionary Travels*, page 83.

Old Makololo warrior

into battle himself. When he saw the enemy he felt the edge of his battle-axe and said: 'Aha! It is sharp and whoever turns his back on the enemy will feel its edge.' He was so fleet of foot that all his people knew that there was no escape for a coward. In some instances of skulking he allowed the individual to return home. Then he summoned him to his presence and said: 'Ah! You prefer dying at home to dying in the field, do you? You shall have your wish.' This was the signal for immediate execution.

He was not the son of a chief, though related closely to the reigning family of the Basúto. He was one of an immense horde of savages driven back by the Griquas from Kuruman in 1824. He then fled north with an insignificant party of men and cattle. At Melita the Bangwaketse collected Bakwains, Bakátla, and Bahurutse to 'eat them up.' Placing his men in front and the women behind the cattle, he routed the whole of his enemies at a blow.

After many further adventures Sebituane moved down the Leeambye (or Zambezi) among the Batoka. This people lived in large islands in the river and, feeling perfectly secure in their fastnesses, often allured wandering tribes on to the uninhabited islets on pretence of ferrying them across, and there left them to perish for the sake of their goods. Sebituane, however, with his usual insight requested the island chief to take his seat in the canoe with him, and detained him by his side till all his people and the cattle were safely over.

But the Matabele, a Zulu tribe under Mosilikatse, crossed the Zambezi, attacked Sebituane, and captured his women and cattle. Rallying his men he followed, and recaptured the whole.

A prophet induced him to turn his face again westward. This man, by name Tlapáne, was called a *senoga*, one who has intercourse with the gods. He probably had a touch of insanity, for he was in the habit of retiring, no one knew whither, until the moon was full. He returned emaciated and worked himself up into a state of ecstasy. These 'prophets' stamp, leap, shout, and beat the ground with a club till they induce a kind of fit. They pretend that the utterances they give forth under its influences are unknown to themselves.

Tlapáne, pointing eastward, said: 'There I behold a fire. Shun it. The gods say: "Go not thither." ' Then turning to the west he said: 'I see a city and a nation of black men. Their cattle are red. Thine own tribe, Sebituane, is perishing and will be consumed. Thou wilt govern black men and when thy warriors have captured red cattle let not the owners be killed. They are thy future tribe.'

This vaticination shows an observant mind. The policy recommended was wise. The fire pointed to was evidently the Portuguese fire-arms. The black men were the Barótse. Sebituane spared their chiefs though they attacked him first.

He was pursued by the Matabele, for Mosilikatse could never forgive defeat. Sebituane placed some goats on one of the large islands of the Zambezi as a bait, and some men in canoes to co-operate. When the Matabele were all ferried over·they found themselves in a trap, being unable to swim. After the goats were eaten, they subsisted on the roots of grass, but became so emaciated that when the Makololo landed they had only to perform the part of executioners on the adults and to adopt the rest into the tribe.

Sebituane knew everything that happened in his country, for he had the art of gaining the affection both of his own people and of strangers. When a party of poor men came into the town to sell shoes or skins he soon knew them all. They would be surprised to see him come alone and, sitting down, inquire if they were hungry. He would order an attendant to bring milk, meal, and honey, and mixing them in their sight in order to remove suspicion make them feast, perhaps for the first time in their lives, on a lordly dish. Delighted beyond measure with his affability, they gave all the information in their power; and as he never let a party go without giving everyone, servants and all, a present, his praises sounded far and wide. 'He has a heart.

He is wise' were the usual expressions we heard before we saw him.

The Death of Sebituane and its Consequences

Sebituane was much pleased at the proof of confidence we had shown in bringing our children, and promised to show us his country in order that we might choose a place in which to locate ourselves.

The plan was that I should remain in pursuit of my objects as a missionary while Mr Oswell explored the Zambezi to the east. Poor Sebituane, just after realizing what he had so ardently desired, fell sick of inflammation of the lungs, which originated in and extended from an old wound.[1] I saw his danger, but being a stranger I feared to treat him lest, in the event of his death, I should be blamed by his people. I mentioned this to one of his doctors who said: 'Your fear is prudent and wise. This people would blame you.' He had been cured before by the Barótse, who made a large number of incisions in the chest. The Makololo doctors scarcely cut the skin.

On the Sunday afternoon in which he died, when our usual religious service was over, I visited him with my little boy, Robert. 'Come near,' said Sebituane, 'and see if I am any longer a man. I am done.' He was thus sensible of the dangerous nature of his disease, so I ventured to assent, and added a single sentence regarding hope after death. 'Why do you speak of death?' said one of a relay of fresh doctors. 'Sebituane will never die.' If I had persisted, the impression would have been produced that by speaking about it I wished him to die. After sitting with him for some time and commending him to the mercy of God, I rose to depart, when the dying chieftain, raising himself up a little from his prone position, called a servant and said: 'Take Robert to Maunku (one of his wives) and tell her to give him some milk.' These were the last words of Sebituane.

[1] *Missionary Travels*, page 89.

We were not informed of his death till next day. We spoke to the people, advising them to keep together and support the heir. They took this kindly and in turn told us not to be alarmed as they would not think of ascribing the death of their chief to us; that Sebituane had just gone the way of his fathers.

He was decidedly the best specimen of a native chief I ever met. I never felt so much grieved at the loss of a black man before, and it was impossible not to follow him in thought into the world of which he had just heard before he was called away, and to realize somewhat the feelings of those who pray for the dead. The deep dark question of what is to become of such as he must, however, be left where we find it, believing that assuredly 'the Judge of all the earth will do right.'

At Sebituane's death the chieftainship devolved, as her father intended, on his daughter named Ma-mochisáne. He had promised to show us his country and to select a suitable locality for our residence. We had now to look to his daughter. She gave us perfect liberty to visit any part of the country we chose.

Mr Oswell and I then proceeded one hundred and thirty miles to the north-east, to Seshéke, and at the end of June 1851 we were rewarded by the discovery of the Zambezi in the centre of the continent. This was a most important point, for the river was not previously known to exist there at all. We saw it in the dry season, yet there was a breadth of three hundred to six hundred yards of deep flowing water. Mr Oswell said he had never seen so fine a river, not even in India. At the period of the annual inundation it rises fully twenty feet in perpendicular height, and floods fifteen to twenty miles of lands adjacent to the banks. The Makololo were living in the swamps thus formed for the sake of the protection the deep reedy river afforded them against their enemies. I could not conscientiously ask them to abandon their defences for my convenience.

The healthy districts were defenceless, and the safe

localities were so deleterious to human life that the original
Basúto have nearly all been cut off by fever.   I therefore
feared to subject my family to the scourge.

The abrupt ending of this record shows that the Explorer
realized that from the point of view of his main purpose the
journey had failed.   No site suitable for residence by a European
family had been found, so haste was made to return to Kolobeng.

The discovery of the Zambezi at this point was, however, a
matter of the first geographical importance.   The confirmation
of his dream that there might be a waterway from the coast
deep into the country, stirred his imagination as thus far nothing
had done.   Should this mighty stream prove to be navigable
from the coast, what a splendid solution that would be to all
his problems!

Further, and even more important, it was here that for the
first time Livingstone came into personal contact with the inland
slave traffic and caught a glimpse of its unlimited possibilities
of evil.   He saw that, through the energy of Arab and other
traders, a demand for European manufactures, for guns, and
cotton goods had already been awakened, that was bound to
increase.   It could not, and should not, be stopped.   But he
foresaw that, inasmuch as such trade could be conducted by
barter only, the exchange of human flesh for merchandise would
inevitably follow.   Indeed he saw there before him in the
Makololo country evidence that such barter had already begun.
Only one thing, it seemed to him, could prevent the disaster
and that was what he called 'Christianity and Commerce.'   By
this he meant business conducted on Christian principles by
Christian men; trade in which the interests of the African
would be given a fair place; and the exchange, on terms advantageous to both sides, of European manufactures for ivory and
other local produce.   This idea was, of course, not new but it
became from that day forward one of his dominating thoughts.

The impact of this new conception called for a complete
change in his plans.   Such trade could not be conducted from
the south—the cost of transport made that impossible.   A
'highway' must be found, from east or from west, by road or
by river, so that mission work, and commerce beneficial to the
inhabitants of these densely populated countries, might be

possible. To open such a path became therefore the motive
of his next journey in many respects his greatest—the Trans-
African Expedition.

Obviously children of tender years could not face the rigours
of such travel. They must go home, and Mrs Livingstone with
them. Kolobeng had been the abode of the family for five years
and was left with much regret. Except for a few crowded
months during the first furlough, it was to be their last experience
of family life.

The little company reached Cape Town in April 1852 after
eleven years of up-country life. 'The costumes of the whole
party,' the Missionary records, 'were somewhat on the style of
Robinson Crusoe.' But Oswell, with characteristic open-
handedness, supplied their need. Moreover, he met the family
in England and helped to settle them in. They lived at first
in London and later in Hamilton.

Livingstone remained in Cape Town, to gather equipment for
his great adventure.

BOOK TWO

The Great Trans-African Journey, 1853–1856

Geographical Note

SOUTH AND WEST CENTRAL AFRICA

SOUTH AFRICA is a vast plateau whose edges rise sharply in a series of steps. The plateau is highest in the east where it culminates in the Basúto highlands, reaching 10,000 feet and rearing the mighty Drakensberg escarpment towards the Indian Ocean. The western margin is lower but none the less definite, and while most of the upper surface of the plateau is above 3,000 feet, it sags to just under this level in the lower parts of the Kalahari. The rain-bearing winds are from the east, being mostly the south-east trades, and these rarely fail to produce some rain on the great east-facing scarp edge of the plateau. The smooth upper surface, however, is normally dry until the trades are reinforced in the southern summer by the monsoon of the Indian Ocean. Even then, however, there is adequate rainfall only on the eastern side of the high plateau and the west remains arid, so that much of the Kalahari is wellnigh desert, and for those who do not know how to find water, completely so.

It was on these high, smooth, grassy plains, then, that Livingstone began his journeys into the unknown, pushing north between the obstacles of the Basúto hills to the east of him and the inhospitable Kalahari to the west. Thus guided, he found himself eventually in the sump of this great basin, the marshy area of which, Lake Ngami, was the residue of a once much greater body of water. Though usually reaching the Zambezi at some seasons, the drainage is indeterminate, and thus the area is fairly well watered and comparatively closely peopled. It was here, with the Makololo, that Livingstone paused for some time and achieved perhaps a closer intimacy than with any other African tribe except the Bakwena.

Deciding eventually to explore a route to the west coast, he moved on up the Zambezi, which here flows over one of the high erosion surfaces so characteristic of Africa. Being smooth and open, movement presented little difficulty except in the

43

rains, but as Livingstone went north he was entering regions of higher rainfall, and the proportion of trees to grass in the landscape gradually increased, till finally on leaving the Zambezi and entering the Congo drainage system he was often in forest. He had also moved out of one of Africa's great shallow basins into another, but over a watershed so slight as to be imperceptible, and where in places the waters flow sometimes to the Congo and sometimes to the Zambezi, so inconclusive is the slope. The route to Loanda, however, lay for much of its length along the slope of the country, and so perforce across a series of rivers which, in this better-watered area, formed no mean obstacle.

Having brought his Makololo porters home again, Livingstone turned to explore the Lower Zambezi. At the outset of this phase comes the great Victoria Falls, where in a curtain of water four hundred feet high and one and a quarter miles in length the river falls off the high flat plateau to a more uneven surface at a lower level. The bed-rock at Victoria Falls is a vast pile of lava-flows with two lines of weakness in the rock, crossing each other at a small angle. The river, working back along these lines, has cut a deep gorge, but where it switches from one line of weakness to another, a sharp angle is formed, so that the gorge below the fall forms a spectacular series of zigzags as, by headward erosion, it extends up-stream. Such is the power of the river that the waterfall has receded five miles up-stream since primitive man first settled in the area.

Having dropped off the high smooth surface, the Zambezi's course is through relatively broken country, with gorges and rapids that obstruct navigation for considerable distances and make it necessary, as Livingstone found, to cut across country. With the decrease in height and approach to the coast goes a rise in temperature and humidity, and the tsetse-fly is present, so that whereas on the high plateau Livingstone had sometimes travelled on horseback, he had to walk down to the Indian Ocean.

Cape Town and Linyanti

LIVINGSTONE spent about three months in Cape Town after his family had left. It was an unhappy time, partly because he felt the separation so keenly and partly because of the petty annoyances that grew from his unpopularity. The bitterness arising from the 'Kaffir Rebellion' persisted, and he was well known as a protagonist of the African. He was generally believed to have made a practice of selling guns and powder to Sechele, the chief of the Bakwains. While this was completely untrue, the suspicion was strong enough to make it impossible for him to secure anything like the quantity of ammunition he needed for the journey that was to be his next effort.

Sir Harry Johnston and other experienced travellers have criticized severely the insufficiency of the equipment that he did eventually manage to collect, affirming that the persistent ill health that clogged his movements during the next three years was mainly due to the inadequacy of his furnishings. There is much truth in this, but the blame must rest in the main on the unfriendly, grudging attitude of the authorities of that time. On the other hand, Livingstone would probably have contested this contention. He was fond of stressing the wisdom of travelling 'light,' arguing that a conspicuous equipment excited the cupidity of the tribes.

But if the Explorer was ill furnished materially for the tremendous task before him, this was more than compensated for by his supreme physical and moral competency.

He was in his prime—forty years of age—and in perfect physical condition. He could live without hurt as few Europeans have ever attempted to do. He could say: 'I have drunk water swarming with insects, thick with mud, putrid with rhinoceroses' urine and buffalo dung, and no stinted draughts of it either, and yet felt no inconvenience from it.' He could exist for months on native food.

His missionary apprenticeship had given him the knowledge of how to deal with the African. Politeness, consideration, and firmness, when needed, were his practice. There was in him the power which for lack of a better word might be called demonic, a sense of overpowering personality. Primitive people felt it at once, and since this power was backed by an imperturbable good humour and a patience that was infectious, there were few who could resist him.[1,2]

One important result of this visit to the Cape must be mentioned—one piece of well-deserved good fortune. With the object of fitting himself better for the work of exploration, he approached Sir Thomas Maclear,[3] Astronomer Royal at the Cape, with the request for better instruments than he possessed, and for some instruction in the art of observation, to help him in his geographical surveys. The petition was most cordially received and was the beginning of a fruitful friendship. Maclear came to admire Livingstone greatly, and never missed the opportunity of commenting on the value and accuracy of the observations that the Explorer systematically sent him.

The Doctor took with him a coloured trader called Fleming, who was the representative of a firm in Cape Town. It was hoped that this might be the beginning of a scheme of 'Christian trading.' Fleming stayed with him as far as Linyanti. The attempt had some success, but was not continued. The cost of transport was prohibitive.

In June 1852 then we see Livingstone setting out upon what was probably the greatest journey in African exploration.[4] His wagons, overloaded with other people's goods, took the well-marked north-going track through the colony to Kuruman and

1 *Livingstone the Liberator*, pages 137-8.
2 'Livingstone had the most singular faculty of ingratiating himself with natives wheresoever he travelled. A frank open-handed generosity, combined with a constant jocular way of treating them, that carried him through all.' See *The Search for Livingstone*, by Lieut E. D. Young, page 201.
3 See Notes on Persons, page 405.
4 It should be noted that this great adventure was a completely individual effort. Coupland in his introduction to Chamberlin's *Some Letters from David Livingstone*, page xiii, says: 'Other great explorers were to emulate his example, but most of them ventured into the unknown with the backing of scientific societies, of newspapers or governments, with carefully prepared and costly equipment, with caravans of porters one hundred or even two hundred strong, and an adequate stock of food, beads, and wire to buy their way through greedy and hostile tribes. But nobody financed Livingstone's enterprise. His store of 'trade goods' was pitifully small and he was alone with his Africans, often utterly exhausted and desperately ill.'

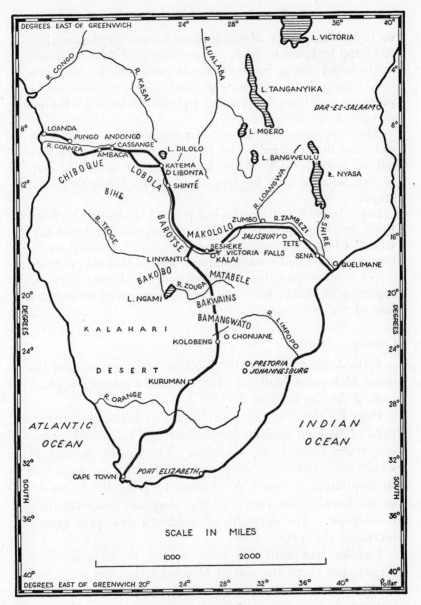

The Transcontinental Journeys

on to Kolobeng, both of which places he saw for the last time.
Kolobeng he found in ruins.   A commando of Boer hot-heads,
in the belief that he had trafficked in arms with the Bakwains,
had, happily in his absence, wreaked their vengeance on his
property, scattering his precious records and looting what was
of value in his furniture.[1]

After the first shock this act of vandalism concerned Livingstone but little, indeed before long he was congratulating himself on being freed from the impediment of household gear,
so that what he calls his 'vagabond' nature might find fuller
scope.

In the beginning of 1853 he had reached his disciple Sechele's
town, and after spending a few days with the 'wretched Bakwains,' whom the commando had also attacked, started on the
long northward trail towards Linyanti and the Makololo country.

We resume quotation from the journal starting with the
beginning of March, when the caravan was passing through the
land of the Bechuana.

Crossing the Chobe

Proceeding to the north of Kama-kama we entered the
dense Mohonono bush, which required the constant application of the axe for two days.[2]

Here for the first time I had leisure to follow the instructions of my kind teacher, Mr Maclear, and calculated several
longitudes from lunar distances.   The hearty manner in
which the astronomer had promised to verify my work was
an inspiration to me.   We wished to avoid the tsetse-fly,
so we kept to the course of the magnetic meridian from
Lurilopepe.   The necessity of making a new path greatly
increased the toil.

Fleming had until this time assisted to drive his own
wagon, but about the end of March he knocked up.   As I
could not drive two wagons, I shared with him the remaining
water and went on, with the intention of coming back to
him as soon as we had reached the next pool.   Heavy rain

[1] See Appendix III, page 408.
[2] *Missionary Travels*, page 167.

now commenced. I employed the whole day in cutting down trees, and every stroke of the axe brought down a thick shower on my back, which during hard work is very refreshing. On returning to the wagon we found that Fleming had managed to come up.

As we went north the country became lovely. The grass was often higher than the wagons. The vines festooned the trees. Among them was the real banian (*Ficus indica*), with its deep roots, the wild date, and palmyra. The hollows contained large patches of water. Next came water courses like small rivers, twenty yards broad and four feet deep. Elephants wading in them made numbers of holes in which the oxen floundered desperately. Our wagon pole broke, and we were compelled to work up to the breast in water for three and a half hours.

At last we came to the Sanshureh, which presented an impassable barrier, so we drew up under a magnificent baobab-tree (lat. 18° 4′ 27″ S., long. 24° 6′ 20″ E.) and resolved to explore the river for a ford. The great quantity of water was part of the annual inundation of the Chobe. In company with the Bushmen I explored the banks. We waded a long way among the reeds in water breast high, but always found a broad, deep space free from vegetation, and unfordable.

We made so many attempts to get over the Sanshureh that my Bushmen friends became quite tired of the work and at last slipped away by night. I was fain to take one of the strongest of my companions and cross the river in a pontoon, the gift of Captains Codrington and Webb. We each carried some provisions and a blanket, and penetrated about twenty miles in the hope of striking the Chobe. The plain was covered with water ankle-deep, and thick grass which reached above the knees.

In the evening we came to an immense wall of reeds six or eight feet high and without any opening. When we tried to enter, the water became so deep that we had to desist. We concluded that we had come to the banks of the river, so we directed our course to some trees towards the south in order to get a bed and a view of the adjacent locality.

Having shot a leche [1] we got a good cup of tea and had a comfortable night. While collecting wood I found a bird's nest consisting of five leaves sewn together with threads of a spider's web. Nothing could exceed the airiness of this pretty contrivance. The threads had to be pushed through small punctures and thickened to resemble a knot.

Next morning, by climbing the highest trees, we could see a fine large sheet of water, but surrounded by the same impenetrable belt of trees. Two tree-covered islands seemed to be nearer to the water than the shore on which we were, so we made an attempt to get to them first. It was not the reeds alone that we had to pass through. A peculiar serrated grass which, at certain angles, cut like a razor was mingled with the reeds, and the climbing convolvulus, with stalks which felt as strong as whipcord, bound the mass together. We felt like pygmies, and often the only way we could get on was by both of us leaning against a part and bending it down till we could stand on it. The perspiration streamed off our bodies, and as there was no ventilation among the reeds the heat was stifling, and the water, which was up to the knees, felt agreeably refreshing.

After some hours of toil we reached one of the islands. Here we met an old friend—the bramble bush. My strong moleskins were quite worn through at the knees, and the leather trousers of my companion were torn and his legs bleeding. Tearing my handkerchief in two, I tied it round my knees and then encountered another difficulty. We were still forty or fifty yards from clear water, but now were opposed by great masses of papyrus, which are like palms in miniature, eight or ten feet high, and an inch and a half in diameter. These were so strongly laced together by convolvulus that the weight of both of us could not make way into the clear water. At last we found a passage

[1] A species of antelope discovered by Oswell and Livingstone.

prepared by a hippopotamus. Eager as soon as we reached
the island to look along the vista to clear water, I stepped
in and found that it took me up to the neck.

Returning nearly worn out, we proceeded up the bank
of the Chobe till we came to the point of departure of the
branch, Sanshureh. We then went in the opposite direction, or down the Chobe, though from the highest trees
we could see nothing but a vast expanse of reed, with here
and there a tree on the islands. This was a hard day's
work, and when we came to a deserted Bayeíye hut on an
ant-hill, not a bit of wood could be got for a fire, except
the grass and sticks of the dwelling itself. I dreaded the
'tampans' so common in old huts; but outside we had
thousands of mosquitoes, and cold dew began to fall, so we
were fain to crawl beneath its shelter.

We were close to the reeds and could listen to the strange
sounds that are often heard there. By day I had seen water-
snakes putting up their heads and swimming about. There
were great numbers of otters which had made little spoors
all over the plain in search of fishes. Curious birds, too,
jerked and wriggled among the reedy masses, and we heard
human-like voices and unearthly sounds with splash, guggle,
jupp, as if rare fun were going on in their uncouth haunts.

At one time something came near us, making a splash
like that of a canoe or hippopotamus. Thinking it to be a
Makololo we shouted, then discharged a gun several times;
but the noise persisted without intermission for an hour.

After a damp cold night we set to early in the morning
to explore, but left the pontoon in order to lighten our
labour. The ant-hills were very high, some thirty feet, and
of a base so broad that trees grew on them. From one of
these ant-hills we discovered an inlet to the Chobe, and
having gone back for the pontoon, we launched ourselves
on a deep river, here from eighty to one hundred yards
wide. I gave my companion strict injunctions to stick by
the pontoon in case a hippopotamus should look at us. Nor
was this caution unnecessary, for one came up at our side

and made a desperate plunge off. We had passed over him.

We paddled on from midday till sunset. There was nothing but a wall of reed on each bank and we saw every prospect of spending a supperless night on our float. But just as the short twilight of these parts was commencing we noticed on the north bank the village of Moremi, one of the Makololo whose acquaintance I had made on our former visit. The villagers looked as we may suppose people do who have seen a ghost, and in their figurative way of speaking said: 'He has dropped among us from the clouds, yet came riding upon a hippopotamus. We Makololo thought no one could cross the Chobe without our knowledge, but here he drops among us like a bird.'

Next day we returned in canoes across the flooded land. A few days later a large party of the Barótse came down from Linyanti to take us across the river. This they did in fine style, swimming and diving among the oxen, more like alligators than men, and taking the wagons to pieces, carried them across on a number of canoes lashed together. We were now among friends, and so, avoiding the flooded lands to the north, we turned west towards Linyanti where we arrived on 23rd May 1853. This is the capital town of the Makololo and only a short distance from our wagon-stand in 1851.

VI

Back among the Makololo

THE whole population of Linyanti, numbering about seven thousand, turned out to see the wagons in motion. They had never witnessed the phenomenon before, for on the former occasion we had departed by night. Sekeletu, now in power, received us in royal style and sent us many pots of *boyalwa*, the beer of the country.

The court herald greeted us. This official issues proclamations, calls assemblies, keeps the *kgotla* [1] clean and the fire burning, and when a person is executed drags away the body. The present herald, an old man, had occupied the post in Sebituane's time. He stood up and roared out some adulatory sentences as: 'Don't I see the white man? Don't I see the comrade of Sebituane? Don't I see the father of Sekeletu? Give thy son sleep, my lord.' The meaning of this last request was that they had heard that the white man had a *pot* (a cannon). If he could only get this weapon, he thought they would be able to sleep in peace.

Sekeletu was eighteen years of age, of the dark yellow, or coffee-and-milk colour, of which the Makololo are so proud, because it distinguishes them from the black tribes on the rivers. To my eye the black skin is much more agreeable than the tawny skin of the half-caste, which the Makololo closely resemble. In height Sekeletu was about five feet seven, not as good-looking as his father but equally friendly.

Sebituane installed his daughter, Ma-mochisáne into the chieftainship long before his death, and to prevent her having a superior in a husband, he told her that all the men were hers, that she might take any one of them but ought to keep to none. According to a saying of the

[1] The village meeting-place.

country 'the tongues of women cannot be governed,' and as she lived this free independent life, they made her miserable by their remarks.   So when her father was dead she declared she would never govern the Makololo while her brother lived.   From fear of the pretensions of another member of the family Sekeletu wished her to retain the authority, and three days were spent in public discussion of the point.   At last the woman stood up and with a womanly gush of tears said to her brother: 'I have been chief only because my father wished it.   I have always preferred to be married and have a family like other women.   You must build your father's house.'

Mpépe, the rival candidate for the chieftainship, favoured the slave-traders.   A large party of Mambari [1] had come to Linyanti while I was floundering on the prairies south of the Chobe.   They fled precipitately when some of the Makololo returned with hats I had given them.   When the cause of their haste was asked they alleged that if I found them there I should take all their slaves and goods from them. They had got this impression from knowledge of what the English cruisers were doing on the coast.

My object being to examine the country for a healthy locality before attempting to make a path to the east or west, I proposed to Sekeletu to ascend the great river that we had discovered in 1851.   He volunteered to accompany us.

We had advanced about sixty miles on the road to Sesheke when we encountered his rival, Mpépe.   Sekeletu and his companions were mounted on oxen.   Mpépe, armed with his little axe, came along a path parallel to but a quarter of a mile distant from ours, and when he saw Sekeletu he ran with all his might towards us, but Sekeletu, being on his guard, galloped off to an adjacent village.   Mpépe had told his party that he would cut down Sekeletu, either at their first meeting or at the breaking up of their first conference.   The former intention having been frustrated, he

[1] A tribe of Portuguese half-caste traders deep in the slave-trade.

then determined to effect his purpose after their first interview.

I happened to sit down between the two in the hut where they met. Being tired with riding all day in the sun, I asked Sekeletu where I should sleep and he replied: 'Come, I will show you.' As we rose together I unconsciously covered Sekeletu's body with mine and saved him from the blow of the assassin. I knew nothing of the plot, but some of Mpépe's attendants divulged it, and Sekeletu put Mpépe to death the same night. It was so quietly managed that, although I was sleeping only a few yards from the scene, I knew nothing of it till the next day.

Nokuáne, one of Sekeletu's friends, went to the fire at which Mpépe sat, with a handful of snuff. Mpépe asked for some and held out his hand. Nokuáne caught hold of it, while another man seized the other hand and, leading him out a mile, speared him. This is the common mode of executing criminals. It being inadvisable for us to go on during this commotion, we returned to Linyanti.

Sekeletu soon asked me to mention the things I hoped to get from him. I explained that my object was to elevate his people and make them Christians. He replied that he did not wish to learn to read the Book, as it might change his heart and make him content with only one wife, like Sechele. He wanted five wives at least. According to the system of the Bechuana he became the possessor of his father's wives and adopted two. A chieftain has always a head wife, a queen.

As I had declined to name anything as a present from Sekeletu except a canoe, he brought me ten fine elephant tusks. He would take no denial. I afterwards gave them to some of his subjects to sell on their own account. I always refused to take presents of ivory, from the idea that a religious instructor degraded himself by accepting gifts from those whose spiritual welfare he professed to seek.

I had brought with me as presents improved breeds of

* C

goats, fowls, and a pair of cats.   The Makololo are fond of
improving the breed of their domestic animals.

Travel with the Chief

On 30th May I was seized with fever for the first time.[1]
We reached the town of Linyanti on the 23rd, and as my
habits were suddenly changed from great exertion to comparative inactivity, at the commencement of the cold season
I suffered from a severe attack of stoppage of secretions,
closely resembling a common cold.   Warm baths and drinks
relieved me, and I had no idea but that I was recovering
from the effects of a chill, got by leaving the warm wagon
in the evening to conduct family worship at my people's
fire.   But on 2nd June a relapse showed to the Makololo,
who know the complaint, that my indisposition was no other
than the fever with which I have since made a more intimate
acquaintance.

Cold east winds prevail at this time, and as they come
over the extensive flats inundated by the Chobe, as well as
many other districts where pools of water are now drying
up, they may be supposed to be loaded with malaria and
watery vapour, and fever often follows.   The usual symptoms of stopped secretion are manifested—shivering and a
feeling of coldness, though the skin is quite hot to the
touch of another.   The heat in the axilla, over the heart,
and in the region of the stomach, was in my case 100°, but
along the spine and at the nape of the neck 103°.   The
internal processes were all, with the exception of the
kidneys and liver, stopped.   The latter, in its effort to free
the blood of noxious particles, often secretes enormous
quantities of bile.   There are pains along the spine, and
frontal headache.

Anxious to know whether the natives had any remedy of
which we were ignorant, I requested the assistance of one
of Sekeletu's doctors.   He placed some roots in a pot of
water, and, when it was boiling, placed it on a spot beneath

[1] *Missionary Travels*, page 194.

a blanket thrown over both me and it. This produced no immediate effect. Then he took a small bundle of medicinal woods and, burning them in a potsherd nearly to ashes, used the smoke and hot vapour as an auxiliary to the other in causing diaphoresis. But after being stewed in their vapour baths, smoked like a red herring over green twigs, and charmed *secundum artem*, I concluded that I could cure fever more quickly than they can. Violent remedies are injurious. There is a good deal in not giving in to this disease. He who is low spirited and apt to despond will die sooner than the man who is not of such a melancholic nature.

Having waited a month at Linyanti we departed for the purpose of ascending the river from Sesheke. Not only Sekeletu but also many of the under-chiefs went with us. The country is perfectly flat except where patches are elevated a few feet above the level and where the termites have thrown up their enormous mounds. No one who has not seen their gigantic structures can imagine the industry of these little labourers.[1] They seem to impart fertility to the soil which they pass through their mouths, for the Makololo find the sides of ant-hills choice places for rearing crops that need more than ordinary care.

Sekeletu is always accompanied by his Mopato,[2] a number of young men of his own age. When he sits down, those who are nearest eat out of the same dish, for the Makololo chiefs pride themselves on eating with their people. He takes a little and then beckons to his neighbours to partake. When they have done so he perhaps beckons to someone at a distance, who starts forward, seizes the pot, and removes it to his own companions.

---

[1] White ants.

[2] *Mopato* (*Mophato*). These are tribal regiments formed every few years. Formerly, and still among some tribes, these were formed by secret initiation on the veldt. After initiation a youth became a warrior and could marry. Nowadays a regiment is formed in the chief's courtyard, and the men are put under special leaders, wherever possible a member of the royal family. To belong to the chief's special corps is a high honour. In these times the purpose of these groups is for tribal service such as road-making.

Sekeletu's comrades, wishing to imitate him as he rode on my old horse, leaped on the backs of half-broken oxen, but having neither saddle nor bridle, the number of tumbles which ensued was a source of much amusement to the rest.

When we arrive at any village, the women all turn out to 'lulliloo' their chief. Their shrill voices, to which they give a tremulous sound by a quick motion of the tongue, peal forth 'Great Lion,' 'Great Chief,' 'Sleep, my Lord.' The men utter similar salutations, all of which are received by Sekeletu with lordly indifference. After the news has been told, the headman of the village, who is always a Makololo, brings forth a number of large pots of beer. Calabashes for use as drinking-cups are handed round, and as many as can partake of the beverage do so. They bring forth also large pots and bowls of thick milk, some of which contain six or eight gallons; and each of these, as well as of the beer, is given to a particular person, who has the power to divide it with whom he pleases.

Spoons not being generally in fashion, the milk is conveyed to the mouth with the hand. I often presented my friends with iron spoons, which pleased them exceedingly, but the old habit of hand-eating prevailed; they lifted out a little with the spoon, then put the milk into the left hand and drank from that.

The chief is expected to feed all who accompany him, and he either selects an ox or two from his numerous cattle stations in every part of the country, or he is presented by the headmen of the villages he visits with as many as he needs. The animals are killed by a thrust from a small javelin in the region of the heart. The wound is made purposely small to avoid loss of blood which, with the internal parts, is the perquisite of the slaughter-man. Hence all are eager to perform the office. Each tribe has its own way of cutting up and distributing an animal. Among the Makololo the hump and ribs belong to the chief; among the Bakwains the breast is his perquisite.

After the oxen are cut up, the joints are placed before

Sekeletu, who apportions them among the gentlemen of the party. The attendants rapidly prepare the meat for cooking by cutting it up into long strips, so many of which are thrown into the fire at once that they nearly put it out. Half broiled and burning hot the meat is quickly handed round; everyone gets a mouthful, but no one except the chief has time to masticate. It is not the enjoyment of eating they aim at, but to get as much of the food into the stomach as possible in the short time allowed. They are eminently gregarious in their eating; and as they despise anyone who eats alone, I always poured out two cups of coffee at my own meals so that the chief or one of the principal men might share it with me. They all became very fond of coffee.

In order to assist in the support of our large party and at the same time to see the adjacent country, I went several times to the north for game. The country is covered with clumps of beautiful trees, between which fine open glades stretch away in every direction. Great numbers of buffaloes, zebras, tsessebes, tahaetsi, and eland, or pohu, grazed undisturbed, so that very little exertion was required to secure a fair supply of meat for our party during the necessary delay.

Hunting on foot in this country is very hard work. Winter though it was, the sun's heat was so great that, had there been anyone to whom I could have assigned the task, he would have been welcome to all the sport. But the Makololo shot so badly that I was obliged to go myself in order to save my powder.

The Valley of the Leeambye

Having at last collected a fleet of thirty-three canoes and about one hundred and sixty men, we began to ascend the river.[1] I had the choice of all the vessels and selected the best, though not the largest. It was thirty feet long by twenty inches wide, and was manned by six paddlers. The

[1] *Missionary Travels*, page 211.

larger canoe of Sekeletu had ten. They stand upright and keep stroke with great precision, though they change from side to side as the course demands. The men at the head and the stern are the strongest and most expert. The canoes are flat-bottomed and can go into very shallow water; and whenever the men can feel the bottom they use the paddles, which are about eight feet long, as punting poles. On land the Makalaka fear the Makololo; on water the Makololo fear them. They love to race each other along at top speed, and place their masters' lives in danger. In the event of a capsize many of the Makololo would sink like stones.

The wind, blowing generally from the east, raises very large waves on the Leeambye.[1] On the first day of our voyage an old doctor had his canoe filled by one of these waves, and, being unable to swim, was lost. The Barótse who were with him saved themselves by swimming, and were afraid of being punished with death for not rescuing the doctor. Had he been a man of more influence they certainly would have been executed.

We proceeded rapidly up-river. The magnificent stream is often more than a mile broad and is adorned by many islands from three to five miles in length.[1] The beauty of the scenery on some of these islands is greatly increased by the date-palm with its gracefully curved fronds and refreshing light-green colour, while the lofty palmyra towers above and casts its feathery foliage against a cloudless sky. The banks of the river are equally covered by forest and most of the trees on the brink of the water send down roots from their branches, like the banian. The adjacent country is rocky and undulating, abounding in elephants and all other large game, except leches and nakongs, which seem generally to avoid stony ground.

From the bend to the north, called Katima-molelo, the bed of the river is rocky and the stream runs fast, forming

[1] The name that Livingstone gives to these upper reaches of the Zambezi at this point is the Leeambye, a name not now in use.

a succession of rapids when the water is low. These are not visible when the river is full, but the cataracts of Nambwe, Bombwe, and Kale must always be dangerous. The fall at each of these is between four and six feet. But the falls of Gonye present a much more serious obstacle. The fall is about thirty feet. We were obliged to take the canoes out of the water and carry them for more than a mile.

Tradition states that a man of the Barótse came down the river and took advantage of the falls for the purposes of irrigation. Such superior minds must have from time to time arisen in these regions but, ignorant of letters, they have left no memorial behind them.

The villages of the Barótse are built on mounds which, during the inundation, when the valley appears like a large lake, look like little islands. There are but few trees. The soil is extremely fertile and produces two crops a year. The Barótse are strongly attached to this fertile district where, they say, 'Hunger is not known.'

This was the first visit Sekeletu had made to these parts since he attained the chieftainship. Those who had taken part with Mpépe were consequently in great terror. Mpépe's father and another man had counselled Ma-mochisáne to kill Sekeletu and marry Mpépe. When we came to their town the two were led forth and tossed into the river. When I protested, the counsellors justified their acts and calmly added: 'You see we are still Boers; we are not yet taught.'

Naliéle, the capital of the Barótse, is built on a mound which was constructed by Santuru to store grain. Santuru was a great hunter, and fond of taming wild animals. He had among others two young hippopotami. These gambolled in the river all day but never failed to go to Naliéle for their suppers of milk and meal. They were the wonder of the country till a stranger, who came on a visit, speared one of them under the idea that it was wild.

While still at Naliéle I walked out to Katongo on the ridge that bounds the valley. It is the commencement of

the lands that are never inundated.   I imagined that because
of its slight elevation Katongo might be a healthy site, but
was informed that no part of this region is exempt from fever.
When the waters begin to retire such masses of decayed
vegetation and mud are exposed to the torrid sun, that even
the natives suffer.   The grass is so rank that it conceals the
black alluvial soil.   The current of the river is about four
and a half miles an hour, and in the higher lands from
which it seems to come I imagined we might find a whole-
some locality.

Determined not to abandon this idea without a complete
search of the Barótse country, I left Sekeletu at Naliéle and
ascended the river.   He furnished me with a herald that
I might enter his villages in what is considered a dignified
manner.   His habit was to shout: 'Here comes the lord,
the great lion,' the latter phrase being *tau e tŏna* which in
his imperfect pronunciation became *sau e tŏna*; and thus so
like 'the great sow' that I had to ask him to be silent, much
to the annoyance of my party.

The river presents the same appearance of low banks
without trees as it had done from 16° 16', until we arrived
at Libonta.   Twenty miles beyond that there is forest down
to the water's edge, and tsetse.   No locality can be inhabited by Europeans where that scourge exists.

The number of large game above Libonta was prodigious,
and they proved remarkably tame.   Eighty-one buffaloes
defiled in slow procession before our fire one evening within
gunshot, and herds of splendid elands stood by day without
fear two hundred yards away.   The lions here roar much
more than in the south.   One of these stood for hours on
the opposite shore roaring as loud as he could, putting his
mouth to the ground, as is usual on such occasions, to make
the sound reverberate.

Sekeletu had gone to his mother's town, Ma-Sekeletu
(mother of Sekeletu), but left us an ox and instructions to
follow him.   Thither we went.   As this was the first visit
which Sekeletu had paid to this part of his dominions, it

was to many a season of great joy. The headmen of each village presented more oxen, milk, and beer than the horde which accompanied him could devour, though their abilities in that line are something wonderful. The people usually show their joy and work off their excitement in dances and songs. The men stand nearly naked in a circle, with clubs or small battle-axes in their hands, each roaring at the top of his voice, while they simultaneously lift one leg, stamp heavily twice with it, then lift the other and stamp once with that. The arms and head are thrown about in every direction. The perspiration streams off their bodies; the noise rends the air; and the continued stamping makes a cloud of dust ascend and leaves a deep ring in the ground. Here grey-headed men joined in the performance with as much zest as the young. The women stand by, clapping their hands, and occasionally one advances into the circle composed of a hundred men, makes a few movements, and then retires.

Motibe asked me what I thought of it. I replied: 'It is very hard work and it brings small profit.' 'It is,' he answered, 'but it is very nice, and Sekeletu will give us an ox for dancing for him.'

As Sekeletu had been waiting for me at his mother's, we left the town as soon as I arrived, and proceeded down the river. Our speed with the stream was very great, for in one day we must have travelled sixty miles. I failed, however, to discover a healthy place and therefore determined to put into execution my second plan and endeavour to open up a path to the coast.

VII

Westward towards the Coast

Linyanti, September 1853. The object proposed to the Makololo seemed so desirable that it was resolved to proceed with it as soon as the cooling influence of the rains should be felt in November. My observations showed that we were much nearer to St Philip de Benguela than to Loanda, and I might have made arrangements with the Mambari to accompany them as far as Bihe, which is on the road to that port. But it is so undesirable to travel a path once trodden by slave-traders, that I preferred to find another line of march. The Mambari had informed me that many English lived at Loanda and thither I prepared to go. The prospect of meeting my countrymen seemed to offset the toils of the longer march.

A *picho* [1] was called to deliberate on the steps proposed. In these assemblies great freedom of speech is allowed, and on this occasion one of the old diviners said: 'Where is he taking you to? This white man is throwing you away. Your garments already smell of blood.' This man was a noted croaker; he always dreamed something dreadful on every expedition, and was certain that an eclipse or comet betokened the propriety of flight. Sekeletu only laughed at him now. The general voice was in my favour, and a band of twenty-seven men was appointed to accompany me. They were not hired, but sent to enable me to accomplish an object as much desired by the chief and most of his people as by me. They were eager to obtain free trade with white men. The prices which the Cape merchants could offer, after paying expenses, were so small that it was scarcely worth while for the natives to collect produce for that market. The desire of the Makololo for direct trade with the sea-coast coincided

---

[1] A consultation.

exactly with my own conviction that no permanent elevation of a people can be effected without commerce.

The three men whom I had brought from Kuruman suffered much from fever, so I decided to send them south with Fleming. I was then entirely dependent on my twenty-seven whom I might call Zambezians, for there were only two Makololo, while the rest consisted of Barótse, Batoka, Bashubia, and two of the Ambŏnda.[1]

The fever had caused me considerable weakness and a strange giddiness when I looked up suddenly at any celestial object. Everything appeared to rush to the left, and if I did not catch hold of some support I fell heavily to the ground.

The Makololo now put the question: 'In the event of your death will not the white people blame us for allowing you to go away into an unhealthy, unknown country?' I replied: 'No,' because I would leave a book with Sekeletu which would explain all that had happened. The book was a volume of my journal which contained valuable notes on the habits of wild animals. As I was detained longer than I had expected at Loanda, it was delivered by Sekeletu to a trader, and unfortunately I have not been able to trace it.[2]

When I committed the wagon and remaining goods to the Makololo they took all the articles except one box into their huts. Two warriors brought forward each a fine heifer calf, and after performing a number of warlike evolutions they asked the chief to be a witness between them that whoever of the two should kill a Matabele warrior first in defence of the wagon should receive the calves.

I had three muskets for my people, a rifle, and a double-barrelled smooth bore for myself; and having seen such great abundance of game on my visit to the Leeba, I imagined that I could easily supply the wants of my party. My ammunition was distributed in portions throughout the luggage, so that if accident should befall one part we should

[1] This is worth noting, as the name Makololo is usually applied to the group indiscriminately. [2] This volume was not recovered.

not be left without supply. I carried about twenty pounds
of beads worth forty shillings. Wishing to avoid heavy loads,
I took only a few biscuits, a few pounds of tea and sugar,
and about twenty of coffee. We carried a small tin canister
fifteen inches square, filled with spare shirting, trousers,
and shoes to be used when we reached civilized life; another
of the same size for medicines; a third for books, my stock
being a Nautical Almanac, Thomson's Logarithm Tables,
and a Bible. A fourth box contained a magic lantern which
we found of much use. The sextant, artificial horizon,
thermometer, and compasses were carried apart. I also
took a small gipsy tent just sufficient to sleep in, a sheepskin
mantle as a blanket, and a horse-rug as a bed.

As I had always found the art of successful travel consisted in taking as few impedimenta as possible and not forgetting to carry my wits about me, the outfit was rather
spare. An array of baggage is apt to excite cupidity among
the tribes.

The Trek to the West begins

11th November 1853. Left the town of Linyanti, accompanied
by Sekeletu and his principal men, to embark on the Chobe.
The chief came to the river to see that all was right at
parting. We crossed five branches of the Chobe before
reaching the main stream. The chief lent me his own canoe.

The Chobe is infested with hippopotami. As a rule they
flee at the approach of man, and are only dangerous if a
canoe passes into the midst of a sleeping herd, when some
of them may strike the vessel in terror. To avoid this, it
is well to travel by day near the bank and by night in the
middle of the stream. Certain elderly males, however,
which have been expelled from the herd, become sour
tempered and attack every canoe that passes near them.

One of the 'bachelors' came out of his lair, and, putting
his head down, ran after some of our company with considerable speed. Another, before we arrived, had smashed
to pieces a canoe with a blow of his hind foot. I was

informed that in the event of such an assault the proper way was to dive to the bottom of the river and remain there a few seconds, because the hippopotamus after breaking a canoe always looks for the people on the surface and, if he finds none, soon moves off. I have seen some fearful gashes made on the legs of men unable to dive. This animal uses its teeth as an offensive weapon, though it is a herbivorous feeder.

The Chobe, like the Zouga, runs through soft calcarious tufa and has cut a deep perpendicular bed. The course is extremely tortuous and carried us to all points of the compass every dozen miles. Some of us walked in six hours a distance which it took the canoes twice that time to reach, though they moved at more than double our speed.

After spending one night at the Makololo village on the island of Mparia we left the Chobe, and turning round began to ascend the Leeambye. On 19th November again reached the town of Sesheke.

I gave many public addresses to the people of Sesheke under the outspreading camel-thorn tree which serves as a shade to the *kgotla* on the high bank of the river. It was pleasant to see the long lines of men, women, and children winding along from different quarters of the town, each party following behind their respective headmen. They often amounted to between five and six hundred souls, and it required an exertion of voice that brought back the complaint for which I got the uvula excised at the Cape.

They were always very attentive. Moriantsane, in order, as he thought, to please me, on one occasion hurled his staff at the heads of some young fellows whom he saw working with a skin instead of listening.[1]

[1] *Livingstone as vernacular preacher.* Livingstone often wondered whether his preaching left any permanent impression, but another Scots missionary, Fred Arnot, famous in his day, wrote in 1884: 'Although thirty years have elapsed since Livingstone first visited the Barótse valley, and more than twenty since he was last seen there, yet remembrance of him, his ways, his words, his physique, is as fresh as yesterday, and his sermons are remembered.' See *Livingstone the Liberator*, page 149.

Recovering partially from a severe attack of fever which had remained with me since our passing the village of Moremi on the Chobe, we made ready for our departure up-river by sending messages before us to the villages to prepare food.   We took four elephants' tusks belonging to Sekeletu as a means of testing the difference in prices between the Portuguese, whom we expected to reach, and the white traders from the south.   The rains were just commencing, but though showers had fallen, sufficient to lay the dust, they had no influence whatever on the amount of water in the river; yet never was there less in any part than three hundred yards of deep-flowing stream.

Our progress up-river was slow. The rapids, having comparatively little water in them, made our passage difficult.   The canoes must never be allowed to come broadside-on to the stream, for, being flat-bottomed, they would at once capsize.   The men worked admirably and were always in good humour: they leaped into the water without the least hesitation to save the canoe from being caught by eddies or dashed against the rocks. Many parts were now quite shallow, and it required great skill to keep the vessel free from rocks that lay just beneath the surface.

30th November 1853. At Gonye Falls. These falls are formed by the passage of the river in a deep fissure in the sandstone rock, a hundred yards wide and several miles long, through which the stream rushes with such violence that not even an expert swimmer could live in it.   Here it is that the river when in flood rises fifty or sixty feet. We felt great lassitude in travelling: no rain had fallen here, so it was excessively hot.

When under way our usual procedure is this: We get up a little before 5 a.m.; it is then beginning to dawn. While I am dressing, coffee is made, and having filled my pannikin, the rest is handed to my companions who relish it greatly.

The next two hours are the most pleasant of the day's
sail. The men paddle most vigorously. The Barótse, being
a tribe of boatmen, have well-developed chests and shoulders,
with indifferent lower extremities. They often engage in
loud scolding of each other in order to relieve the tedium
of their work. About eleven we land and eat any meat
that may have remained over from the previous evening's
meal, or a biscuit with honey, and drink water.

After an hour we again embark and cower under an
umbrella. The heat is oppressive, and being weak with my
last attack of fever I cannot land and supply the camp with
flesh. The men, being quite uncovered in the sun, per-
spire freely, and in the afternoon begin to stop as if waiting
for the canoes that have been left behind. Sometimes we
reach a sleeping-place two hours before sunset and, all being
troubled with languor, we gladly remain for the night.
Coffee again and a biscuit and a piece of coarse bread made
of maize meal, or that of the native corn, make up the bill
of fare for the evening, unless we have been fortunate
enough to kill something, when we boil a potful of flesh.
That is done by cutting it up into long strips and pouring
on water till it is covered. When that is boiled dry the
meat is considered ready.

Rains begin

The people of Gonye carry the canoes over the space
required to avoid the falls by slinging them on poles
tied on diagonally. They are a merry set of mortals—a
feeble joke sets them off into fits of laughter. Here, as
elsewhere, all petitioned for the magic lantern, and,
as it is a good means of conveying instruction, I willingly
complied.

The people in every village treated us most liberally,
presenting besides oxen, butter, milk, and meal, more than
we could stow away in our canoes. The cows in this valley
are now yielding, as they frequently do, more milk than
the people can use, and both men and women present butter

in such quantity that I shall be able to refresh my men as we move along. Anointing the skin prevents excessive evaporation of the fluids of the body and acts as clothing in both sun and shade.

They always made their presents gracefully. When an ox was given the owner would say: 'Here is a little bit of bread for you.' This was pleasant, for I had been accustomed to the Bechuana presenting a miserable goat with the pompous exclamation: 'Behold an ox!'

Nothing worthy of note occurred on our way up to Nameta. There we heard that a party of Makololo, headed by Lerimo, had made a foray to the north and up the Leeba, in the very direction that we were about to proceed. They had taken some of Masiko's subjects prisoner and had destroyed some of the villages of the Balonda, to whom we were going.

The rains began while we were at Naliéle. The showers were refreshing, but the air felt hot and close, the thermometer standing at 90° even in the shade, though in a cool hut it was reduced to 84°. A new attack of fever here caused me excessive languor, but as I am already getting tired of quoting my fevers, I shall henceforth say little about them.

When we reached Litofe, we heard that a fresh foray was in contemplation, but I sent forward orders to disband the party immediately. At Ma-Sekeletu's town we found the head offender, Mpololo himself, and I gave him a piece of my mind. Ma-Sekeletu heartily approved all I said, and suggested that all the captives taken by Lerimo should be returned by my hand. We were pleased to hear that Mpololo agreed to do what was advised. He took all the guilt upon himself before the people and delivered up a captive child whom his wife had in her possession.

Leaving Naliéle amidst abundance of good wishes, we recommenced the ascent of the river. It was now beginning to rise, though the rains had but just commenced in the valley.

17th December 1853. At Libonta. We were detained for days together, collecting contributions of fat and butter, according to the order of Sekeletu, as a present to the Balonda chiefs. Here we demanded the remainder of the captives and got the number increased to nineteen. Libonta is the last town of the Makololo.

Before leaving the villages entirely we may glance at our way of spending the nights. As soon as we land some of the men cut a little grass for my bed, while Mashauana plants the poles of the little tent. These are used by day for carrying burdens, for the Barótse fashion is exactly like that of India, only the burden is fastened near the ends of the poles and not suspended by long cords. The bed is made and boxes ranged on each side of it, and then the tent is pitched over all. Four or five feet in front of my tent is placed the principal or *kgotla* fire, the wood for which must be collected by the man who occupies the post of herald, and takes as his perquisite the heads of all the oxen and game slaughtered. Each person knows his station in reference to the post of honour at the fire.

The two Makololo occupy my right and left, both in eating and sleeping; but Mashauana, my head boatman, makes his bed at the door of the tent as soon as I retire. The rest, divided into small companies according to their tribes, make sheds round the fire, leaving a horseshoe-shaped space in front sufficient for the cattle. The fire gives confidence to the oxen, so the men were always careful to keep them in sight of it.

The sheds are formed by planting two stout forked poles in an inclined direction, and placing another over them in a horizontal position. A number of branches are then stuck in the ground in the direction to which the poles are inclined, the twigs drawn down to the horizontal pole and tied with strips of bark. Long grass is then laid over the branches in sufficient quantity to draw off the rain. In less than an hour we are usually all under cover.

It is a picturesque sight, when the moon lights the sleeping forms, to see the attitudes of profound repose both the men and beasts assume. There is no danger from wild animals on such a night, and the fires are allowed almost to go out. The picture is one of perfect peace.

The cooking is usually done in native style, and as they carefully wash dishes, pots, and the hands before handling food, it is by no means despicable. The cook always comes in for something left in the pot, so all are eager to obtain the office.

I taught several of them to wash my shirts, though their teacher had never been taught that work himself! Frequent changes of linen and sunning my blanket kept me more comfortable than might have been anticipated, and I feel certain that the lessons in cleanliness, rigidly instilled by my mother in childhood, helped to maintain that respect which these people entertain for European ways. It is questionable if a descent to barbarism ever elevates a man in the eyes of savages.

Part of our company marched along the banks with the oxen, and part went in canoes. The pace was regulated by that of the men on shore, whose course was impeded by the numerous branches of the Leeambye, which they were obliged to circumvent or be carried across in the boats. The number of alligators was prodigious, and they were more savage here than elsewhere. Many children are carried off annually; for, notwithstanding the danger, they generally play at the riverside. One of my men while swimming across a stream was caught by the thigh and taken below. He, however, kept his presence of mind, and having a small javelin with him gave the alligator a stab behind the shoulder, the pain of which caused the brute to let go.

I tried to teach my men the use of the gun but they would soon have expended all the ammunition. I was therefore obliged to do all the shooting myself, though a damaged arm handicapped me.[1] The bone had not united

---

[1] His left arm had been crushed by a lion ten years before.

well. Continued labour and some falls from ox-back had lengthened the ligament by which the ends of the bones were united, and a false joint was the consequence. The limb was never painful, but I could not steady the rifle and was obliged to shoot with the piece resting on my left shoulder.

We spent a Sunday on our way up the confluence of the Leeba and the Leeambye. Rains had now fallen, and the woods had put on their gayest hue. Flowers of great beauty and curious forms grow everywhere. Many of the forest trees are palmated and largely developed. The trunks are covered with lichens, and abundance of ferns shows that we are now in a more humid climate. The ground swarms with insect life, and in the cool mornings the welkin rings with the singing of birds, though their notes are not so delightful as the notes of the birds at home, because I have not been familiar with them from infancy. The notes, however, strike the mind by their boldness and variety as the wellings forth from joyous hearts of praise to Him who fills them with overflowing gladness.

Vast shoals of fish come down the Leeambye with the rising waters. The mosala, the mullet, and other fishes spread over the Barótse valley in such numbers that, when the waters retire, all the people are employed in cutting them up and drying them in the sun. The supply exceeds the demand, and the land is said to omit a most offensive smell. The Zambezi everywhere abounds in animal life.

Where Women ruled
27th December 1853. We now began to ascend the Leeba.[1] The water is black and flows placidly. It winds slowly through the most charming meadows, each of which is irrigated by a large pond or trickling rill. The trees were covered with a profusion of the freshest foliage and grouped together in the most graceful manner. The grass, which had been burnt off and was growing after the rain, was

[1] The 'extreme Upper Zambezi' (Sir H. Johnson).

short and green, and all the scenery so like a carefully tended
park that it was difficult to believe that it was the work of
nature alone. I suspect that the level meadows are annually
inundated. Numbers of freshwater shells are scattered all
over the valleys. Beautiful flowers abound, and many bees
sip their nectar. We found plenty of honey in the woods,
and saw the stages on which the Balonda dry their meat
when they come down to hunt and gather the produce of
the wild hives.

A large buffalo was wounded and ran into the thickest
part of the forest, bleeding profusely. The young men
went on his trail, and though the vegetation was so dense
that no one could have run more than a few yards, most of
them went along carelessly, picking and eating fruit of the
melon family called mponko. When the animal heard their
approach he always fled, shifting and doubling his course in
the most cunning manner. Though a heavy, lumbering
animal, his charge is terrific. More accidents happen by
the buffalo and the black rhinoceros than by the lion. Still,
our young men went after him quite carelessly: they never
lose their presence of mind, but, as a buffalo charges, dart
dexterously out of his way behind a tree, and wheeling
round stab him as he passes.

On the 28th we slept at a spot from which there had just
emerged two broods of alligators. We had seen many young
ones as we came up, so this seems to be their time for
coming forth from their nests, for we saw them sunning
themselves in company with the old ones. We made our
fire in one of the deserted nests. On the Zouga we saw
sixty eggs taken out of one such nest alone. They are about
the size of those of a goose; only the eggs of the alligator
are of the same diameter at both ends, and the white shell
is partially elastic from having a strong internal membrane
and but little lime in its composition. The distance from
the water was about ten feet, and there was evidence of the
same place having been used for a similar purpose in former
years. A broad path led up from the water to the nest,

and the dam, it was said by my companions, after depositing the eggs covers them up, and returns afterwards to assist the young out of the place of confinement and out of the egg.

She leads them to the edge of the water and then leaves them to catch small fish for themselves. Assistance to come forth seems necessary, for here, besides the tough membrane of the shell, they had four inches of earth upon them. But they do not require immediate aid for food, because they all retain a portion of yolk equal to that of a hen's egg in a membrane in the abdomen as a stock of nutriment, while only beginning independent existence by catching fish. Fish is the principal food of both small and large, and they are much assisted in catching them by their broad scaly tails. Sometimes an alligator, seeing a man on the opposite bank, rushes across the stream with wonderful agility, as is seen by the high ripple he makes on the surface caused by his rapid motion under water; but in general they act by stealth, sinking underneath as soon as they see man. They seldom leave the water to catch prey, but often come out by day to bask in the sun.

When we reached the part of the river opposite the village of Manenko, the first female chief whom we had encountered, two of the people called Balonda came to us in their little canoe. From them we learned that Kolimbota, one of our party, was believed by the Balonda to have acted as guide to the marauders under Lerimo, whose captives we were now returning. They suspected this from the facility with which their villages had been found. We were in bad repute, but having a captive boy and girl to show that neither Sekeletu nor we were partakers in the guilt of inferior men, I could freely express my desire that all should live in peace. They then went away to report to Manenko.

As it would have been impolitic to pass Manenko without showing some respect and explaining our object in passing through her country, we waited two days for the return of the messengers. We received an answer, together with a basket of manioc roots, that we were to stay where we were till she visited us.   Two days later other messengers arrived with orders for me to come to her; but after four days of rain and negotiation I declined, and proceeded up-river to the Makondo, which enters the Leeba from the east.

1st January 1854. At this point one of my men picked up a piece of a steel watch-chain of English manufacture, and we were told that this was the spot where the Mambari cross in coming to Masiko.   These Mambari are very enterprising merchants: when they mean to trade with a town they begin by building huts, as if they knew that business cannot be done without plenty of time for palaver.   They bring Manchester goods into the heart of Africa, and these cotton prints look so wonderful that the Makololo cannot believe them to be the work of human hands.   The Mambari tell them that English manufacturers come out of the sea and that beads are gathered on its shores.   To Africans our cotton mills are fairy dreams.   'How can iron spin, weave, and print so beautifully?'

On 6th January we reached the village of another female chief named Nyamoána, who is said to be the mother of Manenko and sister of Shinté, the greatest Balonda chief in this part of the country.   Her husband, Samoána, was clothed in a kilt of green and red baize, and was armed with a spear and broadsword of antique form, about eighteen inches long and three broad.

The chief and her husband were sitting on skins placed in the middle of a circle thirty paces in diameter, a little raised above the ordinary level of the ground, and having a trench round it.   Outside the trench sat about a hundred persons of all ages and both sexes.   The men were armed with bows, arrows, spears, and broadswords.   Beside the husband sat an aged woman, having a bad outward squint in the left eye.   We put down our arms about forty yards off, and I walked up to the centre and saluted him in the usual way by clapping hands in their fashion.   He pointed to his wife as much as to say, the honour belongs to her. I saluted her in the same way, and a mat having been brought, I squatted down in front of them.

The talker was then called and I was asked who was my spokesman. Having pointed out Kolimbota the palaver began. I explained simply our objects: I have found that the truthful way of dealing with the uncivilized is always the best. Our man repeated to their talker what I had said. He delivered it all verbatim to the husband, who repeated it again to his wife. It was thus repeated four times in a tone loud enough to be heard by the whole party. The response came back by the same roundabout route, beginning with the lady and then her husband.

After explanations and re-explanations I perceived that my new friends were mixing up my message of peace with Makololo affairs; so I stated that it was delivered on the authority of no one less than their Creator, and that if the Makololo did again break His laws and attack the Balonda, the guilt would rest on the Makololo alone. By way of gaining their confidence I showed them my hair, which is considered a curiosity in this region. They said: 'Is that hair? It is the mane of a lion and not hair at all.' I could not return the joke by telling them that theirs was not hair but wool, for they have no sheep in their country and would not have understood. So I declared that mine was the original hair such as theirs would have been if it had not been scorched and frizzled in the sun. In proof of what the sun could do I compared my bronzed face and hands with the white skin of my chest. They readily believed that we might be of common origin after all.

An Amazon who circumvented Livingstone

As the Leeba seemed to come from the direction in which we wished to go, I was desirous of proceeding farther with the canoes.[1] But Nyamoána was anxious that we should allow her people to conduct us to her brother Shinté; and

[1] *Missionary Travels*, page 275.

when I spoke of the advantage of water-carriage she represented that her brother did not live near the river and,
moreover, that there was a cataract in front, over which
it would be difficult to convey the canoes. She was afraid,
too, that the Balobále, whose country lies to the west of
the river, not knowing the objects for which we had come,
might kill us. This inclined my companions to Nyamoána's
plan of going to her brother's town, and the arrival of
Manenko herself threw so much weight into the scale on
their side that I was forced to yield the point.

Manenko was a tall strapping woman of about twenty,
distinguished by a profusion of ornaments and medicines
hung round her person. The latter supposed to act as
charms. Her body was smeared all over with a mixture of
fat and red ochre, as a protection against the weather; a
necessary precaution, for, like most of the Balonda ladies,
she was otherwise in a state of frightful nudity. This was
not from want of clothing, for being a chief she might
have been as well clad as any of her subjects, but from her
peculiar ideas of elegance in dress.

When she arrived with her husband, Sambánza, they
listened for some time to the statements I was making to
the people of Nyamoána, after which her husband commenced an oration, stating the reasons of their coming.
During every two or three seconds of his delivery he picked
up a little sand and rubbed it on the upper part of his arms
and chest. This is a common mode of salutation in Londa,
and when they wish to be excessively polite they bring a
quantity of ashes or pipe-clay in a piece of skin and, taking
up handfuls, rub it on the chest and upper front part of
each arm. Others, in saluting, drum their ribs with their
elbows.

When Sambánza had finished his oration, he rose up and
showed his ankles ornamented with a bundle of copper
rings. Had they been very heavy they would have caused
him to adopt a staggering walk. Some chiefs have really
so many as to be forced by the weight and size to keep one

foot apart from the other, the weight being a serious inconvenience in walking. The gentlemen like Sambánza,
who wish to imitate their betters, do so in their walk;
so that you see men, with only a few ounces of ornament, strut along as if they had double the number of
pounds.

On the evening of the day in which Manenko arrived we
were delighted by the appearance of an embassy from
Masiko. It consisted of all his under-chiefs, who brought
me a fine elephant's tusk, two calabashes of honey, and a
large piece of blue baize. Masiko expressed his delight at
the return of the captives and at the proposal of peace and
alliance with the Makololo. He stated that he never sold
any of his own people to the Mambari, but only captives
whom his people kidnapped from small neighbouring tribes.
He admitted that two of his men, when hunting, had gone
into Makololo gardens to see if any of their relatives were
there. As the great object in all native disputes is to get
both parties to turn over a new leaf, I urged the wisdom of
forgetting old feuds and avoiding any cause for marauding.
I presented Masiko with an ox furnished by Sekeletu as a
provision for ourselves.

Manenko fell upon our friends from Masiko in a way that
showed she was an accomplished scold. Masiko had on a
former occasion sent to Samoána for a cloth, a common
way of keeping up intercourse, and after receiving it had
sent it back, because it had the appearance of having had
'witchcraft medicine' on it. This was a grave offence, and
now Manenko had a fine excuse to vent her spleen, the
ambassadors having called at her village and slept in one of
the huts without leave. She advanced and receded in true
oratorical style, belabouring her own servants as well for
having allowed the offence. She leaned over the objects of
her ire and screamed forth all their faults and failings ever
since they were born, and her despair of ever seeing them
any better till they were all killed by alligators! Masiko's
people received this torrent of abuse in silence, and as

D

neither we nor they had anything to eat, we parted till next morning.

Manenko gave us some manioc roots in the morning and was determined to carry our baggage to her uncle's, Shinté. We had heard a sample of what she could do with her tongue, and as neither my men nor myself had much inclination to encounter a scolding from this black Mrs Caudle, we made ready the packages. But she came and said the men whom she had ordered for the service would not arrive till to-morrow. Being on low and disagreeable diet, I felt annoyed at this further delay, and ordered a move without her servants; but Manenko was not to be circumvented in that way. She came forward with her people and said her uncle would be angry if she did not carry forward the tusks and goods of Sekeletu, and, seizing the luggage, declared that she would carry it in spite of me.

My men succumbed sooner to this petticoat government than I felt inclined to do; and being unwilling to encounter her tongue, I was moving off to the canoes when she with her hand on my shoulder put on a motherly look and said: 'Now, my little man, just do as the rest have done.' My feelings of annoyance, of course, vanished and I went out to hunt for some meat.

Urged by hunger we followed the trail of some zebra during the greater part of the day. We got within fifty yards of them in a dense thicket and made sure of one when, to my infinite disgust, my gun misfired and off they bounded. The climate is so damp that powder in the gun nipples cannot be kept dry.

11th January 1854. On starting this morning Nyamoána presented a string of beads, and a shell highly valued among them, as an atonement for having assisted Manenko, as they thought. They seemed anxious to avert any evil which might arise from my displeasure. They thought they had vexed me the day before. I replied that I never kept up my anger all night, and they seemed pleased and satisfied.

We had to cross in a canoe a stream which flows past the village. Manenko's doctor waved some charms over Nya-moána, and she took some in her hand and on her body before she ventured upon the water. One of my men spoke rather loudly when near the doctor's basket of medicines. The doctor reproved him and always spoke in a whisper himself, glancing back at the basket, as if afraid of being heard by something therein. So much superstition is quite unknown in the south, and is mentioned here to show the difference in the feelings of this new people and the comparative want of reverence on these points among Kaffirs and Bechuana.

Manenko was accompanied by her husband and her drummer. The latter continued to thump most vigorously until a heavy drizzling mist set in and compelled him to desist. Her husband used various incantations and vociferations to drive away the rain, but down it poured incessantly. On our Amazon went in the very lightest marching order, and at a pace with which few men could keep up. Being on ox-back I kept pretty close to our leader, and asked her why she did not clothe herself during the rain, and learned that it was not considered proper for a chief to appear effeminate. My men, in admiration of her pedestrian powers, every now and again remarked: 'Manenko is a soldier'; and, thoroughly wet and cold, we were all glad when she proposed a halt to prepare our night's lodging on the banks of a stream.

On the 11th and 12th we were detained by incessant and violent rains. I had a little tapioca and a small quantity of Libonta meal, which I reserved for emergencies. The patience of my men under hunger was admirable. Present want is never so painful as the prospect of future starvation.

The forests became more dense as we went north, and we travelled much more in the deep gloom of the forest than in open sunlight. No passage existed on either side of the narrow path made by the axe. Large climbing plants entwined themselves like boa-constrictors around the gigantic trees by which they rise.

This being the rainy season, great quantities of mushrooms were found and eagerly devoured by my companions. The edible variety is always found growing out of ant-hills, and attains the diameter of the crown of a hat. Some, not edible, are of a brilliant red and others a light blue.

In spite of rain and fever, this change of scenery was pleasant. The deep gloom contrasted strongly with the shadeless glare of the Kalahari. Though drenched day by day it was long before I could believe that we were getting too much of a good thing and were not wasting water.[1]

[1] From now on the expedition travelled through true tropical forest, dense and gloomy—West Central Africa.

VIII

West Central Africa

THE number of little villages seemed to equal the number of valleys.[1] At some we stopped and rested, the people becoming more liberal as we advanced. Others were found deserted, a sudden panic having seized the inhabitants, though the drum of Manenko was kept beaten pretty constantly in order to give notice of the approach of great people.

When we decided to remain for the night at any village, the people lent us the roofs of their huts, which resemble in form a Chinaman's hat and can be taken off the walls at pleasure. They lifted them off and brought them to the spot we had selected for our lodging, and when our men had propped them up with stakes they were safely lodged for the night.

Saturday, 14th January, was for a wonder a fine day, and we were able to dry our clothes and other goods. The guns were rusty in spite of being oiled every evening.

On Sunday afternoon messengers arrived from Shinté expressing his approbation of the objects we had in view in our journey through his country.

Manenko now threatened in sport to go on, and I soon afterwards perceived that what now seemed to me the dilly-dallying of this lady was the proper mode of making acquaintance with the Balonda; and much of the favour with which I was received was due to our sending forward messengers to state the object of our coming before entering any place. When we came in sight of a village we sat down under the shade of a tree and sent forward a man to give notice who we were and what were our objects. The headman then

[1] *Missionary Travels*, page 286.

sent out his principal men to bid us welcome and show us
a tree under which we might sleep.

Our friends informed us that Shinté would be highly
honoured by the presence of three white men in his town
at once. Two others had sent notice of their approach
from another quarter. Could it be Barth or Krapf? How
pleasant to meet Europeans in such an out-of-the-way region!
The rush of thoughts made me almost forget my fever.
'Are they of the same colour as I am? Have they the same
hair?' I asked. But as the strangers had, I learned, woolly
hair like themselves, I had to give up the idea of meeting
anything more European than two half-caste Portuguese
engaged in trading for slaves, ivory, and beeswax.

16th January 1854. When Manenko thought the sun high
enough to make a lucky entry, we proceeded. The town
was embowered in banana and other tropical trees. The
streets are straight, and present a complete contrast to
those of the Bechuana, which are tortuous. Here too we
first saw native huts with square walls and round roofs.
The fences or walls of the court are made of upright poles
a few inches apart, with strong grass or leafy branches neatly
woven between. When we made our appearance a crowd
of negroes ran towards us as if they would eat us up. All
were armed and some had guns, but the way in which they
held them showed that the owners were more accustomed to
bows and arrows. After staring at us for an hour they departed.

The two Portuguese traders had erected a little encampment opposite ours. One was a sickly yellow, but his head
was covered with a crop of unmistakable wool. They were
accompanied by a number of Mambari and had a gang of
female slaves whom they had purchased in Lobale. Few of
my men had ever seen slaves in chains before. 'They are
not men,' they exclaimed (meaning they are beasts), 'who
treat their children so.'

Tuesday 17th. We were honoured with a grand reception
by Shinté about eleven o'clock. Sambánza claimed the

honour of presenting us. The *kgotla*, or place of audience, was about a hundred yards square, and two graceful banian-trees stood near one end. Under one of these sat Shinté on a sort of throne covered with a leopard skin. He wore a checked jacket and a kilt of scarlet baize edged with green. Many strings of large beads hung from his neck, and his limbs were covered with iron and copper armlets and bracelets. On his head he wore a helmet of beads woven neatly together and crowned with a great bunch of goose feathers. Close to him sat three lads with large sheaves of arrows over their shoulders.

When we entered the *kgotla* the whole of Manenko's party saluted Shinté by clapping their hands, and Sambánza did obeisance by rubbing his chest and arms with ashes. One of the trees being unoccupied, I retreated to it for the sake of the shade, and my whole party did the same. We were now about forty yards from the chief and could see the whole ceremony.

The different sections of the tribe came forward in the same way as we did, the headman of each making obeisance with ashes which he carried with him for the purpose. Then came the soldiers, all armed to the teeth, running and shouting towards us, with their swords drawn and their faces screwed up so as to appear as savage as possible; for the purpose, I thought, of trying whether they could not make us take to our heels. As we did not they turned round towards Shinté, saluted him, and then retired.

When all had come and were seated, there began the curious capering usually seen in *pichos*. A man starts up and imitates the most approved attitudes observed in actual fighting, as of throwing a javelin, receiving another on the shield, springing to one side to avoid a third, running back-wards and forwards, leaping, etc.

This over, Sambánza and the spokesman of Nyamoána stalked backwards and forwards in front of Shinté and gave forth in a loud voice all that they had been able to learn either from myself or other people of my past history and connection with the Makololo: the return of the captives, the wish to open the country to trade, the Bible as the word from heaven, the white man's desire for the tribes to live in peace. Perhaps, they implied, I was fibbing, perhaps not: they rather thought he was. But as the Balonda had good hearts and Shinté had never done any harm to anyone, he had better receive the white man well and send him on his way. Sambánza was gaily attired, and, besides a profusion of beads, had a cloth so long that a boy carried it after him as a train.

Behind Shinté sat about a hundred women, clothed in their best, which happened to be a profusion of red baize. The chief wife of Shinté, one of the Matabele or Zulus, sat in front with a curious red cap on her head. During the intervals between the speeches these ladies burst forth into a sort of plaintive ditty, but it was impossible to catch whether it was in praise of the speaker, of Shinté, or of themselves. This was the first time that I had ever seen females present at a public assembly: in the south the women are not permitted to enter the *kgotla*. Here they expressed approbation by clapping their hands and laughing, and Shinté frequently turned round and spoke to them.

A party of musicians, consisting of three drummers and four performers on the marimba (a kind of xylophone), went round the *kgotla* several times regaling us with their music.

When nine speakers had concluded their orations Shinté stood up, and so did all his people. He had maintained true African dignity all the time, but my people remarked that he hardly took his eyes off me for a moment. About a thousand people and three hundred soldiers were present. The sun was now hot and the scene ended by the Mambari discharging their guns.

Exchange of Courtesies with Shinté

18th. We were awakened during the night by a message from Shinté requesting a visit at a very unseasonable hour.

As I was just in the sweating stage of intermittent fever
I declined to go. However, at ten o'clock next morning
we went, and were led into the courts of Shinté, the walls
of which consisted of woven rods, all very neat and high.
Numerous trees afforded a grateful shade, while sugar-
cane and bananas, growing outside the enclosure, spread
their large light leaves over the walls.

We took our seat under the broad foliage of a banian-
tree and Shinté soon made his appearance. He seemed in
good humour and said he had expected yesterday 'that a
man who came from the gods would have approached and
talked with him.' That had been my intention in going to
the reception, but when I saw the formidable preparations,
and his own men keeping at least forty yards from him,
I yielded to the solicitations of my men and remained by
the tree opposite that under which he sat. His remark
confirmed my previous opinion that a frank, open, fearless
manner is the most winning way of all with Africans.

I stated the object of my mission and the old gentleman
clapped his hands in approbation. I asked him later if he
had ever seen a white man. 'No, never,' he replied.
'You are the first I have ever seen with white skin and
straight hair.' On learning that Shinté's mouth was 'bitter
for want of ox flesh' I presented him, to his great delight,
with an ox, and as his country is well adapted for cattle,
I advised him to begin a trade in cattle with the Makololo.
He profited by the hint, for when we returned from Loanda
we found that he had got three beasts, one of which was
more like a prize heifer than anything I have seen in
Africa.

Manenko was meanwhile busy erecting a pretty little hut
and courtyard to be her residence. On hearing that we
had given an ox to her uncle she came forward with an
injured air and claimed that 'this white man belonged to
her, therefore the ox was hers.' Upon this she sent her
men for it, had it slaughtered, and presented her uncle
with a leg only. Shinté did not seem to be at all annoyed.

* D

19th. I was awakened at an early hour by a messenger from Shinté, saying that Shinté wished to say all that he had to tell me at once. This was too tempting an offer, and accordingly we went. When we arrived he had a fowl ready in his hand to present, together with a basket of manioc meal and a calabash of mead. On my asking what remedy he would suggest for fever, he answered: 'Drink plenty of mead. As it gets in it will drive the fever out.' It was rather strong, and I suspect he liked the remedy pretty well, though he had no fever. He was highly pleased with the large calabashes of clarified butter that Sekeletu had sent him.

We were particularly struck with the punctiliousness of manners shown by the Balonda. Inferiors on meeting their superiors in the street at once drop on their knees and rub dust on their arms and chests, and continue the salutation of clapping the hands until the great ones have passed. Sambánza knelt down in this manner till the son of Shinté had passed him. We several times saw the woman who holds the office of drawer of water to Shinté; as she passes along she rings a bell to give warning to all to keep out of her way. It would be a grave offence for anyone to exercise an evil influence by approaching the drink of the chief.

I suspect that offences of the slightest character among the poor are made the pretext for selling them or their children to the Mambari. The frequent kidnapping from outlying hamlets explains the stockades we saw round them. The Mambari erect large square huts for the concealment of the stolen ones. Even Shinté seems fond of working in the dark.

One night he sent for me and on my arrival presented me with a slave-girl of about ten years old, saying that he had always been in the habit of presenting his visitors with a child. On my declining the present on the grounds that I thought it wrong to take away children from their parents, he urged that she was 'to be a child' to bring me water, and that a great man ought to have a child for the purpose,

yet I had none. As I replied that I had four children and
should be very sorry if my chief were to take my little girl
and give her away, and that I would prefer this child to
remain and carry water for her mother, he thought I was
dissatisfied with her size and sent me one a head taller.
After many explanations of our horror of slavery and how
displeasing it must be to God to see his children selling
one another, I declined her also.

Shinté was most anxious to see the pictures of the magic
lantern. When I went for the purpose he had his principal
men and the same crowd of court beauties near him as at
the reception. The first picture exhibited was Abraham
about to slaughter his son Isaac. It was shown as large as
life, and the uplifted knife was in the act of striking the lad.
I explained, and the ladies listened with awe, but when I
moved the slide, the uplifted dagger moving towards them,
they thought it was to be sheathed in their bodies instead
of Isaac's. 'Mother! Mother!' all shouted at once, and
off they rushed helter-skelter, tumbling pell-mell over each
other and over the idol-huts and tobacco bushes. We
could not get one of them back again. Shinté, however,
sat bravely through the whole, and afterwards examined
the instrument with interest.

People came long distances for the express purpose of
seeing the objects and hearing the explanations. It was the
only mode of instruction I was ever asked to repeat.

One cannot get away quickly from these chiefs. They
like to have the honour of strangers residing in their villages.
Here we had an additional cause of delay in frequent rains—
twenty-four hours never elapsed without heavy showers.
Everything is affected by the dampness: surgical instruments
became rusty, clothing mildewed, and shoes mouldy. My
little tent was now so rotten and so full of holes that every
sharp shower caused a fine mist to descend on my blanket,
and made me fain to cover the head with it. Heavy dew
lay on everything in the morning, even inside the tent.
There is only a short time of sunshine in the afternoon, and

even that is so interrupted by thunder showers that we cannot dry our bedding.

24th. We expected to have started to-day, but Sambánza, who had been sent off in the early morning for guides, returned at midday without them, and drunk. This was the first case of real, babbling intoxication I had seen in this region. So far as could be collected from his incoherent sentences, Shinté had said the rain was too heavy for our departure and the guides still required time for preparation.

As the last proof of friendship, Shinté came to my tent, though it could scarcely contain more than one person, and looked at all the curiosities, the quicksilver, the looking-glass, hairbrushes, etc., with the greatest interest. Then, closing the tent that none of his own people might see the extravagance of which he was about to be guilty, he drew from his clothing a string of beads and the end of a conical shell, which is considered, in regions far from the sea, of as great value as the Lord Mayor's badge in London. He hung it round my neck and said: 'There, now you *have* a proof of my friendship.'

At our last interview old Shinté pointed out our principal guide, a man of about fifty, who was, he said, ordered to remain with us till we reached the sea; he said that I had now left Sekeletu far behind and must look to Shinté alone for aid, and that it would always be most cheerfully rendered. He gave me a good supply of food and finally a hearty salutation, and we parted with a wish that God would bless him.

Across flooded Plains

26th January 1854. Leaving Shinté with eight of his men to help carry our luggage, we passed in a northerly direction down the lovely valley on which the town stands; then a little to the west through open country and slept in a village of the Balonda.

The country had the same general character of flatness and forest that we had noticed before. The soil was dark, with a tinge of red in places, and appeared fertile.

Our chief guide, Intemese, sent orders to all the villages round our route that Shinté's friends must have abundance of provisions, and we received far more food from Shinté's people than from himself. In return I gave small bunches of our beads.

It was always difficult to get our guides to move away from a place. With the authority of the chief they felt as comfortable as kings' messengers, and were not disposed to forgo the pleasure of living in free quarters.

My Makololo friends were but ill drilled as yet; and since they had never left their own country before, except for purposes of plunder, they did not take readily to the peaceful method we now meant to follow. They either spoke too imperiously to strangers or, when reproved for that, were disposed to follow the dictation of everyone we met.

On 31st January I managed, after considerable opposition on the part of Intemese, to get my party under way. We reached the Leeba, which proved to be only about a hundred yards wide and of the same dark mossy hue as I have already described. The villagers lent us canoes to effect our passage, which took about four hours; and having gone to a village about two miles beyond the river, I had the satisfaction of getting observations and found myself in long. 22° 57' E, lat. 12° 6' 6" S.

In the midst of heavy rain which continued all the morning Intemese sent to say that he was laid up with pains in the stomach and must not be disturbed; but when it cleared up about eleven I saw our friend walking off to the village and talking in loud voice. When I reproached him for telling an untruth, he turned it off with a laugh by saying that he really had a complaint in his stomach which I might cure by killing an ox and allowing him to eat beef.

One of Intemese's men stole a fowl given to us by the lady of the village. When charged with theft all his party shouted with indignation and gesticulated vigorously in defence of his innocence. Then one of my men, Loyanke, brought the lady to identify her fowl, and pointed to the hut where it was hid. Thereupon the Balonda collected round evincing great wrath, but Loyanke seized his battle-axe in the proper manner for striking, and, placing himself on a little hillock, soon moderated their tone. Intemese then called on me to send one of my people to search the huts. The man soon found the bird and brought it out. This incident is mentioned to show that the greater super-stition which exists here does not lead to the practice of virtue.

We entered an extensive plain beyond the Leeba at least twenty miles broad, and covered with water ankle-deep in the shallowest parts. The plains are so perfectly level that rain-water, which this was, stands upon them for months together. Here and there, dotted over the surface, are little islands on which grow stunted date bushes and scraggy trees. The plains themselves are covered with a thick sward of grass, which conceals the water and makes the flats appear like great pale-yellow prairie lands, with a clear horizon except where interrupted by trees. Great numbers of lotus flowers were seen in full bloom.

The continual splashing of the oxen keeps the feet of the rider constantly wet, and my men complained that the perpetual moisture was softening their horny soles. There is no drainage for the prodigious masses of water on these plains, except slow percolation into the different feeders of the Leeba and into the river itself.

These periodically deluged plains have a most important bearing on the physical geography of a very large portion of this country. The plains of Lobale, to the west of this, give rise to a great many streams, which unite to form the deep never-failing Chobe. Similar extensive flats give rise to the Loeti and Kasai and, as we shall see farther on, all the rivers of an extensive region owe their origin not to springs but to oozing bogs.

We made our beds on one of the islands and were

wretchedly supplied with firewood. The booths constructed by the men were but sorry shelter against the rain which poured down without intermission till midday. When released by the cessation of the rain, we marched on till we came to a ridge of dry inhabited land to the north-west. The inhabitants, according to custom, lent us the roofs of some of their huts to save the men the trouble of booth-making. By night it rained so copiously that all our beds were flooded from below, and henceforth we made a furrow round each booth and used the earth to raise our sleeping-places. The men turned out in the wet to work most willingly.

On 7th February we came to the village of Soána Molópo, a half-brother of Katema, whom we found sitting surrounded by about a hundred men.[1] He called on Intemese to give an account of us and gave us a handsome present of food. Intemese raised his hopes of receiving a present of an ox in return for his civility, and on my refusing became sulky and refused to move on.

The following morning we took leave of Molópo, and having been as usual caught by rains, we halted at the house of Mozínkwa, a most intelligent and friendly man, who owned a large garden, well hedged round. He had made the walls of his courtyard constructed of branches of banian, which had taken root and become a hedge. His wife had cotton growing all round her premises, and several plants used as relish to the insipid porridge of the country. His children, very black and comely, were the finest negro family I had ever seen. We were much pleased with their frank friendliness and liberality.

Friday, 10th. As we were crossing the river we were joined by a messenger from Katema, called Shakatwála, a sort of factotum of the chief. Every chief has one attached to his person, generally a poor man, but of great intelligence, and with considerable authority. This man told us that Katema had not received any precise information about

[1] *Missionary Travels*, page 313.

us, but if we were peaceably disposed, as he loved strangers, we were to come to his town. We started forthwith but were turned aside, by the strategy of Intemese, to the village of Quendénde, the father-in-law of Katema. This fine old man was so polite that we did not regret having to spend a Sunday in his village. He expressed his pleasure in having a share in the honour of a visit as well as Katema, though it seemed to us that the conferring of that pleasure required a pretty good stock of impudence, in leading twenty-seven men through the country without the means of purchasing food. My men did a little business of their own in the begging line, but I forbade this at first, believing that as the Makololo had a bad name, the people gave from fear. But after some time it was evident that in many cases maize and manioc were given from pure generosity. In other parts the chiefs attended to my wants, and the common people gave liberally to my men. I presented some of my razors and iron spoons to different headmen, but my men had nothing to give. Yet everyone tried to appropriate an individual in each village as a *molekane*, or comrade, and the villagers often assented. That meant that those who presented food would expect the Makololo to treat them in like manner should they ever be placed in a similar position. Their country, too, is so fertile that they are in no want of food for themselves. However, their generosity was remarkable. Only one woman refused to give some of my men food, but her husband calling out to her to be more liberal, she obeyed, scolding all the time.

In this part of the country buffaloes, elands, koodoos, and various antelopes are to be found, but we did not get any as they are exceedingly wary from being much hunted.

Quendénde's head is a good specimen of the greater crop of wool with which the Negroes of Londa are furnished. The front was parted in the middle and plaited into two thick rolls, which, falling down behind the ears, reached the shoulders. The rest was collected in a large knot which lay on the nape of the neck.

He was an intelligent man, and we had much conversation. He had just come from attending the funeral of one of his people, and I found that the great amount of drum-beating that takes place on these occasions was with the idea that the *barimo*, or spirits, could be drummed to sleep. There is a drum in every village, and we often hear it going from sunset to sunrise. They seem to look on the departed as vindictive beings and are, I suspect, more influenced by fear than love.

We here met with some people just arrived from the town of Matiamvo, who had been sent to announce the death of the late chieftain of that name. Matiamvo is a hereditary title meaning 'lord' or 'chief.' The late Matiamvo seems to have been insane, for he is said to have sometimes indulged the whim of running amok in the town and beheading whomsoever he met, until he had quite a heap of human heads. He explained this by saying that his people were too many. He had absolute power of life and death.

A Laughing Chief

We left the village in company with Quendénde himself and the principal man of the ambassadors of Matiamvo, and after two or three miles' march to the north-west came to the ford of the Lotembwa, which flows southwards. A canoe was waiting to ferry us over, but it was very tedious work; for though the river itself was only eighty yards wide, the whole valley was flooded and we were obliged to paddle more than half a mile to get free of the water.

A fire was lit to warm old Quendénde and enable him to dry his tobacco leaves. The leaves are taken from the plant and spread close to the fire until they are quite dry and crisp. They are then put into a snuff-box which, with a little pestle, serves the purpose of a mill to grind them into powder. It is then used as snuff. As we sat by the fire the ambassadors communicated their thoughts freely respecting the customs of their race. When a chief dies a number of servants are slaughtered with him to form his company in the other world. Quendénde said that he would hide his people so that they might not be slaughtered. As we go north the people become more bloodily superstitious.

We were assured that if the late Matiamvo took a fancy to anything, as for instance my watch-chain, he would order a whole village to be brought up to buy it from the stranger.

After crossing the River Lotembwa we travelled about eight miles and came to Katema's straggling town. It is more a collection of villages than a town. We were led out about a mile from the houses that we might make for ourselves the best lodging we could of the trees and grass, while Intemese was being pumped by Katema as to our past conduct. The chief soon afterwards sent a handsome present of food.

Next morning we were formally presented. We found Katema seated on a sort of throne with about three hundred men on the ground around and thirty women, who were said to be his wives, close behind him. Intemese gave our history, and Katema placed sixteen large baskets of meal and half a dozen fowls and a dozen eggs before us, and expressed regret that we had slept hungry. He did not like any stranger to suffer want in his town, and added: 'Go home, cook and eat, and you will be in a fit state to talk with me to-morrow.'

Katema is a tall man of about forty. He wore a helmet of beads and feathers and a snuff-brown coat with a broad band of tinsel down the arms. In his hand he carried a large tail made of the caudal extremities of a number of gnus. This had charms attached, and he kept waving it in front of him all the time. He seemed in good spirits and laughed heartily several times. This was a good sign, for a man who shakes his sides with mirth is seldom difficult to deal with.[1]

Returning in the morning, Katema addressed me thus: 'I am the great Moéne (lord) Katema, the fellow of Matiamvo.

[1] This is a favourite remark of Livingstone, unlike the Indian proverb that says: 'Truth is found in anger, not in laughter.'

There is no one in this country equal to Matiamvo and me. I have always lived here, and my forefathers too. You found no human skulls near the place where you are encamped. I never killed any traders.' He looked as if he had fallen asleep tipsy and dreamed of his greatness.

We presented a few articles, which pleased him highly. Apologizing for the insignificance of the gift, I asked what I should bring him from Loanda, saying 'not a large thing, but something small.' He laughed heartily at the qualification and replied that everything of the white people would be acceptable, but that his coat was old and he would like another.

I complimented him on the possession of cattle, and pleased him by showing him how he might milk his cows. He had a herd of about thirty, really splendid animals. They were generally white and quite wild, running off gracefully like a herd of elands. When Katema wanted to kill one he had to have it shot like a buffalo.

As Katema did not offer an ox, we slaughtered one of our own and were delighted to get a meal of meat after living so long on light porridge and green maize. When an animal is slaughtered some pieces of meat are in the fire even before the skinning is complete. A frying-pan full of these is quickly handed round. The Balonda, though excessively fond of meat, refused what was offered them because it had been cooked by us. Afterwards my men showed their satisfaction by a dance so uproarious that Katema sent to ask what I had given to produce such excitement.

20th February 1854. We were glad to get away. We went about four or five miles in a north-north-west direction, then two in a westerly one, and came round to the small end of Lake Dilolo. It seemed like a river, a quarter of a mile wide. It is abundantly supplied with fish and hippopotami. The broad part is about three miles wide and the lake almost seven or eight long.

We noticed among Katema's people a love of singing birds. One pretty little songster, named cabazo, a species of canary, is kept in very neatly made cages. They gave as their reason for keeping birds, that 'they sing so sweetly.'

The song-birds here set up quite a merry chorus in the mornings and abound most near the villages. Some sing as loudly as our thrushes, and the king-hunter makes a clear whirring sound like a whistle with a pea in it. During the heat of the day they all remain silent and take their siesta in the shadiest parts of the trees, but in the cool of the evening they again exert themselves. It is remarkable that so many song-birds abound where there is a general paucity of other animal life.

Immediately beyond Dilolo there is a large flat about twenty miles in breadth. On asking the meaning of the name Dilolo, Shakatwála gave the following account of the formation of the lake.

A female chief called Moéne Monénga came one evening to the village of Mosógo, who had gone to hunt with his dogs. She asked for a supply of food, and Mosógo's wife gave her a sufficient quantity. Proceeding to another village standing on the spot now occupied by the water, she preferred the same demand, and was not only refused, but when she uttered a threat for their niggardliness, was taunted with the question: 'What could she do though she were thus treated?' In order to show what she could do she began a song in slow time and uttered her own name, Monénga-Wōō. As she prolonged the last note the village, people, fowls, and dogs sank into the space now called Dilolo. When the headman came home and discovered the catastrophe he cast himself into the lake and is supposed to be there still. Monénga was put to death.

Heavy rains prevented us from crossing the plain in one day, and the constant walking among the grass hurt the men's feet. A path however narrow is a great convenience to all who travel in Africa.

IX

Over the Watershed

24th February 1854. On reaching unflooded lands beyond
the plain we found villages under the authority of a chief
called Katénde, and also found that the plain forms the
watershed between the southern and northern rivers, for
we had now entered a district in which the rivers flowed
in a northerly direction into the Kasai or Loké, while those
hitherto crossed ran southwards. The route to the north-
north-west led us down into a deep valley along the bottom
of which ran a stream from the plain above. This valley,
and another which we reached two hours later, belong to
the water basin of the Kasai.

At different points on the slopes of the valleys there are
oozing fountains surrounded by clumps of the same evergreen, straight, large-leaved trees that we had noted along
the streams. These spots are generally covered with a thick
mat of grassy vegetation.[1] There can be little doubt that
the water, which stands for months on the plains, finds its
way into the rivulets by percolating through the soil and
emerging at these oozing bogs.

In the evening we reached the village of Kabinje, who
sent us a present of tobacco, 'bang,' and maize, but refused
us a guide to the next village because he was at war with it;
though with much persuasion he agreed, provided that the
guide should be allowed to return as soon as he came in
sight of the enemy's village. We felt this a misfortune as
the people all suspect a man who comes telling his own
tale, but we found Kangénke, the headman of a village on
the rivulet Kalómba, a very different man from what his
enemy represented.

[1] These swampy plains are the watershed between the Zambezi and Congo
river systems.

We found that here the idea of buying and selling took the
place of giving for friendship.   As I had nothing with which
to purchase food except a parcel of beads which were
preserved for worse times, I began to fear that we should
soon be compelled to suffer from hunger more than we had
done.   The people demanded gunpowder for everything.
If we had possessed any quantity of that article we should
have got on well, for here it is of great value.   Next to
that, English calico was in great demand, but money was
of no value whatever.   Gold is quite unknown and thought
to be brass.   Trade is carried on by barter alone.

27th February 1854.   Kangénke promptly furnished guides this
morning, so we went on briskly a short distance and came
to a part of the Kasai or Loké, where he had appointed
two canoes to convey us across.[1]

While we were at the ford we were subjected to a trick
of which we had been forewarned by the people of Shinté.
A knife had been dropped by one of Kangénke's people in
order to entrap my men.   It was put down near our encampment as if lost, the owner in the meantime watching
till one of my men picked it up.   Nothing was said until
our party was divided, one half on this and the other on that
bank of the river.   Then the charge was made to me that
one of my men had stolen a knife.   Certain of my people's
honesty, I desired the man, who was making a great noise,
to search the luggage for it.   The unlucky lad who had
taken the bait then came forward and confessed that he had
put the knife in a basket which was already over the river.
When it was returned the owner would not receive it back
unless accompanied by a fine.   The lad offered beads, but
these were refused with scorn.   A shell hanging round his
neck, similar to that which Shinté had given me, was the
object demanded, and the victim of the trick, as we all
knew it to be, was obliged to part with his costly
ornament.

[1] The Kasai is one of the large tributaries of the Congo.

I felt annoyed at the imposition, but the order we in-variably followed in crossing a river forced me to submit. The head of the party remained to be ferried over last, so if I had not come to terms, I would have been, as I always was in crossing rivers which we could not swim, completely in the power of the enemy. It was but rarely we could get a headman so witless as to cross with us and remain on the opposite bank in a convenient position to be seized as a hostage in case of my being caught.

This trick was but one of a number equally dishonourable which are practised by tribes that lie adjacent to the more civilized settlements. The Balonda farther east told us by way of warning that many parties of the more central tribes had at various periods set out in order to trade with the white men themselves instead of through the Mambari, but had always been obliged to return without reaching their destination in consequence of so many pretexts being in-vented by the tribes encountered in the way for fining them of their ivory.

Grasping Headmen

We were now in want of food, for, to the great surprise of my companions, the people of Kangénke gave nothing except by way of sale, and charged the most exorbitant prices for the little meal and manioc they brought. The only article of barter my men had was a little fat from an ox we slaughtered at Katema's, so I was obliged to give them a portion of the stock of beads.

One day (29th) of westing brought us from the Kasai to near the village of Katénde, and we saw we were in a land where no hope could be entertained of getting animal food, for one of our guides caught a light blue coloured mole and two mice for his supper. The care with which he wrapped them up in a leaf and slung them on his spear told us that we could hope for no larger game. On coming to villages beyond this we often saw children digging up these tiny quadrupeds.

Katénde sent for me on the day following our arrival, and I walked for this purpose about three miles from our encampment. When we approached the village we were desired to enter a hut, and, as it was raining at the time, we did so. After a long time spent in giving and receiving messages from the great man, we were told that he wanted either a man, a tusk, beads, copper rings, or a shell, as payment for leave to pass through his country. No one, we were assured, was allowed that liberty, or even to behold him, without something of the sort being presented. Having humbly explained our circumstances, and that he could not expect to 'catch a humble cow by the horns'— a proverb similar to ours that 'you cannot draw milk from a stone'—we were told to go home and he would speak to us again next day. I could not avoid a hearty laugh at the cool impudence of the savage, and made the best of my way home in the still pouring rain.

My men were rather nettled at this want of hospitality, but after talking the matter over with one of Katénde's servants, he proposed that some small article should be given and an attempt made to please Katénde. I turned out my shirts, selected the worst one as a sop to him, and invited Katénde to come and choose anything else I had. I added that when I reached my own chief naked and was asked what I had done with my clothes, I should be obliged to confess that I had left them with Katénde. The shirt was dispatched, and accepted with the message that food would be sent the next day.

My men were as astonished as I was at this demand for payment for leave to pass, and the almost entire neglect of the rules of hospitality. Katénde gave us only a little meal and manioc, and a fowl. Being detained two days by heavy rains, we felt that a good stock of patience was necessary in passing through this country in the rainy season.

Passing onward without seeing Katénde, we crossed a small rivulet, the Sengko, by which we had encamped, and after two hours came to another, the Totélo, which was

larger, and had a bridge over it.   At the farther end of this
structure stood a Negro who demanded fees.   He said the
bridge was his, the path was his; the guides were his
children, and if we did not pay him he would prevent
further progress.   This piece of civilization I was not prepared to meet, and stood a few seconds looking at our bold
toll-keeper, when one of my men took off three copper
bracelets and paid for the whole party.   The Negro was a
better man than he at first seemed, for he immediately
went to his garden and brought us some leaves of tobacco
as a present.

When we had got fairly away from the villages, the guides
from Kangénke sat down and told us that there were three
paths in front, and if we did not at once present them with
a cloth, they would leave us to take whichever we might
like best.   I wished my men to go on without guides,
trusting to ourselves to choose the path which would seem
to lead in the direction we had always followed.   But
Mashauana, fearing we might wander, asked leave to give
his own cloth, and when the guides saw that, they came
forward shouting 'Averié, Averié.'

In the afternoon of this day we came to a valley about a
mile wide filled with clear fast-flowing water.   The men
on foot were chin-deep in crossing, and we three on ox-
back got wet to the middle.   A thunder shower descending
completed the partial drenching of the plain, and gave a
cold uncomfortable 'packing in a wet blanket' that night.
Next day we found another flooded valley about half a mile
wide with a small deep rivulet in the middle.   This was so
rapid that we crossed holding on to the oxen, and the
current soon dashed them to the opposite bank.   We then
jumped off and pulled them to the shallower part.

In the afternoon we came to another stream with a
bridge over it.   The men had to swim to and from each
end of the bridge, and when on it were breast-deep.   Some
preferred to hold the tails of the oxen the whole way across.
I intended to do this too, but before I could dismount the

ox dashed off with its companions, and soon sank so deep that I failed to catch the blanket belt, and was obliged to strike out for the opposite shore. My poor fellows were dreadfully alarmed when they saw me parted from the cattle, and about twenty of them made a simultaneous rush into the water to my rescue, and as I reached the opposite bank one seized my arm and another threw his around my body. When I stood up it was most gratifying to see them all struggling towards me. Some had leaped off the bridge and allowed their cloaks to float down the stream. Great was the pleasure expressed when they found that I could swim, like themselves, without the aid of a tail, and I did and do feel grateful to those poor heathen for the promptitude with which they dashed in to save, as they thought, my life. I found my clothes cumbersome in the water. They could swim quicker from being naked. They swim like dogs, not frog-fashion as we do.

Saturday, 4th March. Came to the outskirts of the territory of the Chiboque. We crossed the Konde and Kalúze rivulets. The valleys are beautifully fertile. My companions were continually lamenting over the uncultivated vales in such words as these: 'What a fine country for cattle. My heart is sore to see such fruitful valleys for corn lying waste.' I had come to believe that the reason why the inhabitants of this fine country possess no herds of cattle, was owing to the despotic sway of their chiefs, and that the common people would not be allowed to keep domestic animals even supposing they could acquire them. But I have been led to the conjecture that the rich fertile country of Londa must formerly have been infested by the tsetse, but that, as the people killed off the game on which, in the absence of man, the tsetse must subsist, the insect was starved out of the country. It is now found only where wild animals abound, and the Balonda, by the possession of guns, having cleared most of the country of all the large game, we may have happened to come just when it was possible to admit of cattle. Hence the success of Katema, Shinté, and Matiamvo with their herds.

The amount of population in the central parts of the country may be called large only in comparison with the Cape Colony or the Bechuana country. The cultivated land is nothing compared with what might be brought under the plough. There are flowing streams in abundance, which could be used for irrigation with little labour. The people are not all quite black in colour. Many incline to be bronze, others are as light in hue as Bushmen, who afford a proof that heat alone does not cause blackness, but that heat and moisture combined do materially deepen colour. Wherever we find people who for ages have continued in a hot, humid district, they are deep black; though to this apparent rule there are exceptions caused by migrations of both tribes and individuals.

An Exciting Moment

Having reached the village of Njambi, one of the chiefs of the Chiboque, as we intended to pass a quiet Sunday and our provisions were quite spent, I ordered a tired ox to be slaughtered.[1] As we wished to be on good terms with all we sent the hump and ribs to Njambi, with the explanation that this was the customary tribute to chiefs in that part of the country from which we came. He returned thanks and promised to send food.

Next morning he sent an impudent message with a very small present of meal, scorning the meat he had accepted and demanding a man, a gun, an ox, powder, cloth, or a shell; and in the event of our refusing his demand he intimated his intention to prevent our further progress. We replied that we should have thought ourselves fools if we had scorned his small present and demanded other food instead; and even supposing we had possessed the articles named, no black man ought to impose tribute on a party that did not trade in slaves. The servants who brought the

[1] *Missionary Travels*, page 339.

message said that when sent to the Mambari they had always got a quantity of cloth from them for their master, and they now expected the same from us.

We heard some of the Chiboque remark, 'They have only five guns,' and about midday Njambi collected all his people and surrounded our encampment. Their object was evidently to plunder us of everything. My men seized their javelins and stood on the defensive, while the young Chiboque had drawn their swords and brandished them with great fury. Some even pointed their guns at me and nodded to each other as much as to say: 'This is the way we shall do with him.'

I sat on my camp-stool with my double-barrelled gun across my knees, and invited the chief to be seated also. When he and his counsellors had sat down on the ground in front of me, I asked what crime we had committed that he had come armed in that way. He replied that one of my men, Pitsane, while sitting at the fire that morning had, in spitting, allowed a small quantity of saliva to fall on the leg of one of his men, and this 'guilt' he wanted to settle by the fine of a man, an ox, or a gun. Pitsane admitted the fact of a little saliva having fallen on the Chiboque, and in proof of its being a pure accident he mentioned that he had given the man a piece of meat, by way of making friends, just before it happened, and wiped it off with his hand as soon as it fell. In reference to a man being given, I declared that we were all ready to die rather than give up one of our number to be a slave; that my men might as well give me up as I give one of them, for we were all free men.

'Then you can give the gun with which the ox was shot.' As we heard some of his people remarking even now that we had only five guns, we declined on the ground that, as they intended to plunder us, giving a gun would help them to do so. This they denied, saying that they wanted the customary tribute only. I asked what right they had to demand payment for leave to tread on the ground of God, our common Father? If we trod on their gardens we would pay, but not for marching on land which was still God's and not theirs. They did not attempt to controvert this, because it was in accordance with their own ideas, but reverted again to the pretended crime of the saliva.

My men now entreated me to give something, and after asking the chief if he really thought the spitting was a matter of guilt, and receiving an answer in the affirmative, I gave him one of my shirts, but the young Chiboque were dissatisfied, and began shouting and brandishing their swords for a greater fine.

As Pitsane felt that he had been the cause of this disagreeable affair, he asked me to add something else. I gave a bunch of beads, but the counsellors objected this time, so I added a large handkerchief.

The more I yielded the more unreasonable their demands became, and at every fresh demand a shout was raised by the armed party and a rush made around us with brandishing of arms. One young man made a charge at my head from behind, but I quickly brought round the muzzle of my gun to his mouth and he retreated. I pointed him out to the chief and he was ordered to retire a little.

I felt anxious to avoid effusion of blood, and though sure of being able with my Makololo, who had been trained by Sebituane, to drive off twice the number of assailants, though now a large body and well armed with spears, swords, arrows, and guns, I strove to avoid actual collision. My men behaved with admirable coolness. The chief and counsellors by accepting my invitation to be seated, had placed themselves in a trap, for my men very quietly surrounded them, and made them feel that there was no chance of escaping their spears.

I then said that, as one thing after another had failed to satisfy them, it was evident that *they* wanted to fight while *we* wanted only to pass peaceably through their country; that they must begin first to bear the guilt before God. We would not fight till they struck the first blow. I then

sat silent for some time. It was rather trying for me because I knew that the Chiboque would aim at the white
man first, but I was careful not to appear flurried, and
having four barrels ready for instant action, looked quietly
at the savage scene around. The Chiboque countenance,
by no means handsome, is not improved by their practice
of filing the teeth to a point.

The chief and counsellors, seeing that they were in more
danger than I, did not choose to follow my decision that
they should strike the first blow and then see what we could
do, and were perhaps influenced by seeing the air of cool
preparedness which some of my men displayed at the
prospect of a work of blood.

The Chiboque at last put the matter before us in this
way: 'You come among us in a new way and say you are
quite friendly. How can we know it unless you give us
some of your food and you take some of ours. If you give
us an ox we will give you whatever you wish and then we
shall be friends.' At the entreaty of my men I gave an ox,
and mentioned food as what we most needed. In the
evening Njambi sent a very small basket of meal and two
or three pounds of the flesh of our own ox, with an apology
that he had no fowls and very little of any other food. It
was impossible to avoid a laugh at the coolness of the
generous creatures. I was truly thankful nevertheless that,
though resolved rather to die than deliver up one of our
number to be a slave, we had so far gained our point as to
be allowed to pass without having shed human blood.

Mutiny and Loyalty
6th March 1854. We were told that the people west of the
Chiboque of Njambi were familiar with the visits of slave-
traders; and it was the opinion of our guides that so many
of my companions would be demanded of me that I should
reach the coast without a single attendant. I therefore
resolved to alter course and strike north-north-east in the
hope that at some point farther north I might find an exit

to the Portuguese settlement of Cassange. We proceeded at first due north, with the Kasabi villages on our right and Kasau on our left.

We could observe the difference in the seasons as we moved northward with the sun. Summer was nearly over at Kuruman, and far advanced at Linyanti, but here we were in the middle of it. Fruits that we had eaten ripe on the Leeambye were here quite green, but we were coming into a region where the inhabitants are favoured with two rainy seasons and two crops, that is, when the sun is going south, and when he comes back on his way to the north, as at present.

In passing through these narrow paths I observed the peculiarities of my ox, Sinbad. He had a softer back than the others, but a much more intractable temper. His horns were bent downwards and hung loosely, so he could do no harm with them; but as he went slowly along the narrow paths he would suddenly dart aside. A string tied to a stick put through the cartilage of his nose serves as a bridle. If you jerk this back it makes him go faster, if you pull it to one side he allows his nose and head to go, but keeps the other eye on the forbidden spot and goes in spite of you. The only way in which he can be brought to a stand is by a stroke of a wand across the nose. Once when he ran in below a climber stretched across the path, so low that I could not stoop under it, I was dragged off and came down on the crown of my head. He never allowed a chance of this sort to pass without trying to inflict a kick, as if I neither had nor deserved his love.

Saturday, 11th. Reached a small village on the banks of a narrow stream. I was too ill to go out of my little covering, except to quell a mutiny that began among some of our party. They grumbled, as they often do against their chiefs, when they think they are partial in their gifts, because they thought I had shown preference in sharing out beads. I explained my reasons and thought them satisfied, and soon sank into a state of stupor that fever sometimes produces. On Sunday the mutineers made a terrible din while preparing a skin. I asked them twice to be more quiet, as the noise pained me; but as they paid no attention I put my head out of the tent and repeated the request but was answered by an impudent laugh. Knowing that our lives depended on vigorously upholding authority, I seized a double-barrelled pistol and darted out looking, I suppose, so savage as to put them to flight. Some remained within hearing, and I told them that as long as we travelled together, I was master. My purpose being plain, they immediately became obedient and never afterwards gave me trouble.

13th. We went forward some miles but were brought to a stand, by the severity of my fever, on the banks of a branch of the Loajima, another tributary of the Kasai. I was in a state of partial coma until late at night, when it became necessary for me to go out. I was surprised to find my men had built a little stockade, and some of them took their spears and acted as a guard. I found that we were surrounded by enemies, and a party of Chiboque lay near the gateway, after having preferred the demand for 'a man, an ox, a gun, or a tusk.' My men had prepared for defence in case of a night attack.

In the morning I went out to the Chiboque and found that they answered me civilly. They admitted that their chiefs would be pleased with the prospect of friendship, and now only wished to exchange tokens of goodwill with me, and offered three pigs which they hoped I would accept. The people here are in the habit of making a present and then demanding whatever they choose in return. I tried to decline by asking if they would eat one of the pigs in company with us. To this proposition they said they durst not accede. I then accepted the present in the hope that the blame of deficient friendly feeling might not rest with me, and presented a razor, two bunches of beads, and twelve copper rings contributed by the men from their arms. They went off to report to their chief, and as I was unable to move from excessive giddiness, we continued in the same spot till Tuesday evening, when they returned with a message stating in plain terms that a man, a gun, or an ox alone would be acceptable. As this was civilly said and there was nothing for it but bloodshed if we refused, I gave a tired riding-ox.

Forest Gloom and Tribal Tactics

Next morning the robber party came with presents. Our guides thought these were only spies of a larger party in the forests through which we must now pass. We prepared for defence by walking in a compact body. We marched through many miles of gloomy forest in gloomier silence, but nothing disturbed us. I was too ill to care. The thick atmosphere prevented my seeing the creeping-plants in time to avoid them, so Pitsane and I, who alone were mounted, were often caught, and as there was no stopping the oxen when they have a chance of giving the rider a tumble, we came frequently to the ground. In addition, Sinbad broke his bridle and brought me down backwards on my head. He gave me a kick on the thigh at the same time. I was none the worse for this rough treatment, but I cannot recommend it as a palliative to fever. This last attack reduced me almost to a skeleton.

On Friday we were met by a hostile party who refused us further passage. I ordered my men to proceed, but our enemies spread themselves out in front of us with loud cries. Our numbers were about equal to theirs this time, so I moved on at the head of my men.

When we came to the edge of the forest an old headman, Ionga Panza, a venerable Negro, came up, and I invited them all to be seated that we might talk the matter over. He soon let me know that he felt himself to have been ill-treated by being passed by. Like all the tribes near the Portuguese settlements, people here think they have a right to demand payment of all passing through the country.

E

The reason is probably that they have seen no traders except those who are engaged in buying slaves; and such traders are at the mercy of the chiefs, for if they afforded a ready asylum to runaway slaves the traders would be stripped of all their property. So they have to curry favour with the chiefs, who thus come to look on white men with great contempt.

During these exciting scenes I always forgot my fever, but a terrible sinking feeling came back with a sense of safety. Old Ionga's demands were not unreasonable, but our guides complicated matters by sending for a body of Bangala traders, in order to force us to sell the tusks of Sekeletu that we were carrying and pay them the price. They made off with two guns and some beads, but my men gave chase, whereupon the guides dropped the guns and rushed into a hut in the village. The door was not much higher than that of a dog's kennel. One of the guides was reached by one of my men as he was in the act of stooping to get in, and a cut was inflicted on a projecting part of the body which would have made anyone in that posture wince. The guns were restored but the beads were lost.

The men offered all their ornaments and I offered all my beads and shirts, but matters could not be arranged without our giving an ox and one of the tusks. We were all becoming disheartened, and my people were now so much discouraged that some proposed to return home. The prospect of being obliged to return just when on the threshold of the Portuguese settlements distressed me exceedingly. After using all my powers of persuasion I declared that I would go on alone, and went into my tent with a mind directed to Him who hears the sighing of the soul; and was soon followed by the head of Mohorisi saying: 'We will never leave you. Do not be disheartened. Wherever you lead we will follow.' Others followed, and with most artless simplicity of manner told me to be comforted: they were all my children; they knew no one but Sekeletu and me, and they would die for me.

One of the oxen offered to the Chiboque had been rejected because it had lost part of its tail. They thought it had been cut off and witchcraft medicine inserted, and some mirth was excited by my proposing to raise a similar objection to all the oxen we still had. The remaining four soon presented a similar shortness in their caudal extremities, and though no one ever asked whether they had medicine in their stumps or no, we were no more troubled by the demand for an ox. We now slaughtered another ox, that the spectacle might not be seen of the owners of the cattle fasting while the Chiboque feasted.

X

Portuguese Territory

24th March 1854. Ionga Panza's sons agreed to act as guides into Portuguese territory if I would give them Shinté's shell. I yielded unwillingly to the entreaties of my people, and gave up the precious shell.

Next morning our guides went only a mile and then told us they would return home. This was just what I expected in paying beforehand. They slipped off into the forest one by one.

26th. We spent Sunday on the banks of the Quilo, or Kweelo, here a stream about ten yards wide. It runs in a deep glen the sides of which are almost five hundred yards of slope, and rocky, the rocks being hardened calcareous tufa lying on clay shale and sandstone, with a capping of ferruginous conglomerate. The scenery would have been very pleasing, but fever took away much of the joy of life and made me very weak and always ready to rest.

The inhabitants of the district live in a state of glorious ease. Food abounds and very little labour is required for its cultivation. The soil is so rich that no manure is required, and when a garden is worn out the owner moves a little farther into the forest, kills the larger trees by fire, cuts down the smaller ones, and has at once a new and rich garden ready for the seed. Hence the gardens usually present the appearance of a number of tall dead trees standing without bark, and maize growing between them. But while vegetable aliment is abundant, there is a want of salt and animal food, so that numberless mouse-traps are seen in all the forests of Londa.

We were travelling west-north-west. All the rivulets

we crossed here had a northerly course, and were reported
to fall into the Kasai. As we were now in the alleged
latitude of the Coanza, I was much astonished at the entire
absence of any knowledge of that river among the natives
of this quarter. But I was then ignorant of the fact that
the Coanza rises considerably to the west of this, and has
a comparatively short course from its source to the sea.

The village on the Kweelo at which we spent Sunday was
that of a civil, lively old man, called Sakandála, who offered
no objection to our progress. We found we should soon
enter on the territory of the Bashinjé. Rains and fever, as
usual, helped to impede our progress, until we were put
on the path which leads from Cassange and Bihe to Matiamvo.
This was a well-beaten footpath, and soon after entering
upon it we met a party of half-caste traders from Bihe.
They presented my men with some tobacco, and marvelled
greatly that I had never been able to teach myself to smoke.

As we were now alone and sure of being on the way to
the abodes of civilization we went on briskly. On the
30th we came to a sudden descent from the high land,
indented by deep narrow valleys over which we had lately
been travelling. It is generally so steep that it can only be
descended at particular points, and even there I was obliged
to dismount, though so weak that I had to be led by my
companions, to prevent my toppling over in walking down.
It was annoying to feel myself so helpless, for I never liked
to see a man, either sick or well, giving in effeminately.

Below us lay the valley of the Quango. If you sit on the
spot where Mary Queen of Scots viewed the Battle of Lang-
side and look down on the Vale of Clyde, you may see in
miniature the glorious sight which a much greater and richer
valley presented to our view.

It is about a hundred miles broad, clothed with dark
forest, except where the light green grass covers meadow-
lands on the Quango, which here and there glances out in
the sun as it wends its way north. The opposite side of
this great valley appears like a range of lofty mountains, and

the descent into it is about a mile, which, measured perpendicularly, may be from a thousand to twelve hundred feet. Emerging from the gloomy forests of Londa, this magnificent prospect made us feel as if a weight had been lifted off our eyelids. A cloud was passing through the middle of the valley from which rolling thunder pealed, while above all was glorious sunlight. When we went down to the part where we saw it passing, we found that a very heavy thunder shower had fallen under the path of the cloud. Looking back from below, the descent appeared as the edge of a tableland with numerous indented dells and spurs jutting out all along, giving a serrated appearance. Both the top and sides of the sierra are covered with trees.

Sunday, 2nd April. We rested beside a small stream, and our hunger being now very severe from having lived on manioc alone since leaving Ionga Panza, we slaughtered one of our four remaining oxen. The Bashinjé refused to sell any food for the poor old ornaments my men had to offer. But we should have been comfortable had not the chief, Sansáwé, pestered us for the usual present. The native traders informed us that a display of force was often necessary before they could pass this man. The more humbly we spoke the more insolent they became, till at last we all felt savage and sulky.

After being wearied with talking all day to different parties, we were honoured by a visit from Sansáwé. He was a young man of rather pleasing countenance. I showed him my watch and pocket compass, and tried to win my way into his confidence by conversation; but when leaving he sent for my spokesman and told him that 'if we did not add a red jacket and a man to our gift, we might turn back. I replied that we would certainly go forward next day, and that if he commenced hostilities, the blame before God would be on him. To which my man added: 'How many white men have you killed?' Hunger has a powerful effect on the temper. After a good meal of meat we could bear annoyances with calm, but as we had suffered much of late, we were rather sour in our feelings.

At daybreak we set off in drizzling rain and passed close to the village. The rain probably damped the ardour of the robbers, for we were not molested. After two hours' march we breathed freely, and my men remarked in thankfulness: 'We are children of Jesus.'

After six hours we halted near the River Quango, the eastern border of Portuguese territory. As I had no change of clothing I was glad of the shelter of my blanket, thankful to God for bringing us thus far without losing one of our party.

An Unexpected Helper

The temptation to use force against these petty tyrants grew greater as, following repeated bouts of fever, his self-restraint waned. To have yielded would, he realized, have spoiled the main purpose of his journey, but when, as on the crossing of the Quango, 'a man, a gun, or an ox' was demanded, he stiffened his attitude.

4th April 1854. The Quango river is here one hundred yards wide and very deep. It is said to contain many venomous water-snakes which congregate round the carcass of any hippopotamus that may have been killed. This may explain why all the villages are situated far from the banks.

The chief of these parts came again and made his demands. My men stripped off the last of their copper rings and gave them; but he was still intent on a man, and kept worrying us till I was tired. I tried in vain to lie down out of sight of my persecutors, but my little tent was in tatters, having a wider hole behind than the door in front.

As I was trying to persuade my men to move on to the bank, in spite of these people, Cypriano di Abreu, a young half-caste Portuguese sergeant of militia, made his appearance

and gave the same advice. He had come across the Quango
in search of beeswax.

When we moved off from the chief who had plagued us
his people opened fire from our sheds, but none of the
bullets reached us. It is probable that they expected that
a demonstration of the abundance of the ammunition they
possessed would make us run, but we moved quietly forward
and they came no farther. Cypriano assisted us in making
a more satisfactory arrangement with the ferryman than
parting with my blanket, and as soon as we reached the
opposite bank we were in the territory of the Bangala, who
are subjects of the Portuguese and often spoken of as
Cassanges, and happily all our difficulties with the border
tribes were at an end.

Passing with light hearts through the high grass by a
narrow pathway for about three miles to the west of the
river, we came to some neat square houses guarded by
cleanly looking half-caste Portuguese. They belonged to a
division of militia stationed here under command of my
friend, Cypriano.

I pitched my little tent in front of Cypriano's dwelling
for the night. In the morning he generously supplied my
men with pumpkins and maize, and then invited me to a
magnificent breakfast, consisting of ground-nuts and roasted
maize, then boiled manioc roots, and concluding with
guavas and honey as a dessert. At dinner he was equally
bountiful, and several of his friends joined us in doing
justice to his hospitality. Before eating, water was poured
on the hands of each by a female slave. This proceeding
was necessary because forks and spoons were used only for
carving and not for eating.

Much of the civility shown us here was, no doubt, owing
to the flattering letters of recommendation I carried from
Chevalier Du Prat of Cape Town, but I am sure that our
new friend was also moved by feelings of real kindness, for
he quite bared his garden in feeding us during the few days
we were there. He killed an ox for us, and his mother

and maids prepared farina for us for the four or five days of our journey and never hinted at payment. My wretched appearance must have excited his compassion.

We were detained by rains, but after three days' pretty hard travelling reached Cassange, the farthest inland station of the Portuguese in Western Africa. I made my entrance among our Portuguese allies in a somewhat forlorn state as to clothing. The first gentleman I met asked me for my passport and said he must take me to the authorities. Like the people who commit petty depredations in order to obtain food and shelter in a prison, in the hope of a meal I went with him gladly to the house of the commandant, Senhor de Silva Rego, who politely asked me to supper. As we had eaten nothing but farina since the Quango, I expect I appeared particularly ravenous to the other gentlemen around the table. They seemed, however, to understand my position pretty well, from all having travelled extensively themselves. Had they not been present I might have put some in my pocket to eat by night, for after fever the appetite is excessively keen, and manioc is one of the most unsatisfying of foods.

Captain Antonio Rodrigues Neves then kindly invited me to take up my abode in his house. Next morning this generous man arrayed me in decent clothing, and continued during the whole period of my stay to treat me as if I had been his brother. I am deeply grateful to him for his disinterested kindness. He not only attended to my wants but also furnished food to my famishing party free of charge.

Portuguese Hospitality. Cassange

The village of Cassange is composed of thirty or forty traders' houses, scattered about without any regularity on an elevated spot in the great Quango or Cassange valley.[1] They are built of wattle and daub, and surrounded by plantations of manioc and maize. Behind them there are usually kitchen gardens, in which the common European

[1] *Missionary Travels*, page 369.

* E

vegetables, such as potatoes, peas, cabbages, onions, tomatoes, etc., grow. Guavas and bananas appear, from the size and abundance of the trees, to have been introduced many years ago, while the land was still in the possession of the natives, but pineapples, orange, fig, and cashew-trees have been more lately tried.

There are about forty Portuguese traders in this district, all of whom are officers of the militia, and many have become rich by adopting the plan of sending out Pombeiros, or native traders, to trade in the more remote parts of the country. Some of the governors of Loanda have insisted on the observance of a law which forbids, from motives of humanity, the Portuguese themselves from passing beyond the boundary. They seem to take it for granted that in cases where the white trader was killed, the aggression had been made by him, and they wished to avoid the necessity of punishing those who had been provoked to shed Portuguese blood. This indicated a far greater impartiality than has obtained in our own dealings with the Kaffirs, for we engaged in the most expensive wars with them without once inquiring whether any of the fault lay with our frontier colonists.

As I have always preferred to appear in my own proper character, I was an object of curiosity to these hospitable Portuguese. They evidently looked upon me as an agent of the English Government, engaged in some new movement for the suppression of slavery. They could not divine what a *missionario* had to do with latitudes and longitudes, which I was intent on observing.

When we became a little familiar, the questions put to me were rather amusing. 'Is it common for missionaries to be doctors? Are you a doctor of medicine or a *Doutor mathematico* too? You must be more than a missionary to be able to calculate the longitude. Tell us at once what rank you hold in the English army.' They may have given credit to my reason for wearing a moustache, as that explains why men have beards and women have none; but that which puzzled many besides my Cassange friends was the anomaly of my being a 'sacerdote' with a wife and four children! I usually got rid of the last question by asking another: 'Is it not better to have children with a wife than to have children without a wife?' But all were most kind and hospitable, and as one of their festivals was near they invited me to partake in the feast.

On the sixteenth I witnessed the celebration of the anniversary of our Lord's resurrection. The coloured population dressed up a figure intended to represent Judas Iscariot, and paraded it on a riding-ox about the village amidst sneers and maledictions. The natives, whether slaves or free, dressed in their gayest clothing, made visits to the principal merchants to wish them a good feast, and expected a present in return.

At 10 a.m. we went to the residence of the commandant, and at a given signal two brass guns began firing, to the great admiration of my men, whose ideas of the power of a cannon were very exalted. The Portuguese flag was hoisted and trumpets were sounded, and Captain Neves invited the principal inhabitants of the place and feasted them in princely style.

None of these gentlemen had Portuguese wives. They usually come to Africa to make a little money and return to Lisbon. Hence they seldom bring their wives with them, and never can make successful colonists in consequence. It is common for them to have families by native women. It was particularly gratifying to me, who have been familiar with the stupid prejudice against colour, entertained only by those who are themselves becoming tawny, to view the liberality with which the people of colour were treated by the Portuguese. Instances, so common in the south, of half-caste children being abandoned, are here extremely rare. They are acknowledged at table and provided for by their fathers. The coloured clerks of the merchants sit at the same table as their employers without embarrassment. Nowhere in Africa is there so much goodwill between Europeans and natives as here.

From the village of Cassange we had a good view of the surrounding country. It is gently undulating plain, covered with grass and patches of forest.

As the traders of Cassange were the first white men we had come to, we sold the tusks belonging to Sekeletu, which we had brought to test the difference in the prices in Makololo and white men's country. The result was highly satisfactory to my companions, as the Portuguese give much larger prices for ivory than the traders of the Cape can possibly do because of overland expenses and ruinous restrictions.

The World said : 'I am finished'

The commandant handsomely offered me a soldier as a guard to Ambaca. My men told me that they had been thinking it would be better to turn back here, as they had been informed at Cassange that I was leading them down to the sea-coast only to sell them; and that they would be taken on board a ship, fattened, and eaten by white men, who were cannibals. I told them that if they doubted my intentions they had better not go to the coast, but that I was determined to proceed. They replied that they had no intention of leaving me but would follow wherever I led the way.

This affair being disposed of for the time, the commandant gave them an ox and entertained me to a friendly dinner before starting. All the merchants accompanied me to the edge of the plateau on which the village stands, and I parted with them feeling that I should never forget their disinterested kindness. May God remember them in their day of need!

From Cassange we had still about three hundred miles before we reached the coast. We had a black militia corporal as a guide. He had three slaves, and was carried by them in his hammock slung from a pole. We left on the 21st, and traversed the remaining portion of the valley to the foot of the Tala Mungongo, the ascent of which was not so arduous as I had been led to suppose. We accomplished it in the course of an hour by a steep slippery path, bordered on each side by a deep gorge, and at the summit found a tableland similar to that on the other side of the valley.

The people here may be called true Negroes. The dark colour, thick lips, heads elongated backwards and upwards and covered with wool, flat noses, and other Negro peculiarities, are general. All have a certain thickness and prominence of lip, but many are met with in every village in whom thickness and projection are not more marked than in Europeans. All are dark, but the colour is shaded off in individuals from deep black to light yellow.

In crossing the Lombe my ox, Sinbad, in his love of finding out a new path for himself, plunged head first into a deep hole, and so soused me that I was obliged to pass on without calling on the Europeans who lived on the bank. I was sorry, for the Portuguese, like the Boers, feel it a slight to be passed without a word of salutation.

We crossed the Lucalla by means of a large canoe kept there by a man who farms the ferry from the Government, and charges about a penny per head. A few miles beyond we came to Ambaca, once an important place, but now a paltry village. We were most kindly received by the commandant, Arsenio de Cargo, who spoke a little English. He recommended wine for my debility, and gave me the first glass of that beverage I had ever taken in Africa. The weakening effects of fever were most extraordinary. For instance, in taking lunar observations I could not avoid confusion of time and distance. I could not hold the instrument steady nor perform a simple calculation. I forgot the days of the week and the names of my companions, and, had I been asked, probably could not have told my own. When sleeping in the house of the commandant, I was bitten in the foot by a kind of tick, known in the southern country by the name of tampan, and common in all native huts in this country. It varies in size from that of a pin's head to that of a pea, and its skin is so tough and yielding that it is impossible to burst it by any amount of squeezing with the fingers. The effects of the bite are a tingling sensation of mingled pain and itching, which gradually ascends the limb until it reaches the abdomen, where it causes violent vomiting and purging.

12th May 1854. As we were about to start this morning the commandant provided bread and meat most bountifully for my use on the way to the next station, and in parting gave me a glass of wine which prevented the violent fit of shivering I expected that afternoon.

There is something so exhilarating to one of Highland blood in being near, or on, high mountains that I forgot my fever as we wended our way among the lofty tree-covered masses of mica schist, which form the highlands around the romantic residence of the Chefe of Golungo Alto. The whole district is extremely beautiful. The hills are be-decked with trees of various hues of foliage, and among them towers the graceful palm, which yields the oil of commerce for making soaps and the intoxicating toddy. Some clusters of the hills look like waves of the sea driven into a narrow open bay, and have assumed the same form as if, when all were chopping up perpendicularly, they had suddenly been congealed.

We were most kindly received by the commandant, Lieutenant Antonio Canto e Castro, a young gentleman whose whole subsequent conduct will ever make me regard him with affection. Like every other person of intelligence whom I met, he lamented deeply the neglect with which this fine country had been treated. The district contained a population of 104,000. The number of carriers who may be ordered out at the pleasure of the Government to convey merchandise to the coast, in this district alone, is about 6,000, yet there are no good roads in existence. This system of compulsory carriage of goods was adopted in consequence of the activity of our cruisers. Each trader who went previously into the interior in pursuit of his calling proceeded on the plan of purchasing ivory and bees-wax, and enough slaves to carry these commodities. But when our cruisers made the export of slaves impossible, a new system of compulsory carriage was resorted to. The system worked in the following manner.

A trader who requires two or three hundred carriers to convey his merchandise to the coast, applies to the General Government for aid. An order is sent to the commandant of a district, and each headman must furnish from five to twenty or thirty men. For this accommodation the trader must pay to the Government a tax of about three shillings a load. The expense of compulsory labour is very heavy, yet no effort has been made to form a great line of road for wheel traffic.

Farther on, we left the mountainous country, and as we descended towards the west coast, saw the lands assuming a more sterile and uninviting aspect. On the right ran the River Senza, which nearer the sea takes the name of Bengo. The banks are infested by myriads of the most ferocious mosquitoes I ever met. Not one of our party could get a snatch of sleep. I was taken into the house of a Portuguese, but was soon glad to make my escape and lie across the path in the lee of a fire where the smoke blew over my body. My host wondered at my want of taste, and I at his want of feeling, for to my astonishment, he and the other inhabitants had actually become used to what was at least equal to a nail through the heel of one's boot or the toothache.

We were now drawing near to the sea and my men were growing apprehensive. One of them asked if we should have the opportunity of watching each other at Loanda: might they not be kidnapped? I replied: 'I am as ignorant of Loanda as you are, but nothing will happen to you that does not happen to me.'

The plains around Loanda are somewhat elevated. On coming across there we caught our first glimpse of the sea. My companions looked upon the boundless ocean with awe.

On describing their feelings afterwards they said: 'We marched along with our father, believing that what the ancients had always told us was true, that the world had no end. But all at once the world said to us: "I am finished; there is no more of me." '

Welcome in Loanda

My men were apprehensive of suffering want, and I was unable to allay their fears, for my own mind was depressed by disease. The fever had induced a state of chronic dysentery, so troublesome that I could not remain on the ox for more than ten minutes at a time; and I was labouring under great depression of spirits, as I had learned that in the population of twelve thousand souls there was but one genuine Englishman. I naturally felt anxious to know whether he was possessed of good nature, or was one of those crusty mortals one would rather not meet.

This gentleman, Mr Gabriel, our commissioner for the suppression of the slave-trade, had kindly forwarded an invitation to meet me on the way from Cassange, but unfortunately it crossed me on the road. When we entered his porch I was delighted to see the number of flowers cultivated carefully, and inferred from this circumstance that he was, as I soon discovered him to be, a real wholehearted Englishman.

Seeing me ill, he benevolently offered me his bed. Never shall I forget the luxurious pleasure I enjoyed in feeling myself again on a good English couch after six months sleeping on the ground.

I was soon asleep, and Mr Gabriel, coming in almost immediately, rejoiced at the soundness of my repose.

The date of Livingstone's arrival at the hospitable home of Mr Gabriel, the British consul of Loanda, was 31st May 1854. His physical condition was serious. He had heavily overtaxed himself. Repeated bouts of malaria had sapped his strength to a dangerous degree, and dysentery, grown almost chronic, had added a painful complication. Fortunately he soon had the attendance of the surgeon of the *Polyphemus*, one of the frigates engaged in the blockade of the slave traffic on that coast. He did not, however, recover quickly. The consul's kindness was unstinted, and the Portuguese authorities were most helpful, in spite of the fact that Loanda, till recently the great centre of the East Coast slave traffic, was being steadily strangled by the British blockade and that Livingstone was well known as the outspoken enemy of their most profitable occupation. No doubt part of the reason for this was that they realized, as clearly as did the missionary, the benefit of opening trade relations with the interior.

Livingstone occupied his time in writing up his journals and dispatches, while his men found employment, at what they considered surprising wages, on various jobs in the port. Loanda was to them a place of endless marvels. Stone houses were wonders to them. They were shown over a frigate, and one of them was allowed to fire a cannon. The sailors treated them with much good humour. 'This is not a canoe,' the men exclaimed, 'it is a town.'

Livingstone was disappointed that there was no news awaiting him from his family. There could hardly have been, since his movements could not have been predicted, but it was two years since he had heard from them and he did not even know that they had reached England.

When, after about four months of rest, he felt able to resume his travel, he had to face what must have been one of the hardest decisions of his life. The strongest pressure was put upon him to accept a passage home by sea, and the reasons for accepting the offer seemed overwhelming, but there is no indication that he ever hesitated as to how his duty lay. He had given his word to his people that he would bring them back, and he never broke a promise, whatever the consequences.

And so, on 20th September 1854, the return journey began. The caravan was much better fitted up than before. The sailors had made him a sturdy little tent that was to prove a great comfort. He carried presents to Sekeletu from the Portuguese merchants and from the acting governor of the province. There was a horse for the chief, and each of the bearers was given a semi-military uniform.

This brief visit to Loanda had effects far more wide-reaching than Livingstone could have dreamed. Great prominence was given in the home press to his achievements as an explorer. The Royal Geographical Society bestowed on him its blue ribbon, the gold medal. The University of Glasgow honoured him with the degree of LL.D.—the first of a long list of academic distinctions.

But perhaps the most important effect of all was that made on the public mind by his refusing, after all that he had gone through, the passage home, and by his facing equal and perhaps greater danger and suffering simply because he had given his promise to 'black men.' It was admiration of this action that accounted, in no small degree, for the amazing reception that was given him when at last he arrived in the home country.

XI

The Return Journey

THE objects I had in view in opening up the country so commended themselves to the General Government and merchants of Loanda, that, at the instance of His Excellency the Bishop, a handsome present to Sekeletu was granted by the Board of Public Works.[1] It consisted of a colonel's complete uniform and a horse for the chief, and suits of clothing for all the men who accompanied me. The merchants also made a present of handsome specimens of all their articles of trade, and two donkeys for the purpose of introducing the breed into his country, as tsetse cannot kill this beast of burden.

I took with me a good supply of cotton cloth, fresh supplies of ammunition and beads, and gave each of my men a musket. As my companions had amassed considerable quantities of goods, they were unable to carry mine, but the bishop furnished me with twenty carriers, and forwarded orders to all the commandants of the districts through which we were to pass, to render me every assistance in their power.

Being supplied with a good new tent made by my friends on board the *Philomel*, we left Loanda on 20th September 1854, and passed round by sea to the mouth of the River Bengo. Ascending this river, we went through the district in which stands the ruins of the convent of St Antonio, and thence into Icollo i Bengo. The commandant of this place, Laurence José Marquis, is a frank old soldier and a most hospitable man. He is one of the few who secure the universal approbation by stern unflinching honesty. We were accompanied thus far by our generous host, Edmund Gabriel, whose unwearying attention and liberality had endeared him to all our hearts.

[1] *Missionary Travels*, page 397.

28th September 1854. Kalungwembo. We were still on the same path by which we came and, there being no mosquitoes, we could now better enjoy the scenery.

Being anxious to obtain some knowledge of this interesting country and its ancient missionary establishments, I resolved to visit the town of Massangano. This led me through the district of Cazengo, famous for its coffee. The Jesuits are known to have brought some fine mocha seed and these have propagated themselves far and wide.

Accompanied by the Commandant of Cazengo we went by canoe down the River Lucalla to Massangano. Near its junction with the Luinha stand the massive ruins of an iron-foundry built in 1768 by order of the famous Marquis of Pombal. But the eight Swedish and Spanish workmen, brought here to instruct the natives in the art of smelting iron, fell victim to disease and 'irregularities,' and the efforts of the marquis were thus rendered abortive.

The fort of Massangano is small but in good repair. It contains some very ancient breech-loading guns. The natives have a remarkable dread of great guns, and this tends much to the permanence of Portuguese authority. The fort of Pungo Andongo is kept securely by cannon perched on cross-sticks alone.

On returning to Golungo Alto I found several of my men laid up with fever. One of my reasons for leaving them there was that they might recover from fatigue of the journey which had affected their feet. They had always been used to moisture in their own well-watered land, and we certainly had an abundance of that in Loanda. But the roads here were both hard and dry, and they suffered severely in consequence. Yet they were composing songs to be sung when they reached home. The Argonauts were nothing to them, and they remarked very impressively to me: 'It is well you came with Makololo, for no tribe could have accomplished what we have done in coming to the white man's country. We are the true ancients who can tell wonderful things.'

The Portuguese take advantage of all the gradations into which native society is divided. Bango, who is the *sova*, or chief, for instance, still has his counsellors, and maintains the same state as when the country was independent. When any of his people are guilty of theft he pays down the amount of the stolen goods at once, and reimburses himself out of the property of the thief so effectively as to benefit by the transaction. The people under him are divided into a number of classes. There are his counsellors, as the highest, who are generally headmen of several villages. The carriers are the lowest free men. One class above the last has the privilege of wearing shoes, and pays for it. Another, the soldiers and militia, pay for the privilege of serving, the advantage being that they are not liable to be made carriers.

They are also divided into gentlemen and little gentlemen, and though quite black speak of themselves as white men, and of the others, who may not wear shoes, as 'blacks.' The men of all these classes trust to their wives for food, and spend most of their time in drinking palm-toddy.

My friend Mr Canto having been seized with fever in a severe form, it afforded me great pleasure to attend him. During his illness I, having charge of his establishment, had a chance of seeing the workings of slavery. When the master is ill the slaves run riot among the eatables. I did not know this till I observed that every time the sugar-basin came to the table, it was empty, and later I came unexpectedly on the washerwoman eating pineapple and sugar. All sweetmeats are devoured, and it was difficult for me to get, till I locked the pantry door, even bread and butter. Probably they thought that, as both they and their property were their master's property, there was no good reason why they should be kept apart.

14th December 1854. My men and myself having recovered, we left Mr Canto's house with a deep sense of his kindness and proceeded on our way to Ambaca. We were able, however, to march but short distances, but we soon passed out into bright sunlight, the whole country looking fresh and green after the rains, and very cheering. One could but wonder to find it so feverish.

We made a detour to the south in order to visit the famous rocks of Pungo Andongo.

As soon as we crossed the rivulet Lotete a change in the vegetation of the country was apparent. We found trees identical with those seen south of the Chobe.

The asserted existence of petroleum springs at Dande, near Cambambe, would seem to indicate the presence of this useful mineral, though I am not aware of anyone having seen a seam of coal tilted up to the surface in Angola as we have since at Tete. The gigantic pillars of Pungo Andongo have been formed by a current of the sea coming from the south-south-east, for seen from the top they appear ranged in that direction and must have withstood the surges of the ocean at a period of the world 'when the morning stars sang together, and all the sons of God shouted for joy.'

While enjoying the hospitality of Colonel Pires in his commodious residence, I learned that all my dispatches, maps, and journals had gone to the bottom of the sea in the mail packet *Forerunner*. I felt so glad that my friend, Lieutenant Bedingfield,[1] to whom I had committed them, had not shared a similar fate, that I was reconciled to the labour of rewriting. I availed myself of the kindness of my host to remain to the end of the year, reproducing my lost papers.

Heading Eastwards

1st January 1855. Having reproduced some of my papers, I left Pungo Andongo on the first day of this year. Our path lay along the right bank of the Coanza. The land was level, with much open forest, and is well adapted to pasturage.

On reaching the confluence of the Lombe we proceeded in a north-east direction through fine open country to Malande, where we struck our former path. We daily met

[1] See Notes on Persons, page 404.

long lines of carriers bearing large square masses of bees-
wax and numbers of elephants' tusks, the property of
Angolese merchants. We bought fowls from them at a
penny each.

My men took care to celebrate their own daring in having
actually entered ships, while the people who had before
tried to frighten them had only seen them from a distance.
The poor fellows were more than ever attentive to me; all
their care was bestowed on making me comfortable.
Mashauana lay with his head close to my feet, and never
during the entire journey did I have to call him twice for
anything that I needed.

15th January 1855. We came down in an hour from the
heights of Tala Mungongo to the valley of Cassange. I was
most kindly welcomed by my friend, Captain Neves, whom
I found labouring under a violent inflammation and abscess
of the hand.

The intercourse which the natives have had with the
white man does not seem to have ameliorated their condition to any great extent. Very many lives are annually
sacrificed to their superstitions without interference from
the Portuguese authorities. The use of ordeal prevails.
Persons accused of witchcraft, in order to assert their innocence, will often travel from distant districts to a river on
the Cassange, the Dua, and there drink the infusion of a
poisonous tree and perish. Hundreds die thus every year
in the valley of Cassange.

How painful is the contrast between this inward gloom
and the brightness of the outer world, between the un-
defined terrors of the spirit and the peace and beauty that
pervade the scenes around us.[1] I have often thought, in
travelling through this land, that it presents pictures of
beauty which angels might enjoy.   How often have I beheld,
in still mornings, scenes the very essence of beauty, and all
bathed in an atmosphere of delicious warmth, to which the

[1] *Missionary Travels*, page 431.

soft breeze imparts a pleasing sensation of coolness, as from a fan.   Green grassy meadows, the cattle feeding, the goats browsing, the kids skipping, the groups of herdboys with miniature bows, arrows, and spears; the women wending their way to the water with watering-pots poised jauntily on their heads; men sewing under shady banians and old grey-headed fathers sitting on the ground, with staff in hand, listening to the morning gossip, while others carry branches to repair their hedges.   Such scenes, flooded with bright African sunshine, and enlivened with the songs of the birds before the heat of the day becomes intense, form pictures which can never be forgotten.

While here I reproduced the last of my lost papers, and as there is a post twice a month from Loanda, I had the happiness to receive a packet of *The Times*, and amongst other news an account of the Russian war up to the terrible charge of the light cavalry.   The intense anxiety I felt to hear more may be imagined by every true patriot; but I was forced to brood in silent thought, and utter my poor prayers for friends who perchance were now no more, until I reached the other side of the continent.

In crossing the Quango the ferryman demanded thirty yards of calico, but accepted six thankfully.   The canoes were wretched, carrying only two persons at a time, but by our men being well acquainted with the water we all got over in about two and a half hours.   They excited the admiration of the inhabitants by the way they managed the cattle and donkeys in crossing; five or six, seizing hold of one, bundled him into the stream, where he found it best policy to give in and swim.   The men sometimes swam with the cattle, or forced them to go on by dashing water at their heads.

We had rain every day.   The heavens were often over-cast by large, white, motionless masses which stood for hours in the same position.   The intervening spaces were filled with a milk-and-water-looking haze.   I obtained good observations.

On reaching Sansáwé's village, he ran out to meet us with wonderful urbanity, and said he would come to receive his dues in the evening. I replied that he had treated us so scurvily that if he did not bring a fowl and some eggs, he would get no present from me. When he came it was in the usual Londa way of showing his exalted position, mounted on the shoulders of his spokesman, which amused my companions greatly. I spoke to him of the impolicy of the treatment we had received at his hands, and concluded by denying his rights to any payment for passing through uncultivated land. To all this he agreed, and then I gave him as a token of friendship some small things. This chief was a man of no power, but in our former ignorance he plagued us a whole day in passing.

A 'Little Skirmish'

We climbed the eastern slope that bounds the Cassange valley, and found that the last ascent, though apparently not so high as that at Tala Mungongo, is actually much higher. The top is about 5,500 feet. Now we began to descend towards the centre of the country. But on 19th April the intermittent (fever), which had begun on 16th March, changed into an extremely severe attack of rheumatic fever. This was brought on by having to sleep on an extensive plain covered with water. The rain poured incessantly, but we formed our beds by dragging up the earth into oblong mounds, somewhat like graves in a country churchyard, and then placing grass over them. We were unable to leave for two days, but as soon as it became fair we continued our march. The heavy dew upon the high grass was so cold as to cause shivering, and I was forced to lie by for eight days, tossing and groaning with a violent pain in my head. This was the most severe attack I had endured. It made me quite unfit to move or even to know what was going on outside my tent. Leeches, which abound in the rivulets, were applied to the nape of my neck and to my loins. This partially relieved the pain. After many days I began to recover and wished to move on, but my men objected to the attempt on account of my weakness.

It happened that the headman of the village where I had lain, while bargaining and quarrelling in my camp for a piece of meat, had been struck on the mouth by one of my men. My principal men paid five pieces of cloth and a gun as an atonement, but the more they yielded the more exorbitant he became, and he sent to all the surrounding villages for aid to avenge the affront of a 'blow on the beard.' As their courage usually rises with success I resolved to yield no more, and departed.

In passing through a forest in the country beyond, we were startled by a body of men rushing after us. They began by knocking down the burdens of the hindermost of my men, and several shots were fired, each party spreading out on both sides of the path. I fortunately had a six-barrelled revolver. Taking this in my hand and forgetting fever, I staggered quickly along the path with two or three of my men, and fortunately encountered the chief. The sight of the six barrels gaping into his stomach, and my own ghastly visage looking daggers in his face, seemed to produce an instant revolution in his martial feelings, for he cried out: 'Oh, I have only come to speak to you and wish peace only.' Mashauana had hold of him by the hand and found him shaking. We examined his gun and found that it had been discharged. Both parties crowded up to their chiefs. One of the opposite party coming too near, one of my men drove him back with a battle-axe.

The enemy protested their amicable intentions. But the knocking down of the goods was evidence to the contrary. Without waiting long I requested all to sit down, and Pitsane by placing his hand on the revolver somewhat allayed their fears. I then said to the chief: 'If you have come with peaceful intentions, we have no other. Go away home to your village.' He replied: 'I am afraid lest you shoot me in the back.' I rejoined: 'If I wanted to kill you I could shoot you in the face as well.' Mosantu called out to me:

'It is only a Makalaka trick; don't give him your back.' But I said: 'Tell him to observe that I am not afraid of him,' and turning, mounted my ox. There was not much danger in the fire that was opened at first, there being so many trees. The villagers were no doubt pleased with being allowed to retire unscathed, and we were also glad to get away without shedding a drop of blood. My men were delighted with their own bravery, and made the woods ring by telling each other how brilliantly they would have behaved before the enemy, had hostilities not suddenly closed. I do not mention this little skirmish as a very frightful affair. The Negro character in these parts is essentially cowardly.

I was so weak and had become so deaf from the effects of quinine that I was glad to avail myself of the company of native traders. Our rate of travelling was only two miles an hour, and the average number of hours three and a half a day, or seven miles. Two-thirds of the month were spent in stoppages, there being only ten travelling days each month. The stoppages were caused by sickness or by purchase of food, and because, when one carrier was sick, the rest refused to carry his load.

We made a little detour to the south in order to get provisions in a cheaper market. This led us amongst a people that had not been visited so frequently as the rest, and who were therefore rather timid and very civil. It was agreeable to get again amongst the uncontaminated, and see natives without that air of superciliousness, which is so unpleasant and common in the beaten track.

The same olive colour prevailed. They file their teeth to a point, which makes the smile of the women frightful, as it reminds one of the grin of an alligator. The inhabitants of this country exhibit just as great a variety of taste as any civilized community. Many of the men are dandies, their shoulders dripping with the oil from their lubricated hair, and everything about them ornamented in one way or an- other. Some spent the whole day, and even portions of the night, in thrumming a musical instrument to their own sole gratification. Others never go anywhere without a canary in a cage. Ladies may be seen tending lapdogs which are intended to be eaten. Round baskets are laid on the thatch of the huts for hens to lay in. Animal food is very scarce; moles and mice constitute important articles in their diet.

The want of life in the scenery made me long to tread the banks of the Zambezi, and see the graceful antelopes feeding beside the dark buffaloes and sleek elands. Here hippopotami are known to exist only by their footprints on the banks. Not one is ever seen to blow or put his head up at all: they have learned to breathe in silence and keep out of sight. We never heard one uttering the snorting sound so common on the Zambezi.

As soon as we got away from the tracks of the slave-traders the kindly spirit of the Balonda appeared. One old man brought a large present of food and volunteered to go as guide himself. At one village they would not show us the path at all unless we would remain at least one day with them. We refused and took a path that led us into an inextricable thicket. We returned and tried another footpath in a similar direction, with the same result. So we were forced to come back. Beyond the next village we met a woman chief who treated us most handsomely, made us a present of food, and sent her son as guide without payment.

In this return journey Livingstone, with the exception of one considerable digression, travelled back the way he had come, and met in general the same kind of adventure. Hence it is not necessary to quote fully from the diaries. There was this difference, however—that the caravan was much more fully armed; and though the guns were carried for show only, they made a deep impression. The chiefs still attempted to exact tribute, it is true, but they were in no position to enforce their demands, and were usually content to accept whatever was given them.

One incident should be recorded because it tickled the sense of humour of the carriers, reinforcing their self-respect, and became one of their favourite yarns.

On 2nd June they reached the Kasai, there a considerable stream. Kawawa, the chief, threatened to oppose their passage unless an ox was given, and ostentatiously removed his canoes to the farther side. Pitsane, the headman, noted carefully where in the reeds the canoes were hid, swam over after dark, and abstracted one. Then in the night the whole party was quietly ferried over. The description of the chagrin of the enemy at what the morning revealed lost nothing in the telling.

An Important Watershed

After leaving the Kasai we entered the wide level plains which we had formerly found flooded. The water had not yet dried up.

During the second day on this plain I had my twenty-seventh attack of fever, at a part where no surface water was to be found. We never thought it necessary to carry water in that region, and now, when I was quite unable to move on, my men found the water to allay my thirst by digging with sticks a few feet below the surface.

The Lotembwa is here about a mile wide. I did not observe the course in which the water flowed while crossing, but having noticed before that the Lotembwa, on the other side of Lake Dilolo, flowed in a southerly direction, I supposed that this was simply a prolongation of the same river beyond the lake, and that it rose in this large march. When we came to the Southern Lotembwa we were told by Shakatwála that the river we had crossed flowed in the opposite direction, not into Dilolo but into the Kasai.

This phenomenon of a river running in opposite directions struck even Shakatwála's mind as strange; but I have no doubt that this assertion is correct, and that Dilolo is actually the watershed between the two systems that flow east and west. I would have returned to examine more carefully this most interesting point, but having caught a chill I was seized with vomiting of blood. Besides, I saw no reason to doubt the native testimony.

I state the fact exactly as it opened to my mind, for it was only now that I apprehended the true form of the river systems and continent. I had seen the various rivers of this country on the western side flowing from the subtending ridges into the centre, and had received information from natives and Arabs that most of the rivers on the eastern side of that same great region took a similar course from an elevated ridge there, and that all united in two main drains, one flowing to the north and the other to the south, and that the northern drain found its way out by the Congo to the west, and the southern by the Zambezi to the east. I was thus on the watershed, or highest point, of two great systems, but still not more than 4,000 feet above the level of the sea, and 1,000 feet lower than the top of the western ridge we had already crossed; yet instead of lofty snow-clad mountains appearing to verify the conjectures of the speculative, we had extensive plains over which one may travel for a month without seeing anything higher than an ant-hill or a tree.

After crossing the Northern Lotembwa we went on to Lake Dilolo. It is a fine sheet of water, six or eight miles long and one or two broad, and somewhat triangular in shape. A branch proceeds from one of the angles and flows into the Southern Lotembwa. Though labouring under fever, the sight of blue waters and the waves lashing the shore had a soothing influence on the mind, after so much of lifeless, flat, and gloomy forest. The heart yearned for the vivid impressions which are always created by the sight of the broad expanse of the grand old ocean. That has life in it, but the flat uniformities over which we had roamed made me feel as if buried alive.

We found Moéne Dilolo (the Lord of the Lake) a fat jolly fellow, who lamented that when there were no strangers there was always plenty of beer, and always none when they came. He gave us a handsome present of meal and putrid buffalo flesh. Meat cannot be too far gone for them, as it is used only in small quantities as sauce for their tasteless manioc.

Back amongst Old Friends

14th June 1855. We reached the collection of straggling villages over which Katema rules and were thankful to see the old familiar faces. Next day Katema came home from his hunting. He wished me to rest and eat abundantly, for, being a great man, I must feel tired, and he took care to give the means of doing so.

I presented him with a cloak of red baize, ornamented with golden tinsel, which cost thirty shillings, and other small things. He seemed greatly pleased. On parting, he mounted on the shoulders of his spokesman. The spokesman being a slender man, and the chief being six feet and stout in proportion, there would have been a breakdown if he had not been well accustomed to the weight.

Leaving Katema's town on the 19th we forded the southern branch of Lake Dilolo. The ford was waist-deep and very difficult from masses of arum and rushes. Going to the westward from here we came to the Southern Lotembwa, itself here eighty or ninety yards wide. We did not find our friend Mosinkwa at his pleasant home. His wife was dead and he had removed elsewhere. He followed us some distance, and our reappearance seemed to stir up his sorrows.

We reached our friend Shinté, and received a hearty welcome from this friendly old man, and abundant provisions of the best he had.

As I wished to introduce some of the fruit trees from Angola, we had carried a pot containing a little plantation of orange- and cashew-trees, custard apple-trees, and a fig-tree, with coffee, areca, and papaws. Fearing that if we took them farther south they might be killed by the cold, we planted them out in an enclosure of one of Shinté's principal men and, at his request, promised to give Shinté a share when grown. At present they had only wild fruits. The tribes in Central Africa are fond of agriculture.

We parted on the best possible terms with Shinté, and

took the path to the village of his sister Nyamoána, who was now a widow.   She received us with much feeling and said: 'When we left the home where you found us, we had no idea that it was at that spot that my husband was to die.' She had come to the River Lofujé, as they never remain in a place where death has once visited them.   We received a loan of five small canoes from her.

Before reaching the Makondo rivulet we came upon the tsetse in such numbers that many bites were inflicted on my poor ox.   The next morning the bites were marked with patches of hair about half an inch broad, being wetted with exudation.   Poor Sinbad had carried me all the way from the Leeba to Golungo Alto and all the way back again without losing any of his peculiarities, or ever becoming reconciled to our perversity in forcing him away each morning from the pleasant pasturage on which he had fed. I wished to give the climax to his usefulness and allay our craving for animal food at the same time, but my men having some compunction, we carried him to end his days in peace at Naliéle.

On leaving this place we were deserted by one of our party, Mboenga, an Ambonda man, who had accompanied us all the way to Loanda and back.   He went off honestly and I was sorry to part with him thus, and sent him notice that he need not have run away, and that if he wished to come to Sekeletu again he was welcome.

Though in these parts game was wonderfully abundant I had got quite out of the way of shooting and missed perpetually.   Once I went determined to get so close to a zebra that I could not miss it.   I fired, but unfortunately only broke its hind leg.   My two men pursued it, but the loss of a leg does not prevent this animal from a gallop. As I walked slowly after the men on an extensive plain covered with a great crop of grass, I noticed that a solitary buffalo, disturbed by others of our party, was coming at me at a gallop.   I glanced around, but the only tree was a hundred yards off, and there was no escape elsewhere.   I therefore cocked my rifle with the intention of giving him a steady shot on the forehead when he should come within three or four yards of me. The thought flashed through my mind: 'What if my gun misses fire?' I placed it to my shoulder as he came on at full speed, and that is tremendous, though generally he is a lumbering-looking animal in his paces. A small bush and a bunch of grass fifteen yards off made him swerve a little, and exposed his shoulder. I just heard the ball crack there as I fell flat on my face. The pain must have made him renounce his purpose, for he bounded close past me on to the water, where he was found dead. In expressing my thankfulness to God among my men, they were very offended with themselves for not being present to shield me from this danger.

27th July 1855. We reached the town of Libonta and were received with demonstrations of joy such as I had never seen before. The women came forth to meet us, making their curious dancing gestures and loud 'lulliloos.' Some carried a mat and a stick in imitation of a spear and a shield. Others rushed forward and kissed the hands and cheeks of the different persons of their acquaintance amongst us, raising such a dust that it was quite a relief to get the men assembled, and sitting with proper African decorum in the *kgotla*. We were looked upon as men risen from the dead, for the most skilful of their diviners had pronounced us to have perished long ago.

After many expressions of joy at meeting, I arose, and thanking them, explained the causes of our delay, but left the report to be made by their own countrymen. Pitsane then delivered a speech of upwards of an hour in length, giving a highly flattering picture of the whole journey, and the kindness of the white men in general and of Mr Gabriel in particular. He concluded by saying that I had done more for them than they expected, that I had not only opened a path for them to the other white men, but had conciliated all the chiefs on the route.

F

The following day we observed as our thanksgiving to God for his goodness in bringing us all back in safety to our friends. My men decked themselves out in their best, and I found that although their goods were finished, they had managed to save suits of European clothing, which, being white, with their red caps, gave them rather a dashing appearance. They tried to walk like the soldiers they had seen at Loanda, and called themselves my braves. During the service they sat with their guns over their shoulders and excited the unbounded admiration of the women and children.

I addressed them on the goodness of God in preserving us from the dangers of strange tribes and disease. The men gave us two fine oxen for slaughter, and the women supplied us with abundance of milk, meal, and butter. It was all quite gratuitous. Strangers came flocking from a distance, and seldom empty-handed. Their presents I distributed amongst my men.

Our progress down the Barótse valley was just like this. Every village gave us an ox, and sometimes two. I felt, and still feel, most deeply grateful.

We had expended all our stock, and all the goods the men had earned in Loanda, and returned as poor as we had set out. Yet no distrust was shown, and my poverty did not lessen my influence. They saw that I had exerted myself for their benefit alone, and even my men remarked: 'Though we return as poor as we went we have not gone in vain.' They began immediately to collect ivory for the second journey.

The Return of the Makololo Braves

On 31st July we parted from our Libonta friends. We planted some palm-tree seeds in the different villages of the valley, but unfortunately they were destroyed by mice.

We reached Naliéle on 1st August, and found Mpololo in great distress on account of the death of his daughter, who had been murdered by one of the Makololo, out of spite to him.

My men were delighted with the cordial reception we met everywhere, but a source of annoyance was found where it was not expected. Many of their wives had married other men during the two years' absence. Mashauana's wife, who had borne him two children, was among the number. He wished to appear not to feel it much, saying: 'Wives are as plentiful as grass. I can get another. Let her go.' But he would add: 'If I had that fellow I would open his ears for him.' As most of them had more wives than one, I tried to console them by saying that they had enough yet; but they felt the reflection to be galling, that while they were toiling another had been devouring their corn. Some of the wives came with very young infants in their arms. That excited no discontent, and for some I had to speak to the chief, to order the men who had married the only wives some of my companions ever had, to restore them.

Sunday, 5th August. A large audience listened most attentively to my morning address. Surely some will remember the ideas conveyed, and pray to our merciful Father, who would never have thought of Him but for this visit. The invariably kind and respectful treatment that I have received from these and many other heathen tribes in this central country have led me to the belief that, if one exerts himself for their good, he will never be ill-treated.

I left Naliéle on 13th August, and when proceeding along the shore at midday, a hippopotamus struck the canoe with her forehead, lifting one half of it quite out of the water so as nearly to overturn it. The force of the butt she gave tilted Mashauana into the river; the rest of us sprang to the shore, which was only about ten yards off. Glancing back, I saw her come to the surface a short way off, and look at the canoe as if to see if she had done much mischief. There was no damage except the wetting of person and goods. There were eight of us in the canoe at the time, and the shake it received shows the immense power of this animal in the water.

22nd August 1855. This is the end of the winter. The trees that line the banks begin to bud and blossom, and there is some show of the influence of the new sap, which will soon end in buds that push off the old foliage by assuming a very bright orange colour. This orange is so bright that I mistook it for masses of yellow blossom. There is every variety of shade in the leaves—yellow, purple, copper, liver-colour, and even inky black.

Long before reaching Sesheke we had been informed that a party of Matabele had brought some packages of goods for me to the south bank of the river, near the Victoria Falls, and though they declared that they had been sent by Mr Moffat, the Makololo had refused to credit the statement of their sworn enemies. They imagined that the parcels were directed to me as a mere trick whereby to place witch-medicine in the hands of the Makololo. When the Matabele, on the south bank, called on the Makololo, on the north, to come over in canoes and get the goods sent by Moffat to 'Nyake,'[1] the Makololo replied: 'Get along with you. We know better than that. How could he tell Moffat to send things here, he having gone away in the north.' The Matabele answered: 'Here are the goods. If they perish the guilt is yours,' and went off. After they had gone the Makololo, in fear and trembling, went over and carried the packages to an island in the middle of the stream, and, building a hut, left them. There I found them a year after in perfect safety.

I found the news very old, but there were some eatables from Mrs Moffat. Among other things I found that my friend Sir Roderick Murchison,[2] while in his study in London, had arrived at the same conclusion respecting the form of the African continent as I had lately come to on the spot, and that from the study of the geological map of Mr Bain and other material, some of which had been discovered by Mr Oswell and myself. He had not only clearly

[1] One of Livingstone's African names.
[2] See Notes on Persons, page 406.

enunciated the peculiar conformation as an hypothesis in his discourse before the Geographical Society in 1852, but had even the assurance to send me a copy for my information! There was not much use in nursing my chagrin at being thus fairly 'cut out,' for here it was in black and white. In his easy-chair he had forestalled me by three years, though I had been cherishing, since the light dawned on me at Dilolo, the pleasing delusion that I should be the first to suggest the idea that the interior of Africa was a watery plateau of less elevation than the flanking hilly ranges.

Having waited a few days at Sesheke till the horses we had left should arrive, we proceeded to that town and found the wagon and all we had left in November 1853 perfectly safe.

A grand meeting of all the people was called. I asked my men to give a true account of all they had seen. The wonderful stories lost nothing in the telling. The climax always was that they had finished the whole world, and had turned only when there was no more land. The presents were received with delight. On Sunday Sekeletu appeared in church in his uniform. It attracted more attention than the sermon! The kind remarks they made about me made me feel inclined to shut my eyes.[1]

The Makololo expressed great satisfaction with the route we had opened up to the west, and soon after our arrival a *picho* was called in order to discuss the question of removal to the Barótse valley, that they might be nearer the market. Some of them objected, mainly on account of the fever engendered in it, as the water dried up.

Sekeletu at last stood up and said: 'I am perfectly satisfied of the great advantage of trade in the path you have opened, and think we ought to go to the Barótse (valley). But with whom are we to live there? You are going to the white man's country. When you return you will find me near the spot where you wish to dwell.'

[1] Livingstone used the same expression in respect to the extreme laudation he received in Britain later.

Livingstone rested in Linyanti for two months. He was exhausted physically and spiritually. He writes: 'In travelling the heart becomes benumbed. I feared much I was becoming a heathen myself, but a little rest has, thank God, quickened my spiritual feelings.'

Rest and returning health, too, gave him the opportunity to get abreast of his correspondence, which had fallen far into arrears, and also to reduce to some order his many records and discoveries. His diary at this point contains an elaborate review of the geology of Central Africa, the result of endless labour and observation—the first systematic survey of these vast districts.

He had also time to think out plans for the future. He had many visitors, whom he questioned unceasingly. Amongst these there was, by good fortune, a far-travelled intelligent Arab, Ben Habib by name, who could speak from personal experience of Tanganyika, Nyasa, and another large inland sea beyond, and much else that reinforced Livingstone's passion for discovery.

He was very pleased to learn that the two horses that he had left in charge of Sekeletu had survived in spite of hard treatment. These, Sir Harry Johnston thought, were 'the forerunners of the establishment of a regular breed in the Barótse country.'[1]

The journal proceeds:

Having found the path to the west impracticable, we now considered to which part of the east coast we should direct our steps. The Arabs assured us that the powerful chiefs beyond the Casembe on the north-east would have no objection to my passing through their country. The Makololo knew all the country eastward as far as the Kafue, and they all advised this path in preference to that by way of Zanzibar. But as the prospect of permanent water conveyance was good, I decided on going down the Zambezi and keeping to the north bank.

During my whole stay with the Makololo, Sekeletu supplied my wants abundantly.

[1] *Life of Livingstone*, by Sir Harry Johnston, page 181.

Although the Makololo were so confiding, the reader must not imagine that they were so to every individual. Much of my influence depended on the good name given me by the Bakwains, and I secured that only through a course of tolerably good conduct. No one ever gains much influence in this country without purity and uprightness. The acts of a stranger are keenly scrutinized by old and young, and seldom is a judgment pronounced, even by the heathen, unfair or uncharitable.

27th October 1855. The first continuous rain of the season commenced during the night, the wind being from the north-east. The rainy season was thus begun and I made ready to go. The mother of Sekeletu prepared a bag of ground-nuts by frying them in cream with a little salt, as a sort of sandwich for my journey. This is considered food for a chief. Others ground maize from our garden into meal.

Sekeletu pointed out Sekwébu and Kanyata as persons who should head the party intended to form my company. Sekwébu had been captured by the Matabele as a little boy. He had travelled along both the banks of the Zambezi several times, and was intimately acquainted with the dialects spoken there. I found him to be a person of great prudence and sound judgment.

XII

The Victoria Falls and the Zambezi

On 3rd November we bade adieu to our friends at Linyanti, accompanied by Sekeletu and about two hundred followers.[1] We passed through a patch of tsetse by night. Most of our company went on by daylight in order to prepare our beds. Sekeletu and I waited outside the tsetse till dark, and then went forward.[2] About ten o'clock it became so pitch dark that both horses and men were completely blinded. The lightning spread over the sky, forming eight or ten branches at a time, exactly like those of a tree. This, with volumes of sheet lightning, enabled us to see the whole country. The intervals between the flashes were so intensely dark as to convey the idea of stone-blindness. The horses trembled, cried out, and turned round, as if searching for each other, and every new flash revealed the men taking different directions, laughing and stumbling against each other. The thunder was of that tremendously loud kind only heard in the tropics.

Then came a pelting rain which completed our confusion. We soon felt miserably cold and turned aside to a fire we saw in the distance. This had been made by some people on their march. My clothing had gone on, and I lay on the ground expecting a miserable night; but Sekeletu covered me with his own blanket and lay uncovered. I was much affected by this little act of genuine kindness. I was entirely dependent on his generosity, for the goods I had originally brought from the Cape were all expended.

We were here joined by Moriantsane, uncle of Sekeletu, and entered the canoes on the 13th. Some of us sailed down to the Chobe, and others drove the cattle along the banks. The river is here very large and deep.

[1] *Missionary Travels*, page 315.
[2] The tsetse-fly does not bite in the dark.

The Barótse believe that at a certain part of the river a tremendous monster lies hid, that will catch a canoe and hold it motionless in spite of the efforts of the paddlers. They believe that some of them possess the knowledge of the proper prayer to lay the monster. It is strange to find fables like those of the more northern nations even in the heart of Africa. Can these be vestiges of traditions of animals that no longer exist?

As at this point I intended to strike off to the north-east, I resolved the following day to visit the falls of Victoria, called by the natives *Mosi-oa-tunya*. Sekeletu intended to accompany me, but one canoe only having come he resigned it to me. After twenty minutes' sail from Kalai, we came in sight, for the first time, of the columns of vapour appropriately called 'smoke,' rising at a distance of five miles, exactly as when large tracts of grass are burned in Africa. Five columns now rose, and bending in the direction of the wind, they seemed placed against a low ridge covered with trees. The tops of the columns at this distance appeared to mingle with the clouds. They were white below, and higher up they became dark so as to simulate smoke very closely.

The whole scene was extremely beautiful; the banks and the islands dotted over the river are adorned with silvan vegetation of great variety of colour and form. These trees have each their own physiognomy. There, towering over all, stands the great burly baobab, each of whose enormous arms would form the trunk of a large tree; besides, the groups of feathery-shaped leaves depicted on the sky lend beauty to the scene. No one can imagine the beauty from anything seen in England. The falls are bounded on three sides by ridges three or four hundred feet high, which are covered with forest, with red soil appearing through the trees.

When about half a mile from the falls, I left the canoe by which we had come down thus far, and embarked in a lighter one with men well acquainted with the rapids, who,

* F

by passing down the centre of the stream in the eddies and still places caused by many jutting rocks, brought me to an island situated in the middle of the river, and on the edge of the lip over which the water rolls. In coming hither there was danger of being swept down by the streams which rushed along each side of the island, but the river was now low, and we sailed where it is totally impossible to go when the water is high. But though we were within a few yards of the spot, a view from which would have solved the whole problem, I believe that no one could perceive where the vast body of the water went. It seemed to lose itself in the earth, the opposite lip of the fissure into which it disappeared being only eighty feet distant.

At least I did not comprehend it till, creeping in awe to the verge, I peered down into a great rent which had been made from bank to bank, and saw that a stream a thousand yards broad leaped down a hundred feet, and then became suddenly compressed into a space of fifteen or twenty yards. The entire falls are simply a crack made in a hard basaltic rock from the right to the left bank, and then prolonged from the left bank away through thirty or forty miles of hills.

In looking down into the fissure from the right side of the island, one sees nothing but a dense white cloud, which, at the time we visited the spot, had two bright rainbows on it. From this cloud rushed up a great jet of vapour exactly like steam, and it mounted two or three hundred feet high. There, condensing, it changed its hue to that of dark smoke, and came back in a constant shower which soon wetted us to the skin. This shower falls chiefly on the opposite side of the fissure, and a few yards back from the lip there stands a straight hedge of evergreen trees whose leaves are always wet. From their roots a number of little rills run back into the gulf, but as they flow down the steep wall there, the column of vapour, in its ascent, licks them clean off the rock and away they mount again. They are constantly running down but never reach the bottom.

On the left we see the water at the bottom, a white

The Victoria Falls

rolling mass moving away to the prolongation of the fissure which branches off near the left bank. The walls of this gigantic crack are perpendicular, and composed of one homogeneous mass of rock. The edge of that side over which the water falls is worn off two or three feet, and pieces have fallen away so as to give it somewhat of a serrated appearance. On the whole it is nearly in the state in which it was left at the period of its formation. The rock is of dark brown colour.

On the left side the mass of vapour leaps quite clear of the rock, and forms a white unbroken fleece all the way down to the bottom. Its whiteness gives the idea of snow. As it breaks into (if I may use the term) pieces of water, all rushing in the same direction, each gives off several rays of foam, exactly as bits of steel when burnt in oxygen gas give off rays of sparks. The snow-white sheet seems like myriads of small comets rushing on in one direction, each of which leaves behind its nucleus rays of foam. It seems to be the effect of the mass of water leaping at once clear of the rocks, but slowly breaking into spray.

Having feasted my eyes long on this beautiful sight, I returned to Kalai. Next day I saw the falls at low water and the columns of vapour when five or six miles distant. When the river is in flood the columns, it is said, can be seen ten miles off, and the sound is quite distinct about the same distance away.[1]

Down the Zambezi Valley

20th November 1855. Sekeletu and his large party having conveyed me thus far, and furnished me with a company of a hundred and fourteen men to carry the tusks to the coast, we bade farewell to the Makololo and proceeded northwards to the River Lekone.

[1] In Book III, page 221, Livingstone gives a much more detailed description of this colossal phenomenon. On his second visit there was much more water in the river and he was able to study the view from the south bank. The account given here has been curtailed to avoid repetition.

The country around is very beautiful. The Lekone winds through it, flowing back towards the centre of the country, in an opposite direction from the main stream. It was plain that we were ascending as we went eastward, and I estimated the level of the lower portion of the Lekone to be about two hundred feet above that of the Zambezi at the falls. Consequently when the river flowed along this ancient bed, instead of through the rent, the whole country was one vast freshwater lake. The fissure made at the Victoria Falls let out the water of this great valley.

24th. At the village of Moyara we left the valley in which the Lekone flows, as it here trends away to the eastward, while our course is more to the north-east. The father of Moyara was a powerful chief, but the son now sits among the ruins of the town with four or five wives and a few people. In this hamlet I counted fifty-four human skulls hung on stakes. These were Matabele whom his father had overwhelmed when they were suffering from sickness and famine. I remarked that many were the skulls of mere boys, and asked why his father had killed boys. 'To show his fierceness,' was the answer. He was evidently proud of these trophies of his father's ferocity. I was assured that few strangers returned from this quarter.

The Batoka of the Zambezi are dark in colour and very degraded in appearance, and not likely to improve because they are addicted to smoking mutokwane (*Cannabis sativa*); this pernicious weed has a very strong narcotic effect, causing a kind of frenzy. It is extensively used by tribes of the interior, though the violent fits of coughing that follow a couple of puffs appear distressing. The hashish used by the Turks is an extract of this plant. It produces different effects on different individuals. To some everything appears as if it is viewed through the wide end of a telescope, while to others things are wonderfully magnified, and in passing over a straw they will lift up their feet as if about to cross the trunk of a tree.

26th November 1855. As the oxen could move only at night, in consequence of a fear that the buffaloes in this quarter might have introduced tsetse, I usually performed the march by day on foot, while some of the men brought on the oxen by night. We passed the ruins of a very old town.

28th November. After leaving Kaonka we travelled over an uninhabited, gently undulating district, the border country between those who accepted and those who rejected the sway of the Makololo. My people magnified it as a perfect paradise. Sebituane had been driven from it by the Matabele. There were few trees, but fine large shady ones dotted here and there over the country, where towns had formerly stood. One was of the fig family. It was forty feet in circumference. The heart had been burnt out, and someone had made a lodging in it, for I saw the remains of a bed and fire.

The sight of the open country, with the altitude we were attaining, was most refreshing to the spirits. Large game abounded. We saw in the distance buffaloes, elands, hartebeests, gnus, and elephants, all very tame, as no one disturbs them. Lions, which always accompany other large animals, roared about us; but in the moonlight there was no danger. The temperature was pleasant, as the rains had fallen in many places. The temperature at 6 a.m. was 70°, at midday 90°, and in the evening 84°. This is very pleasant on the high lands, with but little moisture in the air.

On the 30th we crossed the River Kalomo, which is about fifty yards broad, and the only stream that never dries up on this ridge. The current is rapid, and its course is towards the south. The Unguesi and Lekone, with their feeders, flow westward. All those to which we are about to come take an eastern direction. We were thus on the apex of the ridge, and found that, as water boiled at 202°, our altitude was over 5,000 feet.

It is impossible to say how much farther to the north these subtending ridges may stretch. The inquiry is worthy of the attention of travellers, as they are known to be favourable to health.   They afford a prospect to Europeans of situations superior in point of salubrity to any of those on the coast.[1]

2nd December 1855.   We remained near a small hill called Maundo where we began to be frequently invited (towards honey) by the honey-guide (*Cuculus indicator*).   Wishing to ascertain the truth of the native assertion that the bird is a deceiver, and by its call sometimes leads to a wild beast and not to honey, I inquired if any of my men had been led by this friendly little bird to anything else but what its name implies.   Only one of the one hundred and fourteen could say that he had been led to an elephant instead of a hive.   I am quite convinced that the majority of people are led to honey, and to it alone.

We were now in the vicinity of those whom the Makololo deem rebels, and felt some anxiety as to how we should be received.   On the 4th we reached their first village. Remaining at a distance of a quarter of a mile, we sent two men on to inform them who we were, and that our purposes were peaceful.   The headman came and spoke civilly, but when it was nearly dark, the people of another village arrived and behaved very differently.

They began by trying to spear a young man who had gone for water.   Then one came forward howling at the top of his voice in the most hideous manner.   His eyes were shot out, his lips covered with foam, and every muscle of his frame quivered.   He came near to me, and having a small battle-axe in his hand, alarmed my men lest he might do violence; but they were afraid to disobey my previous orders, and to follow their own inclination by knocking him on the head.   I felt a little alarmed too, but would not show fear before my own people or strangers, and kept a sharp look-out on the little battle-axe.   It seemed to me a case of ecstasy, or prophetic frenzy, voluntarily produced.

[1] The discovery of these healthy ridges was one of Livingstone's greatest achievements.

I felt it would be a sorry way to leave the world, to get my head chopped off by a mad savage, though that would be perhaps preferable to hydrophobia or *delirium tremens*. Sekwébu took a spear in his hand as if to pierce a bit of leather, but in reality to plunge it into the man if he offered violence to me. After my courage had been sufficiently tested I beckoned with the head to the civil headman to remove him, and he did so by drawing him aside. This man pretended not to know what he was doing. I would fain have felt his pulse to ascertain whether the violent trembling were not feigned, but had not much inclination to go near the battle-axe again. There was, however, a flow of perspiration, and the excitement continued fully half an hour, then gradually subsided.

This second batch of visitors took no pains to conceal their contempt of our small party. 'They have wandered in order to be destroyed. What can they do without shields?' Sekeletu had ordered them not to take their shields, as in the case of my first company. We were looked upon as unarmed, and an easy prey. We prepared against a night attack by discharging and reloading our guns. We were not molested.

The farther we advanced the more we found the country swarming with inhabitants. Great numbers came to see the white men, a sight they had never beheld before. They always brought presents of maize and masuko. Their mode of salutation is quite singular. They throw themselves on their backs on the ground, rolling from side to side, and slap themselves on their thighs as expressions of thankfulness, uttering the words 'Kina bomba.' This method of salutation I disliked, and asked them to stop, but they imagined that I was dissatisfied and only tumbled about more furiously. The men being totally unclothed, this performance gave me a sense of their extreme degradation.

10th December. We spent Sunday at Monze's village. He is considered the chief of all the Batoka we have seen. He came to us with one of his wives. She would have been comely if her teeth had been spared. She had a little battle-axe in her hand and helped her husband to scream. She was much excited, as she had never seen a white man before. We rather liked Monze, for he seemed at home with us.

In our front we had ranges of hills called Chamai covered with trees. We crossed the rivulet Nakachinta, flowing eastward to the Zambezi, and then over ridges of the same mica schist of which we found so much in Golungo Alto.

As we passed along the people continued to supply us with food in great abundance. They had by some means or other got to know that I carried medicine, and somewhat to the disgust of my men, who wished to keep it all to themselves, brought their sick children for cure. Some of them had whooping-cough, which is one of the few epidemics that range through this country.

Through Rich and Friendly Country

Passing the rivulet Losito and through the ranges of hills, we reached the residence of Semalembue on the 18th.[1] His village is situated at the bottom of the ranges through which the Kafue finds a passage, and close to the bank of that river.

Semalembue paid us a visit soon after our arrival, and said that now that he had the pleasure of seeing me, he feared that I should sleep the first night in his village hungry. This is considered a handsome way of introducing a present, for he then handed five or six baskets of meal and maize, and an enormous one of ground-nuts. Next morning he gave about twenty more baskets of meal.

I could make but a poor return for his kindness, but he accepted my apologies politely, saying that he knew that there were no goods in the country from which I had come, and in professing great joy at the words of peace I spoke, he said: 'Now I shall cultivate largely, in the hope of eating and sleeping in peace.'

[1] *Missionary Travels*, page 566.

It is noticeable that all whom we have yet met eagerly caught up the idea of living in peace as a probable effect of the Gospel. They required no explanation of the existence of the Deity. Sekwébu makes use of the term 'Reza,' and they appear to understand at once. Like Negroes in general, they have a strong tendency to worship.

Semalembue was accompanied by about forty people, all large men. They have much wool on their heads, which is sometimes drawn all together up to the crown, and tied there in a large tapering bunch. The forehead and round the ears is shaved close to the base of this tuft. Others draw out the hair on one side and twist it into little strings. The rest is taken over and hangs above the ear, which gives the appearance of having a cap cocked jauntily on the side of the head.

The chief said that he ought to see us over the Kafue, so he accompanied us to a pass about a mile south of his village, and when we entered among the hills we found the ford of the Kafue. On parting I put on him a shirt, and he went away apparently much delighted. The ford was at least two hundred and fifty yards broad, but rocky and shallow. After crossing it in a canoe we went along the left bank and were completely shut in by high hills. Every available spot is under cultivation, and the residence of the people here is intended to secure safety for themselves and their gardens from their enemies.

I ascended a hill called Mabue Asula about nine hundred feet above the river. We can see from here five distinct ranges of which Bolengo is the most westerly, and Komanga the most easterly. Very many conical hills appear among them and they are generally covered with trees.

When we came to the top of the outer range of the hills we had a glorious view. At a short distance below we saw the Kafue wending away over the forest-clad plain to the confluence, and on the other side of the Zambezi, beyond that, lay a long range of dark hills. A line of fleecy clouds appeared lying along the course of the river at their base.

The plain below us had more game on it than anywhere I had seen in Africa. Hundreds of buffaloes and zebras grazed on the open spaces, and there stood lordly elephants feeding majestically, nothing moving apparently but the proboscis. When we descended we found all the animals remarkably tame. The elephants stood beneath the trees, fanning themselves with their large ears, as if they did not see us at two hundred yards' distance. The number of animals was quite astonishing, and made me think that here I could realize an image of the time when megatheria fed undisturbed in the primeval forests.

We tried to leave one morning, but the rain brought us to a stand, and we were fain to retrace our steps. This was the first wetting we had got since we left Seshéke, for I had gained some experience in travelling. In Loanda we braved the rain, and as I despised being carried through running water, I was pretty constantly drenched, but now when we saw a storm coming we invariably halted. The men pulled grass sufficient to make a little shelter for themselves, by placing it on a bush, and I having got my camp-stool and umbrella, with a little grass under my feet was kept perfectly dry. We also lighted large fires, and the men were not chilled by streams of water running down their persons. When it was over they warmed themselves, and we travelled comfortably, and had much less sickness than with the smaller party journeying to Loanda.

Another improvement made from my experience was avoiding an entire change of diet. In going to Loanda I took little European food, in order not to burden my men and make them lose spirit, but trusted entirely to the gun and the liberality of the Balonda. But on this journey I took some flour, and baked my own bread all the way in an extemporaneous oven made of an inverted pot. With these precautions, aided no doubt by the greater healthiness of the district, I enjoyed perfect health.

As we approached nearer the Zambezi, the country became covered with broad-leaved bushes, and we had several times to shout to elephants to get out of our way; and when our eyes were gladdened by a view of its goodly broad waters we found it very much larger than even above the falls. Its flow was more rapid, being often four and a half miles an hour.

As the game was abundant and my party very large, I had still to supply their wants with the gun. We slaughtered oxen only when unsuccessful in hunting. We always entered into friendly relations with the headmen of the different villages, and they presented grain and other food freely. One man gave a basinful of rice, the first we met with in the country. It is never seen in the interior. He said he knew it was 'white man's corn,' and when I wished to buy some more he asked me to give him a slave. This is the first symptom of the slave-trade on this side of the country.

The last of these friendly headmen was named Mobala, and having passed him in peace, we had no anticipation of anything else; but after a few hours we reached the Selole, and found that he had not only considered us enemies but had actually sent an express to raise the tribe of Mburúma against us. All the women had fled, and the few people we met exhibited symptoms of terror. An armed party had come from Mburúma, but the headman of the company, suspecting a hoax, came to our encampment and told us the whole.

The reason why Selole acted in this foolish manner we afterwards found to be this. An Italian called Simoens had married the daughter of a chief living north of Tete. He armed a party of fifty slaves with guns, and ascending the river attacked several inhabited islands beyond, securing a large number of slaves and much ivory. On his return, however, he was attacked, at the instigation of his father-in-law, and killed while trying to escape. Selole imagined I was another Italian.

'The Word of a Gentleman of the Most Sacred Honour'

This dramatic story is given in *Missionary Travels* with the severe reticence that is characteristic of Livingstone's treatment of his

more intimate moments. The narrative as here told is supple-
mented by the more detailed account found in the diary on which
Missionary Travels is based. (See *Livingstone the Liberator*,
page 184.)

14th. We reached the confluence of the Loangwa and the
Zambezi.[1] I walked about some ruins I discovered, built
of stone, and found the remains of a church, a broken bell
with the letters I.H.S., and a cross but no date.

Mburúma's guides had behaved so strangely that we were
suspicious we might be attacked while crossing the Loangwa.
We saw them collect in large numbers, and though they
professed friendship they kept at a distance. They refused
to lend us more canoes than two, though they have many.

Thank God for His mercies thus far. How soon may I
be called to stand before Him, my righteous judge, I know
not. O Jesus, grant me resignation to Thy will and reliance
on Thy powerful hand. But wilt Thou permit me to plead
for Africa? My family is Thine. They are in Thy hands.

It seems a pity that the important facts about two healthy
ridges should not be known to Christendom. Thy will be done.

Evening. Felt some turmoil of spirit in view of having all
my efforts for the welfare of this great region and its teeming
population knocked on the head by savages to-morrow. But
I read that Jesus came and said: 'All power is given unto
me in Heaven and Earth. LO, I AM WITH YOU ALWAYS,
EVEN UNTO THE END OF THE WORLD.'[2] It is the
word of a gentleman of the most sacred and strictest honour,
and there's an end on't. I will not cross furtively by night
as I had intended. I shall take observations for latitude
and longitude to-night, though it be my last. I feel calm
now, thank God.

15th January 1856. Left bank of the Loangwa. The
natives of the surrounding country collected round us this
morning, all armed. The women and children were sent

---

[1] *Missionary Travels*, page 584.
[2] These words are doubly underlined in the original diary.

away, and one of Mburúma's wives, who lives in the vicinity, was not allowed to approach. Only one canoe was lent to us, though we saw two others tied to the bank. The part of the river we crossed was about a mile from the confluence: it is here a good mile broad. We passed all our goods first to an island in the middle, then the cattle and men, I, occupying the post of honour, being the last to enter the canoe. We had by this means an opportunity of helping each other in case of attack. A number of the inhabitants stood armed all the time we were embarking. I showed them my watch and burning-glass, and kept them amused till all were over, except those who could go into the canoe with me. I thanked them for their kindness and wished them peace.

After all, they may have been influenced only by the intention to be ready in case I should play them some false trick, for they have reason to be distrustful of whites.

The guides came over to bid us farewell. I gave them some small presents, a handkerchief, and a few beads, and they were highly pleased with a cloth of red baize for Mburúma. We were thankful to part good friends.

Next morning we passed along the bottom of the range called Mazanzwe, and found the ruins of eight or ten stone houses. They all faced the river and were built on one plan, a house on one side of a large court surrounded by a wall. The work had been performed by slaves ignorant of building. On the opposite bank we saw the remains of a wall on a height, which was probably a fort, and the church stood at the central point. The situation of Zumbo was admirably well suited as a site for commerce. The colonies of the Portuguese were strictly military, and the pay of the commandants very small, so the officers were always obliged to engage in trade.

When we left the Loangwa we thought we had got rid of the hills. Tsetse and the hills had destroyed two riding-oxen, and when the little one I now rode knocked up I was forced to march on foot. The bush being very dense and high, we were going along amongst the trees, when three buffaloes which we had unconsciously passed above the wind, thought they were surrounded by men and dashed through our line. My ox set off at a gallop, and when I could manage to glance back, I saw one of the men about five feet in the air above a buffalo, which was tearing along with a stream of blood running down his flank. When I got back to the poor fellow I found that he had alighted on his face, and though he had been carried on the horns of the buffalo about twenty yards before getting the final toss, the skin was not pierced nor a bone broken. When the beasts appeared, he had thrown down his load and stabbed one in the side. It had turned suddenly on him, and before he could use a tree for defence, carried him off. We shampooed him well, and then went on, and in about a week he was able to join the hunt again.

On the morning of the 17th we were pleased to see a person coming from the island of Shibanga with a jacket and hat on. He was quite black, but had come from the Portuguese settlement at Tete. They had been fighting the natives for the last two years. We had thus got into the midst of a Kaffir war. He told us that Mpende lived on this side, and we had been warned by the guides against him, that he was determined to let no white man pass him.

23rd. This morning at sunrise a party of Mpende's people came close to our encampment, uttering strange cries, and waving some bright substance towards us. They then lighted a fire with charms in it, and departed uttering the same hideous screams as before. This was intended to render us powerless, and probably to frighten us. Ever since dawn armed men had been collecting from all quarters, and numbers passed us while it was yet dark.

They evidently meant to attack us, for no friendly message was sent. I therefore ordered an ox to be slaughtered as a means of inspiring courage. The roasting of meat went on

Watering cattle at a sand-pan

Photo: Rev. A. Sandilands

fast and furious, and some of the young men said to me: 'You have seen us with elephants, but you do not yet know what we can do with men.'

Mpende's whole tribe was assembled at a distance of about half a mile. As the country was covered with trees we did not see them, but every now and again a few came about us as spies. Handing a leg of the ox to two of these, I desired them to take it to Mpende, who in due course sent two old men to inquire who I was. I replied: 'I am a Lekoa' (an Englishman). They said: 'We do not know that tribe. We thought you were a Portuguese.' I showed them my hair and skin and asked if the Bazunga had hair and skin like mine. As the Portuguese have a custom of cutting their hair close, and are somewhat darker than we are, they answered: 'No, we never saw skin as white as that,' and added: 'You must be one of that tribe that loves the black men.' I, of course, gladly agreed.

They returned to the village, and we heard later that one of these old men acted as our advocate, and persuaded Mpende to allow us a passage. We sent Sekwébu to purchase a canoe for one of our men, who had become seriously ill, upon which Mpende remarked: 'That white man is truly our friend, see how he lets us know his afflictions.' He did everything afterwards to aid us in our course, and our departure was widely different from our approach to his village. It gratified us to find the English name respected so far from the coast, and I was most thankful that no collision had occurred to damage its influence.

Even the slaves gave a very high character to the English, and I found afterwards that when I was first reported at Tete, the servants of my friend the commandant said to him in joke: 'This is our brother who is coming. We shall all leave you and go to him.' We had, however, still some difficulties in store before we reached that point.

4th February 1856. We were much detained by rains, which prevented us from advancing more than a few miles a day.

The rain up to this point had always been from the east, but now both rain and wind came generally from the west.

13th. I sent my last fragment of cloth as a present to Nyampungo, the headman of these parts, with the request that we should be furnished with a guide to the next chief. After a long conference the cloth was returned with a promise of compliance, and a request for beads only. He behaved in quite a gentlemanly manner, and presented me with some rice.

14th. We left Nyampungo this morning. The path wound round up the Molinge. When we had been gone a few hours my men espied an elephant, and were soon in full pursuit. They were in want of meat, having tasted nothing but grain for several days. As soon as the animal fell my whole party were engaged in a wild dance round the body.

As we were now in the country of stringent game laws, we were obliged to send all the way back to Nyampungo, to give information to a certain person who had been left there by the real owner of the district to watch over his property, the owner himself living near the Zambezi. The men came back with a basket of corn, a fowl, and a few strings of handsome beads, as a thank-offering for having killed it on their land. Had we begun to cut it up before we got their permission we should have lost the whole. They had brought a large party to eat their half, and they divided it with us in a friendly way. My men were delighted with the feast, though by lying unopened a whole day the carcass was pretty far gone.

On the 20th we came to Monina's village close to the sand-river Tangwe. This man is very popular with the tribe on account of his liberality. When we told him that we had nothing to present except some hoes, he replied that he had no need of these articles, and that, as he had absolute power over the country in front, he could, if he chose, prevent us from proceeding. Monina himself seemed to credit our assertion, but his counsellors evidently thought we had goods concealed about us, and at their suggestion a war-dance was got up in the evening about a hundred yards from our encampment, as if to force presents out of us. Some of Monina's young men were armed with guns, and most had large bows, arrows, and spears. They beat their drums furiously, and occasionally fired off a gun. As this sort of dance is always a prelude to an attack, my men quietly prepared themselves to give them a warm reception. But an hour or two after dark the dance ceased and we went to sleep.

During the night one of my headmen, Monahin, left the encampment, probably in a fit of insanity, brought on by illness. Next morning not a trace of him could be found. I sent to Monina to inform him of the sad event, and he at once ordered the gardens to be searched. He evidently sympathized with our sorrow, and allowed us to move on without further molestation.

Approaching Tete

We were now approaching Tete, passing through very rough country without any path. On the evening of 2nd March I halted about eight miles from Tete, feeling too tired to proceed, and sent forward to the commandant the letters of recommendation, with which I had been favoured in Angola by the bishop and others.

About two o'clock on the morning of the 3rd we were aroused by two officers and a company of soldiers, who had been sent with the materials for a civilized breakfast, and a *masheela* [1] to bring me to Tete. My companions called me in alarm, thinking that we were captured by armed men. When I understood the errand on which they had come, and had partaken of a good breakfast, my fatigue vanished, though I had just before been too tired to sleep. It was the most refreshing breakfast I ever partook of, and I walked the last eight miles without the least feeling of weariness,

[1] A chair, either of wood or canvas, for carrying people.

though the path was so rough that one of the officers remarked to me: 'This is enough to tear a man's life out of him.'

I was most kindly received by the commandant, Tito Augusto d'Araujo Sicard, who did everything in his power to restore me from my emaciated condition.[1]   He generously presented my men with abundance of millet, and gave them lodgings in a house of his own.

The village of Tete is built on a long slope down to the river, the fort being close to the water.   The rock is grey sandstone, and has the appearance of being crushed away from the river.   The strata have thus a crumpled form. The hollow between each crease is a street, the houses being built upon the projecting fold.   The whole adjacent country is rocky and broken, but every available spot is under cultivation.   There are about thirty European houses, the rest are native and of wattle and daub.   A wall of about ten feet high encloses the village, but most of the native inhabitants prefer to live in different spots outside.   Compared with what it was, Tete is now in ruins.

On telling the commandant that I had discovered a small seam of coal, he told me the Portuguese were already aware of nine such seams, and that five of them were on the other side of the river.

The gold-field lies extended in a circle from the north-east to the south-west.   In the south-east there are six well-known washing-places.   To the south-east of this lie the gold-washings of Mashona, and still farther east those of Manica, where gold is found much more abundantly.

I saw gold from this quarter as large as grains of wheat. The people know the value of gold perfectly, but they wash only when they want a little cloth.   When they find a piece or flake of gold they bury it, from the idea that this is the seed of the gold, and they prefer losing it to losing the whole crop.   Besides gold there is iron in this district in abundance, and of excellent quality.

[1] *Missionary Travels*, page 628.

THE VICTORIA FALLS AND THE ZAMBEZI   169

Arrangements for Return to Africa

It was necessary to leave most of my men in this place. Major Sicard gave them a piece of land on which to raise their own food, generously supplying them with corn in the meantime. He also gave my young men permission to hunt elephants with his servants, and to purchase goods with both ivory and dried meat, in order that they might have something to take with them on their return to Sekeletu.

The men were delighted, and soon sixty or seventy of them set out to engage in this enterprise. There was no calico to be had at this time, but the commandant handsomely furnished the men with clothing. I was in want myself, but though I pressed him to take payment in ivory for both myself and my men, he refused. I shall ever remember his kindness with deep gratitude.

Having waited a full month at Quelimane, I would have started at the beginning of April, but tarried a few days in order that the moon might make its appearance, and enable me to take lunar observations. A sudden change of temperature happening on the 4th, simultaneously with the appearance of the new moon, the commandant and myself, and nearly everyone in the house, were laid up with a severe attack of fever. I soon recovered by the use of my wonted remedies, but Major Sicard and his little boy were confined much longer. It gave me great satisfaction to attend the invalids in their sickness, though I was not able to show a tithe of the gratitude I felt for the commandant's increasing kindness.

When Major Sicard was fairly recovered, and I myself strong again, I prepared to descend the Zambezi. He lent me a boat which had been built on the river and sent Lieutenant Miranda to conduct me to the coast. He also provided me most abundantly for the journey and sent messages to his friends to treat me as they would himself, from every one of whom, I am happy to say, I received most disinterested kindness.

We left Tete on the 22nd (April), and on the 24th reached

a small island at the western entrance of the gorge at Lupata.   We passed through the gorge in two hours and found it rather tortuous, between two and three hundred feet wide and excessively deep.   A steamer could, I believe, pass through it at full speed.

Next day we landed at Sirambo, once the residence of a Portuguese brigadier, who spent large sums of money to embellish his house and gardens.   These we found in complete ruin, having been destroyed by his half-caste son, who had rebelled against the Portuguese.

On the afternoon of the 27th we arrived at Sena.   I thought the state of Tete quite lamentable, but that of Sena was much worse.   At Tete there is some life: here everything is stagnation and ruin.   The Landeens visit the village periodically and levy fines on the inhabitants.   They consider the Portuguese a conquered tribe.   When I was there a party of Kisaka's people were ravaging the fine country on the other side of the shore.   They came down with captured prisoners, and the half-castes of Sena went over to buy slaves.   Encouraged by this, Kisaka's people came over into Sena fully armed and beating their drums, and were received into the house of a native Portuguese.   The commandant could only look on with bitter sorrow.

The most pleasant sight I witnessed at Sena was the Negroes of Senhor Isidore building boats after the European model, without anyone superintending them.   They had been taught by a European master.   Now they made very neat boats and launches, valued at from £20 to £100.

On 11th May the whole of the inhabitants accompanied us to the boats.   Slavery and immorality have here done their work.   Nowhere else does the European name stand at so low an ebb.   But what can be expected?   Few Portuguese women are ever taken to the colonies, and here I did not observe the honourable regard for offspring which I noticed in Angola.   The son of a late governor of Tete was pointed out to me in the condition and habit of a slave.   There is neither priest nor school in Sena.

A few miles beyond the Shire [1] we left the hills entirely, and sailed between extensive flats covered with trees. The Zambezi at Mazora is a magnificent river, more than half a mile wide and without islands. The opposite bank is covered with forests of fine timber, but the delta, which begins here, is only an immense flat covered with coarse grass and reeds, with a few mango and coco-nut trees.

At Interra we met Senhor Asevedo, who, seeing that I was suffering from a very severe attack of fever, immediately placed at my disposal his large sailing launch, which had a house at the stern. This was greatly in my favour, for it anchored in the middle of the stream and gave me some rest from mosquitoes, which in the whole of the delta are something frightful.

Sailing comfortably in this commodious launch along the River Quelimane, we reached that village on 20th May 1856, thus having been very nearly four years since I started from Cape Town.

Livingstone arrived at the coast in a very low state of health, and found awaiting him news that for the time depressed him greatly. He learned that H.M.S. Dart, that had been on the look-out for him for some time, had been forced to go on, and he was thus compelled to remain, restive and unoccupied, for six weeks till the arrival of the next ship. He heard, too, that in an attempt to cross the bar of the river, a lieutenant and five seamen of a former boat had been drowned. The tired man took these deaths heavily, and could not rid himself of the feeling that he was in some way responsible for the tragedy.

But what troubled him still more was the receipt of a rather tactless letter from the secretary of the London Missionary Society, which while profuse in its appreciation of his efforts, was read by him as retracting the promise he had received that it would proceed to open up new stations in the Makololo country; and also by inference seeming to cast doubt on the value of exploration as a form of missionary work. This was

[1] The Shire flows out of Lake Nyasa and joins the Zambezi. It was the centre of the exploration of the next expedition.

always the Doctor's tender spot, and evoked the well-known dictum in defence that 'viewed in relation to my calling, the geographical feat is the beginning of the missionary enterprise.'

The sick man read into this epistle more than had been intended, and when he reached London explanations were made and the temporary breach healed. Nevertheless, the result of the incident was that he came to feel that to retain an official connection with a missionary body would cripple his liberty of movement. So he resigned his position with the society, though, to the end of his life, he remained, and zealously claimed to be, a missionary.

Livingstone considered that his work for Africa had only begun, and he left with a fixed intention to come back at an early date. He had formed a very definite opinion that free navigation from the coast to the interior, by solving the transport problem, would hamstring the slave traffic, and he was eager to return to prove that this was a possibility.

He therefore left his men at Tete, in charge of his generous friend Major Sicard, and sailed for Mauritius in the brig *Frolic*, whence, after his health had been restored, he took ship for England, where he landed in December 1856.

How the First Book was written

The story of Livingstone's adventures and privations had preceded him, and he was received in Britain with a fervour of public enthusiasm that took his breath away. His chief wish had been to spend his time with his wife and young children, but that was made almost impossible for him. He was soon wellnigh overwhelmed with public engagements. Universities poured their honours on him; learned societies claimed his services; Queen Victoria granted him an interview. He was for the time the most popular man of his day. Essentially a shy man, he found these experiences, while profoundly gratifying, most embarrassing. He felt himself to have grown out of touch with civilized ways, and even rusty in the use of his native tongue. He longed for quiet.

Pressure was quickly brought on him to publish an account of his travels. He agreed most unwillingly. He had complete confidence in the value of the material that his journals contained, but none in his own capacity as a writer. The work had to be put through in what, for anyone else, would have been most distracting surroundings; in a restricted London lodging and very literally in the midst of his family. Happily, however, he was able to boast that his training in the mill at Blantyre had given him a power of concentration that made it possible for him to disregard all extraneous noises; but he used to declare that he would much rather cross Africa again than write another book.

A word should be said here about the founding of the Universities' Mission that played so large a part in the story of the next expedition.

One of the speeches that Livingstone delivered just before his return to Africa was to the undergraduates of Cambridge University in December 1857. He had a rapturous reception. He was never an accomplished speaker. He lacked fluency, his actions were few and stiff, and his voice somewhat harsh. But on this occasion he made a profound impression.

He ended with an appeal to the youth of England, and finished with these memorable words:

'I direct your attention to Africa. I know that in a few years I shall be cut off in that country which is now open. I go back to try to open up a path to Commerce and Christianity. Do you carry on the work that I have begun. I leave it to you.'

The last two sentences were uttered in a voice that became a shout. The effect was electric. It was largely as a result of this address that the Universities' Mission [1] was founded.

---

[1] *The Universities' Mission.* This mission began in good measure in response to the above challenge. The first purpose was to establish work in the healthy highlands near Lake Nyasa, that Livingstone had just discovered. The leader, Bishop Mackenzie, was a man after the Explorer's own heart (page 405), but from the beginning the attempt was tragically unsuccessful, as the text shows. Bishop Mackenzie was succeeded by Bishop Tozer, who quickly decided that the continuance of the work in that locality, would, in the unsettled state of the country, be unwise, and withdrew his men to Zanzibar. Livingstone felt this retreat keenly, and expressed his feelings, as was his wont, in uncompromising terms. But probably it was the wise policy in the circumstances. Later, with Zanzibar as base, the mission moved inland, and now occupies part of the territory near Lake Nyasa.

BOOK THREE

The Zambezi and its Tributaries, 1858–1864

The full original title of the volume from which this abbreviation is compiled is:

NARRATIVE

of an

EXPEDITION TO THE ZAMBEZI

AND ITS TRIBUTARIES

AND OF THE DISCOVERY OF LAKES SHIRWA

AND NYASSA

1858–1864

BY DAVID AND CHARLES LIVINGSTONE

London
John Murray   Albemarle Street
1865

XIII

The Origin of the Expedition

THE stir made by the publication of *Missionary Travels*, and by Livingstone's public lectures, excited, amongst politicians and merchants, a lively interest in the development of Africa, and especially of the valley of the Zambezi and adjacent regions; and it was not long before the suggestion was put forward that the British Government, in concert with the Portuguese, should sponsor an expedition, with Livingstone in charge, for a more extensive examination of the country and its economic possibilities.

The Portuguese were not enthusiastic about the project. That was to be expected. They considered the hinterland of this coast as their possession, though their nationals had rarely penetrated far inland, and they did not relish the prospect of foreign interference. Nor were their apprehensions lessened by the outspoken denunciations of the slave traffic that were constantly appearing in the Missionary's public speeches.

Livingstone, who, as has been explained, had by this time disconnected himself from the London Missionary Society, welcomed the proposal, and the British Government, with unusual promptitude, appointed him as consul of 'The Eastern Coast of Africa,' voted adequate funds, and ordered the naval patrols in these waters to render him such help as he needed. Livingstone made it a condition of his acceptance that he should still be considered a missionary, and retain full liberty to act as his conscience directed in that capacity.

The Zambezi Expedition differed from his other journeys chiefly in that he had with him European assistants. He would have greatly preferred, as was his wont, to travel alone, but that did not suit the ideas of the authorities, and six white men, to act in various capacities, were selected to accompany him.

The best man of this group was undoubtedly Dr (later Sir) John Kirk.[1] His post was that of botanist and physician. Seven years later he became the British Consul in Zanzibar.

[1] See Notes on Persons, page 404.

Charles Livingstone,[1] a younger brother of the Leader, went with him to act as photographer and general assistant. The artist of the expedition, who was also store-keeper, was Thomas Baines,[2] a man with previous experience of exploration in Africa and elsewhere. A naval officer, Commander Bedingfield,[2] volunteered to act as navigator, but left the party within a few months. The geologist was a young man, Richard Thornton,[3] and, finally, in the company there was included a practical engineer called George Rae, from Blantyre, Livingstone's home village, whose special duty it was to look after the river boats.

The five years that followed were, for various reasons, the least happy of the Explorer's life, and though he does not let the fact appear prominently in the journal, a main reason was lack of harmony among the staff. That the background of the succeeding records may be understood, a brief reference to the dissensions that characterized the early stages is necessary.

Though supremely gifted as a leader of Africans, Livingstone was much less suited to superintend and guide Europeans. He had had no previous experience of the charge of a Government expedition, nor of the leadership of white men, and he was nervous and took his responsibilities very heavily. He spared himself in nothing, and disregarded in his own person the many minor discomforts that a tropical climate causes, and was apt to expect a similar hardiness among his less toughened assistants. He was by nature very retiring, indeed almost secretive, and he found it wellnigh impossible to share his plans with his subordinates. Further, the whole problem was complicated by the almost continual incidence of malaria among them, the depressing effects of which Livingstone [4] so feelingly and graphically describes on page 199.

---

[1] See Notes on Persons, page 405.

[2] See Notes on Persons, page 404.   [3] See Notes on Persons, page 407.

[4] On the title-page of this volume Charles Livingstone's name is printed as joint author. The reason for this is that the Doctor in compiling this book used his brother's notes as well as his own. There are occasional passages, e.g. page 256, where a second hand is easily discerned. In order to give Charles credit as co-author, David adopted the expedient of referring to himself throughout as 'Dr Livingstone.'

This makes for awkward reading and tends in places to obscurity, hence the editor has taken the liberty of transposing all reference to David into the first person, and indicating his brother by name.

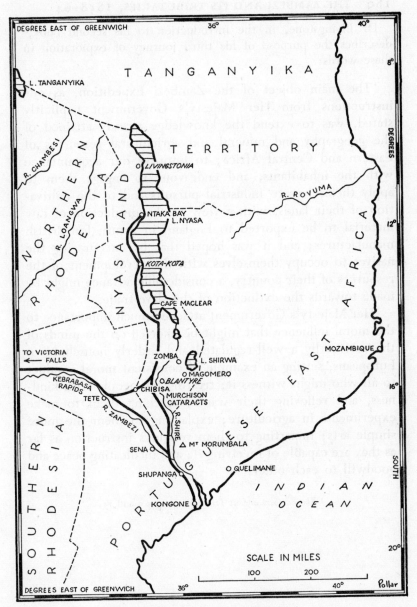

The Second Expedition

Dr Livingstone, in the introduction to his second book,[1] describes the purpose of his third journey of exploration in these words:

'The main object of the Zambezi Expedition, as our instructions from Her Majesty's Government explicitly stated, was to extend the knowledge already attained of the geography and mineral and agricultural resources of Eastern and Central Africa; to improve our acquaintance with the inhabitants, and endeavour to engage them to apply themselves to industrial pursuits and to the cultivation of their lands, with a view to the production of raw material to be exported to England in return for British manufactures; and it was hoped that by encouraging the natives to occupy themselves with the development of the resources of their country, a considerable advance might be made towards the extinction of the slave-trade.

'Her Majesty's Government attached much importance to the moral influence that might be exerted on the minds of the natives by a well-regulated and orderly household of Europeans, setting an example of consistent moral conduct to all who might witness it; treating the people with kindness, and relieving their wants; teaching them to make experiments in agriculture; explaining to them the more simple arts; imparting to them religious instruction as far as they are capable of receiving it; and inculcating peace and goodwill to each other.'

[1] The Zambezi and its Tributaries, pages 9 and 11.

Geographical Note

THE LOWER ZAMBEZI AND NYASALAND

It has been said that Africa leads the world in potential hydro-electric power, but pays for that lead in lack of water communications. The Zambezi, especially from Victoria Falls, is as typical an instance of this as may be found in Africa.

Below the falls, the river is entrenched in a deep gorge for some 50 miles, and though it thereafter opens out slightly, there are many points at which navigation is interrupted at low water and made dangerous at high, while at the Kariba gorge the river is so constricted as to block it to all craft. Below the confluence with its large tributary the Loangwa, the valley opens out and from Zumbo to Chikoa is navigable for over 150 miles, but thereupon crosses another formidable rocky barrier which extends for some 50 miles, and involves a drop of 600 feet, so that violent rapids, the Kebrabasa Falls, occur. Below, the great river, now little above sea level, is a wide placid stream, except for a certain constriction at Loupata. Navigation, however, still has its difficulties, this time from shallow water and shifting sand-banks, and in the delta itself the multiplication of channels so reduces the flow, that entry from the sea is difficult, and normally is effected by the northernmost branch only, on which now stands the Portuguese port of Quelimane.

Knowing these facts, we may perhaps tend to pity the obstinacy with which Livingstone refused to believe that so great a river as the Zambezi could be unnavigable, but we must remember that this very obstinacy was an index of the ignorance of Europe on what we now know to be one of the radical facts of African geography. Indeed, it was this non-navigable character of her rivers that mainly accounted for that ignorance.

Livingstone found the River Shire navigable except in the central section of rapids. The Lower Shire in his time was comparable to the adjacent Zambezi in that both traversed wide flood-plains of which a proportion was swamp. Heat, humidity, mosquitoes, and the fevers they carry, wellnigh wrecked the expedition, and Livingstone was experiencing for the first time conditions very different from the high plains of his first expedition, and more comparable to those which took so heavy a toll of explorers of the Lower Niger.

Lake Nyasa, and indeed the Shire valley also, occupies one of the striking rift valleys that were mentioned earlier as characterizing the way East Africa yielded to earth pressures. So deep is the rift that the maximum depth of the lake, whose surface is some 1,500 feet high, is 700 feet below sea level. The banks rise steeply—a serious defect from man's point of view, for it deprives him of good farm-land—to high plateaus. Two distinct levels, as frequently happens in Africa, can be distinguished, one at 4,000 feet and a higher at 7,000–9,000 feet. These are the highlands which Livingstone immediately recognized as being possible sites for European settlement, and which now carry a town with the name of Livingstone's own birth-place. Even though slave-raiding had disorganized and demoralized the natives, Livingstone accurately envisaged the advantages which Nyasaland's high and varied relief confers upon it, and as he foresaw, the land that was in his time devastated and neglected is now among the most fruitful in East Africa. It still, however, labours under the severe handicap of poor communications with the exterior. Even the lake, which on the map looks so likely an artery of transport, is a disappointment, for while its weather is stormy its steep shores are harbourless, and fluctuations in level of up to 20 feet make the construction of artificial harbours extremely costly. Until the outlet into the Shire River is regularized, neither harbour construction on the lake nor navigation on the Shire can be developed, and water transport must remain almost as unhelpful as in Livingstone's day.

Climate overall is tropical, but the great variations in height and exposure, together with a varied structure from which different soils are derived, ensures that a rich variety of agricultural opportunity offers; and while the natives tend to grow the more typically tropical crops like cotton on the lower ground, and the Europeans to concentrate on the higher, both reach for Africa a very creditable standard. Perhaps nowhere

The Zambezi River, fishermen at work

else would Livingstone find his dreams more satisfactorily realized than in Nyasaland to-day.

The Portuguese discovered the mouth of the Congo in 1484: it was not till 1877 that H. M. Stanley discovered the source. First in the field, they were foremost in the slave-trade, but the territorial ambitions of the Portuguese were small. For centuries their functions were those of traders: from stations on the coast they bartered the products of Europe, America, and Asia, introducing many useful animals and plants but exacting a terrible toll. It has been estimated that, in all, the Portuguese transported some ten to twelve million slaves.

They or their employees must have penetrated the continent on commercial journeys, but in exploration for exploration's sake they are not distinguished. The early date of their settlement in Africa, in days of slow sailing ships, meant long sojourns and infrequent furloughs. Few white women could stand the conditions, and there was consequently much liaison with Africans: of all Europeans, the Portuguese have come closest to the African, for half-castes of all shades form a continuous link from the humblest to the highest. Commendable as may be this lowering of the barriers between the races—and it seems to have paid dividends in tranquillity, if we compare the communal peace of Portuguese possessions with the strife in British —it took with it that perfervid genius which was the hall-mark of north-west European culture; and in respect of which Portugal was, in her day, second to none. In Livingstone's time, Britain was enjoying the first full flush of development of her great natural resources: trade was buoyant, population was increasing by leaps and bounds, her sea power was supreme, and a fine assurance prevailed that progress was inevitable and Britain its prophet, with a special mission to transmit it to the lesser breeds without the law. Portugal, a much older civilization, was not so sure. Her palmy days were so far behind her that she could see them in perspective: she had few mineral resources and was not industrialized. Cultivating her own garden, stability was her motto rather than expansion. If Britain was eager to take up the White Man's Burden, Portugal was concerned rather to make it as little of a burden as possible. Britain, to her undying credit, now led the world in the suppression

*G

of slaving : her zeal and achievements were magnificent. They also tended to obscure from herself the fact that she had but recently been by far the most active slaving power, and the one that had probably made the greatest profits from it.

Livingstone is not noted for co-operation with anyone: little wonder then that his relations with the Portuguese, masters of the Lower Zambezi and Shire, were of the most distant. He must have regarded them, comfortably ensconced in their stations, as cynical and degenerate, and frankly suspected them of slaving behind his back. They in their turn must have regarded him as more than a little crazy voluntarily to incur such hardships, and a distinct liability in that he had on more than one occasion to be rescued from difficulties. In addition he was preaching ideas which they did not regard it necessary to stress. It is to their great credit that they were invariably kind, courteous, and helpful to Livingstone, and he with equal generosity never failed to acknowledge this in his journal.

XIV

The Mouths of the Zambezi and Tete

The Journal Resumed

THE expedition left England on 10th March 1858 in H.M. colonial steamer *Pearl*, and reached the East Coast the following May. The first object was to explore the Zambezi, its mouths and tributaries.

The coast is low and covered with mangrove swamps, among which are sandy patches covered with grass and stunted palms. The land trends east and west, without noticeable feature, and it is difficult to make out the river's mouths. We entered the Luawe first.

A small steam launch, having been brought out in sections, was screwed together. She was called the *Ma Robert* [1] after Mrs Livingstone, to whom the natives, according to their custom, gave the name *Ma* (Mother) of her eldest son.

The Zambezi has four mouths, of which the most western, the Kongone, was found to be the best entrance. The bar is narrow and the passage nearly straight, and were it buoyed, and a beacon placed on Pearl Island, would be always safe for steamers. It is one of the lateral branches, and the safest, inasmuch as the bar has nearly two fathoms on it at low water, and the rise at spring tides is from twelve to fourteen feet. When the wind is from the east and north the bar is smooth; if from the south or south-east it has a heavy break on it, and is not to be attempted by boats. A strong current, setting to the east when the tide is flowing, and to the west when ebbing, may drag a boat or ship into the breakers.

[1] This little vessel was 75 feet long, 8 feet broad, and 3 feet deep, 'being in the shape of a flat-bottomed canoe, having both ends alike, and covered with awning. Her hull was made of three water-tight sections, with curved keel, the draught being only 14 inches. It cost £1,200.' (See *Livingstone's Cambridge Lectures*.)

When a native of the temperate north first lands in the tropics, his feelings resemble in some respects those which the first man may have had on his entrance to the Garden of Eden. He has set his foot in a new world; another state of existence is before him. Everything he sees, every sound that falls upon his ear, has all the freshness and charm of novelty. The trees and the plants are new, the flowers and the fruits, the beasts, the birds, and the insects are curious and strange. The very sky itself is new, glowing with colours and sparkling with constellations never seen in northern climes.

The first twenty miles of the Kongone are enclosed in mangrove jungle. Huge ferns, palm bushes, and occasionally wild date-palms, peer out of the forest; the bunches of bright yellow, though scarcely edible fruit, contrasting prettily with the graceful green leaves. The *Pandanus*, or screw palm, also appears, and some are so tall as in the distance to remind us of the steeples of our native land, and make us relish the remark of an old sailor, that but one thing was wanting to complete the picture—a grog-shop near the church.

The dark woods resound with the exultant song of the kinghunter (*Halcyon striolata*) as he sits perched on high among the trees. As the steamer moves on through the winding channel, a pretty little heron, or bright king-fisher, darts out in alarm, and flies on ahead a short distance. The magnificent fishhawk (*Halietus vocifer*) sits on the top of a mangrove-tree digesting his meal of fresh fish. The glossy ibis, acute of ear, hears from afar the unwonted sound of paddles, and springing from the mud screams out his loud defiant ha, ha, ha, long before the danger appears. Native huts peep out from the bananas and coco-palms. They stand on piles and are entered by ladders. The soil is wonderfully rich. All the tribes are eager traders and come up in swift canoes with every kind of fruit and food they possess.

Finding the *Pearl*'s draught too great, the goods of the

expedition were taken out and placed on a grassy island we called 'Expedition Island,' forty miles from the bar. The country was in a state of war, and we were exposed to the danger of malaria, hence we strained every nerve to finish the work and take the goods away. The weather was fine.

On reaching Mazaro, we found that the Portuguese were at war with a half-caste named Mariano, who, having built a stockade near the mouth of the Shire, owned all the country between the river and Mazaro. He was a keen slave-hunter and kept a large number of men well armed with muskets. So long as his robberies and murders were restricted to the nations at a distance, the authorities did not interfere; but his men, trained in violence, naturally began to practise on the people nearer at hand. A gentleman of high standing told me that it was not uncommon for a slave to rush into his room pursued by one of Mariano's men, with a spear in his hand.

The atrocities of this villain at last became intolerable. All spoke of him as a rare monster of humanity. It is strange why half-castes, such as he, are so much more cruel than the Portuguese, but such is the case.

War was declared against Mariano. It lasted six months and stopped all the trade on the river. When we came into contact with the 'rebels' they seemed well armed and fantastically dressed. When we explained that we were English, some came aboard and called on those on shore to lay down their arms. We saw that many had the branded marks of slaves on their chests. The shout at our departure contrasted strongly with the suspicious questioning on our approach. On arriving at Mazaro I landed to salute some of my old friends among the Portuguese, and found myself in a sickening smell, and among mutilated bodies.

I was requested to take the governor, who was very sick with fever, across to Shupanga, and just as I gave my consent the balls began to whistle about in all directions. After trying in vain to get someone to assist the governor down to the steamer, and being unwilling to leave him in such danger, as the officer sent to bring our Kroomen did not appear, I went into the hut and dragged along his Excellency to the ship.   He was a very tall man, and as he swayed hither and thither from weakness, weighed me down.   It must have looked like one drunken man helping another. The rebels soon retired, and the Portuguese escaped on a sand-bank in the Zambezi.

At Shupanga a one-storeyed house stands on the prettiest site on the river.[1]   In front a sloping lawn, with a fine mango orchard at the southern end, leads down to the broad Zambezi, whose green islands repose on the sunny bosom of the tranquil waters.   Beyond, northwards, lie vast fields and forests of palms and tropical trees, with the massive mountain of Morumbala towering amidst the white clouds.

This beautifully situated house possesses a melancholy interest.   Here in 1826 poor Kirkpatrick of Owen's surveying expedition died of fever, and here in 1862 died, of the same fatal disease, my beloved wife.   A hundred yards east of the house, under a large baobab-tree, both lie buried.

Tete and the Kebrabasa Range

We started for Tete on 17th August 1858.   The navigation was rather difficult, the Zambezi being full of islands. Our steamer's badly constructed furnaces burnt a frightful amount of wood.   Fires were lighted at two in the morning, but steam was seldom up by before six.   A great deal of time was lost in wood-cutting.   The large heavy-laden canoes could nearly keep up with us; the small ones shot ahead, and the paddlers looked back in wonder and pity at the slow, puffing 'Asthmatic.'   For us steam was no labour-saving power.   Boats, or canoes even, could have done for the expedition all that *it* did, with half the toil and expense.

Beyond Pita, farther up the river, we met a small fugitive tribe of hippopotamus hunters.   With the civility so common amongst them, the chief ordered a mat to be spread

---

[1] *The Zambezi and its Tributaries*, page 31.

for us under a shed, and showed us the weapon with which they kill the hippopotamus. It is a short iron harpoon inserted in the end of a long pole, but being intended to unship, it is made fast by a strong cord of bark which is wound closely round the whole shaft, and secured at its opposite end. Two men in a swift canoe steal quietly down on the sleeping animal. The bowman dashes the harpoon into the unconscious victim, while the quick steersman sweeps the light craft back with his broad paddle. The force of the blow separates the harpoon from the corded handle, which appearing above the surface, some-times with an inflated bladder attached, guides the hunters to where the wounded beast lies hid.

The ship anchored in the stream off Tete on 8th September 1858, and I went ashore in the boat. No sooner did the Makololo recognize me than they rushed to the water's edge and manifested great joy at seeing me again. Some were hastening to embrace me, but others cried out: 'Don't touch him you will spoil his new clothes.'

The five headmen came on board and told us that thirty of them had died of smallpox 'having been bewitched by the people of Tete,' who had envied them their good health. Six of their young men had proposed to go to dance before some of the neighbouring chiefs. 'Don't go,' said the others. 'We don't know the people of this country.' But the young men visited a half-caste chief called Bonga. After asking whence they came Bonga rejoined: 'Why do you come from my enemy to me? You have brought witch-craft medicines to bewitch me'; and put them all to death. 'We do not grieve,' said their companions, 'for the victims of smallpox. They were taken away by God. But our hearts are sore for the six youths who were murdered.'

The many slaves of the Portuguese have all the vices of their class, theft, lying, and impurity. In general the real Portuguese are tolerably humane. When they purchase an adult slave they buy, if possible, all his relations, and thus secure him by domestic ties.

Our curiosity had been so much excited by the reports we had heard of the Kebrabasa rapids, that we resolved to make a short examination of them, and seized the opportunity of the Zambezi being unusually low. We reached them on 9th November.

The lofty range of Kebrabasa, consisting chiefly of conical hills covered with scraggy trees, crosses the Zambezi, and confines it within a narrow rocky dell of about a quarter of a mile in breadth. Over this, which may be called the flood-bed of the river, large masses of rock are huddled in indescribable confusion. The chief rock is syenite, some portions of which have a beautiful blue tinge, like lapis lazuli, diffused through them. Others are grey. Blocks of granite also abound, of a pinkish tinge; and these with metamorphic rocks, contorted, twisted, and thrown into every conceivable position, afford a picture of dislocation and unconformability that would gladden a geological lecturer's heart. But at high flood this rough channel is all smoothed over, and it then conforms well with the river below it, which is half a mile wide.

In the dry season the stream runs in a narrow deep groove whose sides are polished and fluted by the boiling action of the water in flood, like the rims of ancient eastern wells by the draw-ropes. The breadth of the groove is often not more than forty to sixty yards, and it has some sharp turnings, double channels, and little cataracts in it. As we steamed up, the masts of the *Ma Robert*, though thirty feet high, did not reach the level of the flood channel above, and the man at the chains sang out: 'No bottom at ten fathoms.' Huge pot-holes, as large as draw-wells, had been worn in the sides, and were so deep that in some instances, when protected from the sun by overhanging boulders, the water in them was quite cool. The sides of the groove of the flood channel were as smooth as if they had gone through the granite mills in Aberdeen. The pressure of the water must have been enormous to produce this polish. It had wedged round pebbles into chinks and crannies so firmly that, though they looked quite loose, they could not be moved except with a hammer. The mighty power of the water gave us an idea of what was going on in thousands of cataracts in the world.

All the information we were able to obtain from our Portuguese friends amounted to this, that some three or four detached rocks jutted out into the river, which though dangerous to the cumbersome native canoes could be easily passed by a steamer; and that if one or two of these obstructions were blasted away by gunpowder, no difficulty would thereafter be experienced.

After we had painfully explored seven or eight miles of the rapids, we returned to the vessel, satisfied that much greater labour was requisite for the mere examination of the cataract than our friends supposed necessary. We therefore went back to make a more serious survey.

The Exploration of the Kebrabasa Rapids

When, in 1851, Livingstone with Cotton Oswell came unexpectedly on the upper reaches of the Zambezi River, the discovery seemed to provide a simple solution to two problems that were at that moment heavily on his mind. If the great river should prove navigable from the mouth upwards, there would be no difficulty in the support of the mission stations that he planned to place in the healthy uplands of that region. And still more important, he believed it would in that case be easily possible to develop his great plan for the establishment of the fair and legitimate trade in European goods, which he was confident would quickly push out the slave-trade. Water-porterage would displace slave-porterage, and all would be well.

So that when it began to dawn upon him that the Kebrabasa rapids might turn out to be impassable, and might write checkmate to his glorious schemes, he returned again and again in an attempt to find a way through, with a dour tenacity that seemed at times to his colleagues near to an obsession.

The same attitude was shown later in his tough conviction that the Rovuma River provided an entry to Lake Nyasa.

The Journal resumed

We set out once more on 22nd November 1858 to examine the Kebrabasa rapids, and anchored in the stream at the foot of the hills.

Canoe men never sleep on the river, but always spend the night on the shore.   Now the people on the right bank are Banyai, and are used to lording it over the Portuguese traders, and were naturally suspicious at our remaining on the water.   They hailed us with: 'Why don't you come and sleep ashore like other people?'   The Makololo replied: 'We are held to the bottom by iron'—a hint that saved us from the usual exactions.

It is pleasant to give a present, but that pleasure the Banyai usually deny by making it a fine, and demanding it in such a supercilious way that only the sorely cowed trader could bear it.   They often throw what is offered on the ground, sneer at the trader's slaves, and refuse a passage until the tribute is raised to the utmost extent of his means.

Next morning we started on foot, with a native Portuguese and his men and a dozen Makololo.   The morning was pleasant and the hills on our right furnished for a time a delightful shade, but soon the path grew terribly rough and the hills no longer shaded us from the blazing sun. Scarcely a vestige of track was now visible, and indeed had our guide not assured us to the contrary, we should have been innocent of even a suspicion of a way along the patches of soft yielding sand, and the great rocks over which we so painfully clambered.

These rocks have a singular appearance from being dislocated and twisted in every direction, and covered with a thin black glaze, as if highly polished and coated with lampblack varnish.   Travellers who have visited the Orinoco and the Congo say that the rocks there have a similar appearance, and it is attributed to some deposit from the water formed only when the current is strong.   The hot rocks burnt the thick soles of the men's feet and sorely fatigued ourselves. Our first day's march did not exceed four miles in a straight line, and that we found more than enough to be pleasant. We slept under the trees in the open air, and suffered no inconvenience from either mosquitoes or dew.

One of the Tete slaves, who wished to be considered a great traveller, gave us, as we sat one evening by our fire, an interesting account of a strange race of men whom he had seen in the interior. They were only three feet high, and had horns growing out of their heads. They lived in a large town and had plenty of food. The Makololo pooh-poohed the story. 'We come from the interior. Are we dwarfs? Have we horns on our heads?' and thus they laughed the fellow to scorn. But he stoutly maintained his point, thus making himself the hero of a traditional story which before and since the time of Herodotus has, with curious persistency, clung to the native mind. The mere fact that such absurd notions are permanent invests the religious ideas of these people with some importance, as fragments of the wreck of a primitive faith floating down the stream of time.

When we reached the foot of a mountain named Chipereziwa, whose perpendicular rocky sides are clothed with many-coloured lichens, our Portuguese companion informed us that there were no more obstructions to navigation, the river being smooth above. He had hunted there and knew. But two natives who came to our camp at night assured us that a cataract, called Morumbwa, did still exist in front. Dr Kirk and I decided to go forward with three Makololo and settled the matter for ourselves. It was as tough a bit of travel as ever I did in Africa, and after some painful marching the guides refused to go farther.

The slopes of the mountains on each side of the river, not now three hundred yards wide, were more than 3,000 feet from the sky-line down, and were covered with thick thorn bush or huge black boulders. This deep trough-like shape caused the sun's rays to converge as into a focus, making the surface so hot that the soles of the feet of the Makololo became blistered. Around, and up and down, the party clambered, amongst those heated blocks, at a pace not exceeding a mile an hour. The strain upon the muscles in jumping from crag to boulder and wriggling round projections took an enormous deal out of them, and they were often glad to cower in the shadow formed by one rock overhanging and resting on another. The shelter induced an overwhelming inclination to sleep, which too much sun sometimes causes. This may be a protection against incipient sunstroke.

The Makololo told me that they always thought I had a heart but now believed that I had none, and tried to persuade Dr Kirk to return, on the ground that it must be evident that in attempting to go where living foot had never trod I was giving sure signs that I was mad. All this was lost on Dr Kirk because he did not understand their language, and I did not enlighten him.

At one part a bare mountain spur barred the way, and had to be surmounted by a perilous and circuitous route, along which the crags were so hot that it was hardly possible to hold on. Yet in this wild region we met a fisherman casting his net into the boiling eddies. He pointed out the cataract of Morumbwa, and within an hour we were trying to measure it from an overhanging rock at a height of about a hundred feet.

When you stand facing the cataract, on the north bank, you see that it is situated in a sudden bend of the river, which is flowing in a short curve. The river above is jammed between two mountains in a channel with perpendicular sides, and less than fifty yards wide. One or two masses of rock jut out, and then there is a sloping fall of about twenty feet in a distance of thirty yards. It would stop all navigation except during the highest floods. The rocks showed that the river rises upwards of eighty feet perpendicularly.

We did not return the way we came, but scaled the

slope of the mountain to the north.   It took us three hours' hard labour cutting our way through the dense thorn bush that covered the ascent.   The face of the slope was often about an angle of 70°, and yet the guide, whose hard horny soles, resembling those of elephants, showed that he was accustomed to this rough hot work, carried a pot of water for us nearly all the way.   We slept that night at a well of tufaceous rock on the north-west of Chipereziwa, and never was sleep more sweet.

A third visit to Kebrabasa was made for the purpose of ascertaining whether it might be navigable when the Zambezi was in flood, the chief point of interest being of course Morumbwa.   It was found that the rapids observed on our first trip had disappeared, and that while they were smoothed over in a few places, the current had increased in strength.

We concluded, therefore, that if the passage were to be forced much greater horse-power was needed, and an application for a more suitable vessel was forwarded to Her Majesty's Government.

XV

Exploration of the Shire River

OUR attention was meanwhile turned to the Shire River, a northern tributary of the Zambezi, which joins it about a hundred miles from the sea.[1] We could find out nothing from the Portuguese about this affluent. They said it was impenetrable because of duckweed. But others hinted that it was not the duckweed that was the obstacle, but the poisonous arrows of the tribes on the banks.

On our first trip up the Shire in January 1859, in the twenty-five miles we found considerable quantities of the weed, but not enough to interrupt navigation. Nearly all of this plant proceeds from a marsh on the west and comes into the river a little beyond a lofty hill called Mount Morumbala.

As we approached, the natives gathered in large numbers, armed with bows and arrows, and some dodged behind trees and were observed taking aim. At the village of a chief named Tingane at least five hundred were collected. I ordered a stop and went ashore, explaining that we were English and had come neither to fight nor to make slaves,[2] but to open up trade in cotton, or in anything else they might have to sell. Tingane became at once quite friendly. The steamer, which showed that they had a new people to deal with, probably helped to the result. The chief was an elderly man and over six feet high. Though somewhat excited, he readily complied with our request to call his people together, that all might know what our objects were.

In beginning a conference we usually referred to the English detestation of slavery. Most already know something of our efforts at sea to suppress the slave-trade. We

[1] *The Zambezi and its Tributaries*, page 74.

[2] This is Livingstone's characteristic way of describing a most plucky act. He stepped into the water and walked slowly ashore, all within easy range of the poisoned arrows.

196

explain that our work is to try to induce them to raise and sell cotton instead of selling their own fellow men. Our efforts appear quite natural, and as a belief in a Supreme Being, the Maker and Ruler of all things, and in the continued existence of departed spirits, is universal, it became natural to explain that we possessed a book containing a revelation of Him. But the difficulty is to make them feel that they have any relation to Him.

In our first ascent of the river our attention was chiefly directed to the river itself. The delight of threading out the meanderings of a hitherto unexplored stream must be felt to be appreciated. All the lower parts we found to be at least two fathoms deep. It became shallower higher up. We had to be most careful lest anything we did might be misunderstood by the crowds that watched us. After having made a straight line of one hundred miles, though the windings fully doubled the distance, we found progress arrested in 15° 55′ by the magnificent cataract we called the 'Murchison,' after one whose name has already world-wide fame, and whose generous kindness we can never repay.

It was deemed imprudent to risk a land journey whilst the natives were so suspicious. The weather also was unfavourable. So after sending presents and messages to the chiefs we returned to Tete. In going down-stream our progress was rapid. The hippopotami never made a mistake, and got out of the way; but crocodiles sometimes rushed with great speed after us, thinking we were some huge animal.

At the end of the hot season everything is dry and dusty. After the rains begin the country changes with surprising rapidity. One sees great distances with ease. The landscape is bathed in a perfect flood of light, and in the morning a delightful sense of freshness is given to everything.

The young foliage of several trees comes out brown, pale red, or pink, and as the leaves increase in size they change to a fresh light green. Bright white, scarlet, pink, and yellow flowers are everywhere, and some are dark crimson. Myriads of bees are busy from morning to night. Brilliant butterflies flit from flower to flower, while the charming little sun-birds, that represent the humming-birds of America, never seem to tire. Multitudes of ants are hard at work hunting for food and bearing it home in triumph. The brown kite with his piping, like a boatswain's whistle, the spotted cuckoo with his call like *pula*,[1] and the roller and hornbill with their loud high notes, are occasionally heard; though generally this harsher music is drowned in the volume of sweet sounds poured forth from many a throbbing throat, which makes the African Christmas seem like an English May.

Some birds of the weaver kind have laid aside their winter garments of brown, and appear in gay summer dress of scarlet and jet-black. Others have passed from green to bright yellow with patches like black velvet. The little cock wydah-bird has graceful plumes attached to his new coat. His finery, as some believe, is to please at least seven hen birds, with which he is said to live. Birds of song have been observed in Africa to congregate round villages, for it is only when we approach the haunts of men that we hear their song. A red-throated black weaver-bird comes in flocks a little later, wearing a long train of magnificent plumes, which seem greatly in his way when working for his dinner in the long grass. The goatsucker or night-jar, only ten inches long from head to tail, attracts the eye in November by a couple of feathers twenty-six inches long in the middle of each wing. They give a slow, wavy motion to his wings, and evidently retard his flight. Males alone possess these feathers, and only for a time.

A good deal of fever comes in March and April. In general the attack does not last long, but it pulls one down

---

[1] *Pula* is a Setswana word that means rain. It is a word of much significance among the Bechuana.

The *Ma Robert*: from a sketch, a photo of which Livingstone sent to William Crosfield in 1858

quickly. The best preventative against fever is plenty of exercise and abundance of good food.

Very curious are the effects of African fever on certain minds. Cheerfulness vanishes, and the whole mind is overcast with black clouds of gloom. The countenance is grave, the eyes suffused, and the few utterances made in the piping voice of a wailing infant. At such times a man feels like a fool, if he does not act like one. He is peevish, prone to find fault and contradict and think himself insulted; he is in fact a man unfit for society.

XVI

The Discovery of Lake Shirwa

In the middle of March 1859 we started again for a second trip on the Shire. The natives were now friendly and readily sold us rice, fowls, and corn. We entered into friendly relations with the chief, Chibisa, whose village was about ten miles below the cataract. He had sent two men on our first visit to invite us to drink beer, but the steamer was such a terrible apparition to them, that after shouting their invitation they jumped ashore, and left their canoe to drift down the stream.

Chibisa is a remarkably shrewd man, the very image, except for his dark hue, of one of our most famous London actors, and the most intelligent chief by far in this quarter. A great deal of fighting had fallen to his lot but it was always the others who began. He was invariably in the right. He was, moreover, a firm believer in the divine right of kings. He was an ordinary man, he said, when his father died and left him the chieftainship: but directly he succeeded to his high office he was conscious of power passing into his head and down his back. He thus knew that he was a chief possessed of authority and wisdom, and his people began to reverence him.

He mentioned this as one would a fact of natural history. His people, too, believed in him, for they bathed in the river without any fear of crocodiles, the chief having a powerful medicine which protects them.

Leaving the vessel opposite Chibisa's village, Dr Kirk and I, with a number of Makololo, started on foot for Lake Shirwa. We travelled north. The people were far from being well disposed and some tried to mislead us. Masa-kasa, a Makololo headman, overheard some remarks which satisfied him that the guide was leading us into trouble.

He came up to me and said: 'That fellow is bad. He is taking us into mischief. My spear is sharp. There is no one here. Shall I cast him into the long grass?' In this case, we found afterwards that there was no treachery, but lack of knowledge of the language.

The party pushed on without guides, or only crazy ones, for oddly enough we were often indebted to madmen. They often guided us well, when no sane man could be hired for love or money.

The bearing of the Manganja (the tribe of the district) at this time was very independent, in striking contrast to their attitude after the scourge of slave-hunting had passed over them. Signals were given from the different villages by means of drums, and notes of intimidation were sounded by day and occasionally all night. We were in constant expectation of attack, but were most anxious that nothing should occur to make the natives look on us as enemies.

Our perseverance was rewarded on 18th April when we discovered Lake Shirwa, a considerable body of bitter water containing leeches, fishes, crocodiles, and hippopotami. Having probably no outlet the water is slightly brackish. It appears to be deep, with islands like hills arising out of it. Our point of view was the base of Mount Pirimiti on the south-south-west side. On the west stood Mount Chikala, which seemed to connect with the great mountain mass of Zomba.

We learned of a much larger lake farther north, separated only by a tongue of land. Shirwa may be sixty to eighty miles by about twenty, and the height above sea level about 1,800 feet. The taste of the water is like a solution of weak Epsom salts. The country is extremely beautiful and clothed in rich vegetation. Lofty mountains, perhaps 8,000 feet, stand near the eastern shore. On the west is Zomba, 7,000 feet in height and some twenty miles long.

Our object being more to gain the confidence of the people than to explore, we considered that we had advanced

far enough for one trip, and so we passed down southwards
to the Shire by the pass Zedi.

It was well that we got to the ship when we did, for
our excellent quartermaster, John Walker, who had been
left in charge, had been down with fever all the time of
our absence. Rowe, his companion, had not given him
any medicine because he did not know what the illness was.
One can scarcely mistake fever, especially as in this country
every complaint is a form of fever, or is modified by malaria.
Walker soon recovered.

The steamer reached Tete on 23rd June, and after repairs
proceeded to the Kongone for provisions from one of
H.M. cruisers. We had been unfortunate in losing a good
many stores and had now to bear privation as best we
could.[1]

On the way we bought some gigantic cabbage and pumpkins. We usually had only one course at dinner, but next
day our cook, from Sierra Leone, brought in a second
course. 'What have you there?' we asked in wonder.
'A tart, sir.' 'A tart! What is it made of?' 'Of cabbage,
sir.' As we had no sugar we could not 'make-believe,'
and so did not enjoy the feast that Tom's genius had
prepared.

H.M. brig *Persian*, Lieutenant Saumarez commanding,
called on her way to the Cape, and though somewhat short
of provisions herself, generously gave us all she could spare.

We now parted with our Kroomen, as, from their inability
to march, we could not use them on land journeys. A
crew was picked from the Makololo, who, besides being
travellers, could cut wood, work the ship, and required
only native food.

While at the Kongone it was found necessary to beach
the steamer for repairs. She was built of a newly invented
sort of steel plate, only a sixteenth of an inch in thickness,

---

[1] Due apparently to the leaky state of the *Ma Robert*. At this time there
was serious friction among the members of the staff, leading to the dismissal
of two. See page 210.

patented but unfortunately never tried before. Some
chemical action on this preparation of steel caused minute
holes. From this point branches like lichens radiated in
all directions. Small holes went through wherever a bend
occurred in these branches. The bottom soon became like
a sieve, which leaked perpetually. The engineer stopped
the larger ones, but the vessel was no sooner afloat than new
ones broke out. The first news in the morning was commonly the unpleasant announcement of another leak in the
forward compartment, or in the middle, which was still
worse.

Frequent showers fell on our way up the Zambezi in the
beginning of August. On the 8th we had three inches.
Sometimes the cabin was nearly flooded, for in addition to
the leakage from below, rain poured through the roof, and
an umbrella had to be used whenever we wished to write.
In trying to form an opinion of the climate it must be
recollected how much of the fever from which we suffered
was caused by sleeping on these wet cushions. Many of
the botanical specimens, laboriously collected and carefully
prepared by Dr Kirk, were destroyed by accidentally falling
into wet places in the cabin.

About the middle of August 1859, after cutting wood at
Shamoara, we again steamed up the Shire, with the intention
of becoming better acquainted with the people and making
another and longer journey in search of Lake Nyasa.

The Shire is much narrower than the Zambezi, but deeper
and more easily navigated. It drains a low and exceedingly
fertile valley from fifteen to twenty miles in breadth.
Ranges of wooded hills bound this valley on both sides.
Morumbala, whose name means 'the lofty watch-tower,'
a detached mountain five hundred yards from the river's
brink, rises with steep sides to the west to 4,000 feet in
height, and is about seven miles in length. It is wooded to
the top and very beautiful. The side which faces the Shire
is steep and rocky.

Beyond Morumbala the Shire comes winding through an

extensive marsh. For miles to the north a broad sea of green grass extends, and is so level that it might be used for taking the meridian altitude of the sun. After steaming through a portion of this marsh we came to a broad belt of palm. Marks of large game were abundant. Elephants had been feeding on palm nuts. Two pythons were observed coiled together among the branches of a large tree and were shot. The larger, the female, was ten feet long. They were harmless and said to be good eating.

The wretched little steamer could not carry all the hands that we needed, so to lighten her we put some into boats and towed them astern. In the dark, one of the boats capsized, but all in it except one poor fellow, who could not swim, were picked up. His loss cast a gloom over us all.

A few miles above Mboma we came again to the village of the chief Tingane, the beat of whose war-drums can speedily muster some hundreds of armed men. The bows and poisoned arrows are here of superior workmanship. Mariano's slave-hunting parties stood in great awe of them and kept aloof.

The Ruo joins the Shire some distance above Tingane's. A short way beyond lies the elephant marsh, which is frequented by vast herds of these animals. We believe we counted eight hundred in sight at once. The choice of such a stronghold shows their usual sagacity, for no hunter can get near them through the swamps. When the steamer first came we steamed into the midst of a herd, and some were shot. But a single lesson was enough to teach them that the puffing monster was a thing to be avoided.

A fine young elephant was caught here alive. When laid hold of, he screamed with so much energy that to escape a visit from his enraged mother we steamed off, and dragged him through the water by his proboscis. As the men were holding his trunk over the gunwale, Monga, a brave Makololo elephant-hunter, rushed aft and drew his knife across it in a sort of frenzy peculiar to the chase.

The wound was skilfully sewn up and the animal became quite tame, but unfortunately breathing prevented the cut from healing, and he died in a few days from loss of blood. Had he lived and we been able to bring him home, he would have been the first African elephant ever seen in England.

The African male elephant is from ten to eleven feet in height, and differs from the Asiatic species more particularly in the convex shape of his forehead and the enormous size of his ears.

Beyond the marsh the country is higher and has a much larger population. On the 25th August we reached Dakanamoio Island, opposite Chibisa's village, and found that he had gone with most of his people to live near the Zambezi. So we returned. Chibisa and his wife, with a natural show of parental feeling, had told me that a few years before some of Chisaka's men had kidnapped and sold their little daughter, and the girl was now a slave to the padre at Tete. I tried hard to ransom the girl and restore her to her parents. The padre was willing, but she could not be found. She had been sold, it would seem, to a distant part of the country.

XVII

The Discovery of Lake Nyasa

WE left the ship on 28th August 1859 for the discovery of
Lake Nyasa.[1] Our party numbered forty-two in all—four
whites, thirty-six Makololo, and two guides. We did not
actually need so many, but took them because we believed
that, human nature being everywhere the same, blacks are
as ready as whites to take advantage of the weak, and are
civil to the powerful. We armed our men with muskets,
which gave us influence rather than strength, as most of
the men had never drawn a trigger and, in any conflict,
would have been more dangerous to us than to the enemy.

Our path crossed the valley in a north-easterly direction
up the course of a beautiful flowing stream. An hour's
march brought us to the foot of the Manganja hills, up which
lay the toilsome road. The vegetation soon changed. As we
rose, bamboos appeared and new trees and plants were met
with, which gave such incessant employment to Dr Kirk
that he travelled the distance three times over. The ascent
became very fatiguing, and we were glad of a rest.

Looking back from an elevation of 1,000 feet we beheld
a lovely prospect: the valley beneath and the many windings
of its silver stream Makubula, from the shady hillside where
it emerges in foaming haste, to where it slowly slides into
the tranquil Shire; then the Shire itself is seen for many a
mile above and below Chibisa's, and the great level country
beyond, with its numerous green woods, until the prospect
is bounded far away by masses of peaked and dome-shaped
blue mountains.

After a weary march we halted at Makolongwe, the
village of Chitimba. It stands in a woody hollow on the
first of the three terraces of the Manganja hills, and, like

[1] *The Zambezi and its Tributaries*, page 104.

Nyasaland: Mlanje Range

all Manganja villages, is surrounded by an impenetrable hedge of poisonous euphorbia.

As strangers are wont to do, we sat down under some fine trees near the entrance of the village. A couple of mats were spread for the white men to sit on, and the headman brought a *seguati*, or present, of a small goat and a basket of meal. The full value in beads and cotton cloth was handed him in return. He measured the cloth, doubled it, and then measured it again. The beads he scrutinized, and after consulting with his comrades, accepted them. Meal and peas were then brought for sale. A fathom of blue cotton cloth, a full dress for a man or woman, was produced. Our headman, thinking a part of it was enough for the meal, proceeded to tear it, when Chitimba remarked that it was a pity to cut such a nice dress for his wife, and offered to bring more meal. 'Right,' said our headman, 'but look, the cloth is very wide, so see that the basket which carries the meal be wide too, and add a cock to make the meal taste nicely.' A brisk trade sprang up at once, and all were in good humour. Women and girls began to pound and grind meal, and men and boys chased the screaming fowls over the village till they ran them down.

We slept under the trees, the air being pleasant, and no mosquitoes on the hills. By early dawn our camp was in motion. We were all charmed with the splendid country. We were a week in crossing the highlands in a northerly direction, and then descended the Upper Shire valley, which is nearly 1,200 feet above sea level.

The Manganja are an industrious race, and in addition to working in iron and cotton and basket-making, they cultivate the soil extensively. All the people turn out to labour in the fields. It is no uncommon thing to see men, women, and children hard at work, with the baby lying close by beneath a shady bush.

Iron ore is dug out of the hills, and its manufacture is the staple trade. Each village has its smelting house, its

H

charcoal-burners, and blacksmiths. They make good axes, spears, needles, arrow-heads, bracelets, and anklets. Many of the men are intelligent looking, with well-shaped heads, agreeable faces, and high foreheads. We soon learned to forget colour, and frequently saw faces like those we knew in England.

The Manganja adorn their bodies extravagantly, wearing rings, bracelets, and much else of brass, copper, and iron, but the most wonderful ornament is the *pelele* or upper-lip ring, of the women.

The middle of the upper lip of the girls is pierced close to the septum of the nose, and a small pin inserted to prevent the puncture closing up. After it has healed the pin is taken out and a larger one is pressed into its place, and so successively for weeks, months, and years till a ring of two inches diameter can be introduced with ease. All highland women wear the *pelele*, and it is common on the Upper and Lower Shire. How this hideous custom originated is an enigma. 'Why do women wear these things?' I asked an old chief. 'For beauty, to be sure. Men wear beards and whiskers. What kind of a creature would a woman be without whiskers and without the *pelele*? She would have a mouth like a man and no beard. Ha! ha!'

The Manganja brew large quantities of beer and like it well. Having no means of checking fermentation, they are obliged to drink the whole brew in a few days. Then drinking, drumming, and dancing continue night and day till the beer is gone.

Our path followed the Shire, above the cataracts, which is now a deep broad river with little current. At one point it expands into a lakelet called Pamalombe, ten or twelve miles long by five or six in breadth.

We discovered Lake Nyasa a little before noon on 16th September 1859. Its southern end is 14° 25′ S. lat., 35° 30′ E. long. At this point the valley is about twelve miles wide. There are hills on both sides of the lake.

A long time after our return from Nyasa we received a letter from Captain R. B. Oldfield, R.N., then commanding H.M.S. *Lyra*, telling us that Dr Roscher, a German, who had lost his life in his zeal for exploration, had also reached the lake, but on 19th November, following our discovery. We were thus two months before Dr Roscher.[1]

The chief of the village near the confluence of the lake and the Shire, hearing that we were sitting under a tree, came and invited us to his village. He told us that a large slave party led by Arabs was encamped close by. Soon after, their leaders came to see us. They were armed with muskets and looked a villainous lot. They evidently thought the same of us, for they offered us several little children for sale, but when told that we were English, decamped during the night.

This is one of the great slave paths from the interior; others cross the Shire a little below. We might have released those slaves, but to liberate and leave them would have been of little good, since the surrounding villagers would have seized them and sold them again.

Our stay at the lake was brief. The trade of Cazembe and Katanga's country crosses Nyasa and Shire. By means of a small steamer above the cataracts, which have a shore line of at least six hundred miles, the slave-trade to the interior would be rendered unprofitable. For it is only by the ivory being carried by slaves, that the latter do not eat up all the profits of the trip. An influence would thus be asserted over an enormous area of country. It seems feasible that a legitimate and thriving trade might in a short time take the place of the present unlawful traffic. Colonel Rigby, Captain Wilson, and other intelligent officers are unanimously of the opinion that one small vessel on the lake would have decidedly more influence, and do more

---

[1] Dr Albert Roscher, of Hamburg. Sent out in 1858 by the King of Bavaria, explored towards Nyasa two months after Livingstone. Was murdered by tribesmen in a village near the lake.

good in suppressing the slave-trade, than a dozen ships of war on the ocean.

After a land journey of forty days we returned to the ship on 6th October 1859 in a somewhat exhausted condition.

The six months that followed had little to show in the way of travel. It was one of the tantalizing occasions, so common during this expedition, when, sometimes because of heavy rain, more often because of the lack of it, and most frequently because of the defects of the boat, the party was marooned in uncomfortable and generally unhealthy surroundings, for weeks and even months on end. It was also the time when the dissensions among the assistants came to a head.[1] The journal of this date is unusually rich in observations on the flora and fauna of the river basin.

The delay, however, gave Livingstone. the opportunity of fulfilling an old promise to his Makololo porters to conduct them back to their chief.

[1] See *Livingstone the Liberator*, p. 259; also *Life of Thomas Baines*, by Professor Wallis, p. 226. (See page 418.)

XVIII

Home with the Makololo

FEELING in honour bound to return home with those who had been my faithful companions in 1856, the requisite steps were taken to convey them to their homes.[1]

We laid the ship alongside of the island Kanyimbe, opposite Tete, and before starting obtained a plot of land to form a garden for the two English sailors who were to remain in charge during our absence. Their first attempt at horticulture was a failure: every seed was dug up by mice. 'Yes,' said an old native next morning on seeing the husks, 'that is what happens this month. This is the mouse-month.' The sailors sowed again next day and this time succeeded.

Everything being ready, on 15th May 1860 we started at 2 p.m. A number of men did not leave with the good-will which their talk had led us to anticipate. Many had taken up with slave women. Some fourteen children had been born to them; and in consequence of having now no chief to order them or claim their services, they thought they were about as well off as they had been in their own country. They knew and regretted that they could call neither wives nor children their own. The slave-owners claimed the whole, but their affection had been so enchained that they cleaved to their domestic ties.

We commenced for a certain number of days with short marches, walking gently until broken in to travel. The nights were cold, with heavy dews and occasional showers, and we had several cases of fever. Some men deserted every night, and we fully expected that all who had children would prefer to return to Tete, for little ones are known to prove the strongest ties even to slaves. By the time

[1] *The Zambezi and its Tributaries*, page 155.

we had got well into the Kebrabasa hills, thirty men, nearly a third of the party, had turned back. At last, when the refuse had fallen away, no more desertions took place.

After fording the rapid Luia, we left our former path on the banks of the Zambezi and struck off in a north-westerly direction. The country was all very dry at the time, and the people poor and always anxious to convince travellers of the fact. We passed immense quantities of ebony and *Lignum vitae*. We slept in a little village near Sindabwe, where our men contrived to purchase plenty of beer, and were uncommonly boisterous all the evening. The last of the deserters, a reputed thief, took French leave of us here. He made off with a musket and most of the brass rings and beads of his comrade, Shirimba, who had unsuspectingly entrusted them to his care.

The remainder of the Kebrabasa path, on to Chicova, was close to the compressed and rocky river. Ranges of lofty tree-covered mountains, with deep narrow valleys in which are flowing rivulets, stretch from the north-west, and are prolonged on the opposite side of the river in a south-easterly direction. Looking back, the mountain scenery in Kebrabasa was magnificent. Conspicuous, from their form and steep sides, are the two gigantic portals of the cataract.

The Makololo who worked on the ship were not sorry at the steamer's being left below, as they were heartily tired of cutting the wood that the insatiable furnace of the 'Asthmatic' required. Mbia, who was a bit of a wag, laughingly exclaimed in broken English: 'Oh, Kebrabasa good, very good. No let shippee go up to Sekeletu. Too much workee. Cuttee woodee. Kebrabasa good.'

A dozen fires are nightly kindled in the camp, being replenished from time to time by the men, who are awakened by the cold. Abundance of hard wood is obtained with little trouble and burns beautifully. After the great business of cooking and eating is over, all sit round the camp-fires and engage in talking or singing. At times

animated political discussions spring up, and the amount of
eloquence expended is amazing. The whole camp is
aroused and the men shout to each other from the different
fires.

The misgovernment of chiefs furnishes an inexhaustible
theme. 'We could govern ourselves better, so what is the
use of chiefs at all? The chief is fat and has plenty of
wives, whilst we, who work hard, have hunger, only one
wife, or, more likely none. This must be bad, unjust,
and wrong.' All shout to this a loud *ehe* (hear! hear!).
Next the headman and Tuba are heard taking up the loyal
side. 'The chief is the father of his people. God made
the chief.' Tuba goes on generally till he has silenced all
opponents, and if his arguments are not always sound, his
voice is the loudest, and he is sure to have the last word.

We average from two to two and a half miles an hour,
and seldom have more than five or six hours a day of actual
travel. This in a hot climate is as much as a man can
accomplish without being oppressed. We were a little
surprised that we could tire our men out. Our experience
tends to prove that the European has the power of endurance,
even in the tropics, greater than that of the hardiest of the
meat-eating Africans. After pitching our camp, one or two
of us would go out to hunt, for the men as well as for
ourselves, as we must have meat.

The intense pleasure that the Explorer had in being once
again on open travel after the confinements and annoyances of
the Shire, is well shown by the fullness and liveliness of the
notes in his journal at this period. A few illustrations are
here quoted.

There must be something in the appearance of white men
frightfully repulsive to the unsophisticated native, on their
entering previously unvisited villages. If we met a child
coming unsuspectingly towards us, the moment he saw men
in 'bags' he would take to his heels in an agony of terror,
as we might feel if we met a live Egyptian mummy at the

door of the British Museum. Alarmed by the child's outcries, the mother rushes out of her hut, but darts back again at the first glimpse of the same apparition. Dogs turn tail and scour off in dismay; and hens leave their chickens and fly screaming to the tops of the houses. The so lately quiet village becomes a scene of confusion and hubbub, until calmed by the laughing assurance of our men that white people do not eat black.

A strong marauding party of large black ants attacked a nest of white ones near the camp. As the contest took place below the surface we could not see the order of battle, but it was soon clear that the blacks had gained the day and had sacked the white town, for they returned bearing off eggs and bits of the bodies of the vanquished.

A gift analogous to language has not been withheld from ants. If part of their building is destroyed an official is seen coming to examine the damage, and after a careful survey, he chirrups a clear and distinct note, and crowds of workers begin at once to repair the breach. When the work is finished another order is given and the workers retire.

I tried to sleep one rainy night in a native hut, but could not because of attacks by a small species of *formica* not more than a sixteenth of an inch in length. It was soon plain that they were under regular discipline, even carrying out the skilful stratagems of some eminent leader. My hands and neck were the first objects of attack. Large bodies of these little pests were massed in silence round the point to be assaulted. I could hear the sharp word of command, two or three times repeated, though till then I had not believed in the vocal powers of the ant. The instant after I felt the storming hosts range over my head and neck, biting the tender skin and clinging with a death grip to the hair, parting with their jaws rather than quit their hold. On my lying down again in the hope of their having been driven off, no sooner was the light out and all still than the manœuvre was repeated. Clear and audible orders were issued and the assault renewed.

The reddish ant, in the west called diggers, crossed our path daily in solid columns an inch wide, and never did the pugnacity of man or beast exceed theirs. It is a sufficient cause for war only to approach them. Some turn out of the ranks and stand with open mandibles, or charging with extended jaws, bite with savage ferocity. When hunting we often get among them. While we are intent on the game, they quietly cover us from head to foot, and all bite at the same instant, seizing a piece of skin in their powerful pincers, and twisting themselves round in it as if set on tearing it out. Their bite is so terribly sharp that the boldest must run, and then strip to pick off those that still cling with their hooked jaws, as with steel forceps. They clear away any dead matter. This appears to be their principal food and their use is clearly in the scavenger line.

Up the Zambezi Valley

Our path led us frequently through vast expanses of apparently solitary scenery.[1] A strange stillness pervades. No sound can be heard; no village is near. The air is still, and earth and sky sunk into deep and sultry repose. We are like a lonely ship on a lonely sea—a long line of weary travellers on the hot glaring plain.

We discover, however, that we are not alone in the wilderness. Other living forms are round us with curious eyes for all our movements. As we enter a piece of wood-land an unexpected herd of *pallah*, or water-buck, suddenly appears, standing as quiet and still as if part of the land-scape. Or we pass a clump of thick thorn and see through the bushes the dim phantom forms of buffaloes, their heads lowered, gazing at us with fierce untamable eyes. Again

[1] *The Zambezi and its Tributaries*, page 196.

*H

a sharp turn brings us upon a native who has seen us from afar, and comes with noiseless footsteps to get a closer view.

Mpende is one of the only two independent chiefs from Kebrabasa to Zumbo, and belongs to the Manganja. Formerly all this tribe was united under their great chief Undi, whose empire stretched from Lake Shirwa to the Loangwa. But after Undi's death it fell to pieces, and large parts were absorbed by their southern neighbours, the Banyai. This has been the inevitable fate of every African empire since time immemorial. A chief of more than ordinary ability rises, conquers his neighbours, and founds a kingdom which he rules till he dies. His successor, not having the talents of the conqueror, cannot hold the dominion.

This may be considered normal and gives rise to frequent and devastating wars, and the people look for a power able to make all dwell in peace. In this light a European colony would be looked upon by natives as an inestimable boon. Thousands of industrious folk would settle round it and engage in peaceful pursuits. To the question 'Would they work for Europeans?' the answer would be affirmative, if these were prepared to pay a reasonable price for labour, and were not of the kind that want only employment for themselves.

On 26th June we breakfasted at Zumbo on the left bank of the Loangwa.[1] It was too deep to be forded and there were no canoes on our side. Seeing two small ones on the opposite shore, we halted for the ferrymen to come over, but it was evident that they were in a state of rollicking drunkenness. We had a waterproof cloak that could be inflated into a tiny boat, so we sent Mantlanyane across. Three half-drunk slaves then brought a shaky canoe over and we manned it with our own men. After four trips the slaves began to clamour for drink, and as we had none to give, they grew insolent, and declared that not another

[1] See page 163.

man should pass that day. Shininyane was remonstrating
with them, when a loaded musket was presented at him by
one of the trio. In an instant the gun was out of his hands
and a rattling shower of blows fell on his back, and he took
an involuntary header into the river. He crawled out a
sad and sober man. The musket was found to have an
enormous charge, enough to blow a man to pieces.

We remained a day by the ruins of Zumbo. The early
traders, guided probably by Jesuit missionaries, were men
of taste and sagacity. They chose the most picturesque
sites. Present-day Portuguese may well be proud of the
enterprise of their ancestors. If ever in the Elysian Fields
the conversation of these honourable men, who dared so
much for Christianity, turns to their African descendants,
it will be difficult for them to reciprocate the feeling. The
chapel, near which lies a broken bell, is in utter ruin, and
desolation broods around. Thorn bushes, rank grass, and
noxious weeds overrun the whole place. The foul hyena
has defiled the sanctuary, and the midnight owl has perched
on the walls to disgorge the undigested remnants of his
prey. One looks with sadness on the utter ruin of the
place where men once met to worship God. A strange
superstition makes natives shun the place as men do
pestilence.

We left the river here and proceeded up the valley which
leads to the Mburuma. The nights were cold and on 30th
June the thermometer was as low as 39° at sunrise. Here
we remained for a couple of days because of the severe
illness of Dr Kirk. He had several times been attacked by
fever, and had been trying several different medicines to
find whether they might not be superior to what we generally used. He suddenly went blind and unable to stand
from faintness. We feared he had overdrugged himself,
but we gave him a dose of our fever pills. On the third
day he rode a skittish donkey, and on the sixth he marched
as well as any of us.

Some Inhabitants of the Jungle

The honey-guide is an extraordinary bird.[1]   How is it that every member of the family has learned that every man, white or black, is fond of honey?   The instant the little fellow gets a glimpse of a man, he hastens to greet him with a hearty invitation to come to a bees' hive and take some honey.   He flies on in the proper direction, perches on a tree, and looks back to see if you are following, and then on to another and another till he guides you to the spot.   If you do not accept his first invitation, he follows you with pressing importunities.   Except when on the march our men always accept the invitation, and have a responsive whistle which means: 'All right; we are coming.'

Our course on 7th July passed over the upper terrace and through a dense thorn jungle.   Here we got separated from one another, and a rhinoceros dashed at me with an angry snort as I was picking a wild fruit; but she stopped stock-still when only her own length distant and gave me time to escape.   A branch pulled out my watch as I ran, and as I was turning half round to grasp it I got a glimpse of her and her calf standing stock-still, as if arrested in the middle of her charge by an unseen hand.

We often met families flitting from one place to another, and marching like ourselves in single file.   The husband at the head carries his bow and arrow, bag and hatchet, and little else.   Next his sons, also armed, but carrying loads. Then follow wife and daughters with bulky loads of house-hold gear on their heads.   They meet us without fear. When we kill an animal these parties are made welcome to a good portion.

On the 9th we tried to send Semalembue a present, but the people refused to incur the responsibility of carrying it.   We who can write cannot realize the danger of being

1 *The Zambezi and its Tributaries*, page 209.

accused of purloining part of the goods carried from one person to another, when one cannot prove that he has delivered all that was put into his charge.

On 14th July we left the river at the mountain range which, lying north-east and south-west across the river, forms the Kariba gorge.   We encamped at the village of the generous chief Moloi, who brought us three immense baskets of fine mapira meal, ten fowls, and two pots of beer. He had visited Mosilikatse a few months before and had seen the English missionaries [1] living in their wagons.   They had told Mosilikatse that they would plough the land and live at their own expense.   He had replied: 'The land is before you.   I shall come and see you plough.'

One might imagine that as mechanical powers are un-known to the heathen, the almost magical operations of machinery, the discoveries of modern science and art, or the presence of the prodigious force which, for instance, is associated with a man-of-war, would have the effect which miracles used to have in arresting the attention and inspiring awe.   But though we have heard natives exclaim at the sight of even small illustrations of what science enables us to do: 'Ye are gods and not men,' yet the heart is un-affected.   In attempting their moral elevation, it is always more conducive to the end desired that the teacher should come unaccompanied by any power to cause either jealousy or fear.

We passed through a fertile country covered with open forest, accompanied by friendly Bawe.   They were very hospitable.   Many of them were named the 'Go nakeds,' their only clothing being a coat of red ochre.   We tried to discover if nudity were a badge of a particular order among the Bawe, but they could only refer to the custom. Some of them had always liked it for no reason in particular. They evidently felt no less decent than we did.   Shame

[1] John and Emily Moffat.

seemed to lie dormant. But whatever may be said in favour of nude statues, it struck us that man in a state of nature is a most ungainly animal.

In travelling from the Kafue to the Zungwe our march was a triumphal progress. We entered and left every village amidst the cheers of the people, the men clapping their hands and the women 'lulliloo-ing,' with the shrill call 'Let us sleep,' or 'Peace.' When we halted it was quite common for the villagers to prepare our camp for us of their own accord.

Men of remarkable ability have arisen among the Africans from time to time, and have attracted much attention by their wisdom; but the total absence of literature leads to the loss of all former experience, and the wisdom is not handed down. They have their minstrels, too, but their effusions are not preserved. One of these, apparently a genuine poet, attached himself to us for several days, and whenever we halted sang our praise in smooth and harmonious numbers. It was a sort of blank verse, each line consisting of five syllables. The song was short at first, but each day he picked up some information about us until our praises made an ode of considerable length.

We reached on 4th August Moachemba, the first of the Batoka villages which now owe allegiance to Sekeletu, and could distinctly see with the naked eye in the great valley spread before us the columns of vapour rising from the Victoria Falls, though upwards of twenty miles distant.

Here all the sad news we had previously heard, of the disastrous results which followed the attempt of a party of missionaries under the Rev. H. Helmore to plant the Gospel in Linyanti, were fully confirmed. Several had succumbed to fever, and the survivors had returned some weeks before our arrival.[1]

---

[1] See Appendix V, page 412.

XIX

A Second View of the Victoria Falls

WE proceeded next morning, 9th August 1860, to see the Victoria Falls.[1] *Mosi-oa-tunya* is the Makololo name, and means 'sounding smoke.'

We embarked in a canoe belonging to Tuba Mokoro, the 'smasher of canoes'—an ominous name. He alone, it seems, knows the medicine which insures one against shipwreck in the rapids above the falls.

For some miles we glided pleasantly over water as clear as crystal, past lovely islands densely covered with tropical vegetation. But our attention was quickly called to the dangerous rapids down which Tuba might unintentionally shoot us.

Before entering the race of waters we were requested not to speak, as our speaking might diminish the virtue of the medicine, and no one with such boiling waters before him would think of disobeying the orders of the 'canoe smasher.' Tuba doubtless thought that talking might divert the attention of the steersman. A slight mistake would be enough to spill us all into the chafing river. There were places where the utmost exertions of both men had to be put forth in order to force the canoe into the only safe part of the rapids, and to prevent it from sweeping down broadside on, where in a twinkling we should have found ourselves foundering among the plotuses and cormorants which were engaged in diving for their breakfast of small fish. At times it looked as if nothing could save us from dashing in our headlong race against the rocks which, now that the river was low, jutted out of the water; but just in the very nick of time, Tuba passed the word to the steersman, and then with a ready pole turned the canoe a little

[1] *The Zambezi and its Tributaries*, page 250.

221

aside, and we glided swiftly past the threatened danger. Never was canoe more admirably managed. Once only did the medicine seem to lose something of its efficacy.

We were driving swiftly down. A black rock, over which the white foam flew, lay directly in our path. The pole was planted against it as readily as ever, but it slipped just as Tuba put forth his strength to turn the bow off. We struck hard and were half full of water in a moment. Tuba, recovering himself speedily, shoved off the bow and shot the canoe into a still, shallow place, to bale out the water. Here we were given to understand that it was not the medicine that was at fault: *that* had lost none of its virtue; the accident was due entirely to Tuba's having started without his breakfast. Need it be said that we never let Tuba go without that meal again!

We landed at the head of Garden Island which is situated in the middle of the river, and on the lip of the falls. On reaching that lip, and peering over the giddy height, the wondrous and unique character of the magnificent cascade at once burst upon us. It is a hopeless task to endeavour to convey an idea of it in words, since an accomplished painter could but impart a faint impression of the glorious scene.

The probable mode of its formation may perhaps help to a conception of its peculiar shape. The Victoria Falls have been formed by a crack right across the river in the hard, black, basaltic rock which there formed the bed of the Zambezi. The lips of the crack are still quite sharp, save about three feet of the edge over which the river rolls. The walls go sheer down from the lips, without any projecting crag or symptom of stratification or dislocation.

When the mighty rift occurred, no change of level took place in the two parts of the bed of the river thus rent asunder; consequently in coming down the river to Garden Island, the water suddenly disappears, and we see the opposite side of the cleft, with grass and trees growing where once the river ran, on the same level as that part of its bed on which we sail. The first crack is, in length, a few yards more than the breadth of the Zambezi, which by measurement we found to be over 1,860 yards. The main stream here runs nearly north and south, and the cleft across it nearly east and west.

The depth of the rift was measured by lowering a line, to the end of which a few bullets and a foot of white cotton cloth were tied. One of us lay with his head over a projecting crag and watched the descending calico till, after his companions had paid out 310 feet, the weight rested upon a sloping projection, probably 50 feet from the water below, the actual bottom being still farther down. The white cloth now appeared the size of a crown-piece. On measuring the width of this deep cleft by sextant, it was found at Garden Island, the narrowest part, to be 80 yards, and at its broadest somewhat more. Into this chasm, of twice the depth of Niagara Falls, the river, a full mile wide, rolls with a deafening roar; and this is *Mosi-oa-tunya*, or the Victoria Falls.

Looking from Garden Island down to the bottom of the abyss, nearly half a mile of water, which has fallen over that portion of the falls to our right, or west of our point of view, is seen collected in a narrow channel 20 to 30 yards wide, and flowing at exactly right angles to its previous course, to our left; while the other half, or that which fell over the eastern portion of the falls, is seen in the left of the narrow channel below, coming towards our right. Both waters unite midway in a fearful, boiling whirlpool, and find an outlet by a crack situated at right angles to the fissure of the falls. This outlet is about 1,170 yards from the western end of the chasm, and some 600 from the eastern end; the whirlpool is at its commencement. The Zambezi, now apparently not more than 20 or 30 yards wide, rushes and surges south, through the narrow escape channel for 130 yards, and then enters a second chasm, somewhat deeper, and nearly parallel to the first. Abandoning the bottom of the eastern half of this second chasm to the growth of large trees, it turns sharply to the west and forms a promontory, with the escape channel at its point, of 1,170 yards long, and 416 yards broad at its base. After reaching this base, the river runs abruptly round the head of another promontory, and flows away to the east, in a third chasm. Then it glides round a third promontory, much narrower than the rest, and away back to the west in a fourth chasm; and we could see in the distance that it appeared to round still another promontory, and bend once more in another chasm towards the east.

The land to the south retains the same level as before the rent was made. The tops of the promontories are flat and covered with trees, and the first is at one place so narrow that it would be dangerous to walk to its extremity, but on the second we found a broad rhinoceros path and a hut.

Garden Island, when the river is low, commands the best view of the Great Fall chasm, and also of the promontory opposite, with its grove of large evergreen trees, and brilliant rainbows of three-quarters of a circle, two, three, and sometimes even four in number, resting on the face of the vast perpendicular rock, down which tiny streams are always running, to be swept back again by the upward-rushing vapour. We have, however, to cross to Mosilikatse's side of the promontory of evergreens, for the best view of the falls.

Beginning, therefore, at the base of this promontory, and facing the cataract at the west end of the chasm, there is first a fall of 36 yards in breadth and upwards of 310 feet in depth. Then Boaruka, a small island, intervenes, and next comes a great fall with a breadth of 573 yards. A projecting rock separates this from the second grand fall of 325 yards broad; in all upwards of 900 yards of perennial falls. Farther east stands Garden Island; then, as the river was at its lowest, came a good deal of the bare rock of its bed, with a score of narrow falls, which at the time of flood constitute an enormous cascade of nearly another half-mile. Near the east end of the chasm are two larger falls, but they are nothing at low water compared with those between the islands.

The whole body of water rolls clear over, quite unbroken, but after a descent of ten or more feet, the entire mass suddenly becomes like a huge sheet of driven snow. Pieces of water leap off in the form of comets, with tails streaming behind, till the whole snowy sheet becomes myriads of rushing, leaping, aqueous comets. This peculiarity was not observed by my brother at Niagara, and here it happens possibly from the dryness of the atmosphere, or whatever the cause may be that makes every drop of Zambezi water appear to possess a sort of individuality. It runs off the ends of the paddles and glides along the smooth surface like drops of quicksilver on a table. Here we see them in conglomeration, each with a train of pure white vapour, racing down till lost in clouds of spray.

This vast body of water, separating in the comet-like forms described, necessarily encloses in its descent a large volume of air which, forced into the cleft to an unknown depth, rebounds and rushes up loaded with vapour to form the three or even six columns as if of steam, visible twenty miles distant. On attaining a height of 200 or at most 300 feet from the level of the river above the cascade, this vapour becomes condensed into a perpetual shower of fine rain. Much of the spray, rising to the west of Garden Island, falls on the groves of evergreen trees opposite; and from their leaves heavy drops are for ever falling, to form sundry little rills which, in running down the face of the rock, are blown off and turned back, or licked off their perpendicular bed, up into the column from which they have just descended.

The morning sun gilds these columns of watery smoke with all the glowing colours of double or treble rainbows. The evening sun from a hot yellow sky imparts a sulphurous hue, and gives one the impression that the yawning gulf might resemble the mouth of the bottomless pit. No bird sits and sings on the branches of the grove of perpetual showers, or ever builds its nest there. The sunshine, else-where so overwhelming, never penetrates the deep gloom of that shade. In the presence of the strange *Mosi-oa-tunya* we can sympathize with those who, when the world was young, peopled earth, air, and river with beings not of human form. Sacred to what deity would be this awful chasm and that dark grove, over which hovers an ever-abiding 'pillar of cloud'?

The ancient Batoka chieftains used Kazeruka, now Garden Island, and Boaruka, the island farther west, as sacred spots for worshipping the Deity. It is no wonder that under the cloudy columns, and near the brilliant rainbows, with the ceaseless roar of the cataract, and with the perpetual flow, as if pouring forth from the hand of the Almighty, their souls should be filled with reverential awe. It inspired wonder in the native mind throughout the interior. It was seen by no European till 1855, when I visited it on my way to the east coast.

The Sick Chief

Marching up the river we crossed the Lekone at its con-fluence about eight miles above the island Kalai. On the 13th we met a party from Sekeletu, who was now in Seshéke.

The headman Mokompa brought a liberal present. He expressed fear that the tribe was breaking up in consequence of Sekeletu's leprosy.

On the 18th we entered Seshéke. The old town, now in ruins, stands on the left bank of the river. Another has been built on the same side a quarter of a mile higher up since their headman, Moriantsane, was put to death for bewitching the chief with leprosy. Sekeletu was on the right bank.

A constant stream of visitors rolled in on us the day after

our arrival. Several of them who had suffered afflictions during my absence, seemed to be much affected by seeing me again. All were in low spirits. A severe drought had cut off the crops and destroyed the pasture of Linyanti, and the people were scattered over the country. Sekeletu's leprosy had brought troops of evils in its train. Believing himself bewitched, he had suspected a number of his chief men, and had put some, with their families, to death. Others had fled to distant tribes and were living in exile. The chief had shut himself up and allowed no one to come near him but his uncle, Mamire. The country was suffering grievously, and Sebituane's grand empire was crumbling to pieces.

Sebituane's wise policy in treating the conquered tribes on equal terms with his own Makololo, as all children of the chief, had been abandoned by his son, who married none but Makololo women, and appointed none to office but Makololo men. He had become unpopular among the black tribes. Strange rumours were afloat respecting the unseen Sekeletu. His fingers were said to have grown like an eagle's claws, and his face so frightfully distorted that no one could recognize him.

The native doctors had given the case up, but an old doctress of the Manyeti tribe had come to see what she could do for him, and on her skill he now hung his last hopes. She had made entire seclusion an essential condition of the much-longed-for cure, but notwithstanding, he sent for me, and the following day we were all three permitted to see him. He was sitting in a covered wagon, which was enclosed by a high wall of close-set reeds. His face was only slightly disfigured by the thickening of the skin in parts. The only peculiarity of his hands was the extreme length of his nails. He has the quiet unassuming manners of his father, speaks distinctly in a pleasant voice, and appears to be a sensible man, except perhaps on the subject of his being bewitched. In this he exhibits as firm a belief as if it were his monomania.

Sekeletu asked us for medicine and medical attendance, but we did not like to take the case out of the hands of the female physician, it being bad policy to appear to undervalue any of the profession.

Having none of the medicines usually employed in skin diseases, we tried local applications of lunar caustic, with hydriodate of potash internally—and with gratifying results.

The disease begins with slight discoloration of the surface, and at first affects only the cuticle, the patches spreading in the manner, and with somewhat of the appearance, of lichens, as if it were a fungus. Small vesicles rise at the outer edge of the patches, and a discharge from the vesicles forms scabs. The true skin next thickens and rises in nodules on the forehead, nose, and ears; and when the disease is far advanced foul fissures appear on the toes and fingers. These eventually fall off, and sometimes the patient recovers. The natives believe it to be hereditary and noncontagious, but while working at this case something like it was transplanted to the hands of Dr Kirk and myself, and was cured only by the liberal use of caustic. The chief's health became better as the skin became thinner, and the deformity of the face disappeared.

The two horses left by me in 1853 had lived, in spite of hard usage and perpetual hunting. A jolly set of young men, the chief's bodyguard, had a rare sort of horse-racing. One mounted with neither saddle, bit, nor bridle, and, spreading out both arms, dashed off at full speed. When he tumbled off, to the great amusement of the bystanders, the servants caught the horse and rode off anywhere, leaving the fallen rider to return rubbing his bruises. The poor horse was kept at this till it was completely exhausted.

The Makololo are by far the most intelligent and enterprising of the tribes I have met. None but brave and daring men remained long with Sebituane

To save the tribe from breaking up by continual losses

it ought at once to remove to the healthy Batoka highlands.

The chief's messengers have most retentive memories.
They carry messages of considerable length for great distances
and deliver them almost word for word. Two or three
usually go together, and when on the way the message is
rehearsed every night in order that the exact words may
be kept to.

The practice of polygamy, though intended to increase,
tends to diminish the tribe. The wealthy old men who
have all the cattle marry all the pretty girls. One ugly old
rich fellow, who was so blind that a servant had to lead
him, had two of the very handsomest wives in the town.
The young men who have no cattle have to do without
wives, or be content with those of few personal attractions.
This state of affairs probably leads to a good deal of
immorality, and children are few.

Wives are not bought and sold among the Makololo,
though marriage looks like a bargain. The husband, in
proportion to his wealth, hands over to his father-in-law
a number of cows, not as purchase money for the wife, but
to buy the right to keep in the family the children she may
bear. Otherwise the children would belong to the family
of the wife's father. A man may have complete control
over his wife without this payment, but not over the
children. Makololo ladies have delicate hands and feet.
Having maidservants to help them, and few children, time
hangs heavily on their hands. The men wickedly aver that
their two great amusements are sipping beer and secretly
smoking bhang, an Indian hemp, here known as *mutokwane*.
Although the men indulge pretty freely in smoking they do
not like their wives to follow their example, and many of
the 'monsters' prohibit it. Nevertheless some of the women
smoke it secretly, and the practice causes a disease known
by a minute eruption of the skin, quite incurable unless the
habit is abandoned. The chief himself is a slave to this

deleterious habit, and could hardly be induced to give it up even during the short time he was under medical treatment.

Two packages from Kuruman, containing newspapers and letters, reached Linyanti previous to our arrival, and Sekeletu, not knowing when we were coming, left them there, but now sent a messenger for them. This man returned on the seventh day, having travelled 240 geographical miles. One of the packages was too heavy for him and he left it behind.

As I wished to get some more medicines and papers out of the wagon left in Linyanti in 1853, I decided to go thither myself. I found everything safe as I left seven years before. The headman received me cordially and lamented that they had so little to give me. 'Oh, had you only arrived the previous year when there was abundance of milk and corn and beer.'

Several loose articles, as the medicine chest, magic-lantern, tools, and books, were given by Sekeletu into the charge of his wives. Everything was safe. Sekeletu's wives gently reproached me for not bringing Ma Robert (Mrs Livingstone), and repeated some of the prattle of the children and said: 'Are we never more to know anything but their names?'

These little points are noted with gratitude, but no one in his senses would suppose such confidence would be inspired by a novice. It ought never to be forgotten that confidence can be inspired only by continuance in well-doing, and that good manners are as necessary among barbarians as among the civilized.

The chief improved greatly in health and spirits during our visit, but he resolutely refused to appear in public till he was completely cured.

As we were expecting another steamer to be at Kongone in November it was impossible to remain at Seshéke more than a month. Before we left, the chief and his principal men expressed in a formal manner their great desire that English people should settle in the Batoka highlands.

The party left Sekeletu's headquarters on 17th September 1860, and Livingstone took a final farewell of the young chief of whom he had grown fond. He did not live much longer, and with his death Sebituane's great empire disintegrated.

Two of his men, Pitsane and Leshore, were appointed to convoy the travellers, and they proved most useful. As this was the third time that Livingstone had traversed this region his diary holds little that is new.

They went by canoe and the tribes were, on the whole, friendly. Hence, compared with the previous trips, travel was easy and rapid, but as not even the Africans were acquainted with the course of the river, nor were, indeed, specially expert canoe men, the party had, twice at least, critical adventures, before they reached Tete.

Down the Zambezi

On the morning of 12th October 1860 we passed through a wild, hilly country with fine wooded scenery on both sides, but thinly inhabited.[1] As we passed several villages without landing the people began to be alarmed, and ran along the banks, spears in hand. We employed one to go forward and tell Mpende of our coming. This allayed their fears, and we landed and took breakfast near a large island with two villages on it, opposite the mouth of the Zungwe. The chief was sorry he had no canoes of his own to sell, but he would lend us two.

Although the hills confine the Zambezi within a narrow channel for a number of miles, there are no rapids beyond those near the entrance. The river is smooth and apparently deep, but large masses of dislocated rock, bent and twisted, attest to some tremendous upheaval.

On emerging we pitched our camp by a small stream, the Pendele, a few miles below the gorge. Game of all kinds is in most extraordinary abundance. The drought drives

[1] *The Zambezi and its Tributaries*, page 321.

all the game to the river to drink. Vast herds of *pallah*, many water-bucks, koodoos, buffaloes, wild pigs, elands, zebras, and monkeys appear; francolins, guinea-fowls, and myriads of turtle-doves, with fresh spoor of elephants and rhinoceroses, which had been at the river during the night. Every few miles we came upon a herd of hippopotami asleep on some shallow sand-bank.

After three hours' sail on the morning of the 29th the river was narrowed again by the mountains of Mburúma, called Karivua, into one channel, and another rapid dimly appeared. It was formed by two currents guided by rocks to the centre.

In going down it the men sent by Sekeletu behaved most nobly. The canoes entered without previous survey, and the huge jostling waves of mid current began at once to fill them. With great presence of mind and without a moment's hesitation two men lightened each by jumping overboard. They then ordered the Batoka man to do the same, as 'the white men must be saved.' 'I cannot swim,' said the Batoka. 'Jump out then and hold on to the canoe' —which he instantly did. Swimming alongside, they guided the swamping canoes down the swift current to the foot of the rapid, and then ran them ashore to bale them out. A boat could have passed down safely, but our canoes were not a foot above the water at the gunwales.

Thanks to the bravery of these poor fellows, nothing was lost, though everything was soaked. The rapid is nearly opposite the west end of the Mburúma mountains. Another soon begins below it. They are said to be all smoothed out when the river rises. The canoes had to be unloaded at this, the worst rapid, and the goods carried about a hundred yards. We found the current to be running six knots, by far the greatest velocity noted in the river.

As the men were bringing the last canoe down close to the shore, the stern swung round into the current, and all except one man let go rather than be dragged off. He clung to the bow and was swept into the middle of the stream. Having held on when he ought to have let go, he now put his life in danger by letting go when he ought to have held on, and was in a few seconds swallowed up in a fearful whirlpool. His comrades launched a canoe below, and caught him as he rose the third time and saved him.

The Karivua narrows are about thirty miles in length. They end at the Roganora mountain.

We reached Zumbo on 1st November and found the river so shallow that it could be waded with ease.

We entered the Kebrabasa rapids at the east end of Chicova, and went down a number of miles till the river narrowed into a groove of forty or sixty yards wide. The navigation then became difficult and dangerous. Two of our canoes passed safely down a narrow channel which, bifurcating, had an ugly whirlpool at the rocky partition between the two branches, the deep hole in the whirls at times opening and shutting. My canoe came next and seemed to be drifting broadside into the vortex, in spite of the utmost exertions of the paddlers.

The rest were expecting to have to pull to the rescue, the men saying: 'Look where these people are going. Look! Look!' when a loud crack was heard. Dr Kirk's canoe was dashed on a projection of the perpendicular rocks by a sudden and mysterious boiling up of the river. Dr Kirk was seen resisting the sucking-down action of the water, which must have been fifteen fathoms deep, and raising himself by his arms on the ledge, while his steersmen, holding on to the same rocks, saved the canoe; but nearly all its contents were swept away by the stream. My canoe, meanwhile, which had distracted the men's attention, was saved by the filling up of a cavity in the whirlpool, just as the fearful eddy was reached.

A few of the things in Dr Kirk's canoe were saved, but all that was valuable, including the chronometer, a barometer, and, to our great sorrow, his notes for the journey and botanical drawings of the fruit trees of the interior, perished. The men had never seen such perilous sailing.

They declared they would carry all the loads rather than risk Kebrabasa any longer. But the fatigue of a day's marching, over hot rocks and burning sand, changed their tune before night.[1]

Panzo, the headman, of the village east of Kebrabasa, received us with great kindness. After the usual salutations he called in a loud voice across the valley to the women of several hamlets to cook supper for us.

We reached Tete on 23rd November, having been absent a little more than six months.

[1] For a very graphic account of this adventure, see *Kirk on the Zambezi*, page 177.

XX

Arrival of the Universities' Mission

As the Zambezi was unusually low we remained at Tete till it rose a little, and then left, on 3rd December, for Kongone.[1] It was hard work to keep the vessel afloat; indeed we never expected her to remain above water. New leaks broke out every day; the engine pump gave way; the bridge broke down; three compartments filled at night; and in a few days we were assured by Rowe that 'she can't be worse than she is.'

The morning of the 21st the uncomfortable 'Asthmatic' grounded on a sand-bank and filled. She could neither be emptied nor got off. The river rose during the night, and all that was visible of the worn-out craft next day was about six feet of her two masts, and we spent the Christmas of 1860 encamped on the island of Chimba. Canoes were sent from Sena, and we reached it on the 27th, to be again hospitably entertained by our friend, Senhor Ferrão.

We reached Kongone on 14th January 1861, and while waiting for a ship we had leisure to read the newspapers and periodicals we found in the mails. Several were a year and a half old.

Kongone is extremely malarial, and the thing most to be dreaded there is inactivity. We had, therefore, to find what exercise we could, when hunting was not required, in peering about fetid swamps. To have gone mooning about in listless idleness would have ensured fever in its worst form, and probably fatal results.

On 31st January 1861 our new ship the *Pioneer* arrived from England. Two of H.M. cruisers came at the same time, bringing Bishop Mackenzie and the Oxford and Cambridge Mission to the tribes of the Shire and Lake Nyasa.

---

[1] *The Zambezi and its Tributaries,* page 338.

The estimable bishop, anxious to commence his work without delay, wished the *Pioneer* to carry the mission up the Shire as far as Chibisa and there leave them. But there were grave objections to this. The *Pioneer* was under orders to explore the Rovuma. She was already two months behind her time and the rainy season was half over. Then, if the party were taken to Chibisa's, the mission would be left without a medical attendant in an unhealthy region at the most unhealthy season of the year, without means of reaching the healthy highlands or of returning to the sea.

The bishop at last consented to take the members of the mission to Johanna, and himself thereafter accompany us up the Rovuma.

On 25th February the *Pioneer* anchored in the mouth of the Rovuma, which unlike most African rivers has a magnificent harbour and no bar.

This, Livingstone's first of three attempts to explore the Rovuma, proved ill-timed. Many inquiries in African sources had convinced him that the river took its rise in Lake Nyasa. If so, then, it might provide the waterway into the interior that was so important to his plans, and which the Zambezi had denied him. Hence his eagerness. But the dry season was on them and the stream already falling, so, after penetrating some thirty miles, it was judged prudent to return, and the *Pioneer* was taken back to Kongone.[1]

The *Pioneer* was a well-appointed, fine little ship but she had, like all the Explorer's vessels, too deep a draught for the work she had to do. To keep her off the sand-banks that abounded was an almost hopeless task, and a vast amount of monotonous labour was needed 'in laying out anchors and toiling at the capstan to keep her off the sand.'

On at last reaching Chibisa's, we heard that there was war in the Manganja country and that the slave-trade was going on briskly. A large gang of enslaved Manganja had recently crossed the river on the way to Tete.

[1] *The Zambezi and its Tributaries*, Chapter XVIII.

With a sufficient number of hired men, we started for the highlands to show the bishop the country. Our first day's march was a long and fatiguing one. The few hamlets we passed were poor. The inhabitants complained that they had no food to sell, but if we would go only a little farther we should come to a village where they had plenty to eat. But we had gone far enough and remained where we were. Before sunset as much food as we could buy was brought, and huts were provided for the whole party.

A Momentous Decision with Serious Consequences

Next forenoon we halted at the village of my old friend Mbame to obtain new carriers. After we had rested a little he told me that a slave party, on the way to Tete, would presently pass through his village. 'Shall we interfere?' we asked one another. We remembered that all our private baggage was at Tete, which if we freed the slaves might be destroyed in retaliation. But this system of slave-hunters dogging us where previously they had not dared to venture, and, on pretence of being 'our children,' setting one tribe against another, to furnish themselves with slaves, would so inevitably thwart all the efforts for which we had the sanction of the Portuguese Government, that we resolved to run all risks and put a stop if possible to the slave-trade, which now followed on the footsteps of our discoveries.

A few minutes after Mbame had spoken to us the slave party, a long line of manacled men, women, and children, came wending their way round the hill into the valley on the side of which the village stood. The black drivers, armed with muskets and bedecked with various articles of finery, marched jauntily in the front, middle, and rear of the line, some of them blowing exultant notes on long tin horns. They seemed to feel that they were doing a very noble thing, and might proudly march with an air of triumph. But the instant the fellows caught a glimpse of the English, they darted off like mad into the forest, so fast, indeed, that we caught but a glimpse of their red caps and the soles of their feet. The chief of the party alone remained, and he, from being in front, had his hand tightly grasped by a Makololo. He proved to be a well-known slave of the late commandant of Tete, and for some time our own attendant while there. On asking how he had obtained these captives, he replied that he had bought them, but on inquiring of the people themselves all, save four, said they had been captured in war. While this inquiry was going on, he bolted too.

The captives knelt down, and in their way of expressing thanks clapped their hands with great vigour. They were thus left entirely in our hands, and knives were soon at work cutting the women and children loose. It was more difficult to cut the men adrift, as each had his neck in the fork of a stout stick, six or seven feet long, and kept in by an iron rod which was riveted at both ends across the throat. With a saw, luckily in the bishop's baggage, one by one the men were sawn out into freedom. The women, on being told to take the meal they were carrying and cook breakfast for themselves and their children, thought the news too good to be true; but after a little coaxing went at it with alacrity, and made a capital fire with which to boil their pots with the slave sticks and bonds, their old acquaintances through many a sad night and weary day.

Many were mere children, about five years of age, and under. One little boy with the simplicity of childhood said to our men: 'The others tied and starved us. You cut the ropes and tell us to eat. What sort of people are you? Where do you come from?' Two of the women had been shot the day before for attempting to untie the thongs. This, the rest told us, was to prevent them from attempting to escape. One woman had her infant's brains knocked out because she could not carry her load and it. And a man was dispatched with an axe because he had broken down with fatigue. Self-interest would have set a watch over the whole, rather than commit murder, but in

Victoria Falls from the air

this traffic we invariably find self-interest overcome by contempt of human life, and by bloodthirstiness.

The bishop was not present at this scene, having gone to bathe in a little stream below the village; but on his return he warmly approved of what had been done. He at first had doubts, but now felt that had he been present he would have joined in the good work. Logic is out of place when the question with a true-hearted man is, whether his brother man is to be saved or not.

Eighty-four, chiefly women and children, were liberated, and on being told that they were now free and might go where they pleased or remain with us, they chose to stay; and the bishop wisely attached them to his mission, to be educated as members of a Christian family. In this way a great difficulty in the commencement of a mission was overcome. Years are usually required before confidence is so far instilled into the natives' minds, as to induce them, young and old, to submit to the guidance of strangers professing to be actuated by motives the reverse of worldly wisdom, and inculcating customs strange and unknown to them and their fathers.

We proceeded next morning to Soche's with our liberated party, the men cheerfully carrying the bishop's goods. As we had begun, it was no use doing things by halves, so eight others were freed in a hamlet on our path. But a party of traders with nearly a hundred slaves fled on hearing of our proceedings. Dr Kirk and four Makololo followed them with great energy, but they made clear off to Tete. Two slave-traders were detained for the night to prevent them from carrying information to a large party still in front. Two of the bishop's black men from the Cape, having been slaves themselves, were now zealous emancipators, and volunteered to guard the prisoners during the night. So anxious were our heroes to keep them safe, that instead of relieving each other and keeping watch and watch, both kept watch together till about four, when sleep stole over them and the wakeful prisoners escaped.

I

One of the guards, seeing the loss, rushed out of the hut shouting: 'They are gone. They have taken my rifle with them. Fire! Fire!' The rifle was, however, safe enough, the slavers being only too glad to escape alone.

Resort to Arms

The part of the highlands which the bishop wished to look at before deciding on a settlement belonged to Chigunda, and this chief asked him to come and live with him at Mago-mero. This seemed to decide the question. A place nearer the Shire would have been chosen if he had expected his supplies to come up the river, but the Portuguese had closed it.

Our hopes were, therefore, turned to the Rovuma as a free highway into Lake Nyasa and the vast interior. A steamer was already ordered for the lake, and the bishop, seeing the advantageous nature of the highlands that stretch an immense way to the north, was more anxious to be near the lake and the Rovuma than the Shire.

The decision having been made it was thought desirable, to prevent the country from being depopulated, to visit the Ajawa chief and try to persuade him to give up his slaving and kidnapping course, and turn the energies of his people to peaceful ways.

On the morning of the 22nd (July), we were informed that the Ajawa were near and were burning a village a few miles off. Leaving the rescued slaves, we moved off to seek an interview with these scourges of the country. On the way we met crowds of Manganja fleeing from the war in front. These poor fugitives from the slave-hunt had as usual to leave all the food they possessed, except the little they could carry on their heads. We passed field after field of Indian corn or beans standing ripe for harvesting, but the owners were away. The villages were all deserted; one, where we had breakfasted two years before and saw a number of men peacefully weaving cloth, and among our-selves called it the 'Paisley of the Hills,' was burnt. The stores of corn were poured out in cart-loads and scattered all over the plain, and all along the paths, neither conquerors nor conquered having been able to convey it away.

About two o'clock we saw the smoke of burning villages, and heard triumphant shouts mingled with the wail of Manganja women, lamenting over their slain. The bishop then engaged us in fervent prayer, and on rising from our knees we saw a long line of Ajawa warriors, with their captives, coming round the hillside. The first of the returning conquerors were entering their own village below, and we heard the women welcoming them back with 'lulliloo-ings.' The Ajawa headman left the path on seeing us, and stood on an ant-hill to obtain a complete view of our party.

We called out that we had come to have an interview with them, but some of the Manganja who followed us shouted: 'Our Chibisa is come': Chibisa being well known as a great conjurer and general. Hearing this, the Ajawa ran off yelling and screaming: 'Nkondo! Nkondo!' (War! War!).

We heard the words of the Manganja, but they did not strike us at the moment as neutralizing our assertions of peace. The captives threw down their loads on the path and fled to the hills, and a large body of armed men came running up from the village, and in a few seconds they were all round us, though mostly concealed by projecting rocks and long grass. In vain we protested that we had not come to fight but to talk with them. They would not listen, having, as we remembered afterwards, good reason, in the cry of 'Our Chibisa.' Flushed with the recent victory over three villages and confident in an easy triumph over a mere handful of men, they began to shoot their poisoned arrows, sending them with great force upwards of a hundred yards, wounding one of our followers through the arm.

Our retiring slowly up the ascent from the village only made them more eager to prevent our escape; and, in the belief that this retreat was the evidence of fear, they closed upon us in bloodthirsty fury. Some came within fifty yards, dancing hideously.   Others having quite surrounded us and availing themselves of the rocks and long grass hard by, were intent on cutting us off, while others made off with their women and a large body of slaves.   Four were armed with muskets, and we were obliged, in self-defence, to return their fire and drive them off.   When they saw the range of the rifles they very soon desisted and ran away, but some shouted to us from the hills the consoling intimation that they would follow and kill us where we slept. Only two of the captives escaped to us, but probably most of those made prisoner that day fled elsewhere in the confusion.   We returned to the village which we had left in the morning, after a hungry, fatiguing, and most unpleasant day.

Though we could not blame ourselves for the course we had followed, we felt sorry for what had happened.   It was the first time we had been attacked by natives or had come into collision with them.   Though we had always taken it for granted that we might be called upon to act in self-defence, we were on this occasion less prepared than usual. No game having been expected here, the men had only a single round of cartridge each.   I had no revolver, and the rifle I usually fired was left at the ship to save it from the damp of the season.   Had we known better the effect of slavery and murder on the tempers of these bloodthirsty marauders, we should have tried messages and presents before going near them.

The old chief, Chinsunse, came on a visit to us next day and pressed the bishop to come and live with him.   But the old man's object was so evidently to have the mission as a shield against the Ajawa that his invitation was declined.

The bishop, feeling as most Englishmen would at the prospect of the people now in his charge being swept off into slavery by hordes of men-stealers, proposed to go at once to the rescue of the captive Manganja and drive the marauding Ajawa out of the country.   All were warmly in favour of this except myself, who opposed it on the grounds that it would be better for the bishop to wait to see the effect of the check the slave-hunters had just experienced. The Ajawa were evidently goaded on by the Portuguese agents from Tete, and there was no bond of union among the Ajawa on which to work.

On the bishop's inquiring whether, in the event of the Manganja again asking aid against the Ajawa, it would be his duty to accede to their request, 'No,' I replied, 'you will be oppressed by their importunities, but do not interfere in native quarrels.' This advice the good man honourably mentions in his journal.

I have been rather minute in relating what occurred during the few days of our connection with the Mission of the English Universities, on the hills, because the recorded advice having been disregarded, blame was thrown on my shoulders, as if the missionaries had no individual responsibility for their subsequent conduct. This, unquestionably, the good Bishop Mackenzie had too much manliness to have allowed. The connection of the members of the Zambezi Expedition with the acts of the bishop's mission now ceased, for we returned to the ship and prepared for our journey to Lake Nyasa. We cheerfully, if necessary, will bear all responsibility up to this point; and if the bishop afterwards made mistakes in certain collisions with the slavers, he had the votes of all his party with him, and those who best knew the peculiar circumstances and the loving disposition of the good-hearted man, will blame him least.

In this position, and in these circumstances, we left our friends at the mission station.

XXI

First Exploration of Lake Nyasa

On 6th August 1861, a few days after returning from Magomero, Dr Kirk, my brother Charles, and I, started for Nyasa with a light four-oared gig, a white sailor, and a score of attendants.[1]

We hired people along the path to carry the boat past forty miles of the Murchison Cataracts, for a cubit of cloth a day. This was deemed great wages, and more than twice the men required eagerly offered their services. The men of one village carried the boat to the next, and all we had to do was to tell the headman that we wanted fresh men in the morning. The country was rough and with little soil on it, but covered with grass and open forest. The inhabitants on both banks were now civil and obliging. Our possession of a boat, and the consequent power of crossing independently of the canoes, helped to develop their good manners.

We followed the river, availing ourselves for the most part of the still reaches for sailing, but a comparatively smooth country lies farther inland, over which a good road could be made. Some of the five main cataracts are very grand, the river falling 1,200 feet in forty miles.

After passing the last cataracts we launched our boat for good in the broad waters of the Upper Shire, and were virtually on the lake, for the gentle current shows but little difference of level. The bed is deep and broad, but the course is rather tortuous at first, and makes a long bend to the east till it comes within five or six miles of the base of Mount Zomba. Seldom does the current here exceed a knot an hour, while that of the Lower Shire is from two to two and a half knots. Our land party of Makololo

[1] *The Zambezi and its Tributaries,* page 365.

accompanied us along the right bank and passed thousands
of Manganja fugitives living in huts on that side, who had
been recently driven from their villages on the opposite
hills by the Ajawa.

As we sailed along we disturbed many white-breasted
cormorants. Here, with many other wild fowl, they find
a subsistence on the smooth water by night, and sit sleepily
on the trees and in the reeds by day. Many hippopotami
were seen on the river, and one of them stretched its wide
jaws as if to swallow the whole stern of the boat close to
Dr Kirk's back, and was so near that in opening its mouth
it lashed a quantity of water on to the stern-sheets, but did
no damage. To avoid large marauding parties of the Ajawa
on the left bank of the Shire, we continued on the right or
western side with our land party, along the shore of the
small lake Pamalombe.

This lakelet is ten or twelve miles in length and five or
six broad. It is nearly surrounded by a broad belt of
almost impenetrable papyrus. The plants, ten to twelve
feet high, grew so close together that air was excluded
and so much sulphuretted hydrogen evolved that by one
night's exposure the bottom of the boat was blackened.
Myriads of mosquitoes showed, as probably they always do,
the presence of malaria.[1]

We hastened from this sickly spot, and when on 2nd
September we sailed into Lake Nyasa we felt refreshed by
the greater coolness of the air off this large body of water.
The depth was the first point of interest. This is indicated
by the colour of the water which on a belt along the shore,
varying from a quarter to half a mile in breadth, is light
green, and this is met by the deep blue or indigo tint of the
Indian Ocean, which is the colour of the great body of
Nyasa. We found the Upper Shire from nine to fifteen
feet in depth; but skirting the western side of the lake about
a mile from the shore the water deepened from nine to

---

[1] Livingstone in several places remarks on the connection of mosquitoes
with malaria.

fifteen fathoms. Then as we rounded the grand mountainous promontory which we named Cape Maclear, after
the Astronomer Royal at the Cape of Good Hope, we could
get no bottom with our line of thirty-five fathoms.

Looking back to the southern end of the lake, the arm
from which the Shire flows was found to be about thirty
miles long and from ten to twelve broad. Rounding Cape
Maclear and looking to the south-west, we have another
arm that stretches some eighteen miles southward, and is
from six to twelve miles in breadth. These arms give the
southern end a forked appearance. The length is over two
hundred miles. The direction in which it lies is as near
as possible north and south.

The lake appeared to be surrounded by mountains, but it
was afterwards found that these beautiful tree-covered
heights were, on the west, only the edges of high table-
lands. Like all narrow seas surrounded by highlands, it is
visited by sudden and tremendous storms. We were on
it in September and October, perhaps the stormiest season
of the year, and were repeatedly detained by gales. At
times while sailing pleasantly with a gentle breeze, suddenly and without any warning was heard the sound of a
coming storm, roaring on with crowds of angry waves in
its wake.

We were caught one morning with the sea breaking all
around us, and, unable either to advance or recede, anchored
a mile from shore in seven fathoms. The waves most
dreaded come rolling on in threes, with their crests, driven
into spray, streaming behind them. A short lull followed
each triple charge. Had one of these white-maned seas
struck our frail bark, nothing could have saved us; but we
escaped. For six weary hours we faced those terrible trios.
Our black crew became sick and unable to sit up or keep
the boat's head to the sea. The natives and our land party
stood on the high cliffs looking at us, and exclaiming as the
waves seemed to swallow up the boat: 'They are lost.
They are all dead.' When at last the gale subsided and

we came safely ashore, they saluted us warmly, as after a long absence.

From this time we trusted implicitly the opinions of our seaman, John Neil, who having been a fisherman on the coast of Ireland, understood boating on a stormy coast, and by his advice we often sat cowering on the land for days together, waiting for the surf to go down. He had never seen such waves before. We had to beach the boat every night to save her from being swamped at anchor, and did we not believe the gales to be peculiar to one season of the year, would call Nyasa the 'Lake of Storms.'

Lake Nyasa receives no great affluents from the west. The five rivers we observed in passing did not seem to bring in as much water as the Shire was carrying out. These streams, with others of about the same size from the mountains on the east and north, when swollen by rains may be sufficient to account for the rise of the lake without any large river. The natives nearest the northern end denied the existence of a large river there. Distinct white marks on the rocks showed that, for some time during the rainy season, the water of the lake is three feet above the point to which it falls towards the close of the dry period of the year. The rains begin here in November, and the permanent rise of the Shire does not take place till January.

The western side, with the exception of the great harbour to the west of Cape Maclear, is a succession of similar small bays, each having an open sandy beach and a pebbly shore, separated from its neighbours by a rocky headland with detached rocks extending some distance out to sea. The great south-western bay would form a magnificent harbour.[1]

[1] In his private correspondence at this time, Livingstone writes much and eagerly of a plan to found a colony in the Nyasa highlands. The colonists were to be drawn from the 'honest poor of the homeland,' who would, he hoped, prove a strong arm against the slave-trade. He was ready to subscribe two to three thousand pounds to such a scheme. This was an old idea of his. In a letter to Professor A. Sedgwick dated 6th February 1858 (now in the keeping of the Rhodes Livingstone Museum, N. Rhodesia), he wrote that he

*I

Further Exploration of Lake Nyasa

Never before have we seen in Africa anything like the dense population on the shores of Lake Nyasa. In the southern part there is almost an unbroken chain of villages. On the beach of wellnigh every little sandy bay, dark crowds were standing gazing at the novel sight of a boat under sail, and whenever we landed we were surrounded in a few seconds by hundreds of men, women, and children, who hastened to stare at the *chirombo* (wild animals). They crowded round us at meal-times and formed a thicket of dark bodies, but they good-naturedly kept each other to a line that we made on the sand, and left us room to dine. On the whole they were civil.

Twice they went to the length of lifting up the edge of our sail, which we used as a tent, as boys do the curtains of travelling menageries at home. No fines were levied on us nor dues demanded. At one village only were they impudent, but they were 'elevated' by beer. They cultivate the soil pretty extensively, and grow large quantities of rice and sweet potatoes as well as maize, mapira, and millet. In the north, however, cassava is the staple product which, with fish kept till the flavour is high, constituted the main support of the inhabitants.

During a portion of the year the northern dwellers on the lake have a harvest which furnishes a singular sort of food. As we approached our limit in that direction, clouds, as of smoke rising from miles of burning grass, were observed bending in a south-easterly direction, and we thought that the unseen land on the opposite side was closing in, and that we were near the end of the lake. But next morning we sailed through one of the clouds on our

had a plan 'which I tell to none but those in whom I have confidence. I hope it may result in an English colony in the healthy highlands.' But Murchison and Young of Kelly threw cold water on the suggestion, and talked ominously of the Darien scheme. So, very unwillingly he dropped it. See *The Personal Life of David Livingstone*, by W. G. Blaikie, page 243, and *Livingstone the Liberator*, page 231.

own side, and discovered that it was neither smoke nor haze, but countless millions of minute midges called *kungo* (a cloud). They filled the air to an immense height, and swarmed upon the water, too light to sink in it. Eyes and mouth had to be kept closed while passing through this cloud. They struck upon the face like fine drifting snow. The people gather these minute insects by night and boil them into thick cakes to be used as a relish—millions of midges to a cake. A *kungo* cake an inch thick, and as large as the blue bonnet of a Scotch ploughman, was offered to us. It was very dark in colour and tasted not unlike caviare or salted locusts.

Abundance of good fish is found in the lake, and nearly all were new to us. The mpasa, or sanjika, a kind of carp, spawn like salmon. The largest we saw was over two feet long—the best fish we have eaten in Africa. They ascend the rivers in August and September. Weirs are made full of sluices, in each of which was set a large basket trap, through whose single tortuous opening the fish, once in, has but small chance of escape.

In deep water some sorts are taken by lowering fish-baskets attached by a long cord to a float, around which is often tied a mass of grass or weeds as an alluring shade for the deep-sea fish. Fleets of fine canoes are engaged in the fisheries. The men have long paddles and stand erect while using them. They sometimes venture out when a considerable sea is running.

Though there are many crocodiles, and some of extra-ordinary size, they rarely attack the fisherman. There is abundance of fish, which is their natural food. But when the muddiness of the water makes them unable to see to catch their prey, then they are dangerous.

The Lake people are by no means handsome. The women are, to use our mildest terms for the fair sex, very plain, and really make themselves hideous by the means they adopt to render themselves attractive. The *pelele*, or ornament for the upper lip, is universally worn by ladies. The most valuable is of pure tin, hammered into the shape of a small dish. Some go to extremes, as ladies will, and insert another in the under lip almost opposite the gums.

By Chitanda, near one of the slave crossings, we were robbed for the first time in Africa. It may only be a coincidence, but we never suffered impudence, loss of property, or were endangered, unless among people familiar with slaving. We had such a general sense of security that we did not set watch at night.

Our native companions had on this occasion been carousing on beer, and had removed to a distance of some thirty yards, that we might not hear their free and easy after-dinner remarks, and two of us had fever. Between three and four in the morning, while we slept ingloriously —rifles and revolvers all ready—some light-fingered gentry relieved us of most of our goods. The boat's sail, under which we all slept, was open all round, so the feat was easy. The rogues left on the beach, close to our beds, the aneroid barometer and a pair of boots. They shoved back some dried plants and fishes into one bag, but carried off many other specimens we had collected, some of our notes also, and nearly all our clothing.

One of us was indebted to female curiosity for the safety of his best suit. On the day previous, Sunday, he had retired to have a bath and change among the reeds, but looked about before being quite undressed, and found a crowd of ladies peering at the apparition. He retired without either bath or change of apparel. (One feels ashamed of the white skin! It seems unnatural, like blanched celery or white mice!) On returning to the camp he changed into and slept in his best, as it was too late to change it again. So the worst only was lost. Our rifles and revolvers were left untouched, but we felt it most humiliating for armed men to have been so thoroughly fleeced by a few black rascals.

Pursuing our exploration, we found that the northern part of the lake was the abode of lawlessness and bloodshed,

The Mazitu live on the highlands and make sudden swoops on the villages of the plains. These are Zulus who came originally from the south, and are of the same family as those who levy tribute from the Portuguese on the Zambezi. All the villages north of Mankambira's had been recently destroyed by these terrible marauders, but they were foiled in their attacks upon that chief and Marenga. The thickets and stockades round their villages enabled the bowmen to pick off the Mazitu in security, while they were afraid to venture near any place where they could not use their shields. Beyond we saw burnt villages and putrid bodies. Our land party was afraid to go farther, and dreaded meeting the inflictors of this terrible vengeance.

'How far is it to the end of the lake?' we asked of an intelligent native at the south part. He exclaimed in feigned or real surprise: 'Whoever heard of such a thing? If one set off as a boy he would be an old man before he got there.' As regards the Rovuma's flowing out of Nyasa, opinions differed.

The Lake slave-trade was going on at a terrible rate. Two enterprising Arabs had built a dhow, and were running her, crowded with slaves, regularly across the lake. We were told that she sailed the day before we reached their head-quarters. Some ivory was offered for sale, but the chief traffic was in human chattels.

Would that we could give a comprehensive account of the horrors of the slave-trade, with an approximation of the number of lives it yearly destroys! For we feel sure that were only half the truth told and recognized, the feelings of men would be so thoroughly roused that this devilish traffic in human flesh would be put down at all risks. But no one has the necessary statistics.

Let us state what we do know of one portion of Africa. We were informed by Colonel Rigby,[1] late H.M. political agent, and consul at Zanzibar, that 19,000 slaves from this

[1] See Notes on Persons, page 417.

Nyasa country alone pass annually through the custom-house of that island. This is exclusive, of course, of those sent to the Portuguese slave ports. Let it not be supposed that this number represents all the victims. Those taken out of the country are but a small section of the sufferers. Besides those actually captured, thousands are killed and die of their wounds and famine, driven from their villages by the slave raid proper. Thousands perish in internecine war, waged for slaves, with their own clansmen, slain for the lust of gain. It is our deliberate opinion, from what we have seen, that not one-fifth of the victims ever become slaves. Taking the Shire valley as an average we should say that not even one-tenth arrive at their destination.

A small armed steamer on Lake Nyasa could easily, by exercising a control and furnishing goods in exchange for ivory and other products, break the neck of this infamous traffic in this quarter, for nearly all must cross the lake or the Upper Shire.

Our exploration of the lake extended from 2nd September to 27th October 1861; and having expended or lost most of the goods we had brought, it was necessary to go back to the ship.

XXII

Africa takes Toll

WE reached the ship on 8th November 1861 in a very weak condition, having suffered more from hunger than on any previous trip. Heavy rains commenced on the 9th, and continued several days; the river rose rapidly and became highly coloured.[1]

Bishop Mackenzie came down to the ship with some of the *Pioneer*'s men, who had been at Magomero for the benefit of their health, and also for the purpose of assisting the mission. The bishop appeared to be in excellent spirits, and thought that the future promised fair for peace and usefulness. The Ajawa, having been defeated and driven off while we were on the lake, had sent word that they desired to live at peace with the English. Many of the Manganja had settled round Magomero, in order to be under the protection of the bishop, and it was hoped that the slave-trade would soon cease in the highlands, and the people be left to enjoy the fruits of their industry. The mission, it was anticipated, might soon become, to a considerable degree, self-supporting, and raise certain kinds of foods.

Mr Burrup, an energetic young man, had arrived at Chibisa's the day before the bishop, having come up the Shire in a canoe. A surgeon and a lay brother followed behind in another canoe. The *Pioneer*'s draught being too much for the Upper Shire, it was not deemed advisable to bring her up on the next trip farther than the Ruo. The bishop, therefore, resolved to explore the country from Magomero to the mouth of that river, and to meet the ship with his sisters and Mrs Burrup, in January. This was arranged before parting, and when the good bishop and Burrup, whom we were never to meet again, left us, they

[1] *The Zambezi and its Tributaries*, page 400.

253

gave and received three hearty English cheers as they went ashore and we steamed off.

The rains ceased on the 14th, and the waters of the Shire fell even more rapidly than they had risen.   A shoal twenty miles below Chibisa's checked our further progress, and we lay there five weary weeks, till the permanent rise of the river took place.   During this detention, with a large marsh on each side, the first death occurred in the expedition, which had now been three and a half years in the country.

The carpenter's mate, a fine healthy young man, was seized with fever.   The usual remedies had no effect, and he died suddenly while we were at evening prayers and was buried ashore.   He came out in the *Pioneer*, and, with the exception of a touch of fever at the mouth of the Rovuma, had enjoyed perfect health.

We entered the Zambezi on 11th January and steamed down towards the coast.   We anchored at the great Luabo mouth, because wood was much more easily obtained there than at Kongone.

On the 30th H.M.S. *Gorgon* arrived, towing the brig which brought Mrs Livingstone, some ladies about to join the Universities' Mission, and twenty-four sections of the new iron steamer intended for navigation on Lake Nyasa.   The new steamer we called the *Lady Nyasa*.[1]

The ladies included Mrs Livingstone, Miss Mackenzie, and Jessie Lennox, who later became one of Florence Nightingale's nurses and lived to be a hundred.   Also Mrs Burrup, the young wife of the recently arrived recruit to the mission.   Their coming, so eagerly anticipated, was to prove the prelude to a succession of tragedies.

The Doctor was most anxious to have the women removed from the malaria-saturated valley of the Shire to the healthy highlands, but was blocked by the customary series of delays. The *Pioneer's* engines badly needed overhauling, and the *Lady Nyasa* had to be fitted together.

[1] This little vessel, built on the Clyde, was Livingstone's private venture and was built at his expense from the royalties on his books.

The mission ladies were, however, anxious to push on, and accepted the offer of Captain Wilson of the *Gorgon*, to conduct them in the ship's gig to the mouth of the Ruo River, that joins the Shire sixty miles below the cataracts. It had been arranged that the bishop should await them there.

At Ruo there was no one to meet them, so they went on to Chibisa's village. There they were met with the shattering news that both the bishop and his young colleague were dead.

The circumstances of the tragedy were as follows. Mackenzie and young Burrup had just returned from rescuing some of their people who had been captured, and had reached their station, Magomero, weakened by dysentery, aggravated by hunger and repeated soakings. Instead of resting, as prudence commanded, they, fearing to be late for their womenfolk, set out at once and took the route down the flooded Shire. The country between was waterlogged, and on the way they were drenched many times.

The Manganja, the customary boatmen, refused to risk the turgid river, but three Makololo volunteered. These men paddled all the day, and towards sunset landed for the night, but, finding the mosquitoes unbearable, insisted on going on. Very unwillingly, permission was given. In the darkness the boat ran into a boiling whirlpool and was upset.

No lives were lost but all their stores, including the precious medicine chest, were swept away. The canoe was secured and in it the party, chilled by the soaking and tormented by mosquitoes, spent the rest of the night.

In the morning they made their way to Malo, an island in the mouth of the Ruo. Here Mackenzie was seized with severe fever, and there being no drugs to check its course, he quickly sank into a stupor and died.

His colleague buried him there, and with the help of the faithful Makololo, struggled back to headquarters, only to die of exhaustion. This was the tragic information that was awaiting the ladies.

The stricken women were as soon as possible taken to the Cape on board the *Gorgon*. Mrs Livingstone remained at Shupanga, where she also, after a few weeks, developed a serious type of malaria, to which she succumbed.

Livingstone's comments on these tragic events are characteristically restrained and unemotional, but the sudden passing
of his much-loved wife was a blow from which he never fully
recovered, while the death of his friend Bishop Mackenzie, and
the subsequent withdrawal of the Universities' Mission, was
perhaps the bitterest disappointment of his life.

Another Attempt on the Rovuma

On the 5th May 1862 Dr Kirk and Charles Livingstone
started in the boat for Tete. They took four Mazaro canoe-
men. These men prefer punting, and in going up the river
chose the shallow parts. On the first day there was little
wind, but towards evening a pleasant breeze got up and the
sail was set. The canoe-men, who were not used to sails,
were of course very pleased to see the boat move without
their exertions. After dark the wind increased and the
boat swept swiftly through the water. The men grew
excited and set up an extempore song. As the breeze
freshened the boat dashed through the waves; then, wild
with excitement, the men sprang to their feet and sang still
louder, gesticulating with might and main. Suddenly the
song ceased and the singers were sprawling on their backs.
The boat was on a sand-bank.[1]

On 23rd June the *Lady Nyasa* was safely launched, the
work of putting her together having been interrupted by
fever and dysentery and many other causes. Natives from
all over the country came to watch, most of them quite
certain that, being made of iron, she must go to the bottom.
'If,' they said, 'we put a hoe into the water it will certainly
sink. How can such a mass of iron float?' But a minority
answered that while that might be true with them, white
men had a medicine for everything. 'They could even
make a woman, all but the speaking. Look at that one on
the figurehead of the vessel!' The unbelievers could hardly
believe their eyes when they saw the ship float gracefully

[1] It is stated in the footnote on page 178 that in the preparation of this
book Charles Livingstone's diary was also used. This passage is obviously his.

on the river. 'Truly,' they said, 'these men have powerful medicine.'

By the time everything was on board the waters had fallen so low that it was useless to take the boat up to the cataracts before the rains in December. The Portuguese were putting obstacles in our way and were establishing river police. So, the Rovuma being outside their claims and a free river, we decided to explore it. To which place we sailed after some repairs and the replenishing of our stores

Captain Gardner, her commander, and several of his officers accompanied us up the river for two days. The water was unusually low, and it was dull work for a few hours in the morning; but the scene was much livelier when the breeze began to blow.

A drowsy herd of hippopotami was suddenly startled by a score of rifle shots, and stared with amazement at the strange objects which were invading their peaceful domains, until a few more bullets made them seek refuge at the bottom of a deep pool. On our return one of the herd retaliated. He followed the boat, came up under it, and twice tried to tear the bottom out of it, but fortunately its bottom was too flat for his jaws to get a good grip, so he merely damaged one of the planks with his tusks, though he lifted the boat right up, with ten men and a ton of ebony in it. There is abundance of large ebony in the neighbourhood.

The valley of the Rovuma, bounded on each side by a range of highlands, is from two to four miles in width and comes in a pretty straight course from the west-south-west, but the channel of the river is winding and, now at its lowest, zigzagged so perversely that frequently the boats had to pass over three miles to make one in a straight line. Few natives were seen during the first week. The villages were concealed in thick jungle on the hillsides, for protection from marauding slave parties.

Though feeling convinced that the river was unfit for

navigation, except for eight months of the year, we pushed on to see if farther inland the accounts we had received from different naval officers of its great capabilities would prove correct.

On 16th September we arrived at the inhabited island of Kichokomane. Before sunrise next morning a large party armed with bows and arrows and muskets came to the camp. It was evidently their intention to attack us at a chosen spot where we had to pass a high bank, but their plan was frustrated by a stiff breeze sweeping the boats past before the majority could get to the place. They disappeared then, but came out again ahead of us on a high wooded bank, near which we were obliged to sail.

An arrow was shot at the foremost boat; and seeing the force at the bend, we pushed out from the side as far as the shoal water would permit, and tried to bring them to a parley by declaring that we had not come to fight but to see the river. 'Why did you fire a gun a little while ago?' they asked. 'We shot a large puff-adder. You may see it lying on the beach.' With great courage our Mokadamo waded out to within thirty yards of the bank, assuring them that we were a peaceable party. While he was talking an old rogue, who appeared to be the ringleader, stole up the bank with a dozen others, waded across to the island near which the boats lay, and came down behind us. Wild with excitement they rushed into the water and danced in our rear with drawn bows, taking aim and making various savage gesticulations. The leader urged them to get behind some snags and then shoot at us. The party on the bank in front had many muskets, and those with bows held them with arrows ready set in the bowstrings. They had a mass of thick bush and trees behind them, into which they could dart, a circumstance that always gives people who use bows and arrows the greatest confidence.

We were exceedingly loath to come to blows. We spent a full half-hour exposed at any moment to be struck by a bullet or a poisoned arrow. With much persuasion we

so far succeeded that the leaders and others laid down their
arms, and waded over to the boat to talk the matter over.
They insisted that this was their river and that they did not
allow white men to use it. We must pay toll for leave to
pass. It was somewhat humiliating to do so; but it was
either pay or fight, and rather than fight we gave them
thirty yards of cloth. They pledged themselves to be our
friends, and said they would have food cooked for us on
our return.

We then hoisted sail, glad the affair was amicably settled.
Those on shore walked up to the bend above, to look at
the boat, as we supposed, but the moment we were abreast
of them they gave us a volley of musket balls and poisoned
arrows, without a word of warning. Fortunately we were
so near that all the arrows passed clear of us, but four
musket balls went through the sail just above our heads.
All our assailants bolted into the bushes and long grass save
two, one of whom was about to discharge a musket and the
other an arrow when arrested by the fire of the second
boat. A few shots were then fired over their heads, and
all fled to the woods. It is only where people are slavers
that the natives of this part of Africa are bloodthirsty.

As we pushed westward we found that the river makes a
little southing, and some reaches are deeper than any near
the sea, but when we had ascended about a hundred and
forty miles by the river's course from the sea, soft tufa
rocks began to appear. Ten miles beyond, the river became more narrow and rocky, and when we had ascended
a hundred and fifty-six miles our further progress was
arrested. We were rather less than two degrees in a
straight line from the coast. When we came to a stand,
just below the island of Nyamatolo, long. 38° 36′ E. and
lat. 11° 53′, the river was narrow and full of rocks, and
these were an effectual barrier to all further progress in
boats.

The Rovuma is remarkable for the high lands that flank
it some eighty miles from the ocean. The cataracts of other

rivers occur in the mountains, those of the Rovuma are found in a level part with hills only in the distance. The natives reported a worse place above our turning-point—the passage being still narrower than this.

We returned to the *Pioneer* on 9th October, having been away one month. The ship's company had used distilled water, and there had not been a single case of sickness on board, though there were so many cases of fever the few days she lay in the same spot last year. Our boat party drank the water of the river, and three white sailors, who had never been on an African river before, had some slight attacks of fever.

Troubled Close of the Expedition

We put to sea on 18th October 1862, and again touching at Johanna obtained a crew and some oxen, and sailed for the Zambezi, but our fuel failing we ran into Quelimane for wood.

Quelimane must have been built solely for the slave-trade, for no one in his senses would have built a village on such a low, muddy, fever-haunted, mosquito-swarming site. Some excellent brick houses still stand, and the owners are generous and hospitable, among them our good friend Colonel Nunez. His disinterested kindness can never be forgotten.

We entered the Zambezi about the end of November, and did not reach Shupanga till the 19th; but by 10th January the Shire had risen and we steamed off with the *Lady Nyasa* in tow. It was not long before we came upon the ravages of the notorious Mariano. The survivors of a village at the foot of Morumbala were in a state of starvation from his raids. Dead bodies floated past us daily, and in the morning the paddles had to be cleared of corpses. For scores of miles the whole population had been swept away. It made the heart sore to see the widespread desolation— the banks, recently so populous, all silent; the villages burnt down, and an oppressive stillness everywhere.

Here and there might be seen on the bank a small dreary
deserted shed where had sat, day after day, a starving
fisherman, until the rising waters drove the fish from their
usual haunts and left him to die.   Many skeletons lay beside
the path.   Ghastly living forms of boys and girls with dull,
dead eyes were crouching beside some of the huts.   A few
more days of terrible hunger and they would be dead.

The Shire fell two feet.   We had two ships to take up
and were detained.   During this detention Mr Thornton [1]
came up to us from Shupanga.   He had left the expedition
in 1859, and had joined Baron van der Decken in a journey
to Kilimanjaro.

Considering the frightful destruction wrought by the
slavers, we have come to believe that if it were possible to
get a steamer upon the lake, we could by means of her put
a check upon the slavers from the east coast, and aid
effectually in the suppression of the trade by introducing,
by way of the Rovuma, a lawful trade in ivory.

We therefore unscrewed the *Lady Nyasa* at a spot below
the first cataract, and began to make a road over the forty
miles of land porterage, over which to carry her piecemeal.

The chief labour of road-making consisted in cutting
down trees.   The land was very much intersected by
ravines, and search had to be made a mile from the bank
for level ground.   Hottentot drivers would have taken
Cape wagons over without any trouble other than occasionally cutting a tree.   There was no tsetse, so our cattle
flourished.   The absence of crowds and the oppressive stillness weighed on our spirits.   No fresh provisions, except
what we shot, could be obtained.

The diet of salt provisions and preserved meats, acting
on our depressed spirits, brought on attacks of dysentery
which went round the company, and Charles Livingstone
and Dr Kirk having suffered most severely, it seemed
advisable that they should be sent home.   Then I myself
was seized in May with a heavy attack, which continuing

[1] See Notes on Persons, page 407.

for a month, reduced me to a shadow. Dr Kirk kindly remained in attendance till the worst was passed. The parting took place on 19th May.

After a few miles of road had been completed and the oxen broken in, we decided to make ourselves independent of the south for fresh provisions, by taking a boat up the Shire beyond the cataracts to reach the tribes at the foot of Lake Nyasa, untouched by the Ajawa invasion.

The *Pioneer* was left in the charge of our active and most trustworthy gunner, Mr Edward Young, R.N.[1] On 16th June we started for the upper cataracts with a mule cart, our road lying a distance of a mile west from the river.

We took several of the men for the sake of change of air and occupation, and also to secure for the ships a supply of buffalo meat. But though we saw their tracks in abundance we could not get a glimpse of them. The grass was taller than we were. Once, at sunrise, we saw a herd slowly wending up the hillside from the water. Sending for a rifle, and stalking with intense eagerness for a fat beef-steak instead of our usual fare of salted provisions, we got so near that we could hear the bulls uttering their hoarse, deep low, but could see nothing except the mass of yellow grass in front. Suddenly the buffalo birds sounded their alarm whistle and away dashed the troop, and we caught sight of neither birds nor beasts.

The animals are wary, from the dread they have of poisoned arrows. The natives follow the game with a steady perseverance and cunning that is quite extraordinary. The arrow makes no noise, and the herd is followed up till the poison takes effect and the wounded animal falls out. A portion of the meat round the wound is cut away, and all the rest is eaten.

The poison used here is called *kombi* and is obtained from a species of *strophanthus* and is very virulent. Dr Kirk found by an accidental experiment on himself that it acts

[1] See Notes on Persons, page 407.

by lowering the pulse.   In using his toothbrush, which had
been in a pocket containing a little of the poison, he noticed
a bitter taste, but attributed it to having sometimes used
the handle for taking quinine.   Though the quantity was
small it immediately showed its power by lowering the
pulse, which at that time had been raised by a cold, and
next day he was perfectly restored.   Not much can be
inferred from one case, but it is possible that *kombi* may
turn out a valuable remedy.[1]

It was the Explorer's intention to use a boat that at the end
of the last Nyasa expedition he had left hidden in a tree on the
river bank.   To his dismay he found that it had been burnt,
probably in a bush fire.   It had been intended by this means
to 'make themselves independent of the south for provisions,'
but being thus disappointed they turned back.

On arriving at the ship they found a dispatch from Lord
Russell withdrawing the expedition.[2]   'All things considered,
and remembering that we had not found the Rovuma fit for
navigation, as we had expected, it is impossible not to coincide
with the wisdom of the withdrawal.'

[1] Strophanthin, now a recognized cardiac tonic.

[2] Amongst the reasons for the withdrawal of the expedition there was
undoubtedly a political one.   'The Prince Consort was King Pedro of
Portugal's cousin, and he made no secret of his displeasure at any interference with the Portuguese.'   (See *Kirk on the Zambezi*, page 268.)   Livingstone remarked some months later on the coldness of his reception by Lord
Russell in London.

XXIII

A Trip towards Lake Bangweulu

To add to the many depressing experiences of this period, Livingstone found himself once more trapped by a fall in the water of the Shire, which kept the *Pioneer* prisoner till the floods of December. Six months of inactivity was more than the Explorer could face, so he decided on a final examination of the lake country. All his staff had, by this time, for reasons of health, gone home, and as it was not wise in his present state of health for him to travel alone, he took with him a ship-steward and a few of his Makololo. Besides a more detailed examination of the south-west coast of the lake, he planned to turn west at Kota-Kota and go some distance along the great slave road that reached Nyasa at this point.

As usual with him, travel restored his physical tone, and his spirits revived. But the trip began badly. The first task was to carry the boat he meant to use past the Murchison Cataracts, but this proved more difficult than he had expected.

Our party consisted of twenty natives. The river was here very narrow and the current strong, and the men were often obliged to haul the boat along by the reeds on the bank. The reeds were full of cowitch (*Dolochos pruriens*), the pods of which are covered with fine prickles and caused an itching and stinging on the naked bodies of the men, and made them wriggle as if stung by a whole bed of nettles. So it was thought wiser to carry the boat.

Five Zambezi men, who all their life had been accustomed to heavy canoes, were very anxious to show how much better they could manage the boats than the Makololo. Three jumped aboard her when our backs were turned, and three hauled her up for a little way. The tide then caught her bow and we heard a shout of distress. The rope was out of their hands in a minute and there she was

264

bottom upwards. A turn or two in an eddy, and then away she went like an arrow down the cataracts. One of the men in swimming ashore saved a rifle. The whole party ran along the bank with all their might, but never again did we see the boat.

The five performers of this catastrophe approached us with penitential looks. They bent down slowly and touched our feet with both hands. They had nothing to say—nor had we.

While the men have been sent back to the ship for provisions, cloth, and beads, may we say a little about the cataracts.

They begin in lat. 15° 20′ S. and end in lat. 15° 55′ S.; the difference of latitude is therefore 35′. The river runs in this space nearly north and south till we pass Malango. So the entire distance is under forty miles. The principal cataracts are five in number. Besides these, three or four smaller ones might be mentioned. While these lesser cataracts descend at an angle of scarcely 20°, the greater fall 100 feet in 100 yards, at an angle of 45°, and one at an angle of about 70°. One part of the Pamozima (fall) is perpendicular, and when the river is in flood causes a cloud of vapour to ascend which, on our journey to Lake Shirwa, we saw at a distance of at least eight miles. The entire descent, from the Upper to the Lower Shire, is 1,200 feet. Only on one spot in all the distance, namely above Tedzane (fall), is the current moderate. The rest is all rapid, and being only fifty to eighty yards wide, it gives the impression of water-power, sufficient to drive all the mills of Manchester, running to waste.

The rock lowest down in the series is a dark reddish-grey syenite. This seems to have been the upheaving agent, for the mica schists above it are much disturbed. Dark trappean rocks full of hornblende have in many places burst through these schists, and appear in nodules on the surface. The highest rock seen is a fine sandstone of closer grain than that at Tete, and quite metamorphosed where it comes

into touch with the igneous rocks below it.   It sometimes
gives place to quartz and reddish-clay schists, much baked
by heat.   This is the usual geological condition of the right
bank of the river.   On the other side we pass over masses
of porphyrytic trap in contact with the same mica schists,
and these probably give the soil the great fertility we
observed.   The great body of the mountain is syenite.   So
much mica is washed into the stream that one sees myriads
of particles floating and glancing in the sun.

Our object was to get away to the north-north-west;
proceed parallel with Lake Nyasa, but at a considerable
distance west of it, so as to pass by the Mazitu without
contact; ascertain whether any large river flowed into it
from the west; visit Lake Moero if time permitted; and
collect information about the trade on the great slave route,
which crosses the lake at the southern end and at Tsenga
and Kota-Kota.

The Great Central African Slave Route

We arrived at Kota-Kota bay in the afternoon of 10th
September 1863,[1] and sat down under a magnificent fig-tree
with leaves ten inches long by five broad, about a quarter
of a mile from the village of Juma ben Saidi, whom we had
met on our first exploration of the lake.

We had rested but a short time when Juma came to salute
us and invited us to take up our quarters in his village, and
presented us with food.   We returned his visit the following
day and found him engaged in building a dhow.

When we met these same Arabs in 1861 they had few
attendants.   Now they had in the village and in the adjoining country 1,500 souls.   Tens of thousands had fled to
them for protection, and all their influence must be attributed to guns.   This crowding of refugees, with the hope
of security, is very common in this region, and knowledge
of this makes our hopes beat high for the success of a peaceful
mission on the shores of the lake.   The rate, however, at

[1] *The Zambezi and its Tributaries*, page 511.

which these people will perish in the next famine, or be exported by Juma and others, will, we fear, depopulate these parts. Hunger will compel them to sell each other.

Leaving Kota-Kota we turned west on the great slave route to Katanga's and Casembe's country in Londa. Juma lent us his servant Selele to lead us for the first day's march. This took us over a rich well-cultivated plain which was succeeded by highlands, undulating, stony, and covered with scraggy trees. Many banks of well-rounded shingle appeared. The disintegration of the rocks, now going on, does not round off the angles; they are split up by heat and cold into angular fragments. On these high downs we crossed the River Kaombe. Beyond it we came among the upland vegetation—rhododendrons, proteas, masuko, and molompi. At the foot of the hill Kasuko-Suko we found the River Bua, running north to join the Kaombe. We had to go a mile out of our way for a ford. The various streams crossed in this journey led us to the conclusion that no large river ran into the north end of the lake. No such affluent was needed to account for the Shire's perennial flow.

In looking forward we seemed to be ascending the long slope of a range of mountains, but the nearer view consisted of a succession of beautiful tree-covered hills. The narrow footpaths were perpetually leading up steep inclines and down descents to running rills, whose sides were fringed with large evergreen trees. The deciduous trees, having parted with their leaves, were enjoying the rest of winter, though only twelve degrees from the equator.

On 15th September we reached the top of the ascent, which had often made us puff and blow as if broken-winded. We had now reached the summit of Ndonda, where the boiling point of water showed an altitude of 3,400 feet above the sea. Looking back we had a magnificent view of the lake, but the haze prevented our seeing beyond the sea horizon. The scene was beautiful, but it was impossible to dissociate the lovely landscape from the sad fact that this was part of the great slave route now actually in use. By this road many 'ten thousands' had seen 'the sea,' but with sinking hearts, for the universal idea among the captive gangs is that they are going to be fattened and eaten by the whites.

Looking westward we perceived that what from below had the appearance of mountains, was only the edge of a tableland, which though at first undulating soon became smooth and sloped towards the centre of the country. To the south a prominent mountain called Chipata, and to the south-west another called Ngalla, by which the Bua is said to rise, gave character to the landscape. To the north, masses of hills prevented our seeing more than eight or ten miles.

The air, which was exhilarating to Europeans, had the opposite effect on five men who had been born and reared in the malaria of the delta of the Zambezi. No sooner had they reached the edge of the plateau than they lay down prostrate and complained of pains all over. The temperature was not much below that on the shores of the lake. Of the symptoms they complained of, nothing could be made, and yet it was obvious that they had good reason for saying they were ill. Medicine had no effect, and in two days one of them did actually, in consequence, die.

The power ascribed to certain medicines made from plants known only to the initiated, is the most prominent feature in African religion. According to their belief there is not only a specific to every ill that flesh is heir to, but for every woe of the wounded spirit. The good spirits of the departed, *Azimo* or *Bazimo*, may be propitiated by medicines or honoured by offerings of beer and meal, or anything they loved while in the body. A man with a headache was heard to say: 'My departed father is now scolding me. I feel his power in my head'; and then was seen to go aside and offer a little food on a leaf, and pray, looking upwards, to where he supposed his father to be. They speak of the spirit world with much reverence, and court the shade and silence for their worship.

The primitive African faith seems to be that there is one Almighty Maker of Heaven and Earth, and that he has given the various plants of the earth to be employed as mediators between him and the spirit world, where all who have ever been or died continue to live; that sin consists of offences against their fellow men either here or amongst the departed; and that death is often the punishment of guilt such as witchcraft.   Their idea of moral evil differs in no respect from ours, but they consider themselves amenable only to inferior beings and not to the Supreme.   Evil speaking, hatred, lying, disobedience to parents, neglect of them, are said by the intelligent to have all been known as sin, as well as theft, murder, or adultery, before they knew aught of Europeans or their teaching.   The only addition to their moral code is that it is wrong to have more wives than one.   This, until the arrival of Europeans, never entered into their minds even as a doubt.

Everything not to be accounted for by common causes, whether good or evil, is ascribed to the Deity.   Men are inseparably connected with the spirits of the departed, and when one dies he is believed to have joined the hosts of his ancestors.   All the Africans we have met are as firmly convinced of their future existence as of their present life. When they pass into the unseen world they do not seem to be possessed with any fear of punishment.   The utensils placed on the grave are all broken, to indicate that they will never be used again.   The body is put in the grave in a sitting posture, and the hands folded in front.

We could hardly obtain food for the men, but neither want of food nor dysentery nor slave wars would have prevented our working our way to the lake (Bemba) had we had time, but we had received orders from the Foreign Office to take the *Pioneer* down to the sea in the previous April.   The salaries of all the men ceased by 31st December.

We decided, therefore, to return, and though we had

afterwards the mortification to find that we were detained two full months at the ship, waiting for the flood, the chagrin was lessened by the consciousness that we had acted in a fair, honest, and above-board manner.

Thus concludes the account of the Zambezi Expedition, and it ends on a note of disappointment. As compared with his previous travels there seemed little to show and the cost had been heavy. Earl Russell was critical, if not indeed, for political reasons, unfriendly, and even Livingstone's best friends were not enthusiastic. That made all the more bitter the thought that if he had been able to continue his last trip only a few stages farther west, he would have been able to bring to light the existence of the great Lake Bangweulu (Bemba), of which he had heard so much. That would have been a success sufficient to outweigh a score of failures. As it was he had sorrowfully to accept the general verdict, and admit that the expedition had not achieved its purpose.

Later and better-informed opinion, however, reverses this judgment completely. There is now no question that, except perhaps from the point of view of mere exploration, the discoveries of this expedition were the most valuable that Livingstone made.

'There was, it is true, little that was spectacular in the discoveries, but their consequences far exceeded in importance those of his first journey. The expedition made history by discovering the central part of the great highland backbone which, beginning at the Red Sea, stretches to Cape Town. Out of this discovery all later colonization has grown.' [1]

It was while waiting dejectedly for the Shire waters to rise sufficiently to float the ships that the Doctor received news that must have seemed to him the keenest of all his disappointments. He learned that Bishop Tozer—the 'good Bishop Mackenzie's' successor—had decided to withdraw the mission to the coast. Livingstone had built so much of his hope for the uplift of the people of the Nyasa highlands on the mission, that he felt the withdrawal as a breach of trust, and, as was his way, he expressed his feeling strongly.

---

[1] See *Livingstone the Liberator*, page 275.

It is now generally admitted the decision was wise. The district had become completely disorganized as a result of the slave-trade, and the work of the mission could not have been, at that time, conducted without the prospect of occasional resort to arms, a policy manifestly inconsistent with missionary aims.

A Foolhardy Adventure at Sea

After a hurried visit to Sena, in order to settle with Major Sicard and Senhor Ferrão for the supplies we had drawn, we proceeded down the Zambezi, and were fortunate in meeting on 13th February 1864 H.M.S. *Orestes*.[1] She was joined next day by H.M.S. *Ariel*. The *Orestes* took the *Pioneer*, and the *Ariel* the *Lady Nyasa*, in tow for Mozambique.

On the 16th a circular storm proved the sea-going qualities of the *Lady Nyasa*, for on this day a hurricane struck the *Ariel* and drove her nearly backwards at the rate of six knots an hour. The towing hawser wound round her screw and stopped her engines. No sooner had she recovered from this shock than she was again taken aback on another tack, and driven stem on towards the *Lady Nyasa*'s broadside. We who were on board the little vessel saw no chance of escape unless the crew of the *Ariel* should heave ropes when the big ship went over us, but she glided past our bow and we breathed again freely.

Captain Chapman, though his engines were disabled, crossed our bows again and again, dropping a cask with a line to give us another hawser. We might never have picked it up had not a Krooman jumped overboard and fastened a second line to the cask, and then we drew the hawser on board and were again in tow. During the whole time the little vessel never shipped a green sea. When the *Ariel* pitched forward we could see a large part of the bottom. When the stern went down we could see all her deck. A boat hung on her stern davits was stove in by the

[1] *The Zambezi and its Tributaries*, page 578.

K

waves. The officers on board the *Ariel* thought it was all over with us. Captain Chapman pronounced the *Lady Nyasa* the finest little sea boat they had ever seen.

On 16th April we steamed out of Mozambique, and reached Zanzibar in a week. We were anxious to dispose of the *Lady Nyasa*, and the only market we could reach was Bombay, though Dr Seward was very doubtful if we could get to India. We resolved to run the risk of getting there before the breaking of the monsoon. The break occurs usually between the end of May and 12th June. So after taking on board fourteen tons of coal, we started on 30th April from Zanzibar.

Our complement consisted of seven native Zambezians, two boys, and four Europeans, namely one stoker, one sailor, one carpenter, and myself as navigator. The *Lady Nyasa* had shown herself to be a good sea boat. The natives had proved themselves capital sailors, though before volunteering not one of them had seen the sea. They were not picked men but were taken at random from several hundreds who offered to accompany us. Their wages were ten shillings per mensem, and it was curious to observe that, so eager were they to do their duty, that only one of them lay down from seasickness during the whole voyage. They took in and set sail very cleverly in a short time, and would climb out along a boom, reeve a rope through a block, and come back with the rope in their teeth, though at each lurch the performer was dipped in the sea. The sailor and the carpenter, though anxious to do their utmost, had a week's severe illness each, and were unfit for duty.

It is pleasant enough to take the wheel for an hour or two, or even for a watch, but when it comes to be every alternate four hours, it is utterly wearisome. We set our black men to steer, showing them which arm of the compass needle was to be kept towards the vessel's head, and soon three of them could manage very well, and they only needed watching. We passed up to about ten degrees north of the equator and then steamed out from the coast.

Zanzibar in Livingstone's day

Here Maury's wind chart showed that the calm belt had
long been passed, but we were in it still, and instead of a
current carrying us north, we had a contrary current that
bore us every day four miles to the south.   We steamed
as long as we dared, knowing that we must use our engines
on the coast of India.

After losing many days tossing on the silent sea with
innumerable dolphins, flying fish, and sharks around us, we
had six days of strong breezes.   Then calms again tried
our patience, and the near approach of that period 'the
break of the monsoon,' in which we believed that no boat
could live, made us sometimes think our epitaph would be:
'Left Zanzibar 30th April 1864, and never more heard of.'

At last, in the beginning of June, chronometers showed
that we were near the Indian coast.   The black men began
to dance for joy as they saw seaweed and serpents floating
past.   The serpents are peculiar to these parts and are
mentioned in the sailing directions.   We ventured to pre-
dict that we should see land next morning, and at midday
the coast hove in sight, wonderfully like the coast of Africa
before the rains begin.   Then a haze covered the land, and
a heavy swell beat towards it.   A rock was seen, and a
latitude showed it to be the Choule Rock.   Making that
a fresh starting point, we soon found the lightship, and then
the forest of masts loomed through the haze of Bombay
harbour.

We had sailed 2,500 miles.   The vessel was so small that
no one noticed our arrival.

The *Lady Nyasa* reached port only just in time.   The monsoon
broke in full force a day or two after.   Tight little ship as she
was, she was quite unsuited to face the fury of the north-west
monsoon.   She swung round at every sharp gust and all but
capsized.   It had been a most foolhardy trip, and the diary on
which the journal is based showed that it had been much more
risky and anxious than is here indicated.

The boat was so insignificant in size that she slipped into
Bombay harbour, under cover of a sea fog, quite unnoticed.

274 THE ZAMBEZI AND ITS TRIBUTARIES, 1858–64

Livingstone's arrival, when known, created no small stir. He became the guest of Sir Bartle Frere, the Governor, and was received with every honour. Especially did the Bombay merchants acclaim him. They controlled, at that time, most of the East African trade, and the Explorer looked to them to assist him by the extension of an honourable trade that would help to counteract the slave traffic.

The Doctor's stay in Bombay was brief. He was anxious about his family, of whose fortunes he had had no recent news. He had no definite plans for the future beyond a determination to return in some capacity to his beloved Africa.

He was received by the British public once more with fervent enthusiasm, though he was not perhaps quite so much the general hero he had been. Official circles, notably Lord Russell, were cold. His mother was still alive, but grown senile, and he was soon to learn that his eldest boy, Robert,[1] who had run off to America and joined in the civil war there, had died of wounds received in battle.

Once again he was overwhelmed with university and civic honours, and was constantly and wearisomely in demand as a speaker. These public appearances he found trying, and he refused them when he could. An important exception was the historic speech he made before the British Association at Bath in September 1864, on the connection of the Portuguese Government with the slave traffic. He opened out on them his full broadside. Inevitably his charges were resented in Portugal, and he was subjected to bitter personal attacks in reply.

Some time during this furlough period the plan was mooted, probably originally at the suggestion of Sir Roderick Murchison, that Livingstone should be sent out by the Royal Geographical Society to explore the sources of the great African rivers—especially of the Nile—a matter much in the thought of geographers at that time. The Doctor accepted eagerly. The urge to explore was still as strong in him as ever. It suited him well that he was to go alone, and that, while he would retain his position as consul, he would still be counted a missionary.

Arrangements were made without delay, but the financial

[1] See *Livingstone the Liberator*, page 282 et seq.

provision was most inadequate.   The R.G.S. put up only £500, and the Government the same.   If it had not been for the munificence of the old friend of his student days, Young of Kelly, now a wealthy man, the scheme would have been still-born.

Livingstone devoted the last eight months to the writing of this, his second book.   The composition was done under ideal circumstances, and thereby hangs a romantic tale.   One day, back in the Kolobeng time, news was brought to Livingstone that a 'white traveller' was lying seriously ill some distance away.   He hurried to help, and was in time to save the sick man's life.   He was W. F. Webb, a well-known hunter.   The friendship thus made continued through life, and led to an invitation to stay at Newstead Abbey, Lord Byron's old home, which had come into the possession of the Webb family.   The visit lasted seven months and was a restful time.   The book, *The Zambezi and its Tributaries*, was written during this interval. It was published after he had sailed for Bombay.   The reception was hearty and the first edition sold quickly, but it was not greeted with quite the enthusiasm that was given to *Missionary Travels*.

BOOK FOUR

The Central African Rivers
1866–1873

XXIV

To Lake Nyasa from the East

LIVINGSTONE left Britain for the last time in August 1865. He passed through Egypt on his way to India, and saw the beginnings of the work on the Suez Canal. In Bombay his chief business was to sell the little *Lady Nyasa*, and this he did, though at a disappointing price.[1]

The Governor, Sir Bartle Frere, sympathized actively with the new enterprise, and made him his unofficial representative. He granted him a free passage to Zanzibar on the luxuriously equipped vessel, the *Thule*, with instructions to hand the steamer over to the Sultan as a gift from the Government of India. The gift was received with much gratification, and a firman was presented to Livingstone by the Sultan, that commended him to all his subjects. This document proved of great use. While in Zanzibar the Missionary visited the famous slave market of which he had heard so much.

And so it seemed to the Explorer as if this, which was to be his last journey, had begun under the most happy circumstances. He was back in the bush he had craved for, and among the people he loved, and he was alone and thus free from the restrictions that European company put upon him. But in his enthusiasm he underestimated the difficulties that lay before him. He thought he could finish the task in two years. It took him seven, and then was not completed.

He was now fifty-one years of age, but actually older than his years. To all appearance his furlough had restored him to full health, but the extreme hardships that he had exposed himself to had depleted his reserves of strength. 'I am very old and grey,' he told Oswell. 'My face is wrinkled like a gridiron. A barber offered to dye my hair for ten and six! I must be very good-tempered, for I did not offer to fight him!'[2]

---

[1] The price did not matter. The Indian bank in which he deposited the money failed, and he lost it all.

[2] *Livingstone the Liberator*, page 292.

The first task was to recruit sufficient and suitable porters, and it cannot be said that he was successful in this essential matter. A considerable part of the diary of the first eight months of the travel is filled, rather monotonously, with the record of weary struggles against the laziness and cruelty of the unsatisfactory group that he eventually gathered at Zanzibar. To obviate repetition, a short description of the men is given here. They were a most heterogeneous crowd, with no mutual loyalties and, with the exception of the faithful few, no attachment to the Leader.

First, there were thirteen Indian sepoys of a marine battalion. They, rather curiously, were supposed to have special skill with draught animals. They proved a completely unreliable lot and were most brutal in their handling of the cattle. Then there were ten men from the Johanna Islands. They behaved much as the sepoys did, and after eight months deserted in a body. Besides these there were nine so-called 'Nassick' (Nazik) boys; freed negro slaves who had been trained in India. These were better though, not unnaturally, towards the end of the interminable trek they grew disgruntled and mutinous.

Then there remained four or five faithfuls, gathered mostly from his old 'attendants,' of whom two, Susi and Chuma, have become proverbial for their unshakable loyalty.

The reader will notice that Livingstone showed his characteristic tenacity by once more trying to prove the navigability of the Rovuma river, and its connection with Lake Nyasa, hoping thus, as we know, to 'dish' the Portuguese.

New Conditions of Travel

It was not long before the Explorer sensed a change, and an increasing hardness, in the circumstances of the march that lay before him. For this stiffening there were various reasons. The tribes that he was to meet were different, and much more difficult to manage, than in his previous experience. The southern districts, that he knew so well, were in the main covered by large tribes and governed by powerful chiefs. Hence fighting between the groups was rare, and friendship with a big chieftain carried a widespread advantage. But in the central regions there were many small tribes, and these were often

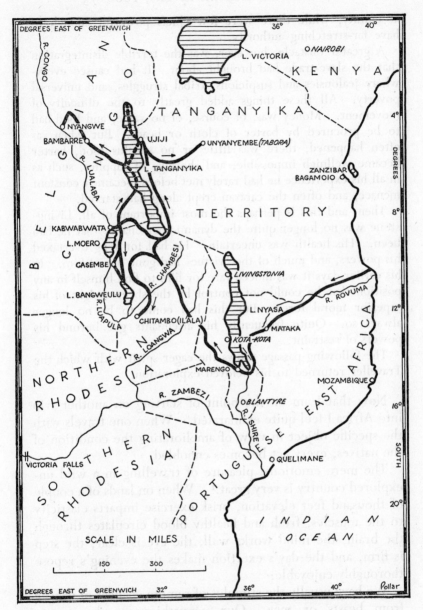

The Last Journey

at enmity, while there were few chiefs powerful enough to have far-stretching authority.

A greater obstacle, however, was the terrible disintegration that the slave-trade had brought about. It had caused everywhere jealousies and suspicions, tribal struggles, and universal poverty. All these things added greatly to the difficulty of movement. Money was, of course, of no value, and food had to be procured by barter of cloth or beads. But when, as often happened, there was little or no surplus food, barter became wellnigh impossible, and shortage of supplies, such as in all his experience he had rarely met before, became a constant menace, and often the caravan crept along half starved.

Then, and this is perhaps the most important of all, Livingstone was no longer quite the dynamic personality that he had been. His health was uncertain. He had for long overtaxed his powers, and much of the 'virtue' had gone out of him. In his earlier days it was indeed rare for him to find himself in any position that he could not control by the sheer weight of his superior moral force. But this had come to be no longer always so. Quite frequently his attendants got beyond his powers of restraint.

The following passage shows the eager spirit with which the Traveller returned to his beloved exploration.

Now that I am on the point of starting on another trip into Africa I feel quite exhilarated. When one travels with the specific object in view of ameliorating the condition of the natives, every act becomes ennobled.

The mere emotional pleasure of travelling in a wild unexplored country is very great.[1] When on lands of a couple of thousand feet elevation, brisk exercise imparts elasticity to the muscles, fresh and healthy blood circulates through the brain, the mind works well, the eye is clear, the step is firm, and the day's exertion makes the evening's repose thoroughly enjoyable.

We have usually the stimulus of remote chances of danger from beasts or men. Our sympathies are drawn out towards our humble, hardy companions by a community

[1] *Livingstone's Last Journals*, vol. i, page 13.

of interests, and it may be of perils, which make us all friends.   The effect of travel on a man whose heart is in the right place is that the mind is made more self-reliant. It becomes more confident of its own resources—there is greater presence of mind.   The body is soon well knit, the muscles and limbs grow hard as a board, and seem to have no fat.   The countenance is bronzed and there is no dyspepsia.

Africa is a most wonderful country for appetite, and it is only when one gloats over marrow bones or elephants' feet that indigestion is possible.   No doubt much toil is involved, and fatigue, of which travellers in the more temperate climes can form but a faint conception; but the sweat of one's brow is no longer a curse when one works for God. It proves a tonic to the system and is actually a blessing. No one truly appreciates the charm of repose, unless he has undergone severe exertion.

Geographical Note

THE EAST AFRICAN PLATEAU

In his last expedition, Livingstone found himself in an environment rather different from that which he had previously experienced in Africa. On the whole, it was a better environment: the tragedy is that by now Livingstone was too spent physically to be able to take advantage of it.

In many ways, East Africa is unique: it has elements in common with the rest of Africa, but in sum it stands apart. The same age-old smooth surface, worn in some of the world's oldest rocks, can be distinguished here, but it does not, as elsewhere, extend in featureless monotony over thousands of square miles. Powerful earth movements heaved up the area so that it is sometimes called the roof of Africa—it certainly is the watershed, for its rivers flow to the Mediterranean and to the Indian and Atlantic oceans. Under the strain, however, the old surface sagged and cracked. Where it sagged, wide shallow basins were formed, of which the greatest is now occupied by Lake Victoria and one of the lesser by Lake Bangweulu. Neither is deep; the latter in fact is so shallow that its disappearance by infilling with sediments and decayed vegetation must occur within foreseeable time. It now has less open water and more swamp than in Livingstone's time, though fluctuations in papyrus growth may be partly responsible. Elsewhere, where cracking took place, the great East African rifts, beyond comparison on earth, were formed. From Lake Nyasa one branch runs north and west and holds in its hollows Lakes Tanganyika, Kivu, Edward, and Albert; the other runs due north through drier country (and is therefore poorer in lakes, although the basins are there), by Lake Rudolf out to the Red Sea, and so to the Dead Sea and Jordan which are part of the system. Between and around the rifts, the old surface was fragmented and disarranged, its component parts tilting in every direction, some moving up, some down, to the great disorganization of the drainage. Lake Moero occupies one such hollow formed by

284

the up-tilting of a block of the earth's crust in the path of a pre-existing river, but there are many other examples, not necessarily so completely enclosed (or so well watered) as to form lakes. The resulting inconsequential behaviour of the streams and the absence of a dominant pattern is reflected in the apparently confused track of Livingstone's expedition.

There is, however, yet another element in the landscape— the great volcanoes poured out from vents associated with the major earth fractures, and forming little islands of high ground with elevations among the world's greatest. Though he knew of them, Livingstone refused to avail himself of the climatic relief they offered, and concentrated on his main objective— the discovery of the Nile-Congo headwaters.

The region thus has a richer variety of topography than is usual in Africa. Great slabs of the smooth old surface are to be found, but where their edges are up-tilted, the steepening of streams has brought about a deep incision of their valleys, and elsewhere also, where drainage channels have been upset, there are falls, rapids, and gorges. Though the whole area is subjected to similar climatic factors, mainly the monsoon and trades from the Indian Ocean, the variety of altitude and exposure causes local variations in rainfall and thus in natural vegetation. While most of the area is under scrub, there are on the one hand pockets and sometime blocks of park-land and even forest, and on the other steppe and even desert. This varied environment offers richer opportunities both in farming and stock-rearing, and the population of the area is now, and probably was in Livingstone's time, denser than in the monotony of either the forests of the Congo or the high grassy plains of the south.

In yet another respect this section of East Africa is unique. It is a cross-roads. Africa was peopled from the north-east: successive waves of immigrants moved south but not over a front of continental width, for the forests of the Congo blocked two-thirds of the way, constricting the routes into the east. As might be expected, representatives of the successive migrations settled in the area and contributed to its variety. Although high and presenting a bold front to the east, and though there is no major river-valley, many smaller valleys break through the scarp and render access from the east coast fairly easy. The coast itself is not typically African, and with its estuaries and islands and sheltering coral reefs, presents quite a contrast to the smooth harbourless coasts to north and south, and indeed elsewhere in Africa. Bases for penetration exist then, and in addition, the regularly reversing monsoon wind, mentioned earlier, supplied the motive power for an overseas commerce to India, the Persian Gulf, and Arabia. This commerce was in the hands of Arabs, who regularly penetrated from their major base at Zanzibar right to Lake Tanganyika and beyond, and even on occasions to the Atlantic. Outside influences, then, were widespread, as is evidenced by the occurrence all over the region of the language—Swahili—and the religion—Islam—of the coast. The major axis of penetration, now followed by the Dar es Salaam–Tabora–Kigoma railway, was even in Livingstone's time a well-beaten path, and one which afforded him a relatively quick, easy, and regular means of communication with the coast. Unfortunately, of course, the majority of the Arab traders were seriously brutalized by the slave-trade, and their contacts with the outside world in Livingstone's time served but to render the natives sophisticated in the worse sense of the word.

XXV

The Rovuma again

19th March 1866. We start this morning at 10 a.m.

I have a dhow to take my animals: six camels, three buffaloes and a calf, two mules, and four donkeys.

I have thirteen sepoys, ten Johanna men, nine Nassick boys, two Shupanga men, two Waiyaus, Wekatani, and Chuma.

I trust the Most High may prosper me in this work, granting me influence in the eyes of the heathen and helping me to make my influence beneficial to them.

23rd March. I went up the left bank to see if the gullies had altered so as to allow the camels to cross. We found three formidable ones, so thick with bush date-palms and twining bamboos and hooked thorns that one could scarcely get along. Farther inland it was sticky mud, thickly planted over with mangrove roots, and gullies in whose soft banks one sank up to the ankles. No camel could have moved.

24th March. During the night it occurred to me that we should be in a mess if, after exploration, we should find no path. The captain of the dhow strongly recommended the port of Mikindany, as near to the Rovuma, Nyasa, and the country I wished to visit, besides being a good landing-place.

Livingstone took the captain's advice, and had his unwieldy caravan transferred to Mikindany Bay, a fine harbour which lies twenty-five miles north of the Rovuma. Here he hired a house at 'four dollars a month, landed all the goods,' and completed his arrangements. His plan was to go some miles inland at this point and then turn south, thus avoiding difficult country. The party was guided by a Somali guide called Ben Ali. Soon troubles began. The buffaloes and camels were bitten by the tsetse-fly which abounded on the route. The jungle was heavy and close, and much cutting of the bush was needed to widen the paths. They pushed on but slowly.

We began to descend the northern slope down to the Rovuma, and a glimpse could occasionally be had of the country. It seemed covered with great masses of dark green forest. More frequently our view was restricted to a few yards. Taking bearings was difficult. So long as we remained within the vegetation that is fed from the Indian Ocean, the steaming smothery air, the dank, rank, luxurious vegetation, made me feel like struggling for existence, and no more capable of taking bearings than if I had been in a hogshead and observing through the bung-hole.

14th April. To-day we succeeded in reaching the Rovuma where some very red cliffs appear on the opposite side, and close to where the *Pioneer* turned back in 1861.

Our course now lay westward along the side of that ragged outline of tableland which we had seen from the river as flanking both sides. Sometimes we went round the hills, sometimes we rose and descended their western sides, and then a great deal of woodcutting was required. We came on many gardens and could buy plenty of rice for the sepoys.

18th April. Ben Ali (the guide) misled us away to the north in spite of my protests. He declared it was the proper path. We had much woodcutting, and found that our course that day and next was to enable him to visit and return from one of his wives, a comely Makondé woman. He brought her to call on me and I had to be polite to her, though we had lost a day by the zigzag. This is one of the ways in which the Arabs gain influence. A great many light-coloured people are strewn among the Makondé, and only one of them had Arab hair.

19th April. We were led over a hill again and on to the level of the plateau, and tasted water of agreeable coldness for the first time this journey. The people, especially the women, are very rude, and the men are very eager to be employed as woodcutters. Very merry they are at it, and every now and then one raises a cheerful shout in which all join. Tsetse are biting the buffaloes again. Elephants, hippopotami, and pigs are the only game here. The tsetse-fly feeds on them.

21st April. After a great deal of cutting we reached the valley of Mehambwé to spend Sunday. All were glad that it had come round again. A wall-eyed, ill-looking fellow that helped to urge on the attack on our first visit in 1861,[1] and the man to whom I gave cloth to prevent a collision, came to us disguised in a jacket. I knew him well but said nothing to him.

25th April. A serpent bit our dog Jack above the eye. The upper eyelids swelled very much, but no other symptoms were to be seen and next day the swelling was gone. The serpent was either harmless or the quantity of venom small. The pace of the camels is distressingly slow.

28th April. The hills to the north now retire out of sight. A gap in the southern plateau gives passage to a small river which rises in a lakelet of some size, eight or ten miles inland. The river and the lakelet are both called Nangadi. The latter is deep and abounds in large fish. The people who live here are Mabiha.

30th April. Many ulcers have burst forth on the camels. Some seem old dhow bruises. They come back from pasture bleeding in a way that no rubbing against a tree would account for. I am sorry to suspect foul play. The buffaloes and mules are badly used, but I cannot be always there to prevent it.

The Upper Reaches of the Rovuma
1st to 3rd May. We now came along through a country free of wood and could move on without perpetual cutting

---

[1] *The Zambezi and its Tributaries*, Chap. XXI.

and clearing. It is beautiful to get a good glimpse out on the surrounding scenery, though it still seems nearly all covered with great masses of umbrageous foliage, mostly of a deep green colour, for nearly all the individual trees possess glossy leaves like laurel. We passed a gigantic specimen of the gum-copal tree.

Our poodle dog Chitané chased the village dogs with unrelenting fury. His fierce looks inspired terror among the wretched pariah dogs of yellow and white colour; and those looks were entirely owing to the difficulty of distinguishing at which end his head or tail lay. He enjoyed the chase of the yelping curs immensely, but if one of them had turned he would have bolted the other way.

12th May. About 4' east-north-east of Matawatawa, our former turning point.[1] We halted at the village. A pleasant-looking lady, with her face profusely tattooed, came forward with a bunch of sweet reed and laid it at my feet saying: 'I met you here before'—pointing to the spot on the river where we turned   I remember her coming then, and that I asked the boat to wait while she went to bring us a basket of food, and no return made. It is sheer kindness that prompts them sometimes, though occasionally people do make presents with a view to getting a larger one in return. She had a quiet dignified manner both in talking and walking, and I now gave her a small looking-glass; and she went and brought me her only fowl and a basket of cucumber seed, from which oil is made. The carriers are very useless from hunger, and we could not buy anything for them, for the country is all dried up.

19th May. Coming on with what carriers we could find at the crossing place, we reached the confluence without seeing it; and Matumora being about two miles up the Loendi, we sent over to him for aid. He came over this morning early—a tall well-made man with a somewhat severe expression of countenance. He took us over the Loendi,

---

[1] See *The Zambezi and its Tributaries*, Chap. XXI.

which is decidedly the parent stream of the Rovuma. Both
rivers are rapid, shoal, and sandy. Matumora says that both
the Loendi and the Rovuma come out of Lake Nyasa.
A boat could not ascend, however, because there are many
waterfalls. It is strange if all this is a myth.

20th May. Abraham, one of the Nassick boys, came up and
said he had been sent by the sepoys to say that they would
come no farther; it was with the utmost difficulty that they
had come so far, and that the havildar had forced them on.
They would not obey him—would not get up in the
mornings, lay in the paths, gave their pouches and muskets
to the natives to carry, and made themselves utterly useless.
The black buffalo is dead, one camel ditto, and one mule
is left behind, ill. Were I not aware of the existence of the
tsetse I would say they had died of sheer bad treatment and
hard work.

19th June. We passed a woman tied by the neck to
a tree, and dead. The people of the country explained
that she had been unable to keep up with the other slaves
in a gang, and her master had determined that she should
not become the property of anyone else, if she recovered
after resting for a time. I may say that we saw others tied
in a similar manner. The explanation we invariably got
was that the Arab, who owned these victims, was enraged
at losing his money by the slaves being unable to walk, and
gave vent to his spleen by murdering them.

20th June. Having returned to Metaba, we were told by the
chief that no one had grain to sell but himself,[1] that he had

---

[1] *Food shortage.* The chief trouble was that the slave traffic has so ruined
the country that the tribes had no grain to spare, and would not sell for ordinary
trade goods. Among the relics on view at the memorial at Livingstone's
birth-place, Blantyre, Scotland, is an old coat that has this illuminating story
attached:
'In 1877 Bishop Chauncey Maples met at Newala, in the uplands of the
Rovuma valley, an old man who with much ceremony presented him with a
coat, mouldy and partially eaten by white ants, that had been given him, he
said, ten years before by a white man "who treated black men as brothers,

plenty of powder and common cloth from the Arabs, and
that our only chance with him was parting with our finer
cloths. He magnified the scarcity in front, in order to
induce us to buy all that we could from him. But he gave
me an ample meal of porridge and guinea-fowl before starting.

26th June. My last mule died. In coming along (after
leaving Chirikaloma's village) we were loudly accosted by
a well-dressed woman who had just had a very heavy slave-
stick put on her neck. She called in such an authoritative
tone to us to witness the flagrant injustice of which she was
the victim, that all the men stood still to hear the case.
She was a near relative of Chirikaloma, and was going up
the river to her husband, when the old man (at whose house
she was now a prisoner) caught her and took her servant
away from her, and kept her in the degraded state we saw.
The withes with which she was bound were green and sappy.
The old man said in justification that she was running away
from Chirikaloma, and he would be offended with him if he
did not secure her. I asked the officious old gentleman
what he expected to receive from the chief, and he said
'Nothing.'

Several slaver-looking fellows came about, and I felt sure
the woman had been seized in order to sell her to them;
so I gave the captor a cloth to give to Chirikaloma, if he
were offended, and told him to say I, feeling ashamed to
see one of his relatives in a slave stick, had released her and
would take her to her husband. She is evidently a lady
amongst them, having many fine beads, and some strung on
elephant's hair. She has a good deal of spirit too, for on
being liberated she went into the old man's house and took
her basket and calabash. A virago of a wife shut the door
and tried to prevent her, as well as cut off her beads, but

and whose memory would be cherished; a short man with bushy moustache
and keen piercing eye, whose ways were always gentle, and whose words
were always kind, whom, as a leader, it was a privilege to follow, and who
knew the way to the heart of all men." ' From *Livingstone the Liberator,*
page 302.

she resisted like a good one, and my men thrust the door open and let her out, but minus her slave.

29th June. The woman whom we had liberated—Akosakone was her name—now arrived at the residence of her husband. She behaved like a lady all through, sleeping at a fire apart from the men. The ladies of the different villages we passed consoled with her, and she related to them the indignity that had been done to her. Besides this she did us many services. She bought food for us, because having a good address, we saw that she could get double what any of our men could purchase for the same cloth. She took leave of us with many expressions of thankfulness, and we were glad that we had not mistaken her position, or lavished kindness on the undeserving.

The farther up the river they moved the clearer it became that the Rovuma was becoming more and more impossible for navigation, and that, in consequence, Livingstone's confident hope that this stream might supersede the Zambezi as the waterway into the interior, was without foundation. He says hardly anything about this in his journal, but the disappointment must have been bitter.

As they approached Mtarika's place the surface became increasingly mountainous. This man, an important local chief, is described as 'a big ugly man with a large mouth and receding forehead,' and as closely linked up with the slave traffic. All along the path there were innumerable signs of this infernal trade—human bones and slave sticks were everywhere. The constant difficulty they experienced in buying food showed that poverty had resulted. After a good eight days' march, however, and an approach to Mataka's town, prospects improved.

Welcome and Plenty
14th July. We found Mataka's town, Moembe, situated in an elevated valley surrounded by mountains. The houses numbered at least a thousand, and there were many villages around. The mountains were of a pleasant green.

Mataka kept us waiting some time on the veranda of his large square house, and then made his appearance smiling with his good-natured face.   He was about sixty years of age, dressed like an Arab, and if we may judge by the laughter with which his remarks were always greeted, some-what humorous.   He had never seen any but Arabs before, and he imitated them in everything.   Peas and tobacco were the chief products raised by irrigation, but batatas and maize were often planted.   English peas have been introduced.   The altitude is about 2,700 feet above the sea.

Mataka sent us a good meal of porridge and cooked beef. He has plenty of cattle and sheep, and next day sent us an abundance of milk.   We stand a good deal of staring un-moved though it is often accompanied by remarks by no means complimentary.   They think that we do not under-stand, and probably I do misunderstand them sometimes.

Some time after our arrival we heard that a number of Waiyau had, without our knowledge, gone to Nyasa, and in a foray had carried off cattle and people.   When they came with the spoil Mataka ordered them all to be sent back whence they had come.   I told the chief that his decision was the best piece of news I had heard in the country.   He was evidently pleased with my approbation.

The change from hard and scanty fare to the present plenty caused illness to several of our party.   I had tasted no animal food, except what turtle-doves and guinea-fowls could be shot, since we passed Matawatawa.

An immense tract of country lies uninhabited.   To the north-east of Moembe we have at least fifty miles of as fine land as can be seen anywhere, still bearing all the marks of having once supported a prodigious iron-smelting and grain-growing population.   The ridges on which they planted maize, beans, cassava, and sorghum still remain unlevelled, to attest the industry of the former inhabitants.   There is water in abundance.

The Waiyau are far from a handsome race, but they are not the prognathous beings one sees on the west coast either.

Their heads are of a round shape; compact forehead, not particularly receding; the *alae nasi* are flattened out; lips full. Their style of beauty is exactly that which was in fashion when the stone deities were made in the caves of Elephanta and Kenora near Bombay. The men are large strong-boned fellows, and capable of enduring great fatigue.

28th July. We proposed to start to-day, but Mataka said he was not ready yet. The flour had to be ground, and he had given us no meat. He had sent plenty of cooked food almost every day. He asked if we would slaughter the ox he would give here, or take it on. We preferred to kill it at once. He gave us men to guide us to Nyasa, telling us that his district extended all the way to the lake. In general the chiefs have shown an anxiety to promote our safety.

The country is a mass of mountains. On leaving Mataka we ascended considerably, and about the end of the first day's march, near Magola's village, the barometer showed our greatest altitude, about 3,400 feet above the sea.

When we ascended the Rovuma about sixty miles a great many pieces and blocks of silicified wood appeared on the surface of the soil at the bottom of the slope up the plateau. This in Africa is a sure indication of coal beneath. In the sands of the Loendi, pieces of coal are quite common.

30th July. A short march brought us to Pezimba's village, which consists of two hundred huts. A very large Arab slave party was close to our encampment, and I wished to speak to them, but as soon as they knew of our being near they set off in a pathless course, across country, and were six days in the wilderness. Next day we saw the encampment of another Arab party. It consisted of ten pens, each of which, from the number of fires it contained, may have held eighty or a hundred slaves.

XXVI

Round the South End of Lake Nyasa

8th August 1866. We came to the lake at the confluence of the Misinje, and felt grateful to the Hand that had protected us thus far on our journey. It was as if I had come back to an old home I had never expected to see again, and it was pleasant to bathe in the delicious waters once more, and hear the roar of the sea, and dash in the rollers. Temperature 71° at 8 a.m., while the air was 65°. I felt quite exhilarated.

Livingstone had at this point expected to have his party ferried across to the western side of the lake, thus saving a long detour. He had sent a letter to Jumbe, a chief on the farther side, who owned a dhow, but had received no reply. He was thus compelled to take the route round the south end of Nyasa. All the Arabs, from fear, kept out of his way. Such was his reputation.

13th September. In the course of this day's march we pushed close to the lake by Mount Gome, being within three miles of the end of the lake. We could see the whole plainly. There we first saw the Shire entrance, and there also we gazed on the broad waters of Lake Nyasa. Many hopes have been disappointed there. Far down on the right bank of the Zambezi lies the dust of her whose death changed all my prospects, and now, instead of a check being given to the slave-trade by lawful commerce on the lake, the slave dhows prosper.

In the evening we reached the village of Cherekalongwa on the brook Pamchololo, and were very jovially received with beer by the headman. The chief had heard much about us. He had been as far as Mozambique, but had never seen an Englishman before.

After nearly giving up the search for the point where Dr Roscher reached the lake, I discovered it in Lesséfa. He arrived at this point two months after we discovered Lake Nyasa. He deserves all the credit due to finding the way hither, but he travelled as an Arab, and no one suspected him to be anything else.

15th September. We are now a short distance south of the lake and might have gone west to Mosauka's to cross the Shire there, but I thought that my visit to Mukaté, a Waiyau chief still farther south, might do good. He still carries on raids against the Manganja at the instigation of the Arabs.

We marched three hours southwards, and then up the hills that flank all the lower parts of the lake. The population was very large, and all the heights, as far as the eye could reach, were covered with villages. The people live in plenty. Mukaté never saw a European before, and everything about us is an immense curiosity to his people.

We had long discussions about the slave-trade. It is but little that we can do but to lodge a protest in the heart against the vile system, and time will ripen it. At the present rate of destruction of the population the whole country will soon be desert.

18th September. We embarked the whole party in eight canoes, and went up the lake to the point of junction between it and the prolongation of Nyasa above it, called Massangano (meetings), which took us two hours.

Musa and the Johanna Men desert

21st September. We marched westward, making for the base of Cape Maclear. Two men employed as guides and carriers went along grumbling that their dignity was outraged by working. 'Only fancy. Waiyau carrying like slaves.' They went but a small distance, and taking advantage of my being in front, laid down their loads, and paid themselves. One of these was the havildar's bed and cooking things, the gallant havildar sitting and looking on.

He has never been of the slightest use. I found that he had been stealing and selling his ammunition, preparatory to returning to the coast.

It was probably at this point that Livingstone's patience with the sepoys gave out, and that he sent them back.

22nd to 24th September. The hills we crossed were about 700 feet above Nyasa, generally covered with trees. No people were seen. We had a Waiyau party with us; six handsomely attired women carried huge pots of beer for their husbands, who liberally invited us to partake. After seven hours' hard travelling we came to the village where we spent Sunday, by the torrent, Usangazi, and near the remarkable mountain, Namasi. Next day we went on two and a half miles to the village of Marengo, a very large one, situated at the eastern edge of the bottom of the heel of the lake. The chief is ill from a loathsome disease derived from the Arabs.

The bogs or earthern sponges of this country occupy a most important part of its physical geography, and probably explain the annual inundations of most of the rivers.[1] Wherever a plain, sloping towards a narrow opening in hills or higher ground exists, there we have conditions requisite for the formation of an African 'sponge.' The vegetation, not being of a healthy and peat-forming kind, falls down, rots, and then forms a rich black loam. In many cases a mass of this loam, two or three feet thick, rests on a bed of pure river sand, which is revealed by crabs and other aquatic animals bringing it to the surface. The black loam forms soft slush, and floats on the sand. The narrow opening prevents it from moving off in a landslip, but an oozing spring rises at that spot. All the pools in the lower portion of this spring-course are filled in the first rains, which happen south of the equator when the sun goes vertically over any spot. The second and greater rains happen in his

[1] This description should be noted in view of the constant references, in later travel farther north, to the obstruction caused by these 'sponges.'

course north again, when all the bogs and river-courses being wet, the supply runs off and forms the inundation. This was certainly the case as observed on the Zambezi and the Shire, and taking the different times for the sun's passage north of the equator, it explains the inundation of the Nile.

25th September. Marengo came dressed in a red figured silk shawl, and attended by ten court beauties who spread a mat for him, then a cloth above. He asked me to examine him inside a hut. He exhibited his loathsome skin disease, and the blotches with which he was covered made him appear very ugly.

26th September. An Arab told Musa yesterday that all the country in front was full of Mazitu, that forty-four Arabs and their followers had been killed by them at Kasungu, and he only escaped. Musa and all the Johanna men declared that they would go no farther. I took him to Marengo and asked the chief about the Mazitu. He explained that the disturbance was caused by the Manganja finding that Jumbe brought Arabs and ammunition into the country every year, and that their nation was being destroyed.

I explained to Musa that we should avoid the Mazitu. Marengo added: 'There are no Mazitu near where you are going.' But Musa's eyes stood out with terror, and he said: 'I no can believe that man.'

When we started, all the Johanna men walked off, leaving the goods on the ground. They have been such inveterate thieves that I am not sorry to get rid of them. For though my party is now inconveniently small, I could not trust them with flints in their guns, nor allow them to remain behind, for their object was invariably to plunder their loads.

The sequel to this incident is as follows:

Musa and the Johanna men reached Zanzibar safely, where, to cover up their desertion without forfeit of pay, they told a circumstantially concocted yarn describing the murder of Livingstone and his men. So watertight was the story that even Dr Kirk, now the consul here, was deceived. It was accepted, amid popular lamentation, by the authorities at home.

But there were some who doubted. Lieutenant E. D. Young, R.N.,[1] under whom Musa had worked on the Shire, knew him to be a liar of genius. Neither did Horace Waller nor Murchison credit the report. The result was that Young made a rapid run in a steel boat *The Search* up to the south end of Lake Nyasa, where he found abundant evidence to disprove the story. But meanwhile Livingstone had disappeared into deep central Africa, and it was not for over four years that he heard of the commotion that Musa had caused.

Moving North.   A Convivial Friend

28th September to 21st October. We reached Kimsusa, below Mount Mulundini of Kirk's range.[2]   The chief was absent, but came two days later and seemed glad to see an old friend. He brought an immense ram, which had either killed or seriously injured a man. The animal came tied to a pole to keep him off the man who held him, while a lot more carried him. He was prodigiously fat. This is the African way of showing love—plenty of fat and beer. He brought also a huge basket of *pombe*, the native beer, and another of porridge, and a pot of cooked meat. More food was brought to us than we could carry. Kimsusa said that by following my advice and not selling his people, his village was now three times its former size.

2nd October. Kimsusa made his appearance early with a huge basket of beer, eighteen inches high and fifteen inches in diameter. He served it out for a time, taking deep draughts himself, and becoming very loquacious in consequence. He took us to a dense thicket behind the town among a number of lofty trees. A space had been cleared, and we were

[1] See Notes on Persons, page 407.
[2] So named by Livingstone in recognition of Sir John Kirk's fine work.

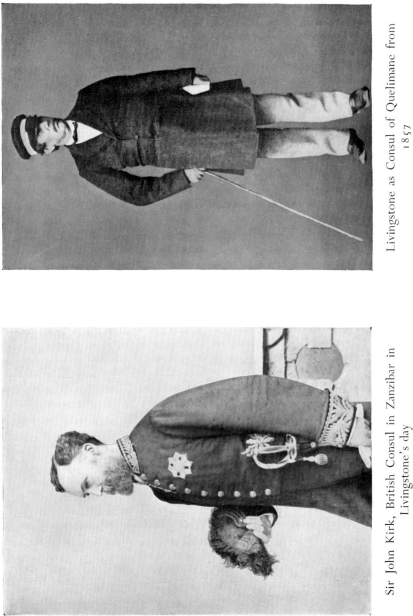

Livingstone as Consul of Quelimane from 1857

Sir John Kirk, British Consul in Zanzibar in Livingstone's day

taken into this shady spot as the one in which business of importance and secrecy is transacted. Another enormous basket of beer was brought here by his wives, but there was little need of it, for Kimsusa talked incessantly and no business was done.

3rd October. The chief came early, and sober. I rallied him on his previous loquacity, and said one ought to find time in the morning if business was to be done. He took it in good part, and one of his wives joined in bantering him.

I proposed to him to send men with me to the Babisa country, and I would pay them there, where they could buy ivory for him with the pay, and, bringing it back, he would be able to purchase clothing without selling his people. He said his people could not be trusted. They would not bring the pay or anything else back. Kimsusa said he would give me carriers to go up to Maravi, but he wished to be prepaid. To this I agreed, but even then he could not prevail on anyone to go.

5th October. The chief came early with an immense basket of beer as usual. We were ready to start, but he did not relish this, and asked us to stay over to-day, and he would himself go, with his wives, to-morrow. I was his friend, and he would not see me in difficulties without doing his utmost.

6th October. We marched about seven miles north to a village opposite the pass Tapiri. It was very hot. Kimsusa behaved like a king. His strapping wives came to carry the loads and shame his people. One wife carried beer, another meal, and as soon as we arrived cooking commenced. Kimsusa delights in showing me to his people as his friend. If I could have used his beer I could have put some fat on my bones, but it requires a strong digestion. Many of the chiefs and their wives live on it almost entirely.

In three and a quarter hours we had made a clear ascent

of 2,200 feet above the lake.   Kimsusa came to the bottom of the range.   I paid his wives for carrying our things. They had done well, and after we had gained the village where we slept, sang and clapped their hands vigorously till one o'clock in the morning, when I advised them to go to sleep.

9th October.   Both barometer and boiling point showed an altitude of 4,000 feet.   This is the hottest time of the year, but the air is delightfully clear and delicious.   The country is very fine, lying in long slopes with mountains rising all around, from 2,000 to 3,000 feet above this upland.   They are mostly jagged and rough.   The long slopes are nearly denuded of trees, and the patches of cultivation are so large and often squarish in form, that little imagination is required to transform the whole into the cultivated fields of England; but no hedgerows exist.   Just now the young leaves are out, but are not yet green.   In some lights they look brown, but when one is near them crimson prevails.   Yellowish green is met sometimes in young leaves, and brown, pink, and orange-red.   The soil is rich and the grass is generally short.

Gombwa, the chief, a laughing man, invited me to speak to his people, and I took the opportunity to give a general discourse on our relationship to our Father, and on the guilt of selling His children.

12th October.   We marched westerly, with a good deal of southing.   We came close to several squarish mountains having perpendicular sides.   One, called 'Ulazo pa Malungo,' is used by the people whose villages cluster round its base as a storehouse for grain.   Large granaries stand on its top, containing food to be used in case of war.   A large cow is kept up there, which is supposed capable of knowing, and letting the owners know, when war is coming.

We started, with Chitikola as our guide, on 22nd October, and he led us westward across the Lilongwe River, and then turned north.

We came to a herd of about fifteen elephants, and many trees laid down by these animals. They seem to relish the roots of some kinds, and spend a good deal of time in digging them up. They chew woody roots and branches as thick as the handle of a spade. Many buffaloes feed here, and we viewed a herd of elands. They kept out of bow-shot only. A herd of hartebeest stood at two hundred paces, and one was shot.

While we were rejoicing over the meat, we got news from the inhabitants of a large village, in full flight, that the Mazitu were out on a foray. The people were running straight for the Zalanyama range, regardless of their feet, making a path for themselves through the forest. The hard grass, with stalks nearly as thick as quills, must have hurt their feet sorely, but what was that in comparison with dear life!

We meant to take our stand on the hill, and defend our property in case of the Mazitu coming near, but we heard next morning that the enemy had gone south.

25th October. Came along northwards to Chimuna's town, a large one of Chipeta, with many villages around. As we emerged into the open strath in which the villages lie, we saw the large ant-hills, each the size of the end of a one-storey cottage, covered with men on guard watching for the Mazitu. Chimuna came in the evening and begged me to remain a day in his village. All the people crowded to see the strangers. They know very little beyond their own affairs, though these require a good deal of knowledge. One toothless patriarch had heard of books and umbrellas, but had never seen either. The oldest inhabitant had never travelled far from the spot in which he was born, yet he had a good knowledge of soils and agriculture, hut-building, basket-making, pottery, and the manufacture of bark cloth and skins for clothing, as also making nets, traps, and cordage.

Chimuna had a most ungainly countenance, yet did well

L

enough.   He was very thankful for a blister on his loins to
ease rheumatic pains, and asked me to fire a gun that the
Mazitu might hear, and know that armed men were here.

Clapping the hands in various ways is a polite way of
saying: 'Allow me'; 'I beg pardon'; 'Permit me to pass';
'Thanks.'   It is resorted to in a respectful introduction or
leave-taking, and also as equivalent to 'Hear! hear!'   When
inferiors are called they respond by two brisk claps of the
hands, meaning: 'I am coming.'   They are very punctilious
amongst each other.

29th October.   The first rain—a thunder shower—fell in the
afternoon; air in the shade before was 92°, wet bulb 74°.
At noon the soil in the sun was 140°, perhaps more, but I
was afraid of bursting the thermometer, as it was graduated
only a few degrees above that.   The rain happened at the
same time that the sun was directly overhead on his way
south.   It was but a quarter of an inch, but its effect was
to deprive us of all chance of getting the five carriers we
needed.   All were off to their gardens to commit the
precious seed to the soil.

9th November.   The country over which we actually travel is
level and elevated, but there are mountains all about, which
when put on the map make it appear as a mountainous region.
We are on the watershed, apparently, between the Loangwa
of Zumbo on the west, and the lake on the east.   The
rivulets on the west flow in deep defiles, and the elevation
on which we travel makes certain that no water can come
from the lower lands on the west.   The natives have a
good idea generally of the rivers into which the streams
flow, but they are very deficient in information of the condition of the people that live on their banks.

13th November.   A lion came last night, and gave a growl or
two on finding that he could not get at our meat.   A man
had lent us a hunting-net to protect it and us from intruders

of this sort.   The people kept up shouting for hours after-
wards, in order to keep him away by the human voice.
Lions sometimes enter huts by breaking through the roof.
Elephants certainly do, for we saw a roof destroyed by one.
The only chance for the inmate is to drive a spear into the
belly of the beast while so engaged.

We might have gone on, but I had a galled heel from
new shoes.

XXVII

Slowly North.   The Upper Loangwa

16th November 1866. We crossed the Bua, eight yards wide and knee-deep. It rises in the northern hills a little above Kanyindula's village, called Kanyenje. The chief came himself in the evening, an active stern-looking man, but we got on very well with him.

18th to 21st November. Rain fell heavily yesterday afternoon, and was very threatening to-day. We remain to sew a calico tent. We left the Bua fountain and made a short march to Mokatoba, a stockaded village where the people refused to admit us till the headman came.

We have been on short commons for some time. Large game abounds but we do not meet it. I divided about fifty pounds of powder amongst my followers to shoot with. This reduces our extra loads to three.

27th November. Zeore's men would not carry without pre-payment, so we left our extra loads as usual and went on, sending men back for them. I groan in spirit and do not know how to make our gear into nine loads only. It is the knowledge that we shall be detained two or three months during the heavy rains that makes me cleave to it as a means of support.

Last night a loud clapping of hands by the men was followed by half-suppressed screams by a woman. They were quite 'eldritch,' as if she could not get them out. Then succeeded a lot of utterances as if she were in ecstasy, to which a man responded *Moio, moio.* The utterances were in five-syllable snatches, abrupt and laboured. I wonder if this 'bubbling and boiling over' has been pre-served as the form in which the true prophets of old gave forth their 'burdens.' One sentence repeated at the end of the effusions was *linyama uta* ('flesh of the bow'), showing that the pythoness loved venison killed by the bow. The people applauded and attended hoping, I suppose, that rain would follow her efforts. Next day she was duly honoured by drumming and dancing.

A continuous tap-tapping in the villages shows that bark cloth is being made. The bark, on being removed from the tree, is steeped in water, or in a muddy hole, till the outer of the two inner barks can be separated. Then commences the tapping with a mallet to separate and soften the fibres. The head of this is often of ebony, with the face cut into small furrows which, without breaking, separate and soften the fibres.

4th December. Marched westward over a hilly dwarf-forest country. We spent a miserable night at Katétté, wetted by a heavy thunderstorm which lasted a good while. Next morning was muggy, and rolling thunder in the distance. Went for three hours with, for a wonder, no water, but made westing chiefly, and got on to the Lukuzhwa again.

6th December. Too ill to march.

7th December. Went on and passed Mesumbé's village. The Babisa have begun to imitate the Mazitu by attacking and plundering Manganja villages. Muasi's brother was so attacked, and now is here and ready to attack in return.

9th December. An alarm of Mazitu sent all the villagers up the side of Mparawe this morning. The affair was a chase of a hyena, but everything is Mazitu! The Babisa came here, but were surrounded and nearly all cut off.

11th December. We are now detained in the forest, at a place called Chondé forest, by 'set-in' rains. It rains every day, and generally in the afternoon, but the country is not wetted till the 'set-in' rains commence. The cracks in the soil fill up, and everything rushes up with astonishing rapidity. The grass is quite crisp and short. The birds now make much melody and noise, all intent on building.

13th December. Reached the Tokosusi. Here I got a *pallah* antelope. Our guide would have crossed the Tokosusi, but always, when we have any difficulty, the 'lazies' exhibit themselves. We had no grain, and the three remained behind, spending four hours at what we did in an hour and a quarter. Our guide became tired, and refused to go over the Loangwa. A 'set-in' rain came on after dark, and we went on through slush, the trees sending down heavier drops than the showers. The people were afraid of us, and it was mortifying to find that food is scarce. The Mazitu had been here three times, and though they were repelled, the fear they inspired has prevented cultivation.

16th December. We could not get food at any price, on the 15th, so we crossed the Loangwa, and judged it to be from seventy to a hundred yards wide. No guide would come, so we went on without one. The 'lazies' of the party seized the opportunity to stay behind—wandering, as they said, though all the cross-paths were marked.[1]

18th December. As the men grumbled at their feet being pierced by thorns in the trackless portions we had passed, I had to accept a guide who would go to Molenga's only, though this led east instead of west. When we arrived I was asked what we wanted. I replied that this was the only way to Casembe's, our next stage. To get rid of us they gave us a guide, and we set forth northwards.

The Mopané forest is perfectly level, and after rains the water stands in pools. The trees are very large and stand twenty or thirty yards apart. As there are no branches on their lower parts, animals see very far. I shot a gnu, but

---

[1] *Waller's note.* At the cross-roads the leader 'marks' all side paths and wrong turnings by making a scratch across them with his spear, or by breaking a branch and laying it across.

wandered in getting back to my party, and did not find them till it was getting dark.

20th December. Reached Casembe,[1] a miserable hamlet of a few huts. The people were very suspicious. We could get no grain or even native herbs, though we rested a day to try.

23rd December. Hunger sent us on, for a meat diet is far from satisfying. We all felt very weak on it, and soon tired on the march. A small present was made by Kavimba, but nothing could be bought except at exorbitant prices. We spent all the day on the 24th haggling and trying to get some grain. He took a fancy to a shirt, and left it to his wife to bargain for. She got to the length of cursing and swearing, and we bore it, but could get only a small price for it. We resolved to hold our Christmas some other day and in a better place!

Christmas Day. We lost our four goats, stolen or strayed in the pathless forest. We do not know which, but the loss I feel very keenly, for whatever kind of food we had, a little milk made all right, and I felt strong and well; but coarse food, hard of digestion without it, was very trying. We spent the 26th searching for them, but all in vain. The loss affected me more than I could have imagined. A little indigestible porridge, of hardly any taste, is now my fare, and it makes me dream of better.

27th December. Our guide asked for his cloth to wear on the way, as it was wet and raining, and his bark cloth was a miserable covering. I consented, and he bolted on the first opportunity; the forest being so dense that he was soon out of reach of pursuit. He had been advised to do this by Kavimba, and nothing else was to be expected. We then followed the track of a travelling party of Babisa, but the grass springs up over the path, and it was soon lost.

[1] Not the great chief of the same name near Lake Moero; the word means 'general.'

28th to 30th December. The Loangwa is said to rise in the Chibalé country, due north of this Malambwé. The chief, Moerwa, came to visit me in my hut, and tried all the usual little arts of getting us to buy all we need here, though the prices are exorbitant. By giving Moerwa a good large cloth he was induced to cook a mess of millet and elephant's stomach. It was so good to get a full meal that I could have given him another cloth. We remained a day at Malambwé, but got nothing save a little *maere*, which grates on the teeth and in the stomach.

The forest resounds with singing birds intent on nidification. Francolins abound, but are wild; also whippoor-wills, and another bird which has a more laboured treble note and a voice 'Oh, oh, oh.' Gay flowers blush unseen, but the people have a good idea of what is eatable and what not. I looked at a woman's basket of leaves which she was collecting for supper, and it contained eight or ten kinds, with mushrooms and orchidaceous flowers. In the evening we encamped beside a little rill and made our shelters, but we had so little to eat that I dreamed the night long of dinners I had eaten, or might have been eating.

I shall make this beautiful land better known, that it may become one of the 'pleasant haunts of men.' It is impossible to describe its luxuriance, but most of it is running to waste, through the slave-trade and internal wars.

31st December. We started this morning after rain, all the trees and grass dripping. A lion roared, but we did not see him. We arrived at Chitembo's village and found it deserted.

We now end 1866. It has not been so fruitful or useful as I intended. Will try to do better in 1867, and be better —more gentle and loving. And may the Almighty, to whom I commit my way, bring my desires to pass, and prosper me. Let all the sins of '66 be blotted out for Jesus' sake.

1st January 1867.[1] A prayer: May He, who is full of grace
and truth, impress His character on mine. Grace, eagerness to show favour, truthfulness, sincerity, honour—for
His mercy's sake.

We remain to-day at Mbulukuta, Chitembo's district, at
the boys' desire, because it is New Year's Day.

4th January. We have remained because of 'set-in' rain.
We got a little *maere* here. We have neither sugar nor
salt, so we have no soluble goods, but cloth and gunpowder
are easily damaged. It is hard fare and scanty. I feel
always hungry, and am constantly dreaming of food when
I am not sleeping.[2] Savoury viands of former days come
vividly before the imagination even in waking hours. This
is odd, as I am not a dreamer. Indeed I scarcely ever dream
but when I am going to be ill, or am actually so.

The people employ these 'set-in' rains for hunting the
elephant, which gets bogged and sinks in fifteen to eighteen
inches in the mud, and finds it difficult to escape.

5th January. Still storm-stayed.

6th January. The country now exhibits extreme leafiness,
and the undulations are masses of green leaves. As far as
the eye can reach with distinctness it rests on a mantle of
that hue, and beyond the scene becomes dark blue. Near
at hand many gay flowers peep out. Here and there are
scarlet martagon (*Lilium chalcedonicum*), bright blue and
yellow, gingers, red, orange, yellow, and pure white
orchids; pale lobelias, etc., but they do not mar the general
greenness. As we ascended higher on the plateau, grasses,
which have pink and reddish brown seed-vessels, imparted
distinct shades of their colour to the lawns, and were
grateful to the eye.

---

[1] The second year of travel begins.

[2] Waller states that Livingstone could sleep when he wished, at the shortest
notice. A mat, a shady tree, would at any time afford him refreshing sleep.

* L

The valleys are very beautiful. The oozes are covered with a species of short wiry grass, which gives the appearance of well-kept gentlemen's parks, but they are full of water to overflowing—immense sponges, in fact—and one has to watch carefully in crossing them, to avoid plunging into deep water-holes made by the feet of elephants and buffaloes. In the ooze the water goes generally half-way up the shoe, and we go plash, plash, plash in the lawn-like glade. There are no people in these lovely wild valleys, but to-day we came to mounds made of old for planting grain, and slag from iron furnaces.

My stock of meal came to an end to-day, but Simon gave me some of his. It is not the unpleasantness of eating un-palatable food that teases one but we are never satisfied. I could brace myself to dispose of a very unsavoury mess, and think no more of it, but this *maere* engenders a craving that plagues day and night.

10th January. We crossed the Muasi flowing strongly to the east, to the Loangwa River. In the afternoon an excessively heavy thunderstorm wetted us to the skin. Four of our men wandered, and remained behind lost. We were in a hollow, and the shots we fired to guide them were not heard till this morning.

Simon gave me a little more of his meal this morning, and went without himself. I took my belt up three holes to relieve hunger.

12th January. Sitting down this morning near a tree, my head was just a yard off from a good-sized cobra, coiled up in the sprouts at its root, but it was benumbed with cold. A very pretty little puff-adder lay in the path, also benumbed. It is seldom that any harm is done by these reptiles here.

We bought up all the food we could get, but it did not suffice for the marches we expect to make to get to the Chambesi, where food is said to be abundant. We were, therefore, again obliged to travel on Sunday. We had prayers before starting, but I always feel that I am not doing

Southern Rhodesia: bush country with clearing for crops

right.   It lessens the sense of obligation in the minds of my companions.

A Twofold Loss

15th January. We had to cross the Chimbwé at its eastern end, where it was fully a mile wide.   I, being the first to cross, neglected to give orders about the poor little dog, Chitané.   The water was waist-deep, and the bottom soft peaty stuff with deep holes in it, the northern side infested with leeches.   The boys were, like myself, too much engaged in preserving their balance to think of the spirited little beast, and he must have swum till he sank.   He was so useful in keeping all the country curs off our huts.   None dared approach and steal, and he never stole himself.   When on the march, he took charge of the whole party, running in front and then in the rear to see that all was right.   He was becoming yellowish-red in colour, and, poor thing, perished in what all the boys call Chitané's river.

20th January. Rain all yesterday.   A guide was refused to-day, so we march without one.   The two Waiyau, who joined us in Kande's village, now deserted.   They had been faithful all the way, and their uniform good conduct made us trust them.   But they left us in the forest, and heavy rain came on and obliterated every vestige of their footsteps.   To make the loss more galling, they took what we could spare least—the medicine-box, which they would only throw away as soon as they came to examine their booty.

One of these deserters exchanged his load that morning with a boy called Baraka, who had charge of the medicine-box because he was so careful.   This was done because with the medicine-box were packed five very large cloths, and all Baraka's clothing and beads, of which he was very careful.   The forest was so dense and high that there was no chance of getting a glimpse of the fugitives, who took all the dishes, a large box of powder, the flour we had purchased dearly to help us as far as the Chambesi, the tools, two guns, and a cartridge pouch; but the medicine-chest was the sorest loss of all. I felt as if I had received the sentence of death, like poor Bishop Mackenzie.

All the other goods I had divided in case of loss, but never dreamed of losing the precious quinine and other remedies. Other losses and annoyances I felt as just parts of the undercurrent of vexation, which is not wanting even in the smoothest life; and certainly not worthy of being moaned over in the experience of an explorer anxious to benefit a country and people; but this loss I feel most keenly. Everything of this kind happens by the permission of One who watches over us with most tender care, and this may turn out for the best, by taking away a source of suspicion among the more superstitious charm-dreading people farther north.

It is difficult to say from the heart: 'Thy will be done.' These Waiyau had few advantages. Sold into slavery in early life, they were in the worst possible school for learning to be honest and honourable. They behaved well for a long time, but having had hard and scanty fare in Lobisa, wet and misery in passing through dripping forests, hungry nights and fatiguing days, their patience must have been worn out, and they had no strong sentiments of honour. They gave way to the temptation which their good conduct had led us to put in their way. Some we have come across in this journey seem born essentially mean and base—a great misfortune to them and all who have to deal with them; but they cannot be so blameworthy as those who have no natural tendency to meanness, and whose education has taught them to abhor it. True; yet this loss of the medicine-box gnaws at the heart terribly.

Returned to Lisunga, and remained for two days.

A Genial Old Rascal

23rd January. A march of five and three-quarter hours brought us to Chibanda's stockade, where 'no food' was the case as usual. We all feel weak and easily tired, and

an incessant hunger teases us, so it is no wonder if so large
a space of this paper is occupied with stomach affairs. It
has not been merely want of nice dishes, but real biting
hunger and faintness.

24th and 25th January. Four hours through unbroken dark
forest brought us to Movushi. Thanks to the Providence
who watches over us, we found at last a good supply of
maere, and some ground-nuts, but through all the region
the trees that yield bark cloth are so abundant that the
people are all well clothed with it, and care little for our
cloth. Red and pink beads are the fashion, and fortunately
we have red. These Babisa are full of suspicion. Everything has to be paid for in advance.

27th January. A 'set-in' rain all morning, but having meat
we are comfortable in the old huts.

In changing my dress this morning I was frightened by
my own emaciation.

30th January. Northwards through almost trackless dripping
forests, and across oozing bogs.

31st January. Through forest, but gardens now appear. A
man offered a thick bar of copper for sale, a foot by three
inches.

At midday we came to the Lopiri, the rivulet that waters
Chitapangwa's stockade, and soon after, found that his
village has a triple stockade, the inner being defended also
by a deep broad ditch, and a hedge of a solanaceous thorny
shrub.

Chitapangwa sent to inquire if we wanted an audience.
I replied: 'Not till evening,' and sent notice at 5 p.m. of
my coming. We passed through the inner stockade, and
then on to an enormous hut where sat Chitapangwa, with
three drummers and ten or more men with rattles in their
hands. The drummers beat furiously, and the rattlers kept
time to the drums, two of them advancing and retreating in
a stooping position, with rattles near the ground, as if doing

obeisance to the chief, and still keeping time with the others. I declined to sit on the ground, and an enormous tusk was brought for me. The chief saluted courteously. He has a fat jolly face, and legs loaded with brass and copper leglets.

After talking awhile he came along with us to a group of cows, and pointing to one: 'That is yours,' he said. The tusk on which I sat was sent after me too, as being mine because I had sat on it. He put on my cloth as token of acceptance. As the chief had behaved, as I thought, handsomely, I went and gave him one of our best cloths, but when we were about to kill the cow, a man interfered and pointed to a smaller one. I asked if this was by the order of the chief. The chief said the man had lied, but I declined to take any cow at all, if he did not give it willingly.

3rd February. I handed this morning to Magaru Mafupi a packet of letters, for which he was to get ten rupees at Zanzibar. I proposed to go on, but Chitapangwa got very angry, and said I came only to show my things and buy nothing. Then he altered his tone and asked me to accept a cow, and as we were much in need I took it. We were only to give what we liked, but this proved a snare. I gave him two more cloths, but he sent them back and demanded a basket. Though it is disagreeable to be thus victimized, it is the first time we have tasted fat for six weeks or more. The boys were sorely afraid of him, and thought talking to him in a cringing manner was the way to win his favour.

I went to his hut and stated that I had given him four times the value of his cow. Chitapangwa replied: 'You are sorry you have given so much for an ox you have eaten. You would not take the smaller, and, therefore, I gratified your heart by giving you the larger. Why should you not gratify my heart by giving me cloth sufficient to cover me, and please me?' I said I had given him cloths that would cover his biggest wife. He laughed, but still blamed me for greediness.

8th February. The chief demands one of my boxes and a blanket. I explain that one day's rain would spoil the contents of the box, and that I cannot take the boys' blankets as they are not slaves.

I am told he terrifies the boys by threats. He thinks we have some self-interest in trying to secure a passage through his country, and, therefore, that he has a right to share in the gain. When told it was for a public benefit, he pulled down the under-lid of his eye.[1]

10th February. I had an open-air service, many looking on, and afterwards spoke to the chief. I explained a little to him, and showed him the woodcuts in the *Bible Dictionary*,[2] which he readily understood.

11th February. The chief sent a basket of hippopotamus flesh, and a large one of green maize. He says a box—a tin one—must be given. He keeps out of my way. He is good-natured and our intercourse is a laughing one, but the boys betray their terrors and render my words powerless.

13th February. I gave one of the boxes at last, and got ready to go; but the chief was very angry, and came with all his force, exclaiming that I wanted to leave against his will, though he wished to adjust matters and send me away nicely. He does not believe that we have no blankets.

It is hard to be kept waiting, but all may be for the best. Though I have nine boys I feel quite alone.

15th February. The chief came in the morning and I showed him that I had no blanket, and he took an old one and said the affair was ended. The chief offered me a cow for a piece of red serge, and I gave that, a cloth, and a few beads. The serge was two fathoms, a portion of that Miss Coutts gave me when leaving England in 1858. The chief is not so bad. It is the boys who are cowardly.

[1] *Waller's note*. 'This looks like the African equivalent of "Do you see any green in my eye?"'

[2] On this journey Livingstone carried with him three books only: the Bible, Smith's *Bible Dictionary*, and a nautical almanac.

17th February. Too ill with rheumatic fever to have service. This is the first attack I have ever had, and no medicine! Chitapangwa begged me to stay another day, that one of the boys might mend his blanket, and I being weak and giddy consented.

20th February. I told the chief on starting that my heart was sore because he was not sending me away as cordially as I liked. He ordered his men to start with us, and gave me a knife with a brass sheath as a memorial. He took a piece of clay off the ground, and rubbed it on his tongue as an oath, and came along with us to see that all was right, and so we parted.

XXVIII

Towards the South of Tanganyika

THE Explorer had been asked by the Royal Geographical Society to investigate the relation of Lakes Nyasa and Tanganyika, in order to prove or disprove the then accepted belief that they belonged to the same river system; and it was for this purpose that Livingstone was now pursuing his laborious, and what appears on the map somewhat erratic, course.

First he turned sharply east for about twenty miles to Moamba's village, after which he followed a route almost steadily north. It was glorious country, but the constant rain made movement hard. Moamba is described as a 'big public-house-looking person with a slight cast of the left eye.' He was hearty and intelligent, however, and his gifts of food were generous. But the Doctor could not shake off his fever.

On 10th March he writes: 'I have been ill of fever ever since we left Moamba. Every step I take jars on the chest, and I am very weak. I can hardly keep up with the march, though formerly I was always first.' Still, they struggled on till they reached Kasonso, and by that time they were already descending into the broad valley of Lake Tanganyika, and beginning to feel the comfort of its warmth. Here he was soon to be rewarded by his first sight of the south end of the great inland lake, which was called by him Liemba.

15th March 1867. We are now making for Kasonso, the chief of the lake and of a large country all round. My long-continued fever ill disposes me to enjoy the beautiful scenery.

19th March. A party of young men came out of the village near which we had encamped, to force us to pay something for not going into their village. I pacified them, and after talking awhile and threatening to do a deal to-morrow, they left.

22nd March. Kasonso gave us a great reception, and after sleeping in various villages we came to Mombo's village, near the ridge overlooking the lake.

31st March and 1st April. I was too ill to march through. I offered to go on the 1st, but Kasonso's son, who was with us, objected. We went up a low range of hills, and soon after passing the summit the blue waters loomed through the trees. This is the southern end of Liemba, or as it is sometimes called, Tanganyika. We had to descend at least 2,000 feet before we got to the level of the lake. It seems about eighteen or twenty miles broad, and we could see about thirty miles to the north. Four considerable rivers flow into the space before us. The nearly perpendicular ridge of 2,000 feet extends with breaks all round, and there, embosomed in tree-covered rocks, reposes the lake peacefully in a huge cup-shaped cavity.

I never saw anything so still and peaceful as it lies all the morning. About noon a gentle breeze springs up and causes the waves to assume a bluish tinge. In the north it seems to narrow into a gateway, but the people can tell us nothing about it. They suspect us. I am deeply thankful in having got so far. I am excessively weak—cannot walk without tottering, and have a constant singing in the head, but the Highest will lead me farther.

Lat. 8° 46′ 54″ S., long. 31° 57′ E., but I only worked out (and my head is out of order) one set of observations. Height above the level of the sea, 2,800 feet. The people won't let me sound the lake.

After being a fortnight at this lake, it still appears one of surpassing loveliness. Its peacefulness is remarkable. It lies in a deep basin whose sides are nearly perpendicular, but covered well with trees. The rocks are bright red argillaceous schist. Down some of these rocks come beautiful cascades, and buffaloes, elephants, and antelopes wander and graze on the more level spots, while lions roar by night. In the morning and evening huge crocodiles may be observed, quietly making their way to their feeding grounds. Hippopotami snort by night, and at early morning.

After I had been a few days here, I had a fit of insensibility, which shows the power of fever without medicine. I found myself floundering outside my hut, and unable to get in. I tried to lift myself from my back by laying hold of the two posts at the entrance, but when I got nearly upright, I let them go and fell heavily on my head on a box. The boys had seen the wretched state I was in, and hung a blanket at the entrance of the hut, that no stranger might see my helplessness. Some hours elapsed before I could recognize where I was.

1st May. We began our return march from Liemba. We intended to go north-west, to see whether the lake narrows or not, for all assert that it maintains its breadth; but when about to start the headman and his wife came and protested so solemnly that by going north-west we should walk into the hands of a party of Mazitu there, that we deferred our departure.

The Mazitu having left, we slept half-way up the ridge. I had another fit of insensibility last night. The muscles of the back lose all power, and there is constant singing in the ears.

At this point the Explorer's plans were interrupted, and a tantalizing delay, and three months of inactivity, followed. It might have been anticipated that, if only to replace his stock of drugs, from stores he expected to find there, he would have moved along the lake to Ujiji, and this was apparently his purpose. But at this juncture he learned of a nasty feud that was in progress between a powerful Arab trading party, and Nsama, the chief of the country to the west and north-west of the point he had reached. The local chief was emphatic as to the great danger of attempting to pass through this disturbed territory. So, most unwillingly, he turned back to Chitimba's village.

The Arabs, when he met them, were friendly. They belonged to 'an influential mercantile house in Zanzibar.' No doubt the sultan's firman that he carried prompted their helpfulness. They enabled him to replenish his stock of trade goods. They too urged him to avoid the disturbed area, and advised him to make his way up the east side of the lake. As, however, this would have taken him far afield from the lakes Moero and Bangweulu, which were his immediate objectives, he declined.

There was nothing to do but to wait. He filled his time by recording in detail his observations and discoveries.

The following entries may be taken as typical.

What we understand by primeval forest is but seldom seen in the interior here, though the country cannot be described otherwise than as generally covered with interminable forest. Insects kill or dwarf some trees, and men maim others for the sake of bark cloth; elephants break down a great number, and so it is only here and there that gigantic specimens are seen. They may be expected in shut-in valleys amongst mountains, but on the whole the trees are scraggy, and their variety not great. The different sorts of birds that sing among the branches seem to me to exceed those of the Zambezi region, but I do not shoot them. The number of new notes I hear astonishes me.

A large spider makes a nest inside the huts. It consists of a piece of pure white paper, an inch and a half broad, stuck close to the wall. Under this some forty or fifty eggs are placed, and then a quarter of an inch of thinner paper is put round it, apparently to fasten the first firmly. When making the paper the spider moves itself over the surface in wavy lines, and then sits on it, with her eight legs spread all over it, for three weeks continuously, catching and eating any insects, as cockroaches, that come her way. After three weeks she leaves it to hunt for food, but always returns at night. The natives do not molest her.

Travelling with Slave-traders

It cannot fail to be noted that, from now on, Livingstone becomes increasingly dependent on the Arab slave-trading parties, and travels much in their company. Though the Hamees —the group with whom he was now consorting—were better than the usual type of slaver, constant association with them must have been, to a man of his outspoken opinions, extremely irksome. Further, as their purpose was trade and not travel, their movements were necessarily slow, and their dilatory progress was to him most trying.

Only some constraining necessity can explain conduct as inconsistent with his general habit. It can hardly have been the need of protection, since the Missionary could be trusted to find his way unharmed through any country, however disturbed. The reason he himself advanced was that he had noticed that his presence kept the traders on their best behaviour. That, without question, was true, but does not alone seem an adequate excuse. Doubtless one main reason was his enfeebled health, and the loss of his drugs. He had some trust, which later experience justified, in the Arab practice of medicine.

30th August. We marched to-day from Chitimba's village, after three months and ten days' delay. On reaching Ponda we found Tipo, the Arab leader, gone on. So we followed him.

2nd to 9th September. When we reached the ford of Lofu we found that we were at least a thousand feet below Chitimba's. The ford was two hundred and ninety-six feet wide. Went seven hours west to a village called Hara, which had been burned by the Hamees because the people would not take a peaceful message to Nsama. Three hours west of Hara we came on Nsama's new stockade. I sent a message to him, and received a message to visit him but to bring no guns.

A large crowd of his people went with us and before we came to the inner stockade they felt my clothes to see that I had no concealed arms. We found Nsama a very old man, with a good head and face and a very large abdomen, showing that he was addicted to beer. I gave him a cloth, and asked for a guide to Moero, which he readily granted. I advise him to live in peace. He sent me a goat, flour, and beer, and next day we returned to Hara.

10th September. Some people of Ujiji have come to Nsama. They report that my goods are safe. I sent a box containing papers, books, and some clothes to Ujiji.

14th September. I remained at Hara, for I was ill. The entire population of the country has received a shock from the conquest of Nsama, and their views on the comparative values of bows and arrows and guns have undergone a great change. Nsama was the Napoleon of the country, hence his defeat has caused a great panic. The people seem intelligent, and will no doubt act on the experience so dearly bought.

30th September. We [i.e. Livingstone with the Arabs] reached Karungu, and found the chief much afraid of us. He kept everyone out of his stockade. But gradually he became friendly.

20th October. (Following a long vexatious delay.) Very ill. I always am so when I have no work—sore bones; much headache; no appetite; much thirst.

27th to 30th October. Off early in fine drizzling rain, and came upon a plain about three miles broad full of large game. Five hours brought us to the Choma River, but the chief and people had fled. No persuasion could prevail on them to come back and sell us food.

2nd November. Still in the same direction. The hills are granite now, and a range on our left from 700 to 1,500 feet high goes all the way to Moero.

These valleys are beautiful, and the clumps of trees often remind me of English park scenery. The long lines of slaves brought up by their Arab employers add life to the scene,

Tanganyika: Kondoa Irangi River

They are in three bodies, and number four hundred and fifty in all. Each party has a guide with a flag, and when that is planted all the company stop till it is lifted, and a drum is beaten and a Kudu-horn sounds. One party is headed by about a dozen leaders, wearing a fantastic head-gear of feathers and beads, red cloth on the bodies, and skins cut into strips and twisted. They take their places in line, the drum beats, the horn sounds harshly, and all fall in. These sounds seem to awaken a sort of *esprit de corps* in those who have once been slaves.

My attendants now jumped up, and would scarcely allow me time to dress, when they heard the sounds of their childhood, and all day they were among the foremost. Africans cannot stand sneers. When any mishap occurs on the march (as when a branch tilts a load off a man's shoulders) all who see it set up a yell of derision. If anything is accidentally spilled, or if one is tired and sits down, the same yell greets him, and all are excited thereby to exert themselves. They hasten on with their loads, and hurry with the sheds they build, the masters only bringing up the rear, and helping anyone who may be sick.

The distances travelled were quite as much as the masters or we could bear. Had frequent halts been made, as for instance a half or quarter of an hour at the end of every hour or two, little distress would have been felt, but five hours at a stretch is more than men can bear in a hot climate. The female slaves held on bravely; nearly all carried loads on their heads. The head, or lady of the party who is also the wife of the Arab, was the only exception; she had a fine white shawl, with ornaments of silver and gold, on her head. These ladies had a jaunty walk, and never gave in on the longest march. Many pounds' weight of fine copper leglets above the anklets seemed only to help the sway of the walk. As soon as they arrive at the sleeping place they begin to cook, and in this art they show a great deal of expertness, making savoury dishes out of wild fruits and other not very likely materials.

7th November. Start for Moero, convoyed by all the Arabs for some distance. They have been extremely kind. We draw to the mountain range on our left called Kakoma. Our course is now nearly south. Villages are thickly studded over the valley. One or two hundred yards is the common distance between these villages. Puta, one of the paramount chiefs, refused us a hut, so we came on to the lake.

XXIX

The Discovery of Lake Moero

8th November 1867. Lake Moero is of goodly size, and is flanked by ranges of mountains on the east and west. Its banks are of coarse sand and slope gradually down to the water. Outside these banks stands a thick belt of tropical vegetation, in which the fishermen build their huts. The country called Rua lies to the west, and is seen as a lofty range of dark mountains. Another range of less height, but more broken, stands on the eastern shore, and in it lies the path to Casembe. We slept in a fisherman's hut on the north shore which has a fine sweep, like an unbent bow. Round its western end flows the water that makes the River Lualaba, which, before it enters Moero, is the Luapula, and that again (if the most intelligent report be true) is the Chambesi, before it enters Lake Bemba or Bangweulu.

We went along the north till we reached the eastern flanking range, then ascended and turned south. The people were suspicious, shutting their gates as we drew near. We were alone, only nine people in all, but they must have had reasons for fear. One headman refused and then relented. We went back and were well entertained.

15th to 18th November. Heavy rain, but we went on. We reached the Kabusi, a sluggish narrow rivulet that runs into the Chungu. On this river Dr Lacerda[1] died. The statement of the people about his death is confused, but the following is what I gleaned from many.

There were some Ujiji people with the Casembe of that time. The Portuguese and the Ujijians began to fight, but Casembe said: 'You are all my guests. Why should you kill each other?' He then gave Lacerda ten slaves, and similar presents to the Ujijians, which quieted them. However, Lacerda was but ten days at Chungu when he died.

[1] See Notes on Persons, page 404.

327

We remained there till Casembe sent one of his counsellors to guide us to his town.   Rain and dense forest
prevented us from seeing Moero as we wished.   There
have been seven Casembes in all.   The name means 'general.'
When one Casembe dies, the man who succeeds invariably
removes and builds his *pembwe*, or court, in another place.

A Great Barbarian

21st November.   The plain extending from the Lundé to the
town of Casembe is level and studded thickly with red
ant-hills.   Casembe has made a broad path from his town
to the Lundé, about a mile and a half long, and as broad as
a carriage path.   The chief's house is enclosed in a wall
of reeds, eight or nine feet high and three hundred yards
square.   The gateway is ornamented by about sixty human
skulls.   A shed stands in the middle of the road before we
come to the gate, with a cannon dressed in gaudy cloths.
A number of noisy fellows stopped our party and demanded
tribute for the cannon.   1 burst through and the rest
followed without giving anything.

The town is on the east side of the lakelet Mofwé, and
one mile from its northern end.   Mohammed bin Saleh
met us with his men, firing guns of welcome.   He conducted us to his reception shed and gave us a hut.   He is
a fine portly black Arab with a pleasant smile and a pure
white beard, and has been more than ten years in these
parts, and has lived with four Casembes.   He has considerable influence.

An Arab trader, Mohammed Bogharib, who arrived seven
days before us with an immense number of slaves, presented
a meal of vermicelli, oil, and honey, also cassava meal
cooked so as to resemble a sweetmeat.   I had not tasted
honey or sugar since we left Lake Nyasa.   They had
coffee too.

Many of Casembe's people appear with ears cropped and
hands lopped.   The present chief has been often guilty
of this barbarity.   One man has just come to us without

ears or hands.   He tried to excite our pity, making chirruping noises by striking his cheeks with the stumps of his
hands.   A dwarf also, with backbone broken, comes about
us.   He talks with an air of authority and is present at
public occurrences.   He is a stranger from a tribe to the
north.   He is three feet nine inches.

24th November.   We were called to be presented to Casembe
in a grand reception.

The present Casembe has a heavy uninteresting countenance, without beard or whiskers, and somewhat of the
Chinese type, and his eyes have an outward squint.   He
smiled but once during the day, and that was pleasant
enough, though the cropped ears and the lopped hands and
the human skulls at the gate, made me indisposed to look
on anything with favour.   His principal wife came, with
her attendants, after he had departed, to look at the Englishman.   She was a fine, tall, good-featured lady with two
spears in her hands.   The principal men made way for her
and called upon me to salute.   I did so, but she being forty
yards off, I involuntarily beckoned her to come nearer.
This upset the gravity of all her attendants.   All burst into
a laugh and ran off.

Casembe's smile was elicited by the dwarf making some
uncouth antics before him.   His executioner also came
forward to look.   He had a broad Lunda sword on his arm,
and a curious scissor-like instrument at his neck for cropping
ears.   On saying to him that his was nasty work, he smiled,
and so did many who were not sure of their ears for a
moment.   Many men of respectability show that, at some
former time, they have been thus punished.

Casembe sat before his hut on a square seat placed on
lion and leopard skins.[1]   He was clothed in a coarse blue-
and-white Manchester print edged with red baize, and
arranged in large folds, so as to look like a crinoline put on

[1] These sections are taken from a dispatch to Lord Clarendon dated
10th December 1867.   See *Livingstone's Last Journals*, vol. i, page 255.

wrong side foremost. His arms, legs, and head were covered with sleeves, leggings, and cap made of various coloured beads in neat patterns; a crown of yellow feathers surmounted his cap. Each of his headmen came forward, shaded by huge ill-made umbrellas, and followed by his dependants, made obeisance to Casembe, and sat down on his right and left. Various bands of musicians did the same.

When called upon I rose and bowed, and an old counsellor with his ears cropped gave the chief as full an account as he had been able to gather during our stay, of the English in general, and my antecedents in particular. My having passed through Lunda, and visited chiefs of whom he knew scarcely anything, excited most attention. He then assured me I was welcome to his country, to go where I liked and do what I chose.

I had another interview, and tried to dissuade him from selling his people as slaves. He listened with a smile, and then broke into a tirade on the greatness of his country, his power and dominion, which Mohammed bin Saleh, who has been here for ten years, turned into ridicule.

When we went on a third occasion to bid farewell, he was much less distant, and gave me the impression that I could soon become friends with him, but he had an ungainly look, and an outward squint in each eye. But thinking of his barbarous ways I could not avoid indulging a prejudice against him.

27th November. Casembe's chief wife passes frequently to her plantation, carried by six, or more commonly by twelve, men in a sort of palanquin. She has European features, but a light brown complexion. A number of men run before her brandishing swords and axes, and one beats a hollow instrument, giving warning to passengers to clear the way. She has two enormous pipes ready filled for smoking. She is very attentive to her agriculture. The people seem more savage than any I have seen. They strike each other barbarously from mere wantonness, but they are civil enough to me.

Mohammed bin Saleh proposes to go to Ujiji next month. He waited when he heard of our coming. He has a very low opinion of the present chief.

An old man named Pérémbé is the owner of the land on which Casembe has built. They always keep up the traditional ownership. If anyone wished to cultivate land, he would apply to the aboriginal chief for it. Old Pérémbé is a sensible man. Mohammed thinks he is a hundred and fifty years old. He is always on the side of liberalty and fairness.

15th December. To-day I told Casembe we were leaving. I am always ill when not working. He said we might go when we chose. On going to say good-bye to Casembe, he tried to be gracious, and said we had eaten but little of his food. He sent a man to escort us.

24th December. Drizzling rain. We are in a wretched spot by the Kabusi, in a bed of brackens four feet high. The guides won't stir in this weather. I gave beads to buy what could be got for Christmas.

27th December. In two hours we crossed the Mandapala. This part was well stocked with people five years ago, but Casembe's severity in cropping ears and other mutilations, selling children on the slightest offences, etc., made all flee to neighbouring tribes. Now he could not collect a thousand men.

28th to 31st December. We came to the Kabukwa, where I was taken ill. Heavy rains kept us back. I have had nothing but coarsely ground sorghum meal for some time back, and am weak.

I am so tired of exploration, without a word from home or anything else for two years, that I must go to Ujiji for letters before anything else.

The Rua Mountains

1st January 1868.[1]   Prayer: Almighty Father, forgive the sins
of the past year for Thy Son's sake.   Help me to be more
profitable during this year.   If I am to die this year prepare
me for it.

My guide to Moero came to-day, and I visited the lake
several times.   The first fifteen miles in the north are from
twelve to thirty-three miles wide.   The great mass of the
Rua mountains confines it.   Thus on a clear day a lower
range is seen, continued from the high point of the first
mass away to the west-south-west.   This ends, and sea
horizon is alone visible away to the south and west.   From
the height we viewed it at, the width must be over forty,
and perhaps sixty, miles.

13th January.   Heavy rains.   Leaving the lake and going
south we soon got on to the plain flooded by the Luao.
We had to wade through very adhesive black mud, generally
ankle-deep with many holes in it.   We had four hours of
this and then came to the ford.   We waded up a branch
of it waist-deep, and then crossed a narrow part by means
of a rude bridge of branches and trees of about forty yards
wide.   This black mud in places smells horribly.

16th January.   On reaching the village of Kabwabwata, a
great demonstration was made by Mohammed's Arab dependants and Wanyamwesi.   The women had their faces
all smeared with pipe clay, and 'lulliloo-ed' with all their
might.   When we came among the huts they cast handfuls
of soil on their heads, while the men fired their guns as
fast as they could load them.   Those connected with
Mohammed kissed his hands, and fired till the sound
was deafening.   Mohammed was quite overcome by the
demonstration.

24th February.   Some slaves who came with Mohammed
Bogharib's agent abused my men this morning, as bringing

[1] The beginning of the third year of the journey.

unclean meat into the camp to sell, though it was killed by a Wanyamwesi man. They called out 'Kaffir, Kaffir,' and Susi, roused by this, launched forth with a stick. Others joined in the row and the offenders were beaten off. But they renewed the assault with increased numbers. One threw a heavy block and struck Simon on the head, making him quite insensible and convulsed for a time. His head wounds may prove serious. This is the first outburst of Mohammedan bigotry that we have met with, and by those who know so little of the creed that they could not repeat any of the formulae.

25th February. Mohammed called this morning to apologize for the outrage, but I wanted no punishment inflicted.

We are waiting in company with a number of Wanyamwesi for the cessation of the rains, which have flooded the country between here and Tanganyika. If there were much slope this water would run off. This makes me suspect that Tanganyika is not so low as Speke's measurement.

16th March. We started for Mpwéto's village, which is situated on the Lualaba, and in our course crossed the Lokinda, a river forty yards broad with a rude bridge over it, as it flows fast away into the Moero. Next day we ascended the Rua mountains and reached the village of Mpwéto, about a mile from the right bank of the Lualaba, where it comes through the mountains.

It then flows about two miles along the base of a mountain lying east and west, before it begins to make northing. Its course is reported to be very winding.

25th March to 11th April. Reached Kabwabwata at noon, and were welcomed by Mohammed and his people.

I am thinking of going to Lake Bemba,[1] because at least two months must be passed here before a passage can be made, but my goods are getting done, and I cannot give presents to the chiefs on our way. Mohammed is strongly

---

[1] Another name for Lake Bangweulu.

against our going. His great argument is the extortionate way of Casembe, who would demand cloth. Were my goods not nearly done I would go, and risk the displeasure of Casembe for the chance of the discovery of Lake Bemba. I fear I must give up the lake for the present.

Livingstone's strongest wish at this time was to reach Ujiji, where he hoped to replenish his stores from the stocks that he believed were awaiting him there. Especially he needed drugs. But the Arabs with whom he must travel had business of their own, and could not move for many weeks. Kabwabwata was in many ways a most uncomfortable camp, and the Doctor's fixed idea was that he could keep good health only when on the move. What follows is thoroughly characteristic of the man.

He let it be known that he intended to visit Lake Bemba. It was a more than usually foolhardy resolve, and provoked immediate and strong opposition. The Arabs, probably because they disliked his exploring what they thought of as their special ivory reserve, protested strenuously, and the Nassick boys, grown stale from the over-protracted wanderings, and influenced by the Arabs, refused to move, and mutinied. His stores were all but exhausted; the country was under flood water, and his health uncertain. But all these difficulties only stiffened his resolve. ('What are difficulties for but to be surmounted.') No doubt he feared that if he missed this chance, no other opportunity of adding this great discovery to his laurels would recur. And so, with only five faithful attendants, he started.

12th April. I think of starting to-morrow for Bangweulu, even if Casembe refuses a passage beyond him. We shall be better there than we are here. Everything in Kabwabwata is scarce and dear.

17th April. We crossed the Luao by a bridge thirty yards long, and more than half a mile of flood on each side. We had four hours' wading, the bottom being generally black tenacious mud. Ruts had been formed in the paths by the feet of passengers. These were filled with soft mud and, as they could not be seen, the foot was often placed on the edge, and when the weight came on to it, down it slumped into the mud, half-way up the calves. It was difficult to draw it out, and very fatiguing. To avoid these ruts we encroached on the grass at the side of the paths, but often stepping on the unseen edge of the rut, we floundered in with both feet to keep the balance, and this was usually followed by a rush of bubbles to the surface, which bursting discharged foul air of frightful faecal odour. When we came near Moero, the water became half-chest and whole-chest deep.

29th April. At the Mandapala River. Some men here made a great outcry against our coming here a second time to Casembe, without waiting at the Kalungosi for permission. I persuaded them to refer the matter to Casembe himself, and send a messenger. On 3rd May he returned with the good news that Casembe was quite gracious.

10th May. I sent to Casembe for a guide to Luapula. He replied that he had not seen me nor given me any food; I must come to-morrow. But next day he was occupied with killing a man for witchcraft, and we did not get our audience. Casembe was friendly, but very dilatory, and several days were lost before food and guides were sent.

10th June. Detained again. Business with Casembe not finished.

24th June. Six men slaves were singing as if they did not feel the degradation of the slave-sticks.[1] When I inquired, they told me that they rejoiced at the idea of coming back after death, and haunting and killing those who had sold them. The burden of the song seemed to be: 'Oh, you sent us off to the sea-coast, but the yoke is off when I die, and back I'll come to haunt and kill you.' Then all joined in the chorus, which was the name of each

---

[1] 'These heavy forked sticks were at night fastened to the ground and lashed together to make escape impossible, and might be kept on for as long as three months.' See *General Rigby, Zanzibar, and the Slave-Trade,* page 29.

M

vendor. The song told not of fun but of bitterness, and of the tears of such as are oppressed.

25th June. We came to a grave in the forest. It was a little rounded mound, as if the occupant sat in it. It was strewn over with flour, and a number of large beads had been put on it. A little path showed that it had visitors. That is the sort of grave I should prefer. To lie in the still, still forest, with no hand ever to disturb my bones. Graves at home seem to me miserable and without elbow-room, especially those in cold damp clay.

But I have nothing to do but wait till He who is over all decides where I may lay me down and die. Poor Mary lies on Shupanga brae 'and beeks fornent the sun.' [1]

[1] 'Beeks fornent the sun'—lies in the face of the sun. From a ballad *Bessie Bell and Mary Gray*, two Perthshire girls who died of plague in the seventeenth century. See *Oxford Book of Ballads*.

XXX

The Discovery of Lake Bangweulu

1st July 1868. I went over to Chikumbi, the paramount chief of this district, and gave him a cloth, begging a man to guide me to Bangweulu. He said I was welcome to his country, and if I waited two days he would select a good man and send some food for me to eat on the journey. His man would take me to the smaller part of the lake, and leave others to forward me to the greater, or Bangweulu. The smaller part is called Bemba, but the name is confusing, because Bemba is the name of the country in which a portion of the lake lies. Therefore it is better to use the name Bangweulu, which is applied to the great mass of the water, though I fear our English folk will boggle at it, or call it 'Bungyhollow!'

2nd July. Writing to the consul at Zanzibar to send supplies of cloth and beads to Ujiji. I ask for soap, coffee, sugar, candles, sardines, French preserved meats, a cheese in tin, *Nautical Almanac* for 1869 and 1870, shoes (two or four pairs), ruled paper, pencils, sealing-wax, ink, powder, flannel-serge.

3rd July. The summary of the sources which I have resolved to report as flowing into the central line of drainage formed by the Chambesi, Luapula, and Lualaba is thirteen in all, each larger than the Isis at Oxford, or the Avon at Hamilton. Five flow into the eastern line of drainage, going towards Tanganyika, and five more into the western line of drainage, or Lufira: twenty-three or more in all. The Lualaba and Lufira unite in the lake of the chief Kinkonza.

5th July. I borrowed some paper from Mohammed Bogharib to write home by some Arabs going to the coast. I will

337

announce my discovery to Lord Clarendon, but I reserve parts of the Lualaba and Tanganyika for future confirmation.

13th July. On resting at a deserted spot, the men from a near village came to us excited and apparently drunk, and began to work themselves up still more by running about, poising their spears at us, taking aim with their bows and arrows, and making as if to strike us with their axes. They thought we were marauders.

There is usually one good soul in such rabbles. In this case a man came to me, and addressing his fellows said: 'This is only your *pombe* (beer). White man, do not stand among them, but go away.' Then he placed himself between me and our assailants, about thirty of whom were making their warlike antics. While I walked quietly away with my good friend, they ran in front, behind bushes and trees, and took aim with bow and arrow, but none shot. The younger men ran away with our three goats. But my friend got them back.

I could not feel the inebriates to be enemies, but in that state they are the worst one can encounter, for they have no fear as they have when sober. One snatched away a fowl from our guide. That too was restored by my friend. I did not load my gun; for any accidental discharge would have inflamed them to rashness. We got away without shedding of blood, and were thankful.

17th and 18th July. Reached the chief village of Mapuni, near the north bank of Bangweulu. On the 18th I walked a little way out, and saw the shores of the lake for the first time, thankful that I had come safely thither.

19th July. Went down to Masantu's village on the shore. The country around the lake is all flat and denuded of trees. The islands, four in number, are also flat, but well populated. The men have many canoes and are expert fishermen. They have many children, as fishermen usually have. We had as spectator a man walking on stilts.

21st July. Canoemen are usually extortionate, because one cannot do without them. The bottom of the lake consists of white sand, and a broad belt of strong rushes, say one hundred yards wide, shows shallow water.

22nd to 25th July. A high wind came with the new moon and prevented our going. Strong south-east wind still blowing, but we embarked on the 25th, and five stout men propelled the canoe quickly towards the opening in Lifungé Island on our south-east. We could see the island Kisi on our east about fifteen miles away. It was all sea horizon to our south and north. The water was a deep sea-green colour, from which we concluded that the depth was not so great as that of Lake Nyasa.

We reached Mpabala after dark. It was bitterly cold, from the amount of moisture in the air. I asked a man for a hut. He led me to the public place of meeting, a large shed with planks around, and open spaces between instead of walls.

Here we cooked a little porridge, and then I lay down on one side, and the canoemen and my attendants at the fire in the middle. I was soon asleep, and dreamed I had apartments in Mivart's hotel. This amused me next day, as I never thought of that hotel in my waking moments— freak of fancy, surely, for I was not at all discontented with my fare or my apartment. I was only afraid of getting a stock of vermin from my associates.

26th to 27th July. We had come to Mpabala at the rate of six knots an hour, and returned at the same rate with six strong paddlers. The latitude was 12′ in a south-east course, which may give 24′ as the actual distance. The land's end running south of Masantu's village is the entrance to the Luapula. The clearest eye cannot see across it there. The Luapula is an arm of the lake for some twenty miles, and beyond that it is never narrower than one hundred and eighty to two hundred yards. I think I am considerably within the mark in setting down Bangweulu as one hundred and fifty miles long by eighty broad.

With the fear before his eyes that Mohammed Bogharib might start without him, Livingstone had to be content with a cursory examination of the great lake, and began his return march on 30th July. He went back by the way he had come but it was not long before he found himself in the middle of a fight in which Casembe, Nsama, and the Arabs were all involved. This made an alteration in his course necessary in order to avoid Casembe's domain, and caused much delay. On one occasion, if not more, he came near to losing his life. 'Confusion prevailed all over the country.' So unsettled was the situation that for six weeks he made no entry in his diary.

By the end of October he was back in Kabwabwata, where he found his rebellious porters penitent, and probably because no other men were available, he re-engaged them.

In spite of all this delay, Mohammed was not, even then, ready to start for Ujiji and, because of the unsettled state of the country to the north, the Doctor did not judge it safe to travel alone. At long last, i.e. on 11th December, the caravan set out. 'It was a motley group, composed of Mohammed and his friends and a gang of Unyamwezi hangers-on, and strings of wretched slaves yoked together in their heavy slave-sticks. Some carried ivory, some copper, some food for the march, whilst hope, fear, misery, and villainy could be read on the various faces that passed in line out of the country, like a serpent dragging its accursed folds away from the victim it has paralysed with its fangs.' [1]

11th December. We marched four hours unmolested by the natives, and next day crossed the Lokinda River. We go between two ranges of tree-covered mountains.

12th December. The tiresome tale of slaves running away was repeated again last night. Not a good-looking slave-woman is left of Mohammed Bogharib's fresh slaves. All the pretty ones obtain favours by their address, beg to be unyoked, and then escape. Rain daily.

[1] Horace Waller's note, *Livingstone's Journals*, vol. i, page 355.

22nd December. We crossed the Lofunso River, wading three branches, neck-deep to men and women of ordinary size. Two were swept away and drowned. Two others were rescued by men leaping in and saving them, one of whom was my man Susi. A crocodile bit one person badly, but was struck and driven off.

25th December. We can buy nothing except the coarsest food—not a goat or fowl—while Syde, having plenty of copper, can get all the luxuries.

31st December. We reached the Lofuko yesterday, in a pelting rain. Not knowing that the camp with huts was near, I stopped and put on a burnous, got wet, and had no dry clothes. Remain to-day to buy food. Clouds cover all the sky from the north-west.

XXXI

Ujiji at last

THE new year—1869—began badly.[1] Health was poor and surroundings most depressing. Frequent wettings and cold affected his lungs, and pneumonia supervened; and this, endured on the march, was an excruciating experience.

Mohammed Bogharib was helpful, and his medical treatment no doubt beneficial, but it was only the marvellous toughness of his constitution that brought the Traveller through.

The brevity of the entries in the diary and the absence of the customary sketch-maps, and perhaps, above all, the absence of the usual New Year prayer, show how low was his strength. Waller thought that Livingstone never completely recovered from the effects of this illness.

1st January 1869. I have been wet times without number, but the wetting of yesterday was once too often. I felt very ill, but fearing that the Lofuko might flood, I resolved to cross it. Cold up to the waist made me worse, but I went on for two and a half hours.

3rd January. After one hour's march I was too ill to go farther. I had pain in the chest and rust of iron sputa. My lungs were affected. We crossed a stream and built sheds. I lost count of the days, weeks, and months after this.

About 7th January.[2] Cannot walk. Pneumonia of the right lung. I cough day and night. Sputa, rust of iron and bloody.

[1] The fourth year of the journey.

[2] *Last Journals*, vol. ii, page 2. When four years later Livingstone was able to check his date with Stanley, he found that he had dropped seventeen days. Probably the miscalculation dated from this time.

Distressing weakness. Ideas flow through the mind with great rapidity and vividness in groups of twos and threes. If I look at a piece of wood the bark seems covered with figures and faces of men, and they remain, though I turn away and turn to the same place again.

I saw myself lying dead in the way to Ujiji, and all the letters I expected there useless. Mohammed Bogharib came up, and I had a cupper, who cupped my chest.

8th and 9th January. Mohammed Bogharib offered to carry me. I am so weak I can hardly speak. Great distress in coughing. Feet swelled and sore. I am carried four hours each day in a *kitanda* or frame, like a cot. Sixteen days of illness. Mohammed Bogharib very kind to me, but carriage is painful. Jolting up and down and sideways. The sun is vertical, blistering any part of the skin exposed, and I try to shelter my face and head with a bunch of leaves, but it is dreadfully fatiguing in my weakness. I had a severe relapse after a very hot day. Mohammed gave me medicine.

14th and 15th February. Arrived at Tanganyika.[1] Syde bin Habib has two or three large canoes at this place. I asked his help. The cough and chest pain diminished, but my body is greatly emaciated. Syde came to-day, and is favourable to sending me up to Ujiji. Thanks to the great Father in heaven.

8th March. Patience was never more needed than now. I am near Ujiji, but the slaves who paddle are tired, and no wonder. They keep up a roaring song all through their work, night and day. I expect to get medicine, food, and milk at Ujiji, but dawdle and do nothing. I have a good appetite, and sleep well, but am dreadfully thin, and I have no medicine. Sputa increases. Hope to hold out to Ujiji. Cough worse. Hope to go to-morrow.

The series of brief entries from 15th January to 8th March

1 At the mouth of the Lofuko, about one hundred and fifty miles from Ujiji.

* M

record a slow progress up the long lake, till at last Ujiji was reached.

It was three years since he had left Zanzibar, and he had had no touch with life beyond Africa; and here he was to meet with a succession of crushing blows. He learned that his stores had been completely plundered; that there were no letters; that food for his enfeebled condition was not available; and, worst of all, that the supply of fresh medicines that he had counted on so eagerly had been left lying at Unyanyembe, one hundred and fifty miles away, and that there was a war in progress in the country lying in between. He took these disappointments with surprising quietness. Perhaps he was too weak to voice the hot anger he must have felt, at the spoiling of his goods.

14th March. Reach Ujiji. Found Haji Thahi's agent in charge of my remaining goods. Medicines, wines, cheese, have been left in Unyanyembe, thirteen days east of this. Milk not to be had, as the cows have not yet calved, but a present of Assam tea, and my own coffee and a little sugar. I bought butter and some four-year-old flour, with which we made bread. I found great benefit from the tea and coffee, and still more from flannel next the skin.

15th March. Took account of all goods left by the plunderer. Sixty-two pieces of cloth out of eighty were stolen, and most of my best beads. The road to Unyanycmbe is blocked by the Mazitu war. So I must wait.

The Musa sent with the buffaloes is a genuine specimen of the ill-conditioned, English-hating Arab. I was accosted on arriving by: 'You must give me five dollars a month for all my time'—this though he had brought nothing (the buffaloes all died), and did nothing but receive stolen goods. He made a regular practice of coming to my house, watching my servants, and going about the village with distorted statements about them. I had to expel him from the house.

13th April. Syde bin Habib refused to allow his men to carry my letters to the coast, as he suspected I would write about his doings at Rua.

27th April. I have been busy writing letters home, and finished forty-two, which in some measure makes up for my long silence. The Ujijians are unwilling to carry my letters. I suspect they fear my exposure of their ways more than anything else.

The intervening days were occupied in resting, and in attempting to recover what remained of his possessions. His strength came back slowly.

26th May. Thani bin Suellim came from Unyanyembe on the 20th. He is a slave who has risen to freedom. He is of the nervous type of African. He brought two light boxes from Unyanyembe, and overcharged heavily. When I paid him he tried to steal, and succeeded with one cloth by slipping it into the hands of a slave.

This is a den of the worst kind of slave-traders. Those whom I met at Urungu and Itawa were gentlemen. The Ujiji slavers, like the Kilwa, are the vilest of the vile. It is not a trade, but a system of consecutive murders. They go to plunder and kidnap, and every trading trip is nothing but a foray.

At this point in his journey Livingstone's plans were uncertain. His movements were severely restricted for many reasons. He found that he could not go where he wished, but for the time being, only where he might. He felt himself hedged in by unscrupulous enemies, and he had good reason so to think. Of the forty-two letters he tells us he had written, only one reached the coast. He believed that the Arabs were in league against him, since they feared the effect of his making public the story of their abominable cruelties.

His immediate hope had been to fulfil one of the tasks that the Royal Geographical Society had set him, viz. to clear up the problem as to whether or not Lake Tanganyika emptied itself to the north. This matter he and Stanley settled later, but at the moment he could get no assistance, and had to give up the thought.

At that time bazaar rumours were rife of the great wealth of ivory that was to be had in the Manyuema country, that lay to the west of the north end of the lake, and the Arabs were flocking in that direction. This seemed a fortunate opening to the Explorer, and he took the chance of going with them.

22nd June. After listening to a great deal of talk, I have come to the conclusion that it will be better for me to go to Manyuema about a fortnight hence, and if possible trace down the western arm of the Nile to the north, if this arm is indeed that of the Nile, and not of the Congo. Nobody here knows anything about it. They all confess that they have but one question in their minds in going anywhere. They ask for ivory and nothing else, and each trip ends as a foray.

The Manyuema are said to be friendly, where they have not been attacked by Arabs. A great chief is reported to be living on a large river flowing northwards. I hope to make my way to him, and feel exhilarated at the thought of getting among people not spoiled by contact with Arab traders. If I return hither from Manyuema, my goods and fresh men from Zanzibar will have arrived, and I shall be better able to judge of the course to be pursued after that.

After much uncertainty, the Doctor decided to accept an invitation from his friend Mohammed Bogharib to travel with his caravan towards the Manyuema country. This offered him a chance, and the only chance, of reaching the great Lualaba River, which had stirred him so greatly when he saw it flowing out of Lake Moero. His hope now was to sail down this stream, in the strong hope that it might lead him to the Nile or its sources.

This invitation had obvious advantages. The Manyuema were a tough people, and had the reputation of being cannibals, and his men were afraid. There would be safety with the Arabs. Then, no doubt, after his recent illness, Livingstone, being without his medicine-chest, was uncertain as to his health, and he had already tested the value of Bogharib's skill as a physician.

But there were obvious penalties of travelling in such company. It was inevitable that he should become identified, as the narrative will show did happen, with the slavers and their evil deeds. He comforted himself with the thought that his new companions conducted their dirty business with less cruelty than did the Portuguese. And there was nothing else to do. Even Livingstone could argue with his conscience!

So very slowly, and without any special incident, the caravan reached the Manyuema country.

XXXII

In the Manyuema Country

1st November 1869. Being now well rested I resolved to go west to Lualaba, and buy a canoe for its exploration. Our course was west and south-west through country surpassingly beautiful and mountainous, with villages perched on the talus of each great mass for the sake of quick drainage. The streets often run east and west, so that the bright blazing sun may lick up the moisture quickly from off them. The dwelling-houses are generally in line; the roofs are low, but well thatched, with a leaf resembling the banana leaf, but tougher. Inside, the dwellings are clean and comfortable, and before the Arabs came bugs were unknown.

5th November. In going, we crossed the River Luela, of twenty yards in width, five times, in a dense dripping forest. The men of one village always refuse to accompany us to the next set of hamlets. They are at war, and afraid of being eaten.

The Manyuema country is all surpassingly beautiful. Palms crown the highest heights of the mountains, and their gracefully bending fronds wave beautifully in the wind. The forests, usually about five miles broad, between the groups of villages, are indescribable. Climbers of cable size, in great numbers, are hung among the gigantic trees; many unknown fruits abound, some the size of children's heads, and strange birds and monkeys are everywhere. The soil is excessively rich, and the people, although isolated by old feuds that are never settled, cultivate largely. The women are naked. They bring loads of provisions to sell, through the rain, and are eager traders for beads. Plantains, cassava, and maize are the chief food.

The first rains have now begun, and the white ants took the hint to swarm and colonize.

6th to 8th November. We came to many large villages, and were variously treated. Some ordered us off, but were coaxed to allow us to remain overnight. They have no restraint. Some came and pushed off the door of my hut with a stick while I was resting, as we should do with a wild-beast cage.

Though reasonably willing to gratify curiosity, it becomes tiresome to be the victim of unlimited staring, by the ugly as well as the good-looking. I can bear the women, but ugly males are uninteresting, and it is as much as I can stand when a crowd follows me wherever I go. Much palm wine to-day made them incapable of reasoning further. They seemed inclined to fight, but after a great deal of talk we departed without collision.

15th November. We came to a country where Dugumbé's slaves had maltreated the people greatly, and they looked on us as of the same tribe, and we had much trouble in consequence. Hassani of Dugumbé got the chief into debt, and then robbed him of ten men and ten goats to clear off the debt.

20th to 25th November. We were now about ten miles from the confluence of the Luamo and Lualaba, but all the people had been plundered, and some killed, by the slaves of Dugumbé. The Luamo is here some two hundred yards broad, and the chiefs everywhere were begged to refuse us a passage. The women were particularly outspoken in asserting our identity with the cruel strangers, and when one lady was asked, in the midst of her vociferations, just to look if I were the same colour as Dugumbé, she replied, with a bitter little laugh: 'Then you must be his father.'

It was no use to try to buy a canoe, for all were our enemies. It is now the rainy season, and I had to move with great caution.

At this point he separated from the Arabs and made Bambarré, the chief town of the Manyuema, his headquarters.

26th December. I got fever severely, and was down all day; but we march, as I have always found moving is the best remedy for fever. I have, however, no medicine whatever. We passed over the neck of Mount Kinyima, through very slippery forest, and encamped on the banks of the Lulwa rivulet. (*31st.*) Heavy rains.

Horrors in Beautiful Surroundings

1st January 1870.[1] Prayer: May the Almighty help me to finish the work in hand, and retire through the Basango before the year is out. Thanks for all last year's loving-kindness.

Our course was due north, with the Luassé flowing in the gentle undulating country on our right, and the rounded mountains in Mbongo's country on the left.

4th January. The villages we passed were civil, but like noisy children they all talked and gazed. When surrounded by three hundred people, some who are not used to the ways of wild men think that a fight is imminent, but poor things, no attack is thought of. Many of Mohammed's men are dreadfully afraid of being killed and eaten. One man lost sight of his companions, and was seen running with all his might to the forest, with no path in it. On the seventh day after he lost his head, he was brought into camp by a headman, after being given up as a victim to the cannibal Manyuema!

5th to 7th January. Wetting by rain and grass overhanging brought on choleraic symptoms, and opium from Mohammed did not stop it. On suspecting water as the cause, I had all I used boiled, and this was effectual.

We proceeded nearly due north. The paths are often

[1] The fifth year of the last journey.

left to be choked by the overbearing vegetation, and then the course of the rill is adopted as the only clear passage. It has also this advantage, it prevents footsteps being followed up by enemies. In fact the object is always to make the approach to human dwellings as difficult as possible. Even hedges round the village sprout out and grow into living fences, and these are covered by a great mass of a species of calabash with broad leaves, so that nothing appears of the hedge to the outsider.

12th to 30th January. Through the hills Chimunémune. We see many albinos and partial lepers, and syphilis is prevalent. It is too trying to travel during the rains.

30th January. Rest from sickness in camp. The country is indescribable, with rank jungle and grass. The elephant alone can pass through it. These are his headquarters.

We came to a village among fine gardens of maize, bananas, and ground-nuts, but the villagers said: 'Go to the next village,' and this means: 'We do not want you here.' But I was weak and sat down at the next hamlet, and asked for a hut to rest in. A woman with leprous hands gave me hers, a nice clean one. Of her own accord she prepared dumplings of green maize, which are sweet, for she said she saw I was hungry. Seeing that I did not eat from fear of leprosy, she kindly pressed me: 'Eat, for you are weak only from hunger. This will strengthen you.' I put it out of her sight and blessed her motherly heart.

2nd February. I am recovering strength. We now climb over the bold hills, Bininango, and turn south-west towards Katomba, to take counsel. He knows more than anyone else about the country, and his people are now scattered everywhere seeking ivory. I do not relish their company.

3rd February. Caught in a drenching rain, which made me fain to sit, exhausted as I was, under an umbrella for an hour trying to keep the trunk dry. As I sat in the rain a little tree-frog, about half an inch long, leaped on to a grassy leaf, and began a tune as loud as many birds, and very sweet. It was surprising to hear so much music out of so small a musician.

The paths are now calf-deep. I crossed a hundred yards of slush waist-deep in mild channel, and full of holes made by elephants' feet, the path hedged in by reedy grass, often intertwined, and very tripping. I stripped off my clothes on reaching my hut in the village, and the fire during the night nearly dried them. At the same time I rubbed my legs with palm oil, and in the morning had a delicious breakfast of sour goats' milk and porridge.

5th February. A drenching told on me sorely. I lay on an enormous boulder under a Muabe palm and slept during the worst of the pelting. I was seven days southing to Mamo-hela, Katomba's camp, and quite exhausted.

I went into winter quarters on 7th February. Rest, shelter, and boiling all the water I used, and above all a new species of potato, called nyumbo, soon put me right. (*The rains continued into June, and fifty-eight inches fell.*)

About this time, though there is no mention of the matter in the journal, the Nassick boys, completely disgruntled, and not unnaturally, by the appalling conditions, deserted once more and joined up with the Arabs.

The Effect of Prolonged Overstrain

26th June. Now my people have failed me; so with only three attendants, Susi, Chuma, and Gardner, I started off north-west for the Lualaba. The number of running rivulets was surprising. We crossed fourteen in one day, some thigh-deep.

July. From Mohammed's people I learned that the Lua-laba was not in the north-west course I had pursued, for in fact it flowed west-south-west in another great bend, and they had gone far north without seeing it.

For the first time in my life my feet failed me, and now having but three attendants, it would have been unwise to go in that direction.   Irritable ulcers fastened on both my feet, and I limped back to Bambarré on the 22nd.

18th August.   Patience is all I can exercise.   These sores hedge me in now, as did my attendants in June, but all will be for the best, for it is in Providence, and not in me.

The watershed is between seven and eight hundred miles long, from west to east, or say from longitude 22° or 23° to 34° or 35° East.   Parts of it are enormous sponges.   In other parts innumerable rills unite into rivulets, which again form rivers.   Lufira, for instance, has nine rivulets, and Lekulwe nine.   The convex surface of the rose in a garden watering-can is a tolerably apt similitude, though the rills do not spring off the face of it, and it is seven hundred miles across the circle; but in the number of rills, coming out at different heights on the slope, there is a faint resemblance.

24th August.   Four gorillas, or sokos, were killed yesterday. An extensive grass-burning forced them out of their usual haunt, and coming on the plain they were speared.   They often go erect, but place the hand on the head as if to steady the body.   When seen thus the soko is an ungainly beast. He is a bandy-legged, pot-bellied, low-looking villain.   His light-yellow face shows off his ugly whiskers and faint apology for a beard.   His forehead, villainously low, with high ears, is well in the background of a great dog-mouth. The teeth are slightly human, but the canines show the beast by their large development.   The hands, or rather fingers, are like those of the natives.

These long weary months were without question the most trying of his life.   He was storm-stayed in mud and incessant rain, lamed by irritable ulcers, and his servants, except only three, were unreliable and discontented.   He was surrounded all the time by brutal paganism, and had no books save his Bible and a Bible dictionary, and there were no special geographical discoveries to balance his hardships.   It is hard to conceive more depressing or indeed more demoralizing circumstances. The Traveller filled in his days as best he could with painstaking observations, but time hung most heavily.

He had, however, one constant preoccupation that kept his horizon illuminated.

He was full of the thought of the Nile at this time. 'The discovery of its sources,' he wrote, 'possesses an element of interest that the North-West Passage never had. The great men of antiquity have recorded their desire to know the fountains of what Homer called 'Egypt's heaven-descended spring.' Moses, too, comes into this exciting picture. There is a fascinating legend that connects him with the sources of the Nile, and with the lost city of Meroë at the junction of the Lualaba rivers. 'An eager desire to discover any evidence of the great Moses having visited these parts held me spellbound.'

Another thought that held him up was the hope of the early arrival of the stores and fresh carriers, that he had asked Dr John Kirk, the consul of Zanzibar, to send. Thus reinforced, he still intended to explore the Lualaba valley. But months passed without news of them, and the delay seemed the last straw.

There were various reasons for this non-arrival, but the most important was a virulent epidemic of cholera, of which the rumour reached Livingstone at this point. It had originated at Zanzibar, where 70,000 people were said to have died, and had spread with heavy casualties along the trade routes from the coast.

10th October. I came out of my hut to-day, after being confined in it since 22nd July, or eighty days, by irritable ulcers on the feet and choleraic trouble.

The great want of the Manyuema is national life, of which they have none. Of industry they have no lack, but if a man from another district ventures among them he is sure to be killed.

25th October. Bambarré. In this journey I have endeavoured to follow the line of duty. I had a strong presentiment, during the first three years, that I should never live through the enterprise, but it weakened as I came near the end of the journey; and an eager desire to discover any evidence of the great Moses having visited these parts bound me—spellbound me, I may say—for if I could bring to light anything to confirm the Sacred Oracles I should not grudge one whit all the labour expended.

28th October. Moenemokata, who has travelled farther than most Arabs, said to me: 'If a man goes with a good-natured civil tongue, he may pass through the worst people in Africa unharmed.' This is true, but time also is required. One must not run through the country, but give the people time to become acquainted with you, and let their first fears subside.

10th November. I am grievously tired of living here. Mohammed is as kind as he can be, but to sit idle, or give up before I finish my work, are both intolerable. Yet I am forced to remain from lack of people.

The strangest disease I have seen in this country seems really to be broken-heartedness. Syde, vowing vengeance for the death of his brother, made a large number of captives. They endured their chains till they saw the broad River Lualaba roll between them and their homes. Then they lost heart. Twenty-one were unchained, as being now safe. However, all ran away, but eight, with many others in chains, died three days after crossing. They ascribed their pain only to the heart, and placed their hands on the right spot. One fine boy, about twelve, who died, said there was nothing wrong with him except a pain in his heart. As it attacks only the free, it seems to be really broken hearts of which they die.

Cholera complicates

1st January 1871.[1] Prayer: O Father! Help me to finish this work to Thine honour.

Still detained at Bambarré, but a caravan of five hundred

---

[1] The sixth year of the last journey.

muskets is reported from the coast. It may bring me men
and goods.

The Manyuema are the most bloodthirsty savages I know.
One puts a scarlet feather from a parrot's tail on the ground,
and challenges those near to stick it in the hair. He who
does so must kill a man or woman.

27th January. My men and goods are reported to be at
Ujiji.

4th February. Ten of my men from the coast will arrive
to-day. I am extremely glad to hear this, as it assures me
that my packet of letters was not destroyed.

Only one letter reached, and forty are missing!

I have sent Dr Kirk a cheque for Rs 4,000. Great havoc
made by cholera, and in the midst of it all my friend has
exerted himself greatly to get me off with my goods. The
first gang of porters all died.

8th February. Ten men, influenced probably by Shereef and
my two ringleaders, are refusing to go north, and have
struck work for more wages. I consented to give six
dollars a month.

The ten men sent are all slaves of the Banians,[1] who are
English subjects, and they come with a lie in their mouths.
They will not help me, and swear that the consul told them
not to go forward, but to force me back, and they spread
the tale over all the country that a certain letter has been
sent me to return forthwith. But for Bogharib, and fear
of pistol-shot, they would gain their own and their Banian
masters' end, to baffle me completely. Their two headmen, Shereef and Awathé, refused to come past Ujiji, and are
revelling on my goods there.

Friday, 16th. Started to-day. The chief gave me a goat,
and Mohammed another, but on coming through the forest
the men lost three, and have to go back for them and return
to-morrow. Simon and Ibram were bundled out of the

---

[1] Indian merchants.

camp. I told them to be off. They came after me with
inimitable effrontery, believing that, though I said I would
not take them, they were so valuable, I was only saying
what I knew to be false.

25th February. So we went on. I found that it was now
known that the Lualaba flowed west-south-west, and that
our course was to be west across this other great bend of
the river. I had to suspend my judgment, so as to be
prepared, after all, to find it perhaps the Congo.

Katomba presented a young soko, or gorilla, that had
been caught while its mother was killed. She sits eighteen
inches high, and has fine long hair all over. She is the least
mischievous of all the monkey tribe I have seen, and seems
to know that in me she has a friend, and sits quietly on the
mat beside me. In walking, she does not tread on the palms
of her hands, but on the backs of the second line of bones
of the hands. In doing this the nails do not touch the
ground, nor do the knuckles. She uses the arms thus supported crutch fashion, and hitches herself along between
them. Occasionally one hand is put down before the other,
and alternates with the feet. Or she walks upright, and
holds out a hand for anyone to carry her. If she is refused
she turns her face down, and makes grimaces of the most
bitter and human weeping, wringing her hands. Quite like
a spoilt child. She eats everything, covers herself with a
mat to sleep, and makes a nest of grass or leaves, and wipes
her face with a leaf.

I presented my double-barrelled gun, which is at Ujiji,
to Katomba, as he has been very kind. I pay him thus for
all his services.

2nd to 5th March. Left Mamohela and travelled over fine
grassy plains, crossing in six hours six running rills. We
came to Monanbunda's villages. These are very pretty,
standing on slopes. A little veranda is often made in front
of the door, and here the family gathers round a fire to
enjoy the heat, inhale the delicious air, and talk over their

little domestic affairs. The various-shaped leaves of the forest around are bespangled with myriads of dewdrops. The cocks crow vigorously, and strut and ogle; the kids gambol and leap on the backs of their dams, quietly chewing the cud. Other goats make-believe fighting. Thrifty wives often bake their new clay pots in a fire made by lighting a heap of grass roots. Next morning they extract salt from the ashes, and so two birds are killed with one stone. The beauty of the morning scene is indescribable.

Many have found out that I am not a slave-trader, and so in various cases they stand up and call loudly: 'Bolongo, bolongo.' ('Friendship, friendship.') I overheard the Man-yuema telling each other that I am a 'good one.'

20th March. I am heart-sore, and sick of human blood. The prospect of getting slaves overpowers all else, and blood flows in horrid streams. The Lord look on it.

28th March. The Banian slaves are again trying compulsion —I don't know what for. It is excessively trying. So many difficulties put in my way. I doubt whether the Divine favour and will is on my side.[1]

29th March. Crossed the Liya, and came seven and a half miles to sleep at one of the outlying villages of Nyangwé. The region is low compared with Tanganyika. About 2,000 feet above the sea. Crossed the Kunda River, and seven miles brought us to Nyangwé.

31st. I went down to have a good look at the Lualaba. It is at least three thousand yards broad, and always deep. The current is about two miles an hour, away to the north.

A Great Central African Market. Nyangwé

1st April. The banks are well populated, but one must see the gathering of the market of about three thousand, chiefly women, to judge of their numbers. They hold the

[1] This is the only recorded occasion when Livingstone seems temporarily to have lost faith in his mission.

market one day, and then omit attendance here for three days, going to other markets at other points in the intervals. Numbers seem to inspire confidence, and they enforce justice for each other. To-day the market contained over a thousand people carrying pots and cassava, brass, cloth, fishes, and fowls. They were alarmed at my coming among them. The people all fear us and have good reason, for the villainous conduct of many of the blackguard half-castes alarms them.

7th April. Made this ink with the seeds of a plant called by the Arabs *zugifare*.[1] It is known in India, and is here used as a dye.

10th April. Chitoka, or market, to-day. I counted upwards of seven hundred passing my door. With market-women it seems to be a pleasure of life to haggle and joke, laugh and cheat. Many come eagerly, and return with care-worn faces. All carry very heavy loads of dried cassava and earthen pots, which they dispose of very cheaply for palm-oil, fish, salt and pepper, and relishes for their food. The men appear in gaudy lambas and carry little, save their iron wares, fowls, grass cloth, and pigs.

I am at a loss for the day of the month.

12th April. My new house is finished. It is a great comfort, for the one I was in was foul and full of vermin. Bugs, that follow wherever the Arabs go, made me miserable, but the Arabs are insensible to them.

14th April. Kahembe came over, and promised to bring a canoe; but he is not to be trusted. They all think that my buying a canoe means carrying war to the left bank, and now my Banian slaves encourage that idea.

Livingstone still hoped to explore northwards the Lualaba

---

[1] From now on till Stanley appeared, Livingstone was without proper writing paper and ink. He used a dye concocted from seeds the Arabs used, and wrote on scraps of newspapers, or any other odds and ends he could get hold of.

River. But canoes, though often promised, were, in the end, always refused.

24th April. Old feuds lead the Manyuema to entrap the traders to fight. They invite them to go to trade, promising them plenty of ivory. Then when the trader goes with his people, word is sent that he is coming to fight, and he is met by enemies who compel him to fight. We were nearly entrapped by a chief pretending to guide us, but we detected his drift and changed our course, and dismissed him with sharp words.

27th April. Waiting wearily and anxiously. Owners of canoes say: 'Yes, yes, we shall bring them,' but do not stir. They doubt us.

16th May. At least three thousand people at the market to-day, and my going amongst them has taken away the fear engendered by the slanders of the slave-traders. It is pleasant being amongst them compared with being with the slaves, who are all anxiously longing to go back to Zanzibar. I saw no hope of getting on with them, and anxiously longed for the arrival of Dugumbé. At last Abed overheard them plotting for my destruction. If forced to go, they would watch the first difficulty with the Manyuema, and fire off their guns and run away, and as I could not run as fast as they could, leave me to perish. I cannot state how much I was worried by these wretched slaves.

27th May. A stranger in the market had ten human under jaw-bones hung by a string over his shoulder. He claimed to have killed and eaten the owners, and showed with his knife how he had cut up his victims. When I expressed disgust, he and the others only laughed.

18th June. Dugumbé has arrived. He has a large party and five hundred guns. He intends to remain for six or seven years. All know that my goods have been purloined by Shereef, and show me kindness. Dugumbé's first words were: 'Why, your slaves are your greatest enemies. I will buy you a canoe, but the Banian slaves' slanders have put all the Manyuema against you.'

24th June. Hassani (one of the most unscrupulous of the traders), and his canoe party in the river, were foiled by the narrows after they had gone four days. Rocks jut out on both sides, not opposite but alternately to each other, and the vast masses of the water of the great river, jammed in, rush round one promontory on to the other, and a frightful whirlpool is formed, into which the first canoe went and was overturned. Five lives were lost. Had I been there, I would have been in the first canoe, for the traders would have made it a point of honour to have given me precedence. The men in charge were so frightened that they returned.

14th July. I am distressed and perplexed. All seems against me.

XXXIII

Massacre at Nyangwé

15th July 1871. The reports of guns on the other side of the Lualaba all morning, tell of the people of Dugumbé murdering Kimburu, and others who mixed blood with Manilla. About one thousand five hundred people came to the market, though villages on the other side of the river were in flames.

It was a hot, sultry day, and when I went to the market I saw Adie and Manilla and three men who had lately come with Dugumbé. I was surprised to see these three with their guns, but put it down to their ignorance. It being very hot I was walking away to go out of the market, when I saw one of the fellows haggling about a fowl and seizing hold of it.

Before I had got thirty yards out, the discharge of two guns in the middle of the crowd showed me that the slaughter had begun. Crowds dashed off from the place, and threw down their wares in confusion, and ran. At the same time volleys were discharged, from a party down near the creek, on the panic-stricken women who dashed for the canoes. These, fifty or more, were jammed in the creek, and the men forgot their paddles in the terror that seized all. The canoes were not to be got out, for the creek was too small for so many. Men and women, wounded by the balls, poured into them, and leaped and scrambled into the water, shrieking.

A long line of heads in the river showed that great numbers struck out for an island a full mile off. Most of these would inevitably drown. Shot after shot continued to be fired on the helpless and perishing. Some of the long line of heads disappeared quietly, whilst other poor creatures threw their arms high, as if appealing to the great Father

above, and sank. Three canoes, got out in haste, picked
up sinking friends, till all went down together and disappeared. By and by, all heads disappeared.

Dugumbé put people into one of the deserted vessels, to
save those in the water, and saved twenty-one. The Arabs
estimated the loss of life at from three hundred and thirty
to four hundred souls.

My first impulse was to pistol the murderers, but Dugumbé
protested against my getting into a blood-feud, and I was
thankful afterwards that I took his advice.

After the terrible affair in the water, the party of Tagamoio, who were the chief perpetrators, continued to fire on
the people there, and fire their villages. As I write I hear
the loud wails on the left bank over those who were slain.
O, let Thy kingdom come! No one will ever know the
exact loss on this bright sultry morning. It gave me the
impression of being in Hell.

Some escaped to me and were protected; Dugumbé saved
twenty and liberated them. They were brought to me, and
remained overnight near my house. I sent men with our
flag to save some, for without a flag they might have
been victims, for Tagamoio's people were shooting right
and left, like fiends.

I proposed to Dugumbé to catch the murderers and hang
them in the market-place, but he gave reasons for not con-
senting, and promised to send orders to Tagamoio's men to
cease firing. I counted seventeen villages in flames.

My Banian slaves would like to go with Tagamoio, and
share his rapine and get slaves. I tried to go down the
Lualaba, then up it and west, but with bloodhounds it is
out of the question. I see nothing for it but to go back
to Ujiji for other men.

17th July. It is a sore affliction. At least forty-five days in
a straight line, equal to three hundred miles, or by turnings
and twistings, six hundred, and all after feeding the Banian
slaves for twenty-one months. But it is for the best.

18th July. The murderous assault on the market people felt to me like Gehenna, without the fire and brimstone, but the heat was oppressive, and the fire-arms pouring their iron bullets on the fugitives was not an inapt representation of burning in the bottomless pit.

The terrible scenes brought on a severe headache, which might have been serious had it not been relieved by a copious discharge of blood. I was laid up all yesterday afternoon with the depression the blood made—it filled me with unspeakable horror. 'Don't go away,' say the Manyuema chiefs, but I cannot stay here in agony.

Defeat and Retreat

20th July. I started back to Ujiji. All Dugumbé's people came to say good-bye, and convoy us a little way. I made a short march, for being long inactive it is unwise to tire oneself in the first day.

23rd to 24th July. We crossed the River Kunda in two canoes. Crowds followed, all anxious to carry loads for a few beads. Several market people came to salute, who knew that we have no hand in the massacre, as we are different people from the Arabs. We came over a beautiful country, with much cultivation.

31st July. Passed through the defile between Mount Kimazi and Mount Kijila. Below the cave with a stalactite pillar in its door is a fine echo. Came to Mangala's numerous villages and, two slaves being ill, rested on Wednesday.

4th to 6th August. Came through miles of villages, all burned because the people refused a certain Abdullah lodging without payment, with the certainty of getting their food stolen and utensils destroyed. The people evidently suspicious and unfriendly.

7th August. To a village, ill and every step in pain. The people all ran away, and appeared at a distance armed, and refused to come near—then came and threw stones at us, and afterwards tried to kill those who went for water. We slept uncomfortably, the natives watching us all round.

8th August. They would come to no parley. They knew their advantage, and the wrongs they had suffered from Bin Juma and Mohammed's men. In passing along a narrow path, with a wall of dense vegetation touching each hand, we came to a point where an ambush had been placed, and trees cut down to obstruct us while they speared us, but for some reason it was abandoned. Nothing could be detected, but by stooping down to the earth and peering up towards the sun, a dark shade could sometimes be seen. This was an infuriated savage, and a slight rustle in the dense vegetation meant a spear. A large spear from my right lunged past, and almost grazed my back, and stuck firmly into the soil. The two men, from whom it came, appeared in an opening in the forest only ten yards off, and bolted, one looking over his shoulder as he ran. As they are expert with the spear, I don't know how it missed, except that he was too sure of his aim, and the good hand of God was upon me.

I was behind the main body, and all were allowed to pass till I, the leader, who was believed to be Mohammed Bogharib, or Kolokolo himself, came up to the point where they lay. A red jacket, which they had formerly seen me wearing, was proof to them that I was the same that sent Bin Juma to kill five of their men, and capture eleven women and children and twenty-five goats. Another spear was thrown at me by an unseen assailant, and it missed me by about a foot in front. Guns were fired into the dense mass of forest, but with no effect, for nothing could be seen, but we heard men jeering and denouncing us close by. Two of our party were slain.

Coming to a part of the forest cleared for cultivation, I noticed a gigantic tree, made still higher by growing on an ant-hill, twenty feet high. It had fire applied near its roots, and I heard a crack that told that the fire had done its work, but felt no alarm till I saw it come straight for me. I ran a few paces back, and down it came to the ground one yard behind me, and breaking into several lengths, covered me with a cloud of dust.

Three times in one day was I delivered from impending death.

My attendants, who were scattered in all directions, came running back to me, calling: 'Peace! Peace! You will finish your work in spite of these people.' Like them, I took it as an omen of good success to crown me yet, thanks to the Almighty Preserver of men.

We had five hours of running the gauntlet, waylaid by spearmen, who all felt that if they killed me they would be revenging the death of relations. From each hole in the tangled mass we looked for a spear, and each moment expected to hear the rustle that told of deadly weapons hurled at us. I became weary with constant strain of danger —as I suppose happens with soldiers on the field of battle —not courageous, but perfectly indifferent whether I was killed or not.

When at last we got out of the forest to cleared lands near the villages of Muanampunda, we lay down to rest, and soon saw the chief coming walking in a stately manner, unarmed, to meet us. He had heard the firing, and came to ask what was the matter. I explained the misunderstanding.

In the evening he sent to say that if I would give him all my people who had guns, he would call his people together, burn off all the vegetation they could fire, and punish our enemies. He brought me ten goats instead of the three milch goats I had lost. I again explained that the attack was made by mistake, that I had no wish to kill men, and to join in his old feud would make matters worse. This he could perfectly understand.

I lost all my remaining calico, a telescope, umbrella, and five spears.

There followed a long weary trudge in much weakness and

Lake Bangweulu, Northern Rhodesia

physical distress. Still, each day has its entry in the diary, though usually very brief.

23rd September. I was sorely knocked up by the march from Nyangwé back to Ujiji. In the latter part I felt like dying on my feet. Almost every step was pain. The appetite failed, while the mind, sorely depressed, reacted on the body. All the traders were returning successful. I alone had failed, and experienced worry, thwarting, baffling, when almost within sight of the end towards which I had strained.

3rd October. I read the whole Bible through four times whilst I was in Manyuema.

8th October. The road, covered with angular fragments of quartz, was very sore on my feet, which were crammed into ill-made French shoes.

At last the eastern bank of the lake was reached, and the party was ferried over to the opposite bank, and up the coast to Rombola.

XXXIV

Unexpected Relief—H. M. Stanley arrives

23rd October 1871. (Rombola.) At dawn, off to Ujiji. Welcomed by Arabs, particularly by Moenyeghere. I was now reduced to a skeleton. With food available, however, I hoped that rest would soon restore me, but in the evening my people came and told me that Shereef had sold off all my goods, and Moenyeghere confirmed it by saying: 'We protested, but he did not leave a single yard of calico out of three thousand or a single string of beads out of 700 lb.' This was distressing. I had made up my mind, if I could not get people at Ujiji, to wait till men could come from the coast, but to wait in beggary was what I never contemplated, and I now felt miserable.

Shereef was evidently a moral idiot, for he came without shame to shake hands with me, and when I refused, assumed an air of displeasure as having been badly treated, and afterwards came with his 'good luck' salutation twice a day; and on leaving said: 'I am going to pray,' till I told him that if I were an Arab his hands and both ears would be cut off for thieving, and I wanted no salutations from him. In my distress it was annoying to see Shereef's slaves passing from the market with all the good things that my goods had bought.

24th October. My property had been sold to Shereef's friends at nominal prices. Syed bin Majid, a good man, proposed that they should be returned, and the ivory taken from Shereef, but they would not return stolen property, though they knew it to be stolen. But one morning Syed bin Majid said to me: 'Let me, I pray you, sell some ivory and give you goods.' But I said: 'Not now, but by and by.'

I had still some barter goods left, which I had deposited with Mohammed bin Saleh.

But when my spirits were at their lowest ebb, the Good Samaritan was close at hand, for one morning Susi came running at the top of his speed and gasped out: 'An Englishman. I see him,' and darted off to meet him. An American flag at the head of the caravan told the nationality of the stranger. Bales of goods, baths of tin, huge kettles, cooking pots, tents, etc., made me think: 'This must be a luxurious traveller, and not one at his wits' end like me.'

28th October. It was Henry Morton Stanley, the travelling correspondent of the *New York Herald*, sent by James Gordon Bennett, Jr, at the expense of £4,000, to obtain accurate information about Dr Livingstone, and, if dead, to bring home my bones.

The news that he had to tell me, who had been two whole years without any tidings from Europe, made my whole frame thrill. The terrible fate that had befallen France, the telegraphic cables successfully laid in the Atlantic, the election of General Grant, the death of the good Lord Clarendon, my constant friend, the proof that Her Majesty's Government had not forgotten me by voting £1,000 for supplies, and many other points of interest, revived emotions that had remained dormant in Manyuema, appetite returned, instead of the spare tasteless two meals a day, I fed four times daily, and in a week began to feel strong.

I am not a demonstrative man, as cold indeed as we islanders are reputed to be, but this disinterested kindness of Mr Bennett, so nobly carried out by Mr H. M. Stanley, was simply overwhelming. I do feel extremely grateful, and at the same time I am a little ashamed at not being more worthy of the generosity. Mr Stanley has done his part with untiring energy and good judgment, in the teeth of very serious obstacles.

The reader may well feel that Livingstone's account of the

world-famous meeting is hardly adequate for so dramatic an occasion. Indeed, for the three weeks that follow there are no entries in the journal. He was excessively tired, and needed the rest and change that Stanley's company so adequately gave him. The diary had been his resource in loneliness. Now it was not needed. Stanley, on the other hand, recounts the story with journalistic avidity.[1]

Good Food and Good Fellowship

Stanley's arrival was providentially timed. Without his assistance, Livingstone would almost certainly have succumbed. Though he was not, strictly speaking, 'lost,' since Kirk was in touch with him, his long silence had made his innumerable friends in Britain uneasy, but nothing had been done. This gave Gordon Bennett, Jr, of the *New York Herald*, an incomparable opportunity for a journalistic scoop. So he called one of his war correspondents, H. M. Stanley (by birth a Welshman) and ordered him to 'find Livingstone,' regardless of expense.

Stanley landed in Zanzibar in January 1871. He knew little about the Missionary. His interest, in the first place, was news, not philanthropy. He consulted the British Consul, Dr Kirk, but as he kept his purpose secret his reception was stiff. With characteristic drive he got together a well-equipped caravan, and started out in search, with but scanty knowledge of the Missionary's movements. He met great difficulty and hardship, but he faced these with a determination almost equal to that of Livingstone himself. He suffered much from fever and from native opposition, but he was well armed and, unlike the Doctor, he did not hesitate to use force.

Exploration with H. M. Stanley

Three weeks of lively company and of plentiful and appetizing food, restored to the elderly traveller a feeling of good health, and no sooner did he feel comparatively fit than his mind reverted to the task in exploration that had been referred to him by the Royal Geographical Society, and which lay near at hand: that of solving the problem of the northern outlet, if any, of Tanganyika.

[1] For Stanley's account of his meeting with Livingstone, see Appendix VI.

Though in haste to return home with his great news, Stanley was most eager to share in a short piece of exploration with so distinguished an expert, and he gives a detailed account of the adventure in his book *How I found Livingstone.* Canoes were hired, and on 16th November the trip began. Livingstone's account is fragmentary. Stanley, to whom the experience was new, gives a fuller description.

20th and 21st November. Passed a very crowded population, the men calling on us to land and be fleeced and insulted. They threw stones, and one, apparently slung, alighted close to the canoe.

We came on until after dark, and landed under a cliff to rest and cook; but a crowd came and made inquiries. They told us to sleep and to-morrow friendship would be made. We put our luggage on board, and set a watch on the cliff. A number of men came along cowering behind rocks, which then aroused suspicion, and we slipped off quietly. They called after us, as men baulked of their prey.

We went on five hours and slept, and then this morning came on to Magala, where the people are civil. The lake narrows here to about ten miles, as the western mountains come towards the eastern range that is about north-north-west magnetic.

24th November. To point Kizuka in Mukamba's country. A Molongwana asserted most positively, that all the water in Tanganyika flowed into the River Lusizé, and then on to Ukerewé of Mtéza. Nothing could be more clear than his statements.

25th November. We came in about two hours to some villages on a high bank, where Mukamba is living. The chief, a good-looking young man, came and welcomed us. Our friend of yesterday declared, as positively as before, that the waters of the Lusizé flowed *into* Tanganyika, and not the way he said yesterday. I have not the slightest doubt that the Tanganyika discharges somewhere, though we may not be able to find it. Lusizé goes to, or comes from, Luanda and Karagwé. This is hopeful, but I suspend judgment.

28th November. This afternoon Luhinga, the superior of Mukamba, came, and showed himself very intelligent. He named eighteen rivers, four of which enter Tanganyika; all come into, but none leave, the lake.

The problem thus settled, the party, apparently in leisurely fashion, made its way back to Ujiji. Stanley had several bad bouts of fever on the way, which Livingstone treated. The Doctor himself was at one time ill. It was 'rainy and uncomfortable' all the time.

Stanley, however, was in haste to forward his 'story' to his paper, and no sooner was Ujiji reached than preparations were begun for the American's return journey, but between rain and fever they had a 'sorry Christmas.' And so the sixth year ended.

The Parting with H. M. Stanley

1st January 1872.[1] Prayer: May the Almighty help me to finish my work this year for Christ's sake.

The two friends kept company as far as Tabora (Unyanyembé), Stanley on his return journey, Livingstone to collect what might remain of his stores that were there. The route was by canoe to Urimba on the lake, then by the well-worn track for the coast. Livingstone surprised Stanley by his stamina, but except that Stanley had several attacks of malaria, there was little to record. There was, however, one uncomfortably exciting incident.

27th January. On across long land waves, and the only bamboos east of Mpokwa Rill, to breakfast. In going on, a swarm of bees attacked a donkey Mr Stanley bought for me, and instead of galloping off as the others did, the fool of a beast rolled down and over and over. I did the same, and then ran and dashed into a bush, like an ostrich pursued;

[1] The seventh year of the last journey.

and then, whisking a bush round my head. They gave me a sore head and face before I got rid of the angry insects. I never saw men attacked before. The donkey was completely knocked up by the stings on his face, head, and lips, and died two days after in consequence.

Unyanyembé was reached on 18th February.

By the arrival of the fast Ramadan on 14th November, and a nautical almanac, I discovered that I was twenty-one days too fast in my reckoning.

Mr Stanley used some very strong arguments in favour of my going home, recruiting my strength, getting artificial teeth, and then returning to finish my work, but my judgment said: 'All your friends will wish you to make a complete work of the exploration of the Nile before you retire.' My daughter Agnes says: 'Much as I wish you to come home, I would rather have you finish your work to your own satisfaction, than return merely to gratify me.' Rightly and nobly said, my darling Nannie. Vanity whispers pretty loudly: 'She is a chip off the old block.' My blessing on her and all the rest.

I propose to go from Unyanyembé to Fipa, then round the south end of Tanganyika, Tambeté, or Mbeté, then across the Chambesi, round the south of Lake Bangweulu, and due west to the ancient fountains, leaving the underground excavations till after visiting Katanga. This route will serve to certify that no other sources of the Nile can come from the south without being seen by me. No one will cut me out after this exploration has been accomplished, and may the good Lord of all help me to show myself His stout-hearted servant, an honour to my children, and, perhaps, to my country and race.

At Unyanyembé Livingstone discovered, what he feared, that his stores had once again been plundered, but in this case not quite so completely, and as he had come, as he would have said, 'to be content with small mercies,' he has little comment to make.

Stanley, with characteristic generosity, made good the losses, and promised to dispatch fresh carriers from Zanzibar.

20th February. To my great joy I found four flannel shirts from Agnes, and I was delighted to find two pairs of fine English boots from my friend Waller.[1] Heavy rain. I am glad to be in shelter.

14th March. Mr Stanley leaves. Our march extended from 26th December 1871 to 18th February 1872, fifty-four days. This was three hundred miles.

I commit to his care my journal, sealed with five seals. The impressions on them are made by an American gold coin, anna and half-anna, and a cake of paint with royal arms. Positively not to be opened.

Tedious waiting for Reinforcements

19th March. Birthday prayer: My Jesus, my king, my life, my all. Once more I dedicate my whole self to Thee. Accept me and grant, O gracious Father, that ere this year is gone, I may finish my task. In Jesus' name I ask it. Amen, so let it be. David Livingstone.

There followed six months of dreary waiting for the porters that Stanley promised to send. It was a most trying time.

His diaries of this period are full of intimate reflections and careful observation. A selected few of these are given here.

The origin of the primitive faith, in Africans and others, seems always to have been a divine influence on their dark minds, which has proved persistent in all ages. One portion of primitive belief—the continued existence of departed spirits—seems to have no connection whatever with dreams, or, as we should say, with 'ghost-seeing,' for great agony is

---

[1] The Rev. Horace Waller, his friend since the Universities' Mission days, and the editor of these journals.

felt in prospect of bodily mutilations, or burning of the body after death, as they are believed to render return to one's native land impossible. They feel that they would thus lose the power of doing good to those once loved, and evil to those who deserve their revenge.

11th May. A serpent of dark olive colour was found dead at my door this morning, probably killed by a cat. Puss approaches very closely, and strikes her claws into the head with a blow as quick as lightning, then holds the head down with both paws, heedless of the wriggling mass of coils behind it. Then she bites the neck and leaves it, looking with interest at the disfigured head, as if she knew that therein had lain the hidden power of mischief.

13th May. He will keep His word, the gracious One—full of grace and truth. He said: 'Him that cometh unto Me I shall in no wise cast out.' He *will* keep His word. Then I can come humbly and present my petition, and it will be all right. Doubt here is inadmissible, surely. D. L.

21st May. I wish I had some of the assurance possessed by others, but I am oppressed by the apprehension that it may, after all, turn out that I have been following the Congo, and who would risk being put into a cannibal pot and converted into a black man for it?

23rd May. A family of ten whidah-birds (*Vidua purpurea*) come to the pomegranate-trees in our yard. The eight young ones, full-fledged, are fed by the dam as young pigeons are. The food is brought up from the crop, without the bowing and bending of the pigeon. They chirrup briskly for food. The dam gives most, while the red-breasted cock gives to one or two and then knocks the rest away.

25th to 27th May. Two whidah-birds, after their nest has been destroyed several times, now try again in another pomegranate-tree in the yard. They put back their eggs, as they have power to do, and build again.

*N

Another pair of the kind (in which the cock is red-breasted) have ten chickens, and also rebuild afresh.   The cock bird feeds all the brood.   Each little one puts his head on one side as he inserts his bill, chirruping briskly, and bothering him.   The young ones lift up a feather, as a child would a doll, and invite others to do the same in play.   So, too, with another pair.   The cock skips from side to side, with a feather in his bill, and the hen is pleased.   Nature is full of enjoyment.

Cock whidah died in the night.   The brood came and chirruped to it for food, and tried to make it feed them, as if not knowing death!   A wagtail dam refused a young caterpillar, till it had been killed—she ran away from it, but then gave in when ready to be swallowed.   The first smile of an infant, with its toothless gums, is one of the pleasantest sights in nature.   It is innocence claiming kinship, and asking to be loved in its helplessness.

31st May.   In reference to this Nile source I have been kept in perpetual doubt and perplexity.   I know too much to be positive.   Great Lualaba may turn out to be the Congo or Nile, or a shorter river after all.   The fountains flowing north and south seem to favour its being the Nile; great westing is in favour of the Congo.   It would be comfortable to be positive like Baker.   How soothing to be positive.

13th to 15th June.   On 22nd June Stanley will be a hundred days gone.   He must be in London now.   Sangara, one of Stanley's men, reports that my caravan (the expected porters) is at Ugogo.   Lewalé doubts him.   Nothing can be believed in this land, unless it is in black and white, and but little even then.   The most circumstantial details are often mere figments of the brain.   The half one hears may be safely called false, and the other half doubtful, or not proven.

19th June.   Whidahs, though full-fledged still, gladly take food from their dam, putting down the breast to the ground and cocking up the bill, and chirruping in the most engaging manner they know. She still gives them a little, but administers friendly shoves-off too. They all pick up feathers and grass, and hop from side to side of their mates as if saying: 'Come, let us play at making little houses.'

The wagtail has shaken her young off, and has a new nest. She warbles prettily, very much like a canary. The young whidah-birds crouch closely together at night for heat. They look like a woolly ball on a branch. By day they engage in pairing and coaxing each other. They come to the same twig every night. Like children, they try and lift heavy weights of feathers above their strength.

24th June. The medical education has led me to a continual tendency to suspend judgment. What a state of blessedness it would have been if I had possessed the dead certainty of the homoeopathic persuasion, and as soon as I had found Bangweulu, Moero, and Kamolondo flowing down the great central valley, bellowed out: 'Hurrah! Eureka!' and gone home in the honest belief that I had settled it. Instead, I am not even now 'cock-sure' that I am not following down what may, after all, be the Congo.[1]

Livingstone's son, Oswell, with a British Search-party
27th June. Received a letter from Oswell, dated Bagamoio, 14th May, which awakened thankfulness and deep sorrow.

This was apparently Livingstone's first knowledge of the fact that a British search expedition had been sent out, of which his third son, Oswell, was a member. It was in charge of Lieutenant Dawson. On arrival they heard with chagrin that Stanley had forestalled them. The officers in charge immediately resigned, and young Oswell was left alone. He might have gone on with the men that Stanley was sending to Ujiji, but did not feel able to face the journey. For this he was much criticized, but, in fairness, it should be remembered that he was quite inexperienced, and in poor health.

[1] This was true, but he happily never knew.

29th June. Received a packet containing one letter, one *Pall Mall Gazette*, one *Overland Mail*, and four *Punches*. Provision has been made for my daughter by Her Majesty's Government of £300, but I do not understand the matter clearly.[1]

3rd July. Received a note from Oswell, written in April last, containing the sad intelligence of Sir Roderick (Murchison's) departure from amongst us. Alas! Alas! This is the only time in my life that I ever felt inclined to use the word, and it bespeaks a sore heart. The best friend I ever had, true, warm, and abiding—he loved me more than I deserved. He looks down on me still. I must feel resigned to the loss by the Divine Will, but still I regret and mourn.

Wearisome waiting this, and yet the men cannot be here before the middle or end of this month. I have been sorely let and hindered on this journey, but it may be all for the best.

5th July. Weary! Weary!

21st July. Some philosophizing is curious. It represents our Maker as forming the machine of the universe, setting it a-going, and able to do nothing more outside certain of his laws. He, as it were, laid the egg of the whole and, like an ostrich, left it to be hatched by the sun. We can control laws, but He cannot! A fire set to this house would consume it, but we can throw on water and consume the fire. We control the elements, fire and water. Is He debarred from doing the same, and more, who has infinite wisdom and knowledge? He is surely greater than His laws. Civilization is only what has been done with natural laws.

30th July. Weary waiting this, and the best time for travelling passes unused. High winds from the east every day bring cold, and to the thinly clad Arabs fever.

What is the atonement of Christ? It is Himself. It is

[1] This was a belated recognition by the British Government of the value of the Explorer's work.

the inherent and everlasting mercy of God made apparent to human eyes and ears. The everlasting love was disclosed by our Lord's life and death. It showed that God forgives because He loves to forgive. He works by smiles if possible; if not, by frowns. Pain is only a means of enforcing love. If we speak of strength, lo! He is strong. The Almighty. The Over Power. The Mind of the Universe. The heart thrills at the idea of His greatness.

XXXV

The Last Lap. The Journey ends

15th August 1872. The men came yesterday, having been seventy-four days from Bagamoio. I have given them a few days' rest, and then shall start.[1]

25th August. Started and went an hour. The weather clear.

30th August to 7th September. Two Nassickers lost all the cows yesterday, through sheer laziness. They were found a long way off, and one cow missing. Susi gave them ten cuts each with a switch. Leave Chikulu's and pass a large puff-adder on the way. A single blow on the head killed it, so that it did not stir. About three feet long, and as thick as a man's arm. A short tail and flat broad head. Rest the caravan. Several ill.

19th and 20th September. I am ill with bowels, having eaten nothing for eight days.[2] Went to Simba's, three and a half hours north-west. Simba sent a handsome present of food. I gave him three dhotis of superior cloth. Rest here as the complaint does not yield to medicine, but I begin to eat now, which is a favourable symptom.

29th September. Through much bamboo and low hills to M'pokwa ruins and river.[3] The latter a deep rent in alluvial soil. Very hot. Many sick on consequence. Sombala fish abundant.

---

[1] Among the newcomers was Jacob Wainwright, a 'Nassick boy.' This man knew a little English, and we are indebted to him for most of the information about Livingstone's death, and after. He was one of those who carried the bier at the burial in Westminster Abbey.

[2] This is an ominous entry. It shows a return of the old trouble that ended fatally.

[3] Up to this point the caravan had returned over the track that they had covered along with Stanley. Now they leave it and turn south.

3rd to 5th October. Southwards down a steep descent into a rich valley, with much green maize in the ear. Men firing off ammunition had to be punished. We pass the Katuma River. The weather disagreeably hot and sultry. Up and down mountains—very sore on legs and lungs. Trying to save the donkey's strength I climbed and descended, and as soon as I mounted, off he set as hard as he could run, and he felt not the bridle. The saddle was loose, but I stuck on till we reached water.

8th and 9th October. Came on early as the sun was hot, and in two hours saw the Tanganyika from a gentle hill. The land is rough, with angular fragments of quartz. The rocks of mica schist are tilted up, as if away from the lake's longer axis. Some are upright, some have basalt melted into the layers, and crystallized into irregular polygons.

All are very tired, and in coming to a stockade we were refused admittance. So we sat outside in the shade of a single palm (borassus). This heat makes me useless, and constrains me to lie like a log. Inwardly I feel tired too.

13th October. Our course went along the top of hills lying parallel to the lake. They are 1,000 feet above the water, and are covered with trees, rather scraggy. At sunset the red glare of the water made the surface look like a sea of reddish gold. It seemed so near that many went off to drink, and were four or five hours in doing so. A milk-and-water sky portends rain.

15th October. Rest, and kill an ox. The dry heat is distressing, and all feel it sorely. I am right glad to rest, but keep on as constantly as I can. By giving dura and maize to the donkeys, and riding on alternate days, they hold on, but I feel the sun more than if walking. (*18th October.*) Ill with my old complaint again.

24th October. There are many rounded bays in mountainous Fipa. We rested two hours in a deep shady dell, and then came along a very slippery mountain-side to a village in a stockade. It is very hot to-day, and the first thunderstorm away to the east. The name of the village is Lindé.

3rd November. We marched this morning to a village where food was reported. I had to punish two useless men for calling out: '*Posho! Posho!*' (rations) as soon as I came near. One was a confirmed bhang smoker. The blows were lightly given, but I promised the next should be severe.

6th to 8th November. Pass a deep narrow bay and climb a steep mountain. Too much for the best donkey. After a few hours we look down on the lake with its many bays. A sleepy glare floats over it. I sent some to find a path out from the lake mountains, for they will kill us all. Others were dispatched to buy food.

Though this is the very hottest time of the year, and all the plants are burnt off or quite dried, the flowers persist in bursting out of the hot dry surface, generally without leaves. A purple ginger, with two yellow patches inside, is very lovely to behold, and it alternates with one of a bright canary yellow. Many trees, too, put on their blossoms.

The sun makes the soil so hot that the radiation is as if it came from a furnace. It burns the feet of the people and knocks them up. Subcutaneous inflammation in the legs is frequent, and makes some of my most hardy men useless.

The spirit of missions is the spirit of our Master, the very genius of His religion. A diffusive philanthropy is Christianity itself. It requires perpetual propagation to attest its genuineness.

16th November. The donkey died this morning. Its death was evidently caused by tsetse bite and bad usage by one of the men who kept it forty-eight hours without water.

18th November. We were overwhelmed in a pouring rain. One of the men picked up a little girl who had been deserted by her mother. As she was benumbed by cold and wet he carried her, but when I came up, he threw her into the grass. I ordered a man to carry her, and we gave her to one of the childless women. She was about four years old and not at all negro-looking.

19th November. I visited Kampamba. He is still as agreeable as he was when he went with us to Liemba.

20th to 23rd November. The men turn to stringing beads for future use, and to all, except defaulters, I have given a present of two dhotis and a handful of beads. I have diminished the loads considerably, which pleases them much. We have now three and a half loads of calico, and one hundred and twenty bags of beads. Several go idle, but have to do any odd work, such as helping the sick.

3rd December. No food to be got on account of M'toka's and Tipo's raids. A stupid or perverse guide took us away to-day to the north-west. We crossed the Lampussi twice. It is forty yards wide, and knee-deep. We camped and sent men in search of food. My third barometer is injured by a fall. The man who carried it slipped upon clayey soil. My men returned with a present of food from Kafimbe. Very heavy rains.

16th December. Off at 6 a.m., crossed the Lopanza, and came to a group of villages having food; and remain as we got only driblets in the last two camps.

The pugnacious spirit is one of the necessities of life. When people have little or none, they are subjected to indignity and loss. My own men walk into houses without asking leave, and steal without shame. I have to threaten and thrash to keep them honest. But if the villagers are pugnacious my fellows are as meek as sucking-doves. I give little presents to the headmen to heal their hurt sensibilities. This is much appreciated, and produces profound hand-clapping.

19th December. Too cloudy to take observations at this real geographical point.[1] The Kalongwesé is sixty or eighty

[1] At this point the route, which for many days had been due west, turned sharply south.

yards wide and four deep about a mile above the confluence of the Luéna. We crossed in small canoes and swamped one twice. Marched south about one and a quarter hours.

20th December. A wet bed last night, for it was in the canoe that we upset.

21st December. Arrived at Chama's. Heavy clouds drifting past, and falling drizzle. Chama's brother tried to mislead us yesterday in hopes of making us wander hopelessly. Failing this, he ran before us to the chief's stockade. We gave him two handsome cloths, one for Chama and one for himself, and said we wanted food only, and would buy it. They are accustomed to being bullied by half-castes who take what they want for nothing. They are alarmed at our behaviour to-day, so we took quiet possession of the stockade as the place they had put us in was on the open defenceless plain. Seventeen human skulls adorned the stockade. They left fowl and pigeons. There was no bullying. Our women went to grind the food and came away without noise. This flight seems to have been caused by the foolish brother of the chief, and it was difficult to prevent stealing by my horde. The brother came drunk, and was taking off a large sheaf of arrows, when we scolded and prevented him.

24th December. Very wet and drizzling. Sent back Chama's arrows, as his foolish brother cannot use them against us now. There were two hundred and fifteen in the bundle. The people are not afraid of us here, as they were so distressingly elsewhere.

25th December. Christmas Day. I thank the good Lord for the good gift of His Son, Christ Jesus our Lord.

Slaughtered an ox, and gave a fundo and a half to each of the party. This is our great day. So we rest.

27th. No rain fell to-day, for a wonder. I killed a Naia Hadje snake, seven feet long, here. He reared before me, and turned to fight. No observations have been possible through most of this month. A man, ill and unable to come on, was left all night in the rain, without fire. We sent men back to carry him. Wet and cold. We are evidently ascending as we come near the Chambesi. 4 p.m. The man carried in here is very ill. We must carry him to-morrow. (*29th.*) Our man, Chipangawazi, died last night, and was buried this morning. He was a quiet good man.

29th, or 1st January. I am wrong by two days.

Trapped in Flood and Mud
1st to 3rd January 1873 (30th).[1] Came on at 6 a.m. Very cold. The rains have ceased for a time. We have been unable to buy food through the illness and death of Chipangawazi. Our last cow died of injuries received in crossing the Lofubu.

4th January. March south an hour to the Lopopozi stream, twenty-five to thirty feet wide, and now breast-high, flowing fast southwards to join the Chambesi. Camped at Ketebé's.

6th January. Ketebé very civil and generous. He sent three men to guide us to his brother, Chungu. The men drum and sing heartily for him continually. I gave him half a pound of powder, and he lay on his back rolling and clapping his hands, and all his men 'lulliloo-ed.' Then he turned on his front and did the same. The men are very timid, and no wonder. The Arab slaves do as they like with them. The women burst out through the stockade in terror when my men broke into a chorus as they were pitching my tent.

8th January. Detained by heavy continuous rains. We are near Lake Bangweulu, and in a damp region. Got off in the afternoon in a drizzle.

9th January. Mosumba of Chungu. After an hour we crossed the rivulet and sponge Nkulumuna, a hundred feet of rivulet and two hundred yards of flood, besides two hundred yards of sponge, full and running off. We then,

[1] The eighth year of the last journey.

after another hour, crossed a large rivulet Lopopozi, by a bridge which was forty-five feet long, and showed the deep water. Then a hundred yards of flood thigh-deep, and three hundred yards of sponge. After this we crossed two rills called Linkanda, and their sponges, the rills in flood ten or twelve feet broad, and thigh-deep.

From now on the face of the country changes. References to 'sponges' become frequent. His men spoke later of the march's being a constant plunge in and out of morass. To a man weakened by dysentery, the increase in strain may be imagined. His followers must have been under fine discipline to endure such travel, for nothing depresses an African more than constant rain.

10th January. Chungu sent for us at 1 p.m. to come, but on reaching the stockade we heard a great uproar, and found it being shut from terror. We spoke to the inmates, but in vain, so we returned. Chungu says we should put his head on a pole like Casembe! Later (*11th*) Chungu sent a goat and a basket of flour, and excused his fears because guns had routed Casembe, and his head was put upon a pole. Cold and rainy weather; never saw the like.

14th January. The villagers are much afraid of us. After four and a half hours we were brought up by the deep rivulet, Mpanda, to be crossed to-morrow by canoes. There are many flowers in the forest: marigolds, a white jonquil-looking flower without smell, many orchids, white yellow and pink asclepias, with bunches of French-white flowers, clematis, *Methonica gloriosa*, gladioli, and blue and deep purple polygalus; and grasses with white starry seed vessels, and spikelets of brownish red and yellow. Besides these there are beautiful blue flowering bulbs, and new flowers of delicate form but little scent. To this list may be added balsams, *compositae* of blood-red colour and of purple, other flowers of liver colour, and bright canary yellow, pink orchids on spikes, thickly covered all round and three inches in length, and spiderworts of fine blue or yellow and pink;

different-coloured asclepias, beautiful red and yellow um-
belliferous flowering plants; dill and wild parsnips, pretty
flowering aloes, yellow and red in one whorl of blossoms;
peas, and many other flowering plants which I do not know.
Few birds and little game. The people are Babisa.

15th January. Found that Chunga had led us astray into an
angle formed by the Mpanda and the Lopopozi, and the
lake full of rivulets which are crossed with canoes. Chisupa,
a headman on the other side of the Mpanda, sent a present
and denounced Chungu for heartlessness. We went first
north-east and then east to the Mosinga, which we forded
again. We crossed a sponge thigh-deep before we came
to Mosinga. The whole march about east for six hours.

16th January. Away north-east and north, to get out of the
many rivulets near the lake, back to the River Lopopozi,
which now looms large and must be crossed in canoes.
We were treated scurvily by Chungu. He knew that we
were near the Chambesi, but hid the knowledge, and himself
too. It is the terror of the guns.

17th January. We need canoes badly, but have to treat
gently with the owners, or they will run away, fearing that
we should punish their silly headman. By waiting patiently
yesterday we drew about twenty canoes, but all too small
for the donkey, so we had to turn back north-west to the
bridge above Chungu's. The Lopopozi is here quite two
miles wide, and full of rushes.

18th January. We lost a week by going to Chungu's (a
worthless terrified headman), and had to turn back to the
ford of the Lopopozi, which we crossed.

21st and 22nd January. We went two and a half hours, and
were brought up by the River Malalanzi. They tried to
mislead us in vain. A man was sent to lead us from our
south-east course, but he turned back when he saw that
we refused his artifice.

No astronomical observations worth making taken during

December and January; impossible because of the cloud and rain. It is trying beyond measure to be baffled by the natives, lying and misleading us wherever they can. They fear us greatly. We are totally unable to observe our position. I don't know where we are. The people are deceitful in their statements, unaccountably so, though we deal fairly and kindly. Rain, rain, rain, as if it would never tire in this watershed.

24th January. Went on east and north-east to avoid a deep part of a large river, which requires two canoes. Went an hour's journey to a large stream through drizzling rain, at least three hundred yards of deep water, amongst sponges and sedges. One part was neck-deep, and the water cold. We plunged in elephant footprints for an hour and a half, and then came on in one hour to a small rivulet.

Carrying me over one of these deep sedgy rivers is really a very difficult task. One we crossed was at least two thousand feet broad. The first part, the main stream, came up to Susi's mouth, and wetted my seat and legs. One held my pistol behind, then one after another took a turn, and when he sank into a deep elephant's footprint, it took two to lift him so as to gain a footing on the level. Others went on and bent down the grass, to ensure some footing on the side of the elephants' path. Every ten or twelve paces brought us to a clear stream, flowing fast in its own channel, while over all a strong current came bodily through all the rushes and aquatic plants.

Susi had the first spell, then Farijala, then a tall stout Arab-looking man, then Amoda, then Chanda, then Wadé Salé, and each time I was lifted off bodily and put on another pair of stout willing shoulders, and fifty yards put them out of breath. No wonder! It was sore on the women of our party. It took us a full hour and a half for all to cross over, and several came out of turn to help me and their friends. The water was cold, and so was the wind, but no leeches plagued us.

We had to hasten the building of sheds, for rain threatened. At 4 p.m. it came on, a pouring cold rain, when we were all under cover. We are anxious about food. The lake is near, but we are not sure of provisions. Our progress is distressingly slow. Wet, wet, wet, and no observations.

28th January. A dreary wet morning, and no food that we know of near. It is drop, drop, drop, and drizzling from the north-west. We killed our last calf but one last night, to give everyone a mouthful.

29th January. No rain in the night, for a wonder. We tramped one and a quarter hours to a broad sponge, having at least three hundred yards of flood. All the streams flow through rushes, knee- and thigh-deep. I resolved to send out scouts south, south-east, and south-west. The music of singing birds, the cooing of the turtle-doves, and the screaming of the francolin proclaim man to be near.

30th January. Remain waiting for the scouts. Wet evening.

Growing Entanglement

1st to 3rd February. The scouts return unsuccessful— forced to do so by hunger. They did not come across a single soul. Killed our last calf, and turned back for four days of hard travel to Chitunkubwé's. I sent men on before us to bring back food towards us. March back smartly. The people bear their hunger well. They collect mushrooms and plants, and often get lost in this flat country. Tried lunars in vain. Neither sun nor moon in clouds.

5th February. Arrived at Chitunkubwé's, and are now at his mercy. The men who were sent before us slept here last night, and deceived us by going more slowly without loads than we who were loaded. We find the chief more civil than we expected. We were told that we had been near Matipa, and other chiefs.

I got lunars, for a wonder. Visited Chitunkubwé. A fine jolly-looking man, with a European cast of countenance, and very sensible and friendly. I gave him two cloths, for which he seemed thankful, and promised us good guides to Matipa's. It seems that we were close to human habitations, but we did not know. We have lost a month by this wandering.

7th February. The chief showed his leanings by demanding prepayment for his guides. This being the first step to desertion I resisted, and sent men to demand what he meant. He denied all, and said that the people had lied. We take this for what it is worth. (*8th.*) The chief dawdled, but the guides came at last, with quantities of food for bargaining on the way with our people. Slept in a most unwholesome ruined village. Rank vegetation had run over all, and the soil smelled offensively.

10th and 11th February. Back again to our old camp on the Lofu. We were all wetted, but we have food. A drizzly night, followed by a morning of cold wet fog, but in three hours we reached our old camp.

13th February. In four hours we came in sight of Luéna and the lake, and saw plenty of elephants and other game, but very shy. The guides are more at a loss than we are, as they always go by canoe.

14th February. Public punishment to Chirango for stealing beads, fifteen cuts. I sent two men to the first villages of Matipa for large canoes to navigate the lake, or give us guides to go east to the Chambesi, to go round on foot. It was Halima who informed on Chirango as he offered her beads for a cloth of a kind that had not hitherto been taken out of the baggage. It was so far faithful of her, but she has an outrageous tongue.

I remain because of an excessive haemorrhagic discharge. If the good Lord gives me favour, and permits me to finish my work, I shall thank and bless Him, though it has cost me untold toil, pain, and travel. This trip has made my hair all grey.

15th February. Sunday. Service. Killed our last goat while waiting for messengers to return from Matipa's. Evening: a messenger came back having been foiled by deep *tinga-tinga* and *bouga*.[1] He fired his gun three times, but no answer came.

17th February. Suffered a furious attack at midnight from *sirafu*, or driver ants. Our cook fled first. I lighted a candle, and remembering van der Kemp's idea that no animal will attack a man unprovoked, I lay still. The first came on my foot quietly, then some began to bite between the toes; then the larger ones swarmed over the foot and began to bite fiercely, and made the blood start out. I then went out of the tent, and my whole person was instantly covered as close as smallpox on a patient. Grass fires were lighted, and my men picked some off my limbs and tried to save me. After battling for an hour or two they took me into a hut not yet invaded, and I rested till they came and routed me out of there, too. Then came a steady downpour of rain, which held on till noon. I then got back to my tent.

The large *sirafu* have mandibles curved like reaping-hooks, sharp as a bee-sting. Their office is to remove all animal refuse, cockroaches, etc., and they took all my fat. Their appearance sets every cockroach in a flurry, and all ants, white and black, into a panic. On man they insert the sharp mandibles, and then with six legs push their bodies round, so as to force the points by lever power. They collect in masses in their runs, and stand with mandible extended, as if defying attack. They remained with us till late in the afternoon, and we put hot ashes on the defiant hordes.

18th February. We waited, hungry and cold, for the return of the men who have gone to Matipa. They returned to-day, having obeyed the natives who told them to sleep instead of going to Matipa. They bought food, and then believed that

[1] Flat prairie, filled with flowing water.

the islet Chirubé was too far off, a most lame story.   We shall have to make the best of it by going round north-west, to be near the islets and buy food, till we can communicate with Matipa.   If he fails us by fair means, we must seize canoes and go by force.   The men say fear of me makes them act very cowardly.   I have gone amongst the whole population kindly and fairly, but I fear I must now act rigidly, for when they hear that we have submitted to injustice, they at once conclude that we are fair game for all. It is, I can declare, not my nature, nor has it been my practice, to go as if 'my back were up.'

19th February.   A cold wet morning keeps us in this uncomfortable spot.   The people, knowing our need, are extortionate.   We went on at 9 a.m.   I was carried three miles to a canoe, and then went westward down the deep flowing Luéna for three hours.   Camped in an old village of Matipa's where, in the west, we see the Luéna enter Lake Bangweulu; but all is flat prairie filled with fast-flowing water.

A large party in canoes came with food as soon as we reached our new quarters.   They had heard that we were in search of Matipa.   All are eager for calico, though they have only raw cassava to offer.   They are clothed in bark cloth and skins.

22nd February.   A wet morning.   I was never in such misty cloudy weather in Africa.   A man turned up at 9 a.m. to carry our message to Matipa.   Susi and Chuma went with him.

26th February.   Susi returned this morning with good news from Matipa, who declared his willingness to carry us to Kabendé for the five bundles of brass wire I offered.   Matipa is at variance with his brothers on the subject of the lordship of the lands, and the produce of the elephants, which are very numerous.   I am thankful to the Giver of all for favouring me thus far.

1st March. Embarked women and goods, and went three hours south-east to Bangweulu.   The water in this country is prodigiously large.   Plains extending farther than the eye can reach have four or five feet of clear water, and the lake and adjacent lands for twenty or thirty miles are level.   We are on a miserable, dirty, fishy island called Motovinza.

3rd March. I visited Matipa at noon.   He is an old man, slow of tongue, and self-possessed.   He recommended our crossing to the south bank to his brother, who had plenty of cattle, and going along that side where there were few rivers and plenty to eat.

4th March. Sent canoes off to bring our men over to the island of Matipa.   They brought ten, but the donkey could not come so far through the *tinga-tinga.*   So they took it back for fear it should perish.   Matipa promised more canoes.   We moved outside as the town swarms with mice and is very closely built and disagreeable.

7th March. We expect our men to-day.   I tremble for the donkey!   Camp sweet and clean, but it, too, has mosquitoes, from which a curtain protects me completely—a great luxury.   The men came at 3 p.m.   The donkey had to be tied down, as he rolled about on his legs and would have forced his way out.   He came in stiff from being tied all day.   I pressed Matipa for a fleet of canoes equal to our number.

Back again on the Chambesi
11th March. Mapita says: 'Wait; Kabinga is coming.   He has canoes.'   Time is of no value to him.   His wife is making him *pombe,* which will drown his cares, but mine increase.   Matipa and his wife sent me a huge calabash of *pombe.*   I wanted only a little to make bread with.

16th and 17th March. Sunday.   Service.   I spoke sharply to Matipa for his duplicity.   He promises everything and does nothing.   The delay is most trying.   So many detentions have occurred.   They ought to have made me of a patient spirit.

18th March.   Sent off men to reconnoitre at Kabinga's, and make a camp there.   Matipa is acting the villain, and my men are afraid of him.   They are all cowards and say they are afraid of me, but this is only an excuse for their cowardice.

19th March.   (Last birthday.)   Thanks to the Almighty Preserver of men for sparing me thus far on the journey of life.   Can I hope for ultimate success?   So many obstacles have arisen.   Let not Satan prevail over me, O my good Lord Jesus!

8 p.m.   Got about twenty people off to canoes.   Matipa not friendly.   They go over to Kabinga on the south-west side of the Chambesi, and thence we go overland.

9 a.m.   Men came back, and reported Matipa false again. Only one canoe had come.   I made a demonstration by quietly taking possession of his village and house; fired a pistol through the roof and called my men, ten being left to guard the camp.   Matipa fled to another village.   The people sent off at once and brought three canoes, so at 11 a.m. my men embarked quietly.   They go across the Chambesi and build a camp there.

23rd and 24th March.   Men returned at noon.   Kabinga is mourning the death of a son killed by an elephant, and keeps in seclusion.   The camp is formed on the left bank of the Chambesi.   The people took the canoes away, but in fear sent for them.   I got four, and started with all our goods, first giving a present, that no blame should follow me.   We punted six hours, and landed in pitiless pelting rain.   We turned up a canoe for shelter.   The wind tore the tent out of our hands, and damaged it, too.   The loads were all soaked, and with the cold it was bitterly uncomfortable.

25th March. Nothing earthly will make me give up my work in despair. I encourage myself in the Lord my God, and go forward.

26th March. We started at seven-thirty, and got into a large stream out of the Chambesi, called Mabziwa. One canoe sank in it, and we lost a slave-girl of Amoda. Fished up three boxes and two guns, but the boxes being full of cartridges were much injured.

We crossed the Chambesi. It is about four hundred yards wide, with a quick clear current of two knots, and three fathoms deep. The volume of water is enormous. We punted five hours, and then camped. Kabinga keeps his distance from us, and food is scarce.

29th March. I bought a sheep for a hundred strings of beads. I wished to begin the exchange by being generous. Then a small quantity of maize was brought, and I grumbled at the meanness of the present. There is no use in being bashful, as they are not ashamed to grumble too.

30th March (5 p.m.). Men returned, but the large canoe having been broken by the donkey, we have to go back and pay for it, and take away about twenty men now left. Matipa kept all the payment from his own people, and so left us in the lurch. Thus another five days is lost.

3rd April. Very heavy rain last night. Six inches fell in a short time. The men at last have come from Matipa's.[1]

5th and 6th April. March from Kabinga's, our luggage in canoes, and men on land. Next day we leave the same way, but men were sent from Kabinga to steal the canoes, which we had paid his brother handsomely for. The whole country south of the lake was covered with water, thickly

---

[1] The remaining entries in this journal are all found in a small pocket note-book. At first ink is used, but later a stump of a pencil stuck into a steel pen-holder attached to a rough piece of bamboo. The writing grows increasingly feeble and indistinct.

These, and many other relics, are on exhibition at the memorial at Livingstone's birth-place in Blantyre, Lanarkshire.

dotted with lotus leaves and rushes.   The amount of water spread out over the country constantly excites my wonder. It is prodigious.   It is the Nile apparently enacting its inundations, even at its sources.

Pitiless pelting showers wetted everything; but near sunset we saw two fishermen paddling quickly off from an ant-hill, where we found a hut, plenty of fish, and some fire-wood.   There we spent the night watching by turns lest thieves should come and haul away our canoes and goods. Heavy rain.   One canoe sank, wetting everything in her. We did not touch the fish, and I cannot conjecture who has inspired fear in all the inhabitants.

7th April.   Went on south-west, and saw two men who guided us to the River Muanakazi, about the southern borders of the flood.   Men were hunting.   A lion wandered into this world of water and ant-hills, and roared night and morning, as if very much disgusted, and we could sym-pathize with him.   Our guides left us, well pleased with the payment we had given them.

Natives beating a drum on our east made us believe they were of our party.   This misled us, and we went forward through papyrus, tall rushes, arum, and grass, till we were tired out and took refuge on an ant-hill for the night. Lion roared.   We fired a gun in the stillness of the night, but received no answer.   So on the 8th we sent a small canoe at daybreak to ask for information.   Two men came, and at last we unloaded in a village of friendly people.

All hands at the large canoe could move her only a few feet.   Putting all their strength to her, she stopped at every haul with a jerk, as if in a bank of adhesive plaster.

Interminable Grassy Prairies and Morass

9th April.   After two hours' threading the very winding, deep channel of this southern branch of the Muanakazi, we came to where our land party had crossed it and gone on to Gandochité, a chief on the Lolotikila.   My men were

all done up, so I hired a man to call some of his friends to
take the loads; but he was stopped by his relations in the
way, saying: 'You ought to have one of the traveller's own
people with you.'   He returned, but did not tell us plainly
or truly till this morning.

10th April. The headman of the village explained, and we
sent two of our men with the turn-again fellow of yesterday.

   I am pale, and weak from bleeding profusely ever since
31st March.   Oh, how I long to be permitted by the Over
Power to finish my work.

12th April. Cross the Muanakazi. It is about a hundred to a
hundred and thirty yards broad, and deep.   Great loss of
αἷμα made me so weak I could hardly walk, but tottered
along nearly two hours, and then lay down, quite done.
Cooked coffee—our last—and went on, but in an hour I was
compelled to lie down.   Very unwilling to be carried, but
on being pressed I allowed the men to help me along by
relays to Chinama, where there is much cultivation.   We
camped in a garden of dura.

13th April. Found that we had slept on the right bank of
the Lolotikila, a sluggish, marshy-looking river, very winding, but here going south-west.   The country is all so flat
down here that the rivers are of necessity tortuous.   Fish
and other food abundant, and the people are civil and
reasonable.   They usually follow the character of the chief,
and this one is polite.   The sky is clearing.   It is the dry
season well begun.   Seventy-three inches is a higher rainfall than has been observed anywhere else, even in northern
Manyuema; it was lower by inches than here far south on
the watershed.   In fact this is the very heaviest known in
these latitudes—between fifty and sixty is the maximum.

   One sees interminable grassy prairies, with lines of trees
occupying quarters of miles in breadth, and these give way
to *bouga* or prairie again.   The *bouga* is flooded annually.
Other *bouga* extend out from the lake up to forty miles and

are known by aquatic vegetation, such as lotus, papyrus, arums, rushes of various species, and many kinds of purely aquatic subaqueous plants, which send their flowers only to fructify in the sun, and then sink to ripen one bunch after another.   Others, with great cabbage-looking leaves, seem to remain at the bottom.   The young of fish swarm and bob in and out among the leaves.   A species of soft moss grows on most plants, and seems to be good fodder for fishes fitted by hooked or turned-up noses to guide it into their maws.

One species of fish has the lower jaw turned down into a hook, which enables it to hold its mouth close to the plant as it glides up and down, sucking in all the pulpy food. The superabundance of gelatinous nutriment makes these swarmers increase in bulk with extraordinary rapidity, and the food supply of the people is plenteous in consequence. The number of fish caught by weirs, baskets, and nets now, as the waters decline, is prodigious.   The fish feel their element becoming insufficient for comfort, and retire from one *bouga* to another towards the lake.   The narrower parts are duly prepared by weirs to take advantage of their necessities.   The sun seems to oppress them, and forces them to flee.

With the south-east aerial current comes heat and sultriness.   A blanket is scarcely needed till the early hours of the morning, and here, after the turtle-doves and cocks give out their warning calls to the watchful, the fish-eagle lifts up his remarkable voice.   It is pitched in a high falsetto key, very loud, and seems as if he were calling to someone in another world.   Once heard, his weird unearthly voice can never be forgotten.   It sticks to one through life.

15th April. Cross Lolotikila by canoe, and went south-west for an hour.   I being very weak had to be carried part of the way.   Am glad of resting. $A\tilde{\iota}\mu\alpha$ flowed copiously last night.   A woman, the wife of the chief, gave a present of a goat and maize.

Photo: M. L. Maitland Moir

Livingstone's grave at Chitambo, Ilala

Scottish National Memorial to David Livingstone: 'The Last Journey'—
carrying the body to the coast.   Group carved in oak by C. d'O. Pilkington
Jackson

16th April.   Went south-west for two and a half hours, and crossed the Lombatwa River of one hundred yards in width, rush-deep and flowing fast.

17th April.   A tremendous rain after dark burst all our rotten tents into shreds.   Went on at 6.35 a.m. for three hours, and I, who had been suffering severely all night, had to rest.   Our course south-west three and three-quarter hours to a village on the Kazya River.

18th April.   On leaving this village we forded the river, and found it seventy yards broad, waist- to breast-deep all over. Much papyrus and other aquatic plants in it.   Fish are returning now with the falling waters, and are guided into rush-cones set for them.

Crossed two large sponges.   I was forced to stop at a village after travelling south-west for two hours.   Very ill all night, but remembered that bleeding and most other ailments are forms of fever.   Took two scruple doses of quinine, and stopped it quite.

19th April.   A fine bracing south-east breeze kept me on the donkey across the broad sponge, and over white sandy soil and much cultivation, for an hour and a half, when we stopped at a large village on the right bank of the . . .[1] The men went over to the chief, Muanzambamba, to ask the canoes to cross to-morrow.   I am excessively weak, and but for the donkey could not move a hundred yards.   It is not all pleasure, this exploration!   The Lavusi hills are a relief to the eye in this flat upland.   Their form shows an igneous origin.   The River Kazya comes from them, and goes direct into the lake.   No observations now owing to great weakness.   I can scarcely hold the pencil, and my stick is a burden.   Tent gone.   The men built a good hut for me and the luggage.   South-west one and a half hour.

20th April.   Sunday.   Service.   Cross over the sponge, Moenda for food and to be near the headman of these

[1] Probably from weakness no name is inserted.

O

parts. I am excessively weak. Village on Moenda sponge, 7 a.m. Cross Lokulu in a canoe. The river is about thirty yards broad, very deep and flowing in marshes, two knots from south-south-east to north-north-west, into the lake.

The last Journey ends

The search was now over.

It was one of Livingstone's fixed opinions, almost it might be called an obsession, that the best cure for illness, and especially for fever, was always to keep moving, and he held on to this self-imposed course, in spite of the constant protests of his servants, with almost superhuman tenacity. That, in spite of his extreme prostration, he continued to record so painstakingly his observations, is one of the marvels of his wonderful life.

But weakness had at last conquered, and these final words— a few broken sentences—are his last struggle.

All that is further known of the circumstances of his death, and of the events that followed, was gathered with loving care from the African attendants by his friend and editor, Horace Waller.

21st April. Tried to ride, but was forced to lie down, and then they carried me back to the vil[lage] exhausted.

(*Susi's account.* 'In the morning the Doctor tried to ride the donkey, but soon fell to the ground exhausted and faint. When he recovered we carried him gently back to the village, and to the hut he had been occupying.') Later, he sent to the chief for a guide for the next day, as he hoped to be well enough to travel. The answer was friendly.

22nd April. Carried on *kitanda* over Buga, south-west, two and a quarter [hours].

Next day, it being clear that his strength was decreasing, the men made him a *kitanda* of wood, and carried the sick man to the next village through a flooded grassy plain. The exhaustion caused by his dysenteric condition was extreme, and the pain excruciating. A grass hut was built for him here.

On the next four days the diary contains no entry except the date and the hours travelled.

According to Susi's account it would seem as if Livingstone recovered somewhat on the next stage, for while a hut was being built for him in the village, of which the name is not given, he, in the absence of the chief, summoned some of the people and asked them his customary question, as to whether they knew of a hill on which four rivers took their rise. They replied in the negative, so, explaining that he was too ill to continue talking, he dismissed them. In the next village the chief Kalunganjovu came to meet him, dressed in an Arab fez. Here there is reported a little incident that would seem to show that Livingstone had no thought that death was near. He is reported to have ordered his men to bargain for two large tusks. His purpose evidently was that should he run short of trade-goods by the time they got to Ujiji he might exchange the tusks for cloth to carry them on to Zanzibar.

27th April. Knocked up quite and remain—recover—sent to buy milch goats. We are on the banks of the Molilamo.[1]

This is the last entry in the little note-book.

The search for goats was unproductive, though the chief was helpful. 'Everything should be done for his friend,' he had said. A hut was provided for the night.

In the morning, the patient being unable to walk, the wall of the hut was broken down, and he was gently placed on his *kitanda*; and on the next river's being reached, he was very carefully transferred into a canoe. Movement was most painful, especially in the 'lumbar region of the back.'

Across the stream lay Chitambo's village (Ilala). There a hut was rapidly built for him, and a rough bed of sticks and grass. On this he was placed, and there he lay and dozed.

On the 30th Chief Chitambo came to pay his respects, but the sick man was able to speak to him only a few words, and asked him to return the next day.

---

[1] *Waller's note.* The name 'Molilamo' has been allowed to stand, but on Livingstone's map we find 'Lulimalo.'

About eleven that night, Livingstone called Susi and asked how far it was to the Lualaba, and on learning that it was about three days, 'as if in great pain he half sighed and half said: "Oh dear, dear," and then dozed off once more.'

About an hour later Susi was again summoned, and asked to bring the medicine-case. The Doctor now seemed hardly able to see, helped himself with difficulty to a dose of calomel, and then, in a feeble voice, said: 'All right. You can go now.' These were the last words he was heard to speak.

A lad was placed at the door of the hut so as to be within call, and the camp went uneasily to sleep. Some time during the night the boy looked into the hut, and, by the light of a candle, saw his master on his knees by the cot, apparently in prayer, and so withdrew. Early in the morning he peeped in again, and noting that the Bwana had not changed his position, called the senior servants. Together they entered the hut. They found Livingstone 'kneeling by the side of his bed, his body stretched forward, and his head buried on his hands upon the pillow.'

He had died during the night. The exact date is uncertain, but it is generally believed to have been 1st May 1873.

The famous story of how Livingstone's African 'boys' carried the embalmed body of their beloved leader through fifteen hundred miles of unfriendly country, to the coast, and committed it to the keeping of men of his own race, is a fitting epilogue to his own heroic history. It showed how much they had loved him, and how much he had influenced them. The story may be read in detail in any of his many biographies. To allay the fear of dead bodies common among the tribes the corpse was trussed up to look like a bale (see group facing page 399).

Finally, the body was buried in the centre of the nave in Westminster Abbey on 18th April 1874. The pall-bearers were all men who figure honourably in this story: Oswell, Webb, and Steele, associates of his early travel; Kirk and E. D. Young, his assistants on the Zambezi; Horace Waller of the Universities' Mission and, as representing his gallant African colleagues, Jacob Wainwright.

APPENDIX I

The Biography in Brief

1813   David Livingstone born in Blantyre, 19 March.

1823   Began work as cotton-spinner.

1836   Entered college and theological school in Glasgow.

1839   Accepted by the London Missionary Society.

1840   Medical lectures in Charing Cross Hospital, London. Took degree. L.F.P. and S. (Glasgow). Ordained 20 November and sailed 8 December.

1841   Arrived at Cape Town 15 March, and at Kuruman 31 July.

1843   Settled at Mabotsa.

1845–6   Married Mary Moffat and removed to Chonuane.

1847   Settled at Kolobeng.

1849   Crossed the Kalahari Desert and reached Lake Ngami.

1851   Discovery of the Upper Zambezi.

1852   Family went home (April). Boers raided Kolobeng (August).

1853   Started for West Coast (November). Loanda reached May 1854.

1855   Reached Linyanti (September) and left November. Discovered Victoria Falls.

1856   End of great journey (May). First return home (9 December).

1857–8   Published *Missionary Travels*. Overwhelmed with honours. Resigned from London Missionary Society. Appointed Consul. Sailed 10 March.

1859–60   Found Lake Nyasa. Explored valleys of Shire and Zambezi.

1861–2   Explored Lake Nyasa. Mrs Livingstone died, April 1862.

1863–4   Recalled. Sailed *Lady Nyasa* to Bombay. Home (July).

1864–5   Wrote *The Zambezi and its Tributaries*.

1865–6   Sailed for Africa last time, to explore Nile. Zanzibar (January).

1867   Reached Tanganyika. Discovered Lake Moero.

1868   Discovered Lake Bangweulu. Reached Ujiji.

1871   Explored Manyuema. Witnessed massacre on Lualaba. Returned to Ujiji and met H. M. Stanley (October).

1872   Stanley left (March) and Livingstone waited.

1873   Last days of travel. Died in Chitambo's village, Ilala, 1 May.

1874   Buried with national honours in Westminster Abbey (18 April).

APPENDIX II

Notes on Persons

Baines, Thomas (1822–75). Born in King's Lynn. Explored in Australia. Appointed artist to the Zambezi Expedition on recommendation of the Royal Geographical Society. Acted also as store-keeper. Dismissed after about two years. It is generally felt that Livingstone made much of a small fault, and acted over-severely, if not unfairly. (See *Life of Thomas Baines*, by Professor J. P. R. Wallis (Chatto & Windus), and *Livingstone the Liberator* (Collins), page 235.)

Bedingfield, Commander, R.N. Second in charge of Zambezi Expedition. Livingstone had met him at Loanda in 1854. The appointment was unfortunate. The men were uncongenial and Bedingfield showed insubordination, and, after resigning, made his grievances widely known.

Edwards, Rogers, artisan missionary with the London Missionary Society (1825–76). Livingstone's colleague at Mabotsa.

Kirk, Dr John (afterwards *Sir*). Born at Barry, Angus. Studied medicine in Edinburgh. Specialized in botany. Recommended to Livingstone by the Director of Kew Gardens. The Explorer's best helper. Acted as botanist and physician of the expedition. Returned home in 1863, but went out to Zanzibar three years later. Became Consul there, and did more than anyone, except Livingstone, to suppress the East African slave-trade. Was knighted for his good work. (See *Kirk on the Zambezi* (Clarendon Press), *Livingstone's Last Journey* (Collins), both by Sir Reginald Coupland.)

Lacerda, Dr Francesco de, famous Portuguese scientist and geographer. (*Last Journals*, vol. i, page 245.) Born *c.* 1770. Travelled much in South America and elsewhere. Landed in East Africa in 1797, and the following year, hoping to link up East and West Portuguese African colonies, attempted to cross the continent. With great difficulty he reached Casembe's country, where he died of fever. The tradition of his visit still persists locally.

Livingstone, while he had a great respect for this man's work, thought very lightly of the ordinary Portuguese geographers and their maps, which he alleged were fantastic and founded on hearsay. They, on their part, disputed the priority he claimed for his discoveries. In

particular, they denied his claim to have been the first white man to have
crossed Africa, and asserted that two half-caste Portuguese traders,
Pedra Jean Batista and Amaro Joseph, performed the feat in 1806–11.
Livingstone used to claim that he had evidence to prove that these
men had not finished the journey.

Livingstone, Charles (1822–75). David's brother, younger by nine
years. Emigrated to U.S.A. with Livingstone's help in 1840. Studied
in Union College, New York. Became naturalized and held pastoral
charge there. Was included in the Zambezi Expedition as 'Moral
Agent.' Had charge of photography. Was also credited with special
knowledge of cotton. He was not a success or generally popular, and
was, in Kirk's opinion, the cause of the quarrel between Baines and
the Leader. Was later appointed British Consul in Fernando Po,
where he did very useful anti-slavery work. He died of fever.

Mackenzie, Bishop, Charles Frederick (1825–62). Bishop of Central Africa.
Born Portmore, Peebles-shire. Educated at Edinburgh Academy and
Caius College, Cambridge. A fine athlete. Went to Africa in 1851,
and worked under Bishop Colenso in Natal. Appointed head of the
newly established Universities' Mission. Began work in the Nyasa
uplands, 1861. Died of fever within a year. (See *Memorial of Bishop
Mackenzie*, by Goodwin.)

Maclear, Sir Thomas (1794–1879). Educated in medicine, but took up
astronomy as hobby, and was appointed Astronomer Royal at the Cape
in 1834. Did useful survey and other work. Knighted in 1860.
Taught Livingstone the use of the sextant, etc. Maclear greatly
admired the accuracy of the Missionary's observations. These were
sent to him systematically, and are said to fill a large trunk.

Moffat, Dr Robert (1795–1888). Livingstone's father-in-law. Famous
missionary. Born in Ormiston, East Lothian. A trained gardener.
Sent by London Missionary Society to South Africa in 1817. A
shaggy-haired, impressive-looking man of simple nature, he acquired a
marvellous influence over many difficult Africans, such as Afrikander
and Mosilikatse. Spent his life in Kuruman, which he made beautiful.
Did much work on the Setswana language, especially in Bible translation.
Received D.D. degree in 1878. Was present at Livingstone's funeral
in Westminster Abbey. Died at age of 93. (See *The Lives of Robert
and Mary Moffat* (T. Fisher Unwin, 1885) and *The Matabele Journals
of Robert Moffat*, edited by Professor J. P. R. Wallis. (Chatto &
Windus, 1945.))

Mosilikatse. A great Matabele (Zulu) chief, father of Lobengula. A complete autocrat over a great tribe of highly organized fighters; widely feared for his cruelty. The chief enemy of the Boers, and also of the Makololo. Moffat attained an extraordinary influence over this man, and to a considerable extent tamed him. See above.

Murchison, Sir Roderick (1792–1871). Famous geologist. ('The best friend I ever had, true, warm, abiding.'—D. L.) A Scot of Highland extraction. Served under Sir John Moore in Peninsular campaign. President of the Geological Society and of the Royal Geographical Society.

Oswell, William Cotton (1818–93). A most generous friend of the Livingstone family. Pupil of Dr Arnold of Rugby. Joined the East Indian Company, Madras. Went to Africa for health reasons. Discovered along with Livingstone Lake Ngami and the Upper Zambezi. A famous hunter, 'The Nimrod of Africa.' Took part in the Crimean War. Settled in Kent. (See *William Cotton Oswell, Hunter and Explorer*, by W. E. Oswell.)

Rigby, Colonel (1820–95). British Consul, 1858–61, in Zanzibar. A very vigorous opponent of the slave-trade. Livingstone and he corresponded, but did not meet.

Sebituane. Chief of the Makololo. A great ruler of Basuto extraction. Expelled from near Kuruman by the Griquas, he incorporated various Bechuana tribes, but was driven north by the Matabele, though later he held them in check. He created a great Barótse kingdom in the Upper Zambezi valley. A man of unusual gifts.

Sechele. Chief of the Bakwena. Livingstone's first convert. A man of unusual intelligence. He resisted the Boers and incurred their animosity. His town was attacked and destroyed at the time the Missionary's house was destroyed. He re-established his position later.

Sekomi (Sekgoma). Chief of the Bamangwato. Father of the famous Christian chief, Khama.

Stanley, Henry Morton (1841–1904). Born in Denbigh, Wales. Had hard childhood that left its mark on him. His original name was Rowlands. Sailed in youth to New Orleans, where he worked for a friendly merchant, whose name he took. Served on both sides in the American Civil War. Became war correspondent of the *New York Herald*, and in that capacity 'found Livingstone.' Returning to Africa he explored the Lualaba, and found it to lead to the Congo. This region he explored later for the King of the Belgians. In 1886 he led a party to relieve Emin Pasha. He became a British subject in 1892.

Steele, Sir John Montague (1820–90). One of Livingstone's hunting friends. 'The politest of the whole. Well versed in the classics.' Saw much service in the Crimea. Was the Explorer's correspondent with the Royal Geographical Society. One of the pall-bearer's at Livingstone's funeral.

Susi and Chuma. Livingstone's devoted servants. Not related. Susi, who was older and taller, was a Shupanga man, and was first a wood-cutter for the *Pioneer*. Chuma was a Wanyan boy, a slave whom Livingstone had released. He sailed in the *Lady Nyasa* to Bombay. Both were of the small faithful nucleus throughout the last journey. Both led the party that carried the body to the coast, and both were brought to England by Young of Kelly, but arrived too late for the funeral. Stayed at Newstead Abbey, and other places in this country, for some months, and then returned to Zanzibar.

Thornton, Richard (1837–62). The geologist of the Zambezi Expedition. A popular member of the group, but was at first too young to stand up to the hardships and face his duties. At the end of his two years' contract Livingstone 'terminated his engagement,' but left his return open. Thornton thereafter pulled himself together, and joined Baron van der Decken's expedition to explore the Kilimanjaro range, and did other good work. Livingstone later reinstated him, but he died soon after, in a gallant attempt to secure animal food for the Universities' party.

Waller, the Rev. Horace (1833–96). The editor of the *Last Journals*. Born in London. As a member of the Universities' Mission, he met Livingstone on the Shire in 1861 and became a close friend. Retired from the mission after Mackenzie's death (1862). Became vicar of Twywell and elsewhere. A close friend of General Gordon. Wrote largely on African subjects, and especially against the slave-trade.

Young, Lieutenant E. D., R.N. Belonging to H.M.S. *Gorgon*, he joined, in 1859, Livingstone on the Shire, and took command of the *Pioneer*.

*o

He was put in charge of the search expedition in 1867 (see page 300). He published the story of his rapid trip up the Shire. Was one of the pall-bearers at the funeral. He led the party that established in 1875 the 'Livingstonia Mission' and helped to put the first steamer on Lake Nyasa.

APPENDIX III

The Looting of Kolobeng. Livingstone's Conflict with the Boers

As this incident (see page 48), which every decent Boer regretted, passes out of the story it is advisable to say something here of Livingstone's contact with the Dutch during the previous eleven years.

The dispute in which he had become involved was, of course, of fundamental importance, and was only one facet of the colour problem that is the cause of so much of the unrest of the world.

It is impossible to conceive the Missionary's having taken any other stand than that which he took. A born fighter, raised in the Scots tradition of freedom; a member of the London Missionary Society, a body which has always been distinguished as the champion of the black man in Africa—the society of Philip, of Moffat, and John Mackenzie —it was inevitable that he should espouse the cause of the African with all the impetuosity of his Highland nature. This he did, however, from no dislike of the Dutch. Far from that, while criticizing their attitude towards the 'sons of Ham,' he liked and admired the farmers in the settled parts of the country, especially the older men. Both in their theology and in their general outlook on life, they reminded him of his father.

It was with the younger hot-bloods who formed the spearhead of the northern drang that he clashed. Apart from the whole question of white expansion, there was much in their rough methods that offended his sense of justice, and what Livingstone felt he let the world know. In consequence he became noted as an 'agitator,' and attempts were made to have him expelled from the country.

Something of this old prejudice against him still continues in South Africa. Credence is even now given in certain quarters to the charge which was the immediate cause of the outrage at Kolobeng: to the story, namely, that he had been trading in arms with the Bakwena. He was accused of maintaining a private arsenal, and with having even supplied Sechele with a cannon—a formidable list of sins.

There is not the faintest trace of truth in these canards. Nothing could have been more completely out of character, and Livingstone was nothing if not consistent.

There is no vestige of proof that Livingstone ever gave Africans arms, except on such rare occasions as to the young chief Lechulathebe (page 30),[1] when he was forced by circumstances to do so. The so-called arsenal was only a handyman's workshop, and the terrible cannon nothing more formidable than a cooking-pot of unusual size. The story of the black pot became, indeed, one of his favourite jokes.

Surely the fact that when the clash did eventually come, the Bechuana could produce only five guns, was proof enough of the absurdity of the whole report.

In one respect, as he realized later, Livingstone had himself to blame. Though he was well aware that these stories were widely current, he purposely refrained from contradicting them, in the misplaced confidence that the belief that the tribe was well armed would make its enemies chary of attack.

Surely the statement made by Field Marshal Smuts, in his address in Edinburgh in November 1929, might be allowed to provide for this hoary yarn a burial long overdue. He said: 'I once took the opportunity to discuss the matter with President Kruger, and his explanation of the differences which arose between the Boers and Livingstone was, that Gordon Cumming—another of your errant countrymen—had supplied the border tribes with rifles and ammunition in exchange for ivory; and the Boers, finding the natives armed, concluded erroneously that Livingstone had done so, and treated him accordingly.'

It may be permissible to surmise that in the end the victim got more private fun out of the story of the big black pot, than he did pain from the £300 damage that he suffered. Anyhow, that would have been characteristic of the man.

APPENDIX IV

The Inland Slave Traffic

THE sudden intensification, at the end of his first term of service, of Livingstone's hatred of the traffic in slaves, is a good illustration of his mental attitude. He was not a man to whom it came naturally to think and plan far ahead. He found his duty in what lay before him, but once a purpose was clearly formed, he followed it with inflexible tenacity.

[1] *Livingstone the Liberator*, p. 120.

Without question the Explorer was well versed in the story of the earlier stages of the anti-slavery campaign. It is on record, though he himself does not mention the fact, that he was present at the memorable meeting in Exeter Hall in 1840, when, following the publication of T. F. Buxton's book *The African Slave-Trade*, the ill-fated Niger Expedition was inaugurated. But there is no evidence that, in his early days in Africa, the problem of slavery was in the forefront of his mind. His championship of the Bantu, as against the Boer, was, as has been seen, mainly on other grounds.

It was not till the discovery of the Upper Zambezi in 1851, when he had already been ten years in the country, that he was brought up personally against slave exploitation in an organized form. The experience seems to have come to him with all the force of a horrid discovery. He came across there, for the first time, a tribe of half-caste Portuguese traders, the Mambari, who were engaged in the systematic barter of guns and cloth for human flesh. He was to meet them thereafter in many places.

Livingstone perceived immediately the unlimited ramifications of evil that such a trade would necessarily cause, and this prospect added additional urgency to his plan to open a road to the coast, by which honourable trading might be introduced.

During his trans-African journey, though he saw much of the demoralizing effects of slavery and slave raiding, he saw little of its actual practice. Nor did he at that time realize the extent to which the Portuguese authorities were involved in the business. Many of their officials were most friendly and helpful. There were not a few whom he greatly admired, all of whom seemed to share in his abhorrence of traffic. So sure was he of their sympathy, that one of the last things he did before he sailed for home in 1856, was to write to the King of Portugal, thanking him for the kindness of his officers, and pointing out emphatically the demoralizing effects of slavery on the whole economy of his colony. The letter was politely acknowledged, and there the matter rested.

Somewhat before this time the East African slave traffic had assumed a new and more virulent form, which marked it off from the same trade on the west coast. That, though it had been cruel beyond words, had been conducted in the main on peaceful lines, by barter and similar means. Not so that on the east, and for a special reason.

Slave caravanning had been an old institution on that coast, but about this date it was wakened to a new activity by rumours of the vast wealth in ivory and copper stored in Central Africa. This was to be got on easy barter terms for cloth and beads, but the difficulty was carriage. The tsetse-fly made animal transport impossible. Human porterage was costly, and so a simple but brutally barbarous method was largely resorted to by the Arab and half-caste traders interested.

Villages were surrounded during the night and set on fire, and all able-bodied people of both sexes captured and secured by slave-sticks and chains. They were then formed into long gangs, loaded with burdens, and driven mercilessly with whips. The scenes that Livingstone describes so graphically became appallingly common in hitherto peaceful districts. Nowhere are these horrors more vividly sketched than in Livingstone's journals. The horrible sights that he was forced to witness, on the banks of the Shire and along the shores of Lake Nyasa, burnt themselves deep into his mind; and thereafter it became the main purpose of his life to put a stop to the curse which, in a famous phrase, he called 'the open sore of the world.'

It is to be feared, however, that the Explorer found little personal satisfaction in the fight. It often seemed to him that he was likely to bring to his Africans more harm than benefit. Not only did his efforts appear to close no doors to the invaders, they seemed on the other hand to open new ones, since the slavers penetrated into regions that he had opened up, where till then they had been afraid to go, and even did so, calling themselves his children.

It was, however, during his last journey, when not only did he appear to be achieving nothing, but he had been forced to become dependent on the charity of the very men against whom he was fighting, that he felt his ineffectiveness most. It was during his broodings in these depressing days that he began to find comfort in a new hope, that transformed his monotonous attempts to find the sources of the Nile into a holy quest. In a letter from Manyuema to his brother John in America, he writes thus: 'If the good Lord gives me strength to complete the task, I shall not grudge my hunger and toils. Above all, if He permits me to put a stop to the enormous evils of the slave-trade, I shall bless His name with all my heart. The Nile sources are valuable to me only as a means of opening my mouth with power.'

And that is how in the end the deliverance did come. The tremendous impression made upon world opinion by the circumstances of his death, and by the story of the loyalty of his African men, together with the news of the ghastly massacre at Nyangwé (page 362), raised a storm of righteous anger that strengthened immensely the hands of Sir John Kirk, and others, who remained to fight in the same cause, and went far, before many years were passed, in bringing to an end this ancient horror.

APPENDIX V

The Injati Defeat and the Linyanti Tragedy

BEFORE the expedition reached the Falls, news had come to them
(page 220) of the terrible disaster that had overwhelmed the party
sent by the London Missionary Society, to open work among the
Makololo. Two gallant efforts, to reach the Matabele and Makololo
tribes respectively, had resulted from Livingstone's urgency. The
first ended in temporary failure, the second in unrelieved tragedy.

The Explorer's separation from the London Missionary Society did
not lesson his sense of responsibility for the districts he had opened up,
for when what seemed to him a fortune came to him from his books,
he offered to provide funds to send a substitute to work in the districts
he had opened up; and when it seemed to him that the London
Missionary Society were tantalizingly dilatory in making use of his offer,
he made private arrangements with his brother-in-law John, the fourth
son of Dr Robert Moffat. He hastened the wedding of the young man
to Emily Unwin of Brighton; equipped them, and sent them out to
live at Inyati, near the main kraal of Musilikatse, the much-dreaded
paramount chief of the Matabele (p. 36).[1] Out of respect for his
father, the chief treated John with tolerance, but the young people
soon found that they were completely in his hands. They were
practically prisoners, with no freedom for their mission work, and
little for personal movement. Poor and sparse food, and the strain
of living on the doorstep of a capricious barbarian, told on their nerves,
especially on those of Emily, a delicate and cultured woman, and after
six years of brave struggle the attempt was relinquished.

The second party, that which was to settle at Linyanti among the
Makololo, reached Sekeletu's town in 1860, after having crossed the
Kalahari with great difficulty. It consisted of Holloway Helmore, a
missionary of twenty years' experience; his wife and four children;
and Roger Price, a newcomer, with his wife and one child.

There appears to have been some kind of understanding with Livingstone that he should meet them, and introduce them to his 'son,'
Sekeletu, but how far the plan was definite is not clear. Obviously,
between a consul in charge of a Government expedition on the Shire,
and this big family party struggling up from the Cape, there could be
no accurate timing. At any rate, when the little company arrived at the
swampy country of the Upper Zambezi, there was no word from
Livingstone.

[1] See page 418.

Then, to their exceeding embarrassment, they found the young chief most unhelpful, and indeed actively unfriendly. They had been assured that Sekeletu had promised that, if missionaries were sent, he would move the whole tribe from the malaria-saturated valley to the healthy uplands, but this he refused to do. Nor would he permit the party to move. It was not these strangers that he had expected but Livingstone himself, and especially Mary Livingstone. It was protection from the ruthless Matabele that, especially since the death of Sebituane, the tribe most needed. Was not 'Ma Robert' the daughter of the great Moffat, and it was well known that whatever Moffat Bwana said, Mosilikatse did. So the chief argued.

Soon malaria took its toll. One by one the missionary party died. Two of the Helmore children first and next their mother, and soon poor Helmore himself, and then the Price child; and all the while the young chief subjected them to exactions and petty persecutions of many kinds. Hope that Livingstone would come held for three months, but then those who remained turned, in desperation, south. On the way Mrs Price's strength gave out, and only Roger Price and the two remaining Helmore children survived, and they too would have succumbed had they not met John Mackenzie of the London Missionary Society travelling north. Out of a party of nine, six were dead.

There is not a little in this story that will never be cleared up. Many criticized Livingstone, but it is doubtful if he can be fairly blamed. He averred that he had received no word of the movements of the expedition. This lack of information may be explained by the fact that a boat that contained some of his mail had been lost.

Another unpleasant doubt remains, arising from the belief, apparently prevalent among the tribes, that the deaths had been caused not so much by fever, as by poison administered on the instigation of Sekeletu. The Doctor knew of this rumour, but did not believe it, and he was in a good position to know, since within a few months he investigated the matter on the spot.

Livingstone arrived six months too late.

APPENDIX VI

Stanley's Account of his Meeting with Livingstone

(*How I found Livingstone*, page 409 *et seq.*)

WE were about three hundred yards from Ujiji, and the crowds were dense about me. Suddenly I heard a voice on my right say:

'Good morning, sir.'

Startled at hearing this greeting in the midst of a crowd of black people, I turned sharply round and saw him at my side, with the blackest of faces, but animated and joyous—a man dressed in a long white shirt, with a turban of American sheeting round his woolly head, and ask him:

'Who the mischief are you?'

'I am Susi, the servant of Dr Livingstone.'

'What, is Dr Livingstone here?'

'Yes, sir.'

'In this village?'

'Yes, sir.'

'Is the Doctor well?'

'Not very well, sir.'

'Now run and tell the Doctor I am coming'—and off he darted like a madman.

By this time we were within two hundred yards of the village, and the multitude was getting denser. Flags and streamers were out. Soon Susi came running back, and asked me my name. He had told the Doctor that I was coming, but the Doctor was too surprised to believe him.

During Susi's absence, news had been conveyed to the Doctor that it was surely a white man that was coming, and the great Arab magnates of Ujiji had gathered together before the Doctor's house, and the Doctor had come out from his veranda to await my arrival; and the *kirangozi* was out of the ranks, holding his flag aloft, and Selim said to me: 'I see the Doctor, sir. Oh, what an old man! He has got a white beard.' And I—what would I not have given for a bit of friendly wilderness, where, unseen, I might vent my joy in some mad freak, such as idiotically biting my hand, turning a somersault, or slashing at trees, in order to allay the exciting feelings that were well-nigh uncontrollable? My heart beat fast, but I must not let my face betray my emotions, lest it detract from the dignity of a white man appearing under such extraordinary circumstances.

So I did what I thought was most dignified. I pushed back the crowds, and passing from the rear walked down a living avenue of people, till I came in front of the semicircle of Arabs, in front of which stood a white man with a grey beard. As I advanced slowly towards him I noticed he was pale, looked weary, had a grey beard, wore a bluish cap with a faded gold band round it, and had on a red-sleeved waistcoat and a pair of grey tweed trousers. I would have run to him, only I was a coward in the presence of such a mob—would have embraced him, only, he being an Englishman, I did not know how he would receive me; so I did what cowardice and false pride suggested was the best thing—walked deliberately to him, took off my hat, and said:

'Dr Livingstone, I presume?'

'Yes,' he said, with a kind smile, lifting his cap slightly.

I replace my hat on my head, and he puts on his cap, and we both grasp hands; and then I say aloud:

'I thank God I have been permitted to see you.'

He answered: 'I am very thankful I am here to welcome you.'

I turn to the Arabs, take off my hat to them in response to the saluting chorus of *yambos* I receive, and the Doctor introduces them to me by name. And then, oblivious of the crowds, we turn our faces towards his tempe. He points to the mud platform under the broad overhanging eaves, and to his own particular seat, a straw mat with a goatskin over it, and another skin nailed against the wall to protect his back from the cold mud. I protest against taking his seat, but the Doctor will not yield. I must take it.

We are seated. The Arabs take seats on our left. More than a thousand natives are in front of us, filling the whole square. So I found myself gazing at him, conning the wonderful man at whose side I now sat in Central Africa. I cannot repeat what he said. I was too engrossed to take my note-book out.

The Arabs rose up with a delicacy I approved. They intuitively knew that we ought to be left to ourselves.

APPENDIX VII

Source Books

THE main source of information about Livingstone is, naturally, the journals of which this book is an abbreviation (page xi) and the more intimate diaries on which the journals are founded; together with a very large number of letters now in many hands. The most important collections of these last are those in the archives of the London Missionary Society; the Scottish National Memorial to David Livingstone at his birth-place in Blantyre, Lanarkshire; the Rhodes-Livingstone Memorial at Livingstone, Northern Rhodesia; the Rhodes House, Oxford, and those in the keeping of various descendants of the Livingstone family. The principal biographical source books, apart from these, are given below.

The Personal Life of David Livingstone, by W. G. Blaikie (John Murray, 1894).

This is, and always must remain, *the* authoritative biography. The author had access to material, especially in the form of private letters, the location of much of which is not now known. 'Lives,' almost without number, have been and continue to be written, but these, in the main, simply delve what Blaikie ploughed. The book is full, accurate, and on essential points most understanding. To the modern reader, however, its defect is that it reflects too closely the somewhat indiscriminate hero-worship of the mid-Victorian age. Livingstone had his own measure of man's frailty—the reverse side of his titanic strength. There is, on the other hand, in this book little reflection of the remarkable charm of mind and manner, to which his intimate friends often testify. Blaikie did not know Livingstone personally. The resultant picture is grimmer and less human than the reality.

Livingstone, by Sir Harry Johnston (George Philip & Son, 1890). Valuable chiefly because of the author's extensive knowledge of Africa and its people.

Livingstone, by Canon R. J. Campbell (Ernest Benn, 1929). The first biography to use the Kirk material. Valuable mainly because of the help given by David Chamberlin, the editorial secretary of the London Missionary Society, and the most accomplished 'Livingstonian' of his day. Full use is made of the resources of the London Missionary Society archives, and also of the investigations made by Dr Hubert Wilson, the Explorer's grandson, into the Highland origins of the Livingstone family.

Livingstone the Liberator, by James I. Macnair (Collins Classics, 1940). Embodying much new material collected at the Scottish National Memorial to David Livingstone, Blantyre, Lanarkshire.

Livingstone's Last Journey, by Sir Reginald Coupland (Collins, 1945). A skilful retelling of the story of the last seven years, dealing in detail with the dispute between Stanley and Kirk.

The Search for Livingstone, by Lieut E. D. Young (John Murray, 1863.) The story of the expedition to Lake Nyasa to investigate the false report of Livingstone's death.

How I found Livingstone in Central Africa, by H. M. Stanley (Sampson Low & Co., 1872).

Some Letters from David Livingstone, 1840–72, edited by David Chamberlin (Oxford University Press). The correspondence in the London Missionary Society's archives.

Livingstone's Cambridge Lectures, edited by William Monk (Deighton Young & Co., 1860).
Gives full report of the two lectures delivered to the university students in December 1857, which had much to do with the founding of the Universities' Mission, with much other matter, more or less related. Also a large number of valuable letters written from the Shire to various notable people. The book contains, however, little that is not found in his other books.

Livingstone and Newstead, by Mrs A. Z. Frazer (John Murray, 1913). Out of print.
A daughter of Livingstone's hunting friend, W. F. Webb, of Newstead Abbey, Nottinghamshire. Here the Explorer spent seven peaceful months in writing his second book. This delightful volume shows the human side of the great man, his humility, his geniality in private life, his robust sense of humour and playfulness—a charming picture.

After Livingstone, by F. L. M. Moir (Hodder & Stoughton, 1923).
The story of two brothers who followed out in Nyasaland Livingstone's ideal of 'Christianity and Commerce,' and helped in the final fight that ended the slave-trade.

General Rigby, Zanzibar, and the Slave-Trade, by his daughter, Mrs Charles E. B. Russell (George Allen & Unwin, 1935).
Consul in Zanzibar, 1858–61. One of the strongest and most effective opponents of the slave-trade. Correspondent of Livingstone. He set 8,000 slaves free.

William Cotton Oswell, Hunter and Explorer, by W. E. Oswell (Heinemann, 1900).
With extracts from Livingstone's private journal. One of Livingstone's greatest and most helpful friends. Many great hunting stories.

Kirk on the Zambezi, by Sir Reginald Coupland (Clarendon Press, 1928). This book, together, in a lesser degree, with the same author's *Exploitation of East Africa*, contains the most valuable Livingstone research of recent times. Dr Kirk (later Sir John) was Livingstone's most valued assistant on the Zambezi. He admired his chief intensely, but his frankly expressed views on certain weaknesses in his hero, that showed themselves in that very trying time, form a useful supplement to Blaikie's picture.

Bishop Mackenzie, Memorial of, by H. Goodwin (Deighton Bell & Co., 1864).

Life of Thomas Baines, 1822–75, by Professor J. P. R. Wallis (Chatto & Windus).

Gives an account, from Baines's side, of his quarrel with Livingstone.

The Matabele Mission of John and Emily Moffat, 1858–65, published in 1945 for the Southern Rhodesian Government. Edited by Professor J. P. R. Wallis (Chatto & Windus).

The story of Livingstone's brother-in-law and his wife, and their unsuccessful attempt to establish, as the Explorer's substitute, a mission among the Matabele. Contains many letters from Livingstone in a happy vein.

APPENDIX VIII

The Scottish National Memorial to David Livingstone, Blantyre, Scotland

This memorial, to which frequent references are made in this book, was opened by Her Majesty the Queen Mother in October 1929.

The house, which was one in a small township, built to accommodate the workers of a factory that was one of the first results of the industrial age in Scotland, had been allowed to fall into ruins, and its demolition had been ordered.

To prevent this calamity a committee, of which the editor of this book was chairman, was formed, and in 1926 an appeal for funds for its renovation was issued. The response, especially in Scotland, was most generous. The work was entrusted to the late Sir Frank Mears, P.R.S.A., F.R.I.B.A. The result is a memorial that is unique. It is designed especially to interest children and young people, and aims to stabilize at his birth-place the Livingstone tradition.

The general plan is as follows.

The twenty-four small rooms of the tenement of which the Livingstone home was one, have been transformed into what may be called a profusely illustrated biography. Each room has its share in the telling of the history, the story itself being given in brief paragraphs in panels on the walls. The whole is enlivened by pictures, maps, working models, and a wonderfully varied collection of personal relics. The progress round the house becomes thus, especially for children, a kind of voyage of discovery.

The journey begins with the 'Ancestry Room,' where wall panels in tempera by Mr A. E. Haswell Miller, R.S.W.S., tell the romantic stories of Livingstone's highland and lowland ancestors. Next comes the little room (10 ft. by 14 ft.) where the Explorer was born, and which was his home for more than twenty years. In this are several of the original furnishings. There follows the 'Youth Room,' where are shown more of Mr Miller's panels that tell some of the stories of the boyhood, that most Scots children know. Adjoining is the 'Blantyre Room,' which is rich in reminders of Livingstone's youth: the arithmetic book scribbled all over with his signature; the little book of poems that hints at a love story, and much else of personal interest. Close by is the 'Adventure Room,' designed especially for boys, where the wall pictures depict the 'lion' and other thrilling yarns.

From here the visitor descends to the second storey, into the 'Livingstone Gallery.' This may be considered the centre of the museum, and its main attraction. It is by Mr C. d'O. Pilkington Jackson, the sculptor, and is an experiment in art.

To make this gallery, four of the small rooms have been thrown into one to form a long, low apartment where, in the original bed recesses, have been placed eight 'tableaux,' groups of coloured statuary in bas-relief. These are shown under modern lighting conditions. The colour is in part on the figures and in part comes from lights hidden above. They are illuminated by switches operated by the spectator, which cause the beautiful scenes to glow up slowly out of the darkness, to fade away again when the switch is released. The scenes are symbolic, and the whole scheme has been carried out with severe artistic restraint.

The visitor then passes through four rooms where there are on view a collection of relics that for completeness and intimate personal interest have, it may be safely claimed, no equal in the world: the manuscript of *Missionary Travels*, the famous 'consular cap,' the old white-ant-eaten overcoat, the surgical instruments he used, and, most precious of all, the series of little pocket note-books in which Livingstone recorded all that is known of his last seven years. There are hundreds more.

On the ground floor are shown a variety of maps, working models, and African curios, and the beautiful group, the 'Last Journey' (see plate facing page 399, bottom). The 'voyage' ends at the 'Shrine,' on the wall of which hangs a rough-hewn cross, made from part of the tree under which Livingstone's heart was buried.

The memorial became at once popular, with an annual attendance of about 65,000 people. Since the opening there have passed its turnstiles, at the date of the publication of this book, just over a million and a half visitors, equal to about a third of the population of Scotland. About half of these are children, for whom there are wide fields, and a great variety of play apparatus. Blantyre has become the great children's centre of Scotland.

Pilgrims are coming too from, almost literally, every country in the world, and in ever increasing numbers.

Blantyre is eight miles from Glasgow, and is easily reached by bus or train. From Edinburgh the approach is by bus to Bothwell, and then over the Livingstone footbridge to Blantyre.

INDEX

Index